Demonetization, Economic Slowdown
and
Energy Future

About the Editors

Prof. (Dr.) M. R. Biju, currently working as Dean, School of Social Sciences, Dean, School of Legal Studies and Head of the Department of Public Administration and Policy Studies, Central University of Kerala, Kasaragode. He is the Chairperson of the PG Board of Studies and also serving as Member of the Court of the University. Dr. Biju is the Editor of South Asian Journal of Socio-Political Studies (SAJOSPS) and Editor-in-Chief of International Journal of Political Science (IJOPS) is a prolific writer on socio-political and developmental issues. He has published over twenty-nine (29) books, one hundred and sixty (160) research papers, seventeen [17] book chapters, and reviewed over nine hundred books for South Asian Journal of Socio-Political Studies. His teaching and research experience, spanning more than 25 years, includes several achievements such as completion of three major research projects funded by Ministry of Panchayati Raj, Government of India and University Grants Commission, New Delhi and the post-doctoral fellowship awarded by the UGC in 2004. He has also successfully guided doctoral students of the University of Kerala.

He is consistently making professional academic contributions in the capacity of an Associate Board Member of Economics and Management, a prestigious journal published by the Technical University of Liberce, Czech Republic; as the Director and Member Secretary of the Asian Institute of Development Research (AIDR); and as a life Member of several Academic and Professional Bodies. He is also serving on the Editorial Board of International Journal of Business and Innovation, Administration. He is a Member of the PG Board of Studies Political Science and Public Administration of the University of Kerala and Gandhigram Rural Institute, Dindigul. Dr. M.R. Biju is one of the widely cited writers in the field of Social Sciences with 161 citations and H-index of 6 and i10 index of 3. As per UGC Regulations of 2010, 2013 and 2016 Dr. Biju possess a total API Score of 3914 with API Cap of 3739 as on 1.1.2017.

M.R.B. Anantha Padmanabha currently serving as Deputy Editor of South Asian Journal of Socio-Political Studies. He has co-authored two books and published a few research papers. He has also presented papers in national seminars and conferences. He is pursuing masters in Politics and International Relations at the Central University of Pondicherry.

Demonetization, Economic Slowdown and Energy Future

Trends and Challenges

Edited by

M.R. Biju
M.R.B. Anantha Padmanabha

CONCEPT PUBLISHING COMPANY PVT. LTD.
NEW DELHI-110059

ISBN-13: 978-93-88937-42-9

First Published 2021

Published and Printed by

Concept Since 1974

Concept Publishing Company Pvt. Ltd.
A/15-16, Commercial Block, Mohan Garden,
New Delhi-110059 (INDIA)
T: +91 11 25351460, +91 11 25351794
E : publishing@conceptpub.com, *W* : www.conceptpub.com

Cataloging in Publication Data--Courtesy: D.K. Agencies (P) Ltd. <docinfo@dkagencies.com>

Demonetization, economic slowdown and energy future : trends and challenges / edited by M.R. Biju, M.R.B. Anantha Padmanabha.

pages cm
Contributed articles.
Includes bibliographical references and index.
ISBN 9789388937429

1. Demonetization—India. 2. Monetary policy—India. 3. India—Economic conditions—1991- 4. India—Economic policy—2016- 5. India—Social policy. 6. Environmental justice—India. I. Biju, M. R., 1965- editor. II. Anantha Padmanabha, M. R. B., editor.

LCC HG1235.D46 2021 | DDC 332.4954 23

Preface and Acknowledgements

As the clock struck 8 P.M. on November 8, 2016, India came to a standstill and the Prime Minister announced the demonetization of all Rs. 500 and Rs. 1,000 currency notes. The government claimed that the action would curtail the shadow economy and crack down on the use of illicit and counterfeit cash fund illegal activity and terrorism. In fact demonetization was initiated with a wide array of motives like stripping the Indian economy of its black money push people to pay taxes for the unaccounted pile of cash, curb terrorism, promote the digital India movement and, make the nation a cashless economy.

The most important factor that pushed people to support demonetization was its motto to put an end to black money problem in India. The statistics available now shows that either hoarders found a way to legitimatize their black money or did not hold them in the form of cash. But this was known by many before the RBI reports as well. Black money hoarders do not hold the money in cash according to financial experts.

- Another reason to support demonetization was its role in curbing terrorism by increasing obstacles in terror funding. Further, demonetization also aimed at, yet another reason to support demonetization was its role in curbing terrorism by increasing the obstacles in terror funding. Terrorist organisation were known to use fake Indian currency notes for funding their projects and the government believed that this could be contained with the help of demonetization.
- Pushing India towards becoming a cashless economy was yet another reason that demonetization was publicized for. People turned towards digital transactions for everything from buying

groceries from a road side vendor to paying utility bills during the time of demonetization.

- Pushing Indians to deposit and account cash lying in their house also meant a rise in the tax payment for the country. According to government reports, the income tax payers saw a record increase in the post-demonetization era. 9.1 million new tax payers were added to the slab which was an 80 per cent rise over the typical yearly rise.
- The ban of old notes is being cited as one of the key contributors to the economic slowdown with the GDP for the first quarter was slipping to 5.7 per cent, the reality of the economic slowdown could not be ignored. The World Bank has reduced the India GDP growth forecast for 2017-18 owning to demonetization and GST. The slowdown is being cited a delayed consequence of demonetization by the World Bank and while there are various other reasons at play, the steep decline has been credited to be an effect of demonetization.
- Demonetization had a lasting effect on Indians Medium, Small and Micro Enterprises (MSMEs). Various medium and small enterprises turned towards digitalization, however, the micro industries were affected by the worst of its wrath. The micro industry owners were not a part of the black money and they were clearly unprepared for the effects of demonetization. Many micro industry workers returned to villages and the growth rate of these companies went as low as 1 per cent. The MSME sector has been recovering from the drastic changes and its impact on the revenue, but demonetization forced the MSME sector to be a friendlier and more accommodating towards the digital arenas and made them more accommodating towards change.

Keeping this in background, this volume attempts to address the issues pertaining to various aspects of Indian Economy, viz. impact of demonetization of Indian economy, economic slowdown and changes in employment pattern, changing structure of manufacturing sector, socio-economic implications of large scale farmer's suicide, impact of Special Economic Zones, land acquisition, smart cities, women empowerment, social capital, multi-culturalism, environmental justice discourses, environmental determinism, entrepreneurial development, socio-economic vulnerability and citizen centric services. The research papers and articles are contributed by senior academics and developmental activists. In their submissions, they have tried to expose the existing problems in these core areas and present valuable suggestions to restructure the Indian Economy. The views and opinions expressed by the contributors are of immense value for researchers, academics and administrators for framing policies and strategies on demonetization and economic reforms.

Before concluding, I would like to express my gratitude to those who have been kind enough to help me in the preparation of this book. I wish to express a deep sense of gratitude to the esteemed contributors to this anthology of articles. I am also thankful to Shri Ashok Kumar Mittal of Concept Publishing Company Pvt. Ltd., New Delhi, who brought out the book in an elegant form.

Dr. M.R. Biju

Contents

SECTION II
Displaced Identity, Multiculturalism and Social Capital

SECTION III
Environmental Justice and Entrepreneurial Development

List of the Contributors

Dr. Aparna Sajeev, Senior Manager, Research and Insights (Psychometrician), Gray Matters India, Hyderabad. Address: Flat No. I-A, Alliance Tower, DPI Junction, Trivandrum, Kerala, Pin-695014 Mob. 9818479697.
E-mail: aparnasajeev88@gmail.com

Dr. Ashutosh Mohanty, Director, Truman Graduate School-Public Administration (Affairs) Joint Programme of University of Missouri (Truman School of Public Affairs) U.S.A., Mongolia International University, Ulaanbaatar, Mongolia. E-mail: amohantydr@min.edu.mn

Ashutosh Panday, Associate Professor, Department of Political Science and Public Administration, Dr. Shakntala M.N.R. University, Lucknow.
E-mail: ashuparsiya@rediffmail.com

Dr. Ashwani Kumar Dubey, Professor and Head, Department of Political Science & Public Administration, Dr. Shakuntala M.N.R. Univercity, Lucknow.
E-mail: akdubey.16@gmail.com

Dr. Bushra Beegom R.K., Assistant Professor of Sociology, University of Kerala, Kerala. E-mail: bushrabeegom@gmail.com

Dr. Cheruku Jeevan Kumar, Assistant Professor, Department of Public Policy, Law and Governance, Central University of Rajasthan, Rajasthan.
E-mail: jeevanckumar@gamil.com

Dr. D. Indrakumar, National Institute of Labour Economics Research and Development, New Delhi. E-mail: dindrakumar@gamil.com

Dr. G. Palanithurai, Professor, Gandhigram Rural Institute, Dindigul, Tamil Nadu. E-mail: gpalanithurai@gamil.com

Dr. M. Sarngadharan, Emeritus Fellow, and former Professor and Head of Department of Commerce, University of Kerala, Trivandrum, Kerala.
E-mail: dr.sarngadharan@gmail.com

Dr. M.R. Biju, Dean, School of Social Sciences and Head of Department of Public Administration and Policy Studies, Central University of Kerala, Kasaragode, Kerala. mrbijueditor@yahoo.com

M.R.B. Anantha Padmanabha, Deputy Editor, South Asian Journal of Socio-Political Studies (SAJOSPS). E-mail: mrbanantha97@gamil.com

Dr. Madhu Thawani, Professor, Department of Public Administration, VN South Gujarat University, Surat, Gujarat.
E-mail: madhuthawani.2008@rediffmail.com

P.T. Aienla Lemtor, Executive Director, Centre for Human Development and Information Technology, Nagaland. E-mail: aienlemtor@gmail.com

Dr. R.d. Rajnish Saryal, Assistant Professor, Political Sciences, Punjab University Regional Centre, Ludhiana. E-mail: rajnishsaryal@gmail.com

Dr. Raj Kishor Pradhan, Senior Statistical Officer, RO (NSSO)—FO, Sambalpur, Odisha. E-mail: rajkishor81@gamil.com

Dr. Rana Sonia Tez Bahadur, Assistant Professor, Dayalbagh Deemed University, Agra, Uttar Pradesh. E-mail: soniarana872@gamil.com

Dr. Ronald C. Zochin, Head, School of Business, Marist International University College, (A Constituent College of Catholic University of Eastern Africa, Nairobi)

Dr. S.M. Dogga, Assistant Professor of Economics, Central University of Rajasthan, Rajasthan. E-mail: satyanarayana_eco@curaj.ac.in

Dr. S.N. Ambedkar, Dean, School of Social Sciences, Central University of Rajasthan, Rajasthan. E-mail: ambedkarsn@gamil.com

Samseer R.H., Doctoral Fellow in Sociology, University of Kerala, Kerala.

Dr. Shantilin Lazarus, Principal, St. Anne's College of Education, Kattukuppam, Puducherry. E-mail: shatilinlazarus@yahoo.com

Dr. Simrit Kaur, Professor of Public Policy, Faculty of Management Studies, University of Delhi, Delhi. E-mail: kaur.simrit@gmail.com

Prof. Swami Prakash Srivastava, Dean, School of Social Sciences, Dayalbagh Deemed University, Agra, Uttar Pradesh. E-mail: spsdei2008@gamil.com

Introduction

Demonetisation is an act of cancelling the legal tender status of a currency unit in circulation. It can also be described as an act of taking away the legal tender rights of any currency. Further, it is the process of ceasing a unit of money of its status as legal tender. It is a necessary condition for changing the old currency with the new units of money. Anticipating positive changes on the liquidity structure as a whole, nations often adopt demonetisation policy as a measure to counterbalance the current economic situation. Countries across the globe have used demonetisation at some or the other point to control situations such as inflation and efforts to boost the economy.

In India demonetisation has been introduced in three occasions—12th January, 1946, 16th January, 1978 and 8th November, 2016. The latest ban has been introduced due to four vital reasons—to control inflation, to fight against the currency, to remove counterfeit currency and to discourage the cash transaction. Now, let us have a look into the reasons or justifications for demonetisation and its impact on various sectors of the economy.

- *Issues connected with Black Money:* Demonetisation was a bold and revolutionary action taken by the Government of India to curb Black Money. Definitely, it will have deep impact on the parallel economy of the nation. Persons, institutions and other sources connected with black money can be well identified through this move.
- *Online Transactions:* The ultimate objective of demonetisation is to build up a cashless or digital economy. More and more digital transactions will lead to more disclosure of income. It will ultimately increase the direct tax collection in a positive

way. Naturally, with a reduction in cash transactions alternative forms of payments will get more attraction.

- *To put an end to fake currency:* Fake currency notes have been wasted by demonetisation. Withdrawing highest value currency notes will have a serious impact on the fake currency syndicates. Naturally, it will help to put an end to terror funding in Jammu and Kashmir, North Eastern states and Naxalite hit states.
- *Increase in GDP:* Though demonetisation has its negative impact on real estate and property, construction and household conception in general, it is believed that long term benefits for GDP growth will outweigh the short-term transitional impact.

With regard to the impact of demonetisation is concerned it has multi-dimensional effects and consequences. It can be summarised in sector-wise as under:

- Real estate and property sector would be one of the worst affected sectors through the note ban. Demonetisation has no doubt finished the business of the majority of the builders as the major portion of their transactions depends on direct cash transfer rather than bank transfer. Marginal builders are adversely impacted reason being the high involvement of cash components in payment in this sector. Similarly, unorganized builders have also been affected adversely. Builders all-over the nation faced cash crunch due to the unexpected draw in sales.
- With regard to the impact of demonetisation on gems and jewellery is concerned, the substantial portion of the payment by customers involves cash for purchasing jewellery so the impact of demonetisation is quite high. Demonetisation made people with less cash available in their hands for fulfilling their daily needs rather than purchasing jewellery. Smaller retailers in the unorganised sector were the most to be impacted which reduce the demand for jewellery. Many Jewellers started selling gold at more than their market price to take advantage of banned notes which resulted in tax rates on such jewellers.
- Regarding hospitality and tourism sectors are concerned both these sectors have been severely impacted as the majority of their spending is in cash. Most of the luxury foreign trips are sponsored by or sponsored through black money. Due to the cash crunch local tourism get affected.

- As far as automobile sector is concerned it can be treated as the worst affected industry in India. The major decline in demand has been seen in two-wheeler business and four-wheeler business. Similarly, the used cars industry is another segment badly affected by demonetisation.
- Labour intensive sectors are also adversely affected by or through demonetisation. Limitations on the withdrawal amount from the bank affected the weekly payment to contract personal mining textile and leather industries. Further, daily requirements of the factory owners are being affected by the restrictions oh cash withdrawal.
- Regarding the effects of demonetisation on equity and mutual funds are concerned, it is expected to be positive with more money entering the organized system of financial transactions. If cash flow across the nation is fully tracked, equities will strengthen significantly, as more people will invest in equity linked savings schemes to save on taxes.
- Regarding tax to GDP ratio is concerned, in an economic survey conducted last year, the tax to GDP ratio of India was found to be at 16.6 per cent, which is comparatively low when compared to emerging markets across the world. But with deposits drifting away from the unorganized zones and getting channelized to banks, the tax to GDP ratio is expected to rise drastically. Analysts also predict a significant rise in the tax collection percentage, as all financial transactions will be under the scanner. Owing to the same reasons, government may also reduce tax rates.
- With regard to Jan Dhan accounts are concerned at present, the contribution of Jan Dhan accounts in terms of deposits has been significantly low in the overall banking domain. But post-Demonetisation, these idle accounts are witnessing a steep surge in deposits. Another positive side of the Demonetisation is that government's financial inclusion plan will gain momentum with a large number of people—including those from rural areas—opting for bank-based transactions.
- With regard to the impact of demonetisation on digital payments are concerned, e-wallet companies such as Paytm, PayUIndia, Mobikwik, etc. are concerned, it has been witnessing a sudden rise in their daily transactions. Demonetisation will also have an impact on the hiring needs and other business functions of

these companies. Even app-based cab companies are launching their promotional materials to encourage cashless transactions.

- With regard to the effects of demonetisation on interest rates are concerned as a result of increased liquidity, RBI is likely to cut down the rates of interests applicable on fixed deposits, and the like. Since, banks are sure to accumulate huge deposits in the months that follow, the borrowing cost for Banks will be reduced. This benefit will be extended to customers in the form of lower interest rates on loan products.
- With regard to steel and cement industries are concerned a temporary decline in sales can be observed in the cement and steel sectors which are closely linked to real estate. A closer look at the situation reveals sizeable impact of Demonetisation on construction industry—daily wage earners being the worst sufferers. However, with an increase in bank deposits complementing the savings rate, the short-term difficulties will be outstripped soon.
- Finally, as far as agricultural sector is concerned sale, distribution, marketing and transport connected with the sector are dominantly cash dependent. Further, demonetisation disrupted the supply change, this sector has severely impacted by huge wastage of perishables. The small farmers selling their products on daily basis to the wholesale centres were also adversely affected.

The unexpected move of the government to demonetise old currency and replacing it with the new one has been taken as a surprise. The move was an effort to handle the threat of illegal money, corruption, terror funding and counterfeit currency. The decision to introduce demonetisation should be considered as a surgical strike against the unaccounted and undeclared money in the history of Indian economy. No doubt, demonetisation is a bold step towards the establishment or a cashless or digital economy. But one cannot undermine its negative aspects. No doubt the demonetisation is followed by a liquidity crunch throughout the nation and thereby, banks and ATMs across the nation faced severe cash shortages. It has adverse effect on almost all sectors of the Indian economy. Currency ban created confusion and chaos in short term as most people with old currency faced difficulties in exchanging them. The total value of old currency notes in the circulation as of Rs. 14.2 trillion which constitute about 86 per cent of the total value in circulation. The black money has either been accounted by paying, heavy taxes and penalties or has reached the bank accounts through direct and indirect channels. Demonetisation no doubt would bring a positive impact in the long run in the Indian 'economy as it encourages the digital mode of payment.

References

1. Aban, D.K. (2017), A Study on the Impact of Demonetisation over the Banking Sector with Special Reference to Veraval City, *International Journal of Marketing and Financial Manangement*, Vol. V, No. 3, pp. 21-26.
2. Muthulekshmi, E.K. (2017), Impacts of Demonetisation on Indian Economy: Issues and Challenges. *Journal of Humanities and Social Sciences.*
3. Veera Kumar, K., (2017), A Study on People Impact on Demonetisation, *International Journal of Interdisciplinary Research in Arts and Humanities.* Vol. II, No. 1, pp. 9-12.
4. Shah, A.Y. (2017), Impact of Demonetisation on Rural India, *International Journal of Scientific Research Publications.* Vol. VII, No. 3, pp. 220-223.
5. Himanshu Kushwaha, Aswani Kumar and Zaninab Abbas, (2018), *Impact of Demonetisation on Indian Economy: A Critical Study,* Vol. V, Issue 2, April, 2018.
6. Aiswarya Krishnan, Demonetisation Anniversary: Decoding the Effects of Indian Currency Notes Ban.
   www.economictimes.indiatimes.com/tdmc/yourmoney/demonetisation-anniverssary-decoding-the-effects-of-indian-currency-notes-ban/tomorrowmarkershow/61579118 .cms

Section I

Demonetization and Its Future in India

1

Demonetization in India and Its Future Impact on Indian Economy

Swami Prakash Srivastava

Crisil Report

When a currency note of a particular denomination ceases to be a legal tender it is termed as demonetization. But since our government is replacing the old Rs. 500 notes with newer ones and doing away with the Rs. 1,000 notes, it would be more appropriate to call the move as 'scrapping' or 'phasing out' of certain currency notes.

1. Introduction

Demonetization is a radical monetary step in which a currency unit's status as a legal tender is declared invalid. This is usually done whenever there is a change of national currency, replacing the old unit with a new one. Such a step, for example, was taken when the European Monetary Union nations decided to adopt Euro as their currency. However, the old currencies were allowed to convert into Euros for a period of time in order to ensure a smooth transition through demonetization. Zimbabwe, Fiji, Singapore and Philippines were other countries to have opted for currency demonetization.

In India's case, the move has been taken to curb the menace of black money and fake notes by reducing the amount of cash available in the system. It is also interesting to note that this was not the first time the Government of India has gone for the demonetization of high-value currency. It was first implemented in 1946 when the Reserve Bank of

India demonetised the then circulated Rs. 1,000 and Rs. 10,000 notes. The government then introduced higher denomination banknotes in Rs. 1,000, Rs. 5,000 and Rs. 10,000. In January 1978, the Indian Government had demonetised Rs. 1,000, Rs. 5,000 and Rs. 10,000 notes to counter black money in the economy.

Demonetization in India

On November 8 evening, Prime Minister Narendra Modi, in his televised address to the nation, made Rs. 500 and Rs. 1,000 notes invalid, saying that it was aimed at curbing the "disease" of corruption and black money, which have taken deep root. People holding notes of Rs. 500 and Rs. 1,000 can deposit the same in their bank and post office accounts from November 10 till December 30. All notes in lower denomination of Rs. 100, Rs. 50, Rs. 20, Rs. 10, Rs. 5, Rs. 2 and Re 1 and all coins continued to be valid, and new notes of Rs. 2,000 and Rs. 500 were introduced. There was no change in any other form of currency exchange be it cheque, DD, payment *via* credit or debit cards etc. Banks and ATMs have witnessed chaos and long queues as cash-starved people jostled to exchange and withdraw money, even as cash dispensing machines went dry soon after they were stocked due to heavy rush.

2. Review of Literature

The nation, of course, stands divided in its opinion on whether the drastic measure taken by the government—which has plummeted the country (temporarily, the government argues) into a financial paralysis—was an informed step. We have compiled a list of what some of the country's leading economists and experts have to say. Unsurprisingly, the views are divided.

Experts and Economists who are against Demonetization

Amartya Sen: Only an authoritarian government can calmly cause such misery to the people—with millions of innocent people being deprived of their money and being subjected to suffering, inconvenience and indignity in trying to get their own money back.

Kaushik Basu: Leading Economist; Senior Vice-President and Chief Economist at the World Bank: Anyone seeking to convert more than Rs. 2,50,000 must explain why they hold so much cash, or failing that, must pay a penalty. This requirement, has already spawned a "new black market to service people wishing to offload: Large amounts of illicit cash are broken into smaller blocks and deposited by teams of illegal couriers.

Arun Jaitley, Finance Minister of India: A lot of money that operates in the shadow economy will now become a part of the banking structure itself. Banks will have a lot more money to support the economy. Private sector investment, which was so far lacking, will now get back into the economy. The banks which were struggling because of the NPA problem will have a lot more money to lend for agriculture, infrastructure sector, social sector, trade and industry.

Bibek Deb Roy, Member of the NITI Aayog: There have been several arguments pitched by economists as to why the different denomination notes vary in sizes. The difference in sizes are delaying the printing and therefore, taking longer to circulate within the country.

Arvind Virmani, Former Chief Economic Adviser, GoI: This is a useful method of flushing out black money, given that a large percentage of cash holding is in these two denominations. The manner in which it was implemented is not surprising—such actions are always secret till announced, so, that insiders do not take advantage of the information at the cost of the outsiders.

Urjit Patel, RBI Governor: The Demonetization decision was taken after detailed deliberations and not in haste, while nearly Rs. 11.85 lakh crore or 80 per cent of junked notes have come into the system.

Amit Shah: The demonetization move has given a hard blow to terrorism. The terror organisations have been left penniless. The country needed a surgery to cure it from the cancer of black money and the present Central Government has done that.

Anna Hazare: This revolutionary step will curb black money, corruption and terrorism funding to a large extent. The previous governments never showed the will to crackdown on black money. The present dispensation has taken a bold step and this will strengthen the democracy.

New York Times: The decision to scrap the old Rs. 500 and Rs. 1,000 notes had thrown the economy into turmoil. The Government did not appreciate the extent of the pain it would inflict. The government has begun circulating new, Rs. 500 and Rs. 2,000 notes, which means that cash based corruption and tax evasion are almost sure to return as people accumulate the new bills.

Venkaiah Naidu, Parliamentary Affairs Minister: The government recognises this is a problem but it is attempting to paper it over by invoking the spirit of voluntarism and sacrifice. We are told that a measure of "inconvenience" is necessary for the nation; temporary pain is "for larger gain".

3. Present Status of Demonetization in India

Historians will likely mark the current 'cash chaos' as one of the defining moments in independent India. Millions of Indians are making their way to banks to line up and exchange their useless Rs. 500 and Rs. 1,000 notes; those in cities are luckier to find banks and ATMs within reasonable distance but they end up waiting for hours nonetheless. In rural areas, where 833 million Indians or 69 per cent of the population lives, the journeys will be long and arduous. Three in four rural households have incomes less than Rs. 5,000 per month, but there is a strong likelihood that a majority of them have a Rs. 500 note that they need to change. To take a different angle, India has around 248 million households. Even if you assume that 50 million households (200 million people at an average of four per unit) are too poor to have a Rs. 500 note, that is still around 200 million journeys to the bank that need to be immediately made. Members of families will be going to banks more than once before the end of December; millions are thus setting off in India and trudging in different directions, looking for cash just because the government made them. This is a time when all of India is being socialised by everyday experience to understand, interpret and, in many cases, disapprove of the NDA's policy of demonetization.

4. Demonetization Cost and Volume of Currency Notes

As on March 31, 2016, 86 per cent of the value of currency notes issued were in demonetizations of Rs. 500 (48%) and Rs. 1,000 (38%) involving 1,571 crore pieces of Rs. 500 and 633 crore pieces of Rs. 1,000 denomination respectively. Till the October 2016, the volume grew by 5.6 per cent. So, that means the government's measures of November 8 impounded about 1,658 crore Rs. 500 notes and 668 crore of Rs. 1,000 notes—a total of Rs. 2,327 crore pieces of currency notes worth about Rs. 15 lakh crore. When 86 per cent of value of currency in circulation in an economy is impounded overnight, the inevitable outcome is short-term economic contraction. It happened in Indonesia when bank collapsed during the Asian currency crisis and it will happen here—as the hiatus caused by the impounding is unlikely to be shortlived.

The production capacity of Bharatiya Reserve Bank Note Mudran Pvt. Ltd. (BRBNMPL) which used to produce Rs. 1,000 notes and is now printing the new Rs. 2,000 note—is 133 crore pieces a month on a two-shift basis. Even if it can move to three-shift working, the maximum output will be 200 crore pieces a month. So, the minimum time for it to replace the value of impounded Rs. 1,000 notes by new Rs. 2,000 notes will be about two months. That is, at best second half of December 2016.

Now, the task of replacing the Rs. 500 notes is harder. Security Printing and Minting Corporation of India Ltd. (SPMCIL) is printing the Rs. 500 notes. Its capacity is believed to be Rs. 100 crore pieces a month. Assuming that BRBNMPL, a combined resources with SPMCIL, after mid-December, the time line to replace the existing stock of 1,658 crore pieces of Rs. 500 note will run into May 2017. Currency shortages will remain with us for many months and economic contraction will rule this period. At the end of the period, confidence will be at new lows and recovery will take time. This is aside from the human costs. Demonetization, whatever its motives, will exact a sizeable and inescapable cost on the economy.

5. Benami Assets—Transaction Act

The Benami Act provides that the benamidar, the beneficial owner and any other person who abets or induces the Benami transaction, shall be punishable with rigorous imprisonment for a period ranging from 1 to 7 years. The benami amount in the bank account deposited post-demonetization will bc seized and confiscated and the accused will also be liable to fine which extends up to 25 per cent of the fair market value of the benami property.

Warning people against depositing their unaccounted old currency in someone else's bank account, the tax department has decided to slap charges under the newly enforced Benami Transactions Act against violators that carries a penalty, prosecution and rigorous jail term of a maximum seven years. In a related development, the department has detected over Rs. 200 crore in undisclosed income after it conducted over 80 surveys and about 30 searches. Such instances where the suspicion is found to be true will be prosecuted under the Benami Property Transactions Act, 1988, applicable on both movable and immovable property, that has been enforced from November 1 this year.

The Act empowers the taxman to confiscate and prosecute both the depositor and the person whose illegal money he or she has "adjusted" in their account. "The CBDT has asked the Income Tax Department to closely monitor all such transactions. Primarily, the notices will be issued in cases of huge cash deposits beyond the threshold of Rs. 2.5 lakh but in cases where a suspicious report is received from the bank or the Financial Intelligence Unit below this threshold will also be investigated. Already some instances have been reported in this regard and the Department is set to issue notices under the Benami Act."

6. The Trouble with India's Demonetization Gamble

The idea of demonetization is good but it has to be taken into consideration that most of the black money is kept in the form of land, buildings or gold or kept abroad. What is in cash constitutes only 4 per cent of the total amount of black money on which taxes are not being paid. Out of this, a lot of money is in circulation in everyday transaction like if someone is building a house; the bill is not paid through banks for sand, bricks etc. This money goes into the other systems though it has been drawn from bank. These things will come under control with this step. The country is in uproar following the bold and risky move:

1. Small farmers, sellers, merchants, daily wage labourers and traders are suffering because of lack of proper planning, intelligence and foresight such as recalibration of ATM machines. There was need to pile up enough Rs. 100 notes and other smaller denomination notes in the market before taking this step.
2. Demonetization is an established practice in monetary policy to tackle black money. The Prime Minister has explained why this is a financial surgical strike. It was meant to be suddenly implemented.
3. In the past, demonetization has taken place twice, but it fails because the idea is to tackle the black money existing in circulation. This is not tackle corruption *per se* or the Government is not saying that 100 per cent corruption will be tackled. If announcement and time would have been given, this step might not have been successful in controlling black money and counterfeit currency in circulation coming from Pakistan, Nepal or other countries.
4. People are facing problems because the limit of withdrawal has not been kept at a higher level. If this would have been kept at a

higher level, there were chances that the recycling of black money might begin. The ideal money in circulation has to come to the banking channels.

5. It is also being said that what is being attempted is replacement of currency and not demonetization itself which was unnecessary. This is a terrible setback for the international standing of the Indian economy. At this time, the economy is struggling with slowdown. There is demand sluggishness in the economy leading to practically no private sector investment and stagnant industrial growth. If we look at the farm sector, this is the harvest time. Farmers generally deal in cash and India is also largely a cash economy. The cash transactions in this economy are far more than the total number of electronic transactions done on a daily basis.
6. In the tribal heartland of the country, the poor people through middlemen are getting their currencies exchanged for Rs. 300 or Rs. 400 because of lack of proper information which is hitting them.
7. The stock of the black economy constitutes a major part of the GDP is significant. Even if 50 per cent of this amount is withdrawn, the kind of relief that RBI will get on its liabilities and the sort of deposits, commercial banks will get will lead to a rise in the deposit and later on there will be decrease in lending rates plus fiscal deficit.
8. The black money in circulation is like a steroid in the economy which keeps the demand going gives a feeling that everything is working well. The problem is that investment is not taking place in the economy and the rate of growth of capital formation is down. The only way to bring this up is to divert more funds into investments which will happen when the cost of capital comes down.
9. The next question that may be raised is the preparedness of the government and the banks regarding implementation of a move of this scale. The argument provided for why this move was announced and administered overnight is that it denies hoarders of black money the chance to dispose of it. While that may appear to be sound logic, it has also apparently impacted the banking system's ability to ensure a smooth transition.
10. Several ATMs across the nation continue to be useless by virtue of not having enough fresh notes, while the ones that are refilled

are attacked by painfully long lines and eventually emptied at once.

7. Opposition of Political Parties and Bank Unions on Demonstration move

The Chief Ministers of the States of Bihar, Andhra Pradesh, Odisha, and Telengana have openly expressed both support and appreciation for this move in the long run, while the Chief Ministers of Uttar Pradesh, Karnataka, Maharashtra, and West Bengal have expressed varying degrees of criticism and worry at the potentially very harmful short-term impacts. Members of the Congress and the Samajwadi Party have violently opposed this move as well. Some leading Bank Unions have criticized the move as having been improperly planned—resulting in a severe shortage of Rs.100 notes that in turn ensures that the large tender of the new Rs. 2,000 notes is rendered useless for routine everyday transactions.

8. Supreme Court Views on Demonetization

On November 15, the Supreme Court sat down to hear multiple petitions and four Public Interest Litigations regarding this move—some of which requested a complete rollback of this policy due to its severe impact on everyday citizens. The Court decided not to stay the decision right then and instead will examine its legal validity before making a decision. After asking the government to file an affidavit justifying its notification, the Court adjourned the hearing. Meanwhile, government authorities were also asked to ensure that the average citizen was not deeply impacted by this policy.

9. Impact of Demonetization

Growth in cash-intensive sectors such as real estate, construction and FMCG is likely to take a hit in the short-term as consumers are deferring purchases. However, there is a positive side to the story: over the medium-term, there would be benefits through higher government spending and greater financial inclusion. Also, the movement of household savings from physical to financial will help boost growth. The near-term fall in growth on account of spending slowdown, could push inflation down. Also, an increase in fiscal headroom will allow the government to maintain fiscal discipline, which in turn will support inflation target in the medium term.

This in turn is the major question raised against this policy—who is affected the most? The removal of large sums of legal tender unquestionably affects all individuals who need to engage in cash transactions in some form. Those with access to plastic money are less directly impacted even in the short-term, but in both the long and short-term, specific sections have been disproportionately hit. Disenfranchised groups who lack the access to ID documents are chief among these.

1. Impact on Rural People

Farmers in a few eastern states expressed discontent over the drive. This is the sowing season and the farmers have been adversely hit by the cash crunch. Many of them do not have money to pay labourers. The government needs to come up with more measures to help them—including increasing the limit of Kisan Credit Card. The way the scheme has been implemented will hurt agricultural growth in our country, will hurt small industry, will hurt all those people who are in the informal sectors of the economy. After all, 90 per cent of our people work in the informal sector, 55 per cent of our workers in agriculture are reeling in distress. The cooperative banking system, which serves large number of people in the rural areas, is non-functional and has been prevented from handling cash (Dr. Manmohan Singh, Former Prime Minister of India).

The rural poor who lack the infrastructure to set up deposit accounts and who currently hold all their money in cash form have been directly hit. Even those who do have access to accounts among them struggle with ill prepared banks and post offices, small and dispersed in number, and the need to take off several crucial hours from work—sometimes in vain. The lopsided rural-urban spread of ATMs and bank branches has snuffed out economic activity in rural India, with micro, tiny and small enterprises finding it impossible to get cash in Rs. 100 notes for their daily operations. Consider this statistic: every bank branch in a rural and semi-urban centre caters to more than double the number of people in an urban and metropolitan centre. According to a December 2015 Reserve Bank of India report on "Financial Inclusion in India", each rural and semi-urban bank branch serves 12,863 people compared with an urban and metropolitan branch which serves just 5,351 people.

2. Impact on Refugees

Refugees who lack the requisite documents to create accounts are also now seeing months of savings potentially vanish, as they still lack mechanisms to access the banking sector. Socially ostracized communities who are again disproportionately cut off from the banking systems—like transgender communities and sex workers—are other immediate victims. This is in addition to the fact that the government may have overestimated the existing levels of connectivity to banking.

3. Impact on Real Estate

In the short term some sectors such as retail and construction will be adversely hit. In some of the northern and western states, for instance, the construction sector has witnessed a revenue dip by up to 30 per cent. The demonetization scheme is likely to provide the much needed transparency to the real estate sector thus leaving a positive impact on the buyers. As always said, *roti, kapda, makan* being the basic demand for any human being, the housing sector of India, employing the second largest workforce and contributor to GDP, has felt the pressure of demonetization too owing to the huge amount of cash flows in residential, commercial and office space sector. On the flip side, demonetization will exert a bright and promising future.

Realty business works on high capitals as majority of cash is used in purchase of land and material costs. At times, it is also alleged that huge amount of unaccounted cash is traded between the buyer and the trader, especially, in the high end sale of properties. However, after the demonetization the realty companies in all probabilities have to turn towards funding from sources like FDI, non-banking finance companies or private equity funding from institutions leading to transparency. FDI was allowed in the realty sector by the Central Government.

4. Impact on Naxal and Terroism Funds

Demonetization will finish off Naxal funds. All the extortion money in Rs. 500 and Rs. 1,000 notes that they have collected over the years will go waste now. A large part of the cash, which they have kept with them will now become dead money. This will weaken the Naxals in a big way financially and they will feel its impact while buying new arms and ammunition and also in planning future activities. Demonetization is a big step towards ending Naxalism and Terroism.

5. Impact on Tourism

Foreigners are restricted to exchanging currency up to only Rs. 5,000 per week. They want to spend, but Rs. 5,000 is way too little for them. So, they are either postponing their trips or are cancelling them. There has been at least a 24-30 per cent decline in both outbound and inbound travel. Demonetization has also thrown up a whole bunch of obstacles for tourists travelling in India. For instance, lack of point-of-scale machines at monuments, long queues for forex at airports due to fewer counters are some of the problems they have to face. Online tickets for monuments have to be scanned, but there are no scanning machines installed in monuments, however, the situation is expected to get better by February-March 2017.

6. Impact on Inflation

Illicit black money not only finances terrorism but also fuels inflation. There is a possibility that inflation will be contained through demonetization, especially land and housing prices. Counterfeit currency and black money are largely used in the real estate sector (particularly in unorganised sector and for secondary sales), where prices continuously remained high, due to the presence of black money. It is a known fact that a sizeable portion of the transaction value of land and building is done through black money, which is in currency form. Though some have converted a part of this amount into real assets, demonetization is a useful tool to address the amount that is kept in currency form. This will reduce the prices of land and houses and thereby act as a blessing to the poor and middle-income groups. Likewise, there are a number of intermediaries in the fishing sector, agricultural sector and service sector with unaccounted money in currency form. Arresting this phenomenon will be beneficial to the society. However, there should be proper institutional reforms to address these issues. Otherwise, demonetization is not going to produce any wonderful results for the country's economy. Sometimes, a deflationary situation cannot also be neglected which will hamper the economy.

10. "Black Money" and India's Demonetization Project

The decision to demonetize Rs. 500 and Rs. 1,000 notes is misconceived and will not address the problem of black money for the following reasons:

1. If it is the Government's case that high value denomination currency is used to hoard black money, then the decision to reissue new Rs. 500 and Rs. 1,000 notes does not make sense. Issuing even higher value Rs. 2,000 note is completely inexplicable and puzzling.
2. Black money is generated through evasion of taxes on income from lawful activities and money generated from illegal activities. In the absence of steps to curb the generation of black money, demonetization is a futile exercise, as it proved to be in 1978.
3. In the last 5 years, IT raids have found that only 5-6 per cent of black money is kept in hard cash. Moreover, those who have amassed sizable black money are equipped to find ways around demonetization by converting their existing cash to bullion, gold jewellery, real estate and foreign currencies through brokers and middle-men. In fact, organized middle-men and touts have already emerged to convert black money into white for a commission.
4. As per the Indian Statistical Institute, Kolkata study done on behalf of the National Investigation Agency (NIA), Rs. 400 crore worth of fake currency is in circulation in the Indian economy. This is only .028 per cent of Rs. 14,180 billion worth currency demonetized in Rs. 500 and Rs. 1,000 notes.
5. Experts including a former RBI Governor and the current Chief Economist of the World Bank have spoken against demonetization.
6. Eighty six per cent of currency in circulation is in Rs. 500 and Rs. 1,000 notes. Ninety seven per cent of all transactions by volume are done in cash. Summary demonetization has created chaos all over the country with people unable to purchase daily essentials and, in many cases, life-saving goods and services. 5 persons, including one infant, have died as a direct result of the impact of demonetization
7. Only about 30 per cent of the Indian population has access to the banking system as per data compiled by the banking division of the Finance Ministry. Moreover, the distribution of banks is highly skewed with a third of all bank branches in only 60 Tier 1 and Tier 2 cities/towns. Consequently, people in rural India who often also suffer from inadequate information have become the worst victims of demonetization.

8. Reports have started coming in of digital payment systems unable to keep up with the new volume of transactions with credit and debit card servers also going down.
9. All currency has value only because of the inherent trust in the banking system. Summary demonetization has shaken this trust and will likely impact India's economy well beyond the initial and widespread chaos.

It is evident that demonetization will not achieve its stated intent of eliminating black money but has thrown the entire country's economic system in disarray. Related developments also call into question Government's intentions and need clarification:

1. Rs. 1.14 lakh crore of bad debts have been waived by Government Banks in the last 3 years. At the same time, loans worth lakhs of crores of rupees are still outstanding. Why has the Government not made public the names of the beneficiaries of the waiver and the names of the big defaulters, both individuals and corporations?
2. A key campaign promise was to bring back black money stashed abroad and deposit Rs. 15 lakh each from the proceeds in the account of every citizen. Why has the Government not made public the names held by it of Indian account holders in offshore banks?
3. Why did the Government announce that cash deposits higher than Rs. 2.5 lakh will be scrutinised against the tax return with 200 per cent penalty for any tax evasion? This appears to be intended to dissuade people from depositing money so that the Government can claim success of demonetization and forewarn people to split their deposits among different accounts and different depositors.
4. All conversions can be done only after filling a form and attaching ID proof. This has led to major harassment of poor and illiterate people and those who do not have an identity card.
5. It has been estimated that the cost of replacing currency in circulation with new Rs. 500 and Rs. 2,000 notes will be Rs. 20,000 crore. Besides, far greater losses will be incurred by markets predominantly run on cash and the participants (wholesale markets, retail stores, street-vendors, transportation etc.) and in lost productivity.

6. Even if the Government was intent on demonetization, why was it not implemented after careful planning: new notes printed, arrangements made for distribution, ATMs recalibrated etc.? It has been seen that banks are running out of cash within hours of opening and most ATMs are still non-functional.
7. We are all concerned about the use of money power in elections. Why has not the Government proposed state funding of elections?

11. Basic Difference between 1946, 1978 and 2016 Demonetization in India

There are both parallels and differences with 2016 episode:

- Similarities are all three were aimed at curbing black money. Though this time security is an added challenge.
- In the earlier editions, RBI was mostly against the exercise and was proven right. This time it seems RBI has welcomed the idea (though there could be initial differences which will emerge only later). So, will RBI be proven right or wrong given their current view?
- The big difference obviously is the size this time. Previous ones barely impacted common people but this one is huge with 85 per cent of currency out of the system.
- The first demonetization was a case of conversion. Second of cumulation. Third is projected as a demon, but is more of a conversion. Will it be a case of demon? Only time will tell...

12. Demonetization in India and its Impact on GDP Growth Forecast

The RBI cut its GDP growth forecast for this financial year to 7.1 per cent, citing the governments demonetization exercise that sucked out 86

Table 1.1: Gross Domestic Product Forecast

Institutions	*Before Demonetisation (%)*	*After Demonetisation (%)*
RBI	7.6	7.1
Fitch	7.4	6.9
Morgan Stanley	7.7	7.4

Source: RBI Data.

per cent of the currency in circulation. Rating agencies and broking houses also cut their estimates of GDP growth.

FITCH Ratings

FITCH Ratings lowered India's GDP growth forecast for this fiscal year to 6.9 per cent from 7.4 per cent, saying there will be "temporary disruptions" to economic activity post-demonetization. It is said economic activity will be hit in the October-December quarter because of the cash crunch created by withdrawal and replacement of Rs. 500 and Rs. 1,000 notes that accounted for 86 per cent of the value of currency in circulation. Indian growth has also been revised down to reflect temporary disruptions to activity related to the RBI's surprise demonetization of large-denomination bank notes.

"The US-based ratings agency also revised GDP growth forecast for 2017-18 and 2018-19 lower to 7.7 per cent from 8 per cent earlier. Gradual implementation of the structural reform agenda is expected to contribute to higher growth, as will higher real disposable income, supported by an almost 24 per cent hike in civil servants' wages. But the anticipated recovery in investment looks a bit less certain in light of ongoing weakness in the data", FITCH said in its "Global Economic Outlook—November" report.

"Regarding currency ban, it said consumers do not have the cash needed to complete purchases, and there have been reports of supply chains being disrupted and farmers unable to buy seeds and fertiliser for the sowing season. Time spent queuing in banks is also likely to have affected general productivity. The impact on GDP growth will increase the longer the disruption continues", FITCH said, adding the medium-term effect of the currency withdrawal on GDP growth is uncertain, but is unlikely to be large.

Most importantly, demonetization is a one-off event. People who operate in the informal sector will still be able to use the new high-denomination bills and other options (such as gold) to store their wealth.

13. Digital Economy

Cash was king in India, used in an estimated 78 per cent of transactions, compared with 20-25 per cent in industrialized countries like Britain and the US. Many people, in India, do not have bank accounts or credit cards, and even those who do often must use cash because many businesses do not accept other forms of payment. India is still one of the most cash intensive economies in the world with a cash to GDP ratio of 12 per cent, about four times as much as other economies such as Brazil 3.93 per cent, Mexico 5.3 per cent and South Africa 3.73 per cent, according to a report, "Cost of Cash in India", commissioned by Master Card. A boost of electronic payments is welcome as the spin offs include automatic audit trials, transparent accounting and minimising the risk and cost of handling cash. But India is a vastly unbanked country and many among the poor do not have bank accounts. To expect people in rural India to switch to plastic in a short span seems unrealistic. The government is looking to make India cashless economy. But with such transactions accounting for only 2 per cent of total transaction and low ATM penetration the country has a long way to go.

Table 1.2: 'Cashless' around the Globe Countries that Lead in Cashless Transactions and where India Stands

Country	*Cashless Transactions*
Singapore	61%
Netherlands	60%
France	59%
Sweden	59%
Canada	57%
Belgium	56%
UK	52%
USA	45%
Australia	35%
South Korea	29%
Spain	16%
Brazil	15%
Japan	14%
China	10%
India	2%

Source: Master Card Advisers.

There are around 2.17 lakh ATMs in India but they are far and few (*see* Table 1.3).

Digital payment providers have mobilised hundreds of extra workers to enrol small merchants and offered their services for free, betting that severe cash shortages will prove to be the opportunity of a lifetime.

The Prime Minister, whose government supports digital payments, brought in demonetization to crack down on the shadow economy and improve tax collection. Why should India not make a beginning in creating a 'less-cash society?', "Once we embark on our journey to create a 'less-

Table 1.3: ATM per 1,00,000 Adults

Country	ATMs (in Lakhs)
China	254.13
Canada	220.52
USA	172.98
Russia	172.97
Australia	164.62
UK	131.59
Brazil	129.25
Japan	127.64
India	19.71

Source: IMF Financial Access Survey, 2016.

cash society', the goal of 'cashless society' will not remain very far. The companies say results have been promising so far."

Payment and Financial Technology Companies

Demonetization has sent payment and Financial technology companies scrambling for talent to meet the unprecedented increase in digital payments. Since, scrapping of high denomination currency notes on November 8, paytm, mobikwik, CapayU, Free Charge, ItZ Cash and other digital wallet companies have been hiring peoples in key leadership positions. Most payment and fintech companies are reaching to merchants and helping them to go digital. Of about 40 million merchans in the country, only 3,00,000-4,00,000—just one per cent had adopted digital payment method before demonetization, which has now opened up a huge opportunity for growth. Over the last 15 days after demonetization, millions of customers across India have tried mobile wallets as an alternative to cash.

Paytm

Paytm, backed by Chinese Internet giant Alibaba Group Holding Ltd., has added 700 sales representatives since November 8, taking its number of agents to 5,000. The company, which has 4,500 full-time employees, plans to double the number of agents to more than 10,000, as it aggressively expands its network.

It says it has nearly doubled the number of small merchants signed up to its services to 1.5 million in the last few weeks and added eight million clients to the 150 million it had before the banknote ban. Paytm recently slashed fees until December 31, from a system of fees that ranged from 1 to 4 per cent, with the most lucrative coming from telephone and utility bill payments.

MobiKwik

MobiKwik, whose backers include U.S. venture capital firm Sequoia Capital and American Express, said it had increased its agent base to more than 10,000 from about 1,000.

Merchants on its platform have risen to 2,50,000 from 1,50,000 previously. MobiKwik had started offering wallet-to-wallet transfers, though not all rivals were on board. The challenges raise questions about whether the business models of mobile payment providers are sustainable. MobiKwik is not charging fees until March 2017. The company will hire for key services and management positions such as product management, business heads and function heads.

ItZ Cash

ItZ is looking for talent across level, with profile in technology product and sales. If the overall business growth forecast happens at 40-50 per cent, it will have to grow his team at 10-20 per cent.

Credit Suisse

Credit Suisse estimates more than 90 per cent of consumer purchases are made in cash, as millions still do not have bank accounts. Those who do have bank cards mainly use them to withdraw from cash machines. Sales of cheap smartphones have boomed in recent years, but internet networks remain patchy, especially in rural India. Financial literacy and technology usage also remain low. Many businesses have traditionally opted for cash transactions because they are hard for the tax man to trace, given sales taxes are typically at least 10 per cent. Concerns also remain about the infrastructure for mobile payments, as customers or merchants from one platform cannot transfer payments to another.

14. Micro ATMs in Rural and Semi-Urban Areas

Government is pushing for Micro-ATMs in Semi and Urban Areas to ease the cash stress. About two lakh micro ATMs will come to the rescue of people as the government has directed banks to activate nearly 1.1 lakh such ATMs in rural areas and nearly 90,000 in urban and semi-urban areas.

Adhar enabled Micro ATM

With nearly 70,000 transactions being conducted on Aadhar enabled Micro ATMs every weak, the government is hoping that this will reduce some stress on the bank branches and ATM network. Micro ATMs can be extended in the shortest possible time and the more cash-in, cash-out points are there, the more it will help the public.

Micro-ATMs are hand held devices enabled with GPRS and some have a fingerprint scanner attached to them, making them Aadhar Compatible. All that a customer has to do is use the debit card as he would in an ATM and the moment the card is swiped, the Micro ATM connects it to the core banking system and money is either debited or credited from the scanner. The government is planning to increase the number of micro ATMs that will be available in rural and urban areas. In another six months 1.5 to 2.0 lakh new points will be added. So, in another one year government will reach the 4 lakh figure.

PDS-shops as Business Correspondents

Government also plan to make all ration—PDS-shops as business correspondents which are around 5.5 lakh in number.

Postal Payment Banks

The Finance Ministry is also planning to be launched postal payment banks as all its 1.5 lakh points across India will also be designated as business correspondents.

15. Report of the Special Team of Bureaucrats on Demonetization

A special team of bureaucrats sent to states for an on-the-spot assessment of the demonetization drive informed the government that though there was massive support from the people, the implementation was patchy. Cash crunch in banks and ATMs, shortage of smaller denomination and Rs. 500 banknotes, ATMs not recalibrated and post office network not optimally used were some of the key problems that the central team flagged in its report submitted to the Union Finance Ministry. The team was set up to assess the implementation of central measures in the wake of Prime Minister Narendra Modi's November 8 announcement that Rs. 500 and 1,000 banknotes—which accounted for about 86 per cent of the currency in circulation—will no longer be legal tender. Barring some areas in states such as West Bengal and Bihar, where farmers expressed discontent, the central team found that people by and large supported the Prime Minister's decision with the hope that it would weed out black money and rein in corruption. "People in rural and urban areas in states, including Uttar Pradesh, Rajasthan, Himachal Pradesh, North-East, said they are willing to suffer the inconvenience as they feel the end result will be good," said a member of the team that visited a northern state.

16. Modification in Income Tax Laws

Intensifying its black money hunt, the government tabled a Bill to amend the Income Tax Act in the Lok Sabha to impose more tax, penalty and surcharge on deposits made after the demonetization drive was launched on 8th November, 2016. The amendments provide a window to black money holders by proposing to levy a total tax, penalty and surcharge of 50 per cent on the amount deposited post-demonetization, while higher taxes and stiffer penalty of up to 85 per cent await those who do not disclose but are caught. The money from the scheme would be used for projects in irrigation, housing, toilets, infrastructure, primary education, primary health and livelihood, so, that there is justice and equality, said the Statement of Objects and Reasons of the Bill. The key points of the New Taxation Amendment Bill, tabled by Finance Minister in Lok Sabha are:

1. Thirty per cent tax and 10 per cent penalty on undisclosed income.
2. Thirty three per cent (33% of 30%) surcharge for Pradhan Mantri Garib Kalyan Deposit Scheme.
3. Seventy five per cent tax and 10 per cent penalty in case, those who do not disclose but are caught.

17. Demonetization of Currency Notes in other Countries

With the ban of Rs. 500 and Rs. 1,000 currency and introduction of new notes, India is coping with demonetization. The measure is not new, however, as several other countries have embraced it in the past. Some met the purposes, whereas some failed miserably. Here are 11 countries that tried demonetization before India:

1. In 1996, **Australia** became the first country to have a full series of circulating polymer bank notes after replacing all paper-based notes, which the government systemically made non-tender for legal purposes. To stop widespread counterfeiting, the Reserve Bank of Australia had released the world's first long lasting and counterfeit-resistant polymer (plastic) banknotes.
2. To deter counterfeiting, **Switzerland** has a reserve series of notes. A series of Swiss Franc 10 notes were printed by the Swiss National Bank in 1984. But the notes were never issued and the notes are currently still in reserve.
3. Due to chronic hyperinflation in **Zimbabwe**, the government was at one point printing a currency note with a face value of one hundred trillion dollars. This obviously rendered lesser denominations obsolete, which were taken out of circulation quickly in 2010.
4. In 1969, Richard Nixon, the then **United States** President, had, in one go, demonetised $10,000 and $1,000 bills. He kept only $100 as legal tender.
5. **Pakistan** has decided to phase out all currency notes with old designs with a notification dated 4th June, 2015. However, its citizens have nearly a year and half to exchange old notes. The country had earlier demonetised Rs. 5 and Rs. 500 denomination notes. And from 1st December, 2016 it has been decided to phase out all remaining old design banknotes of Rs. 10, 50, 100 and 1,000.
6. **Nigeria**—During the government of Muhammadu Buhari in 1984, Nigeria introduced new currency and banned the old notes. However, the debt-ridden and inflation hit country did not take the change well and the economy collapsed.
7. **Ghana**—In 1982, Ghana ditched their 50 cedis note to tackle tax evasion and empty excess liquidity. This made the people of the country support the black market and they started investing in physical assets which obviously made the economy weak.
8. **North Korea**—The demonetization that happened in North Korea in 2010 left people with no food and shelter. Kim Jong-il introduced a reform that knocked off two zeros from the face value of the old currency in order to banish black market.

9. **Soviet Union**—Mikhail Gorbachev ordered to withdraw large-ruble bills from circulation to take over the black market. The move did not go well with the citizens which resulted into a coup attempt which brought down his authority and that led to Soviet breakup.
10. **Myanmar**—In 1987, Myanmar's military invalidated around 80 per cent value of money to curb black market. The decision led to economic disruption which in turn led to mass protests that killed many people.
11. **Zaire**—Dictator Mobutu Sese Seko's administration laid out back to back currency reforms along with a plan to withdraw obsolescent currency from the system in 1993. The reform was not well received by the public and resulted in increasing economic disruptions. Mobutu was ousted in 1997.

18. Demonetization and Black Money

Recently, Indian Government has demonetized the high value currencies, i.e. currency notes of Rs. 500 and 1,000 with objective to unearth the black money, and to curb the corruption, counterfeit currency as well as terror financing. This decision was considered as biggest cleanliness drive against the black money in the history of Indian economy. But there is various views of experts on demonetization, as some argue that it will hit the black money and other argued in negative.

How it will Curb Black Money

- In India all sections of the society are accustomed to use cash transactions, and this habit is unscrupulously misused by some bad elements of the society. Such habit resulted in even people with accounted money are started using cash transaction for high value transactions.
- It is resulted into parallel economy with unaccounted money, even much stronger than regular economy. The parallel economy black money, corruption, counterfeit currency and terror financing. These issues hampered growth and development of the economy.
- In this background Demonetization of Rs. 500 and Rs. 1,000 currency notes as a master stroke, as the move will address issues

like black money and corruption and also help the economy become more digital.

- The move will either unearth the black money slashed in the form of cash or forces to destroy those unaccounted currencies. Demonetization will curb the menace of black money and will help check stashing of funds to a large extent.
- Similarly, it has major impact on corruption that exists in India and also on financing of terror activities in India. Hence, it was considered as courageous step in the fight against unaccounted money.

Some Argues against it

- Currently high-value currency notes accounts for the value of 86 per cent of the notes in circulation in India.
- According to some estimates the size of the black economy in India range from 20 per cent to 60 per cent of GDP and more and the currency in circulation is just 12 per cent of GDP.
- Even if more than 50 per cent of money in circulation is black money, but most of it will find its way back to the banking system one way or another, and be recycled as new notes.
- According to some experts, the black money holders, tax evaders and corrupt official may not slash these money in cash in their homes due to sheer scale of logistics.
- Generally, many viewed that tax evaded income mostly invested in companies, real estate and these people may not be affected due to demonetization.
- Hence, these experts argue that, demonetization may not yield desired results against black money, rather, it creates inconvenience to the general people.

19. Sources of Black Money and Demonetization

Black money is accumulated through different sources. The three main sources of black money are corruption, *hawala* and crime. Among these, corruption is the chief villain.

Corruption

Corruption is generally defined as the "misuse of public office" to extract an illegal rent. It is a major political and economic issue in India. There was widespread corruption at the top, middle and bottom levels of governance in India during the import substitution regime. Economic reforms could be a source of huge one-time rents to politicians in power, for example, privatisation of public monopolies. This reduces their ability to use the public sector for political patronage in the future. The sources of corruption can be traced to scarcity, property rights and their enforcement, transaction costs and information asymmetries, and political position (Patibandla and Sanyal, 2009).

Corruption through scarcity is generally seen in terms of a mismatch between demand and supply. In the case of goods, the market structure of an industry (monopoly *versus* competition), price regulation, quantity limits, zoning and differential tax treatment in different states result in scarcity, which creates opportunities for rent (corruption). In the case of service sector, a supplier or a government body may refuse to provide a service, unless a bribe is paid. In the post-reform era, some sources of scarcity-related corruption have been magnified, owing to weak property rights and high transaction costs of enforcement. As a result, corruption has been part of the society, including the pre-reform period. In 2011, Corruption Perception Index ranked India 94 among 176 countries with a score of 36. India's rank has now improved to 76. It is not at a satisfactory achievement, as it is evident that cross-border flow of money derived from criminal or corrupt activities is around $1.5 trillion annually. Nearly $40 billion of this is accounted for bribes paid to public officials in developing countries.

Hawala

Money transfer without money movement is an easy definition of *hawala*. *Hawala* works by transferring money without actually moving it. It is estimated that an amount ranging from $100 billion to $300 billion flows through informal remittance systems globally every year. 'White *hawala*' is used to refer to legitimate transactions. 'Black *hawala*' refers to illegitimate transactions, specifically *hawala* money laundering (associated with some serious offence such as narcotics trafficking and fraud). In the case of India, Interpol estimates the size of *hawala* at possibly 40 per cent of the country's GDP. In India, *hawala* is only a civil offence and persons violating its provisions are penalised with fine up to three times the amount detected in a contravention. This is a grossly inadequate deterrence to terrorists indulging in *hawala* for their sustenance and operation. There is fake currency circulated through the *hawala* system. Hence, demonetization would help check the flow of *hawala* money.

Crime

Criminal offence includes drug trafficking, gunrunning, money laundering and extortion, murder for hire, fraud, human trafficking, poaching and prostitution. Many criminal operations engage in black markets, political violence, religiously motivated violence, terrorism and abduction. Other crimes are homicide, robbery, assault etc. Property crimes include burglary, theft, motor vehicle theft and arson. Demonetization will be effective to the extent these activities are carried out with Indian high-denominated currencies. A sizeable volume of business is done by way of high-denominated currencies, though no scientific data is available in this respect.

20. Indian Currency Demonetization: Advantages and Disadvantages

The demonetization of currency after a long period of 38 years was a welcome and bold step taken by the Government of India on November 8, 2016. The last demonetization was implemented in 1978 by withdrawing Rs. 1,000, Rs. 5,000, and Rs. 10,000 notes that were in circulation. Every reform will have its merits and demerits. The question is whether the merits outweigh the demerits. A careful analysis is required to answer the question. Here are some advantages and disadvantages of demonetization:

1. This move will help the government to track unaccounted black money or cash on which income tax has not been paid.
2. Individuals who are sitting on a pile of cash usually do not deposit the amount in the bank or invest anywhere as they would be required to show income or submit PAN for any valid financial transactions. They would hide it somewhere and use it as and when necessary.
3. Banning high-value currency will impact people who will have no option, but, to declare income and pay tax on the same or destroy the cash somehow.
4. Banning high-value currency will halt illegal activity as the cash

provided for such activities has no value now. Black money is usually used to fund the illegal activity, terrorism, and money laundering.

5. Fake currency circulation will come to a halt in a single shot. Corrupt officers, money launderers are under threat as Income tax department is taking all the measures to track such people.
6. Most of the businessmen who have been hiding some income are ready to pay advance tax as current year's income. Tax payers who have been hiding some income can come forward to declare income and pay tax on the same.
7. Individuals are required to submit PAN for any deposit above Rs. 50,000 in cash, which will help tax department to track individuals with high denominations. Also, deposit up to Rs. 2.5 lakh will not come under Income tax scrutiny.
8. Now, individuals are depositing enough cash in their Jan Dhan accounts which they were reluctant to do so a few days back. The amount deposited can be used for the betterment of the country.

Disadvantages

1. It may cause inconvenience for initial few days for those who have to start running to the banks to exchange notes, deposit amount or withdraw the same. The situation can turn chaotic if there is a delay in the circulation of new currency.
2. Individuals who have an upcoming wedding are the ones who have to make alternative arrangements to make payments. However, the government has given higher withdrawal limit in such cases.
3. After the news, many individuals have burnt their cash and discarded the same, which is a loss to the economy. The government has to bear the cost of printing of new currency and its circulation. It makes sense when benefits of demonetization are higher.
4. There are only advantages of demonetization in the long term. The government is taking all the necessary steps and actions to meet the currency demand and ensure the smooth flow of new currency.

21. Conclusion

In conclusion, whoever expects that the demonetization process will be a great success is mistaken. The inherent limitation of demonetization has to be kept in mind, while evaluating it. To make the final point, the effects of demonetization can be split into three periods, such as very short, short and long periods. In the very short period (three to seven days or less than one month), there will be some adverse effects, especially for the poor and middle-income groups. Hence, it will be in a pain economy. In the short period (less than a year), it will produce positive outcomes, barring a few limitations. This period will naturally be in a pleasure economy. In the long period, counterfeit currency and black money (which is not the result of demonetization, but bad governance) may make a comeback, unless proper institutional measures are taken. This coupled with the spread effect of the positives in the short period will usher in a 'neutral economy'. No doubt, demonetization will not produce bad outcomes in the long run, except a few hardships faced by low-income common men for three to five days. The possibility of some positive outcomes like bringing all the black money out of hiding and throttling terror funding in due course cannot be neglected. So far, it can be said that this is a historical step and should be supported by all. One should look at the bigger picture which will definitely fetch results in the long term. This is what the people have been asking for a long time which has finally happened.

References

The Times of India, November 19, 2016, pp. 6 and 11.
The Economic Times, November 11, 2016, p. 5.
The Economic Times, December 6, 2016, p. 8.
The Times of India, December 8, 2016, p. 5.
The Economic Times, November 20-26, 2016, p. 5.
The Economic Times, November 14, 2016, p. 12.
Hindustan Times, November 25, 2016.

2

Impact of Demonetization on Indian Economy

An Empirical Analysis

Satyanarayana Murthy Dogga, S.N. Ambedkar and *Cheruku Jeevan Kumar*

1. Introduction

For the second time in four decades, India has been subjected to shock treatment of overnight demonetization of high-value currency notes. High-value currency notes of Rs. 500 and Rs. 1,000 stopped being legal tender, as part of noble package of measures to combat counterfeit notes and black money in the form of cash. Perhaps, this is the most significant move ever taken to curtail the parallel economy. This change will give a sharp boost to all the official channels of payment which in turn, will help the economy to grow. These sweeping measures will also be disruptive as India's rural and informal economies are largely cash based.

Therefore, here are few of my speculations about the future keeping in view the present decision on demonetization of Rs. 500 and Rs. 1,000 notes. First and foremost, this is one of the bravest decisions taken by any government till now in India which requires extra caliber and backup support as decisions like these do have severe implications. Therefore, we all must consider and note the will power of Prime Minister Narendra Modi irrespective of various views regarding this move. Second, yes, this will be a major blow to a large section of the population holding black money in the form of undisclosed assets which may generally held in the form of cash. What we need to notice here is that there is no good estimate for how much of India's black money is in forms other than currency/physical notes such as gold, jewellery, land or any other form of wealth. Therefore, while banning Rs. 500 and Rs. 1,000 notes will tackle the black money that is in the form of hard cold cash, it won't affect other forms of black money. On similar lines, this move will, obviously, have little effect on black money stash away in foreign tax havens. It is expected that some bold steps will definitely be taken soon for dealing with the money held in foreign accounts. Third, it was actually very disturbing to note that the higher denomination notes of Rs. 500 and Rs. 1,000 made up around 86 per cent of the total currency in circulation as it is a clear indicator of bulk of high-value transactions are taking place in the country as cash transactions which needs to be controlled. In this regard, it would be important to see how RBI will regulate the circulation of new Rs. 500 and Rs. 2,000 notes with minimum disruption to the liquidity situation in the economy.

Theoretically, a fall in currency to deposit ratio boosts money supply, but in India where the bulk of transactions are in cash, it will certainly impact trade and other business activities (can be very much seen today as almost all shops and restaurants are running dry). Critics are of the view that this is not the first time that currency notes of higher denomination have been demonetized (1946 and 1978 witnessed demonetization of Rs. 5,000 and Rs. 10,000 notes). But please note that their demonetization did not and would not have as severe impact as the current case due to the fact that Rs. 5,000 and Rs. 10,000 notes were too big to be used for general transaction as compared to Rs. 500 and Rs. 1,000 notes. The people who had gone to marry in the first three months after the recent demonetization of high value currency notes and their parents might have experienced hardships due to lack of cash balances. Finally, Prime Minister Shri Narendra Modi deserves kudos for the surgical strike on black/fake money. This move is expected to have several spinoffs for Asia's third largest economy including lowering inflation, improving tax GDP ratio, raising public investments and could lead to healthy public finances. But some short-term pains were also on the horizon. It is expected that sectors with a huge exposure to cash like real estate, transportation and food industry had witnessed downward price pressures in the short run. Over a long-term, however, this move could change the face of the Indian economy and improve the government's fiscal position. Let us see first need of this strategic move by the government.

What was the need?

According to World Bank estimation in 2010, the shadow economy for

India increased to 23.2 per cent of the GDP in 2007 from 20.7 per cent in 1999. A parallel shadow economy corrodes and eats into the vitals of the country's economy. It produces inflation which in turn may adversely affect the poor and the middle classes more than others. It also deprives the government of its legitimate revenues which could have been otherwise used for welfare and development activities. Similarly, even though several steps have been initiated by the present government over the last two and-a-half years, India's global ranking on corruption had only marginally improved from 100th to 76th. This may be because the share of large-value notes has been increasing over the years. According to data provided by the Reserve Bank of India (RBI) presented in Figure 2.1, the share of Rs. 1,000 notes in the stock of currency in circulation at the end of the financial year 2014-15 was a whopping 39 per cent, with Rs. 500 notes accounting for a further 45 per cent of currency stock. These two high value notes accounts for nearly one fourth of the all the currency notes in the circulation. In value terms, their share was more than 84 per cent as of the end of the March 2015. Therefore, it is argued that high denomination notes are likely to be used for illegal activities and not much as a medium of regular transaction. That is what, in his speech, Prime Minister, Shri Narendra Modi specifically pointed out that these high-value currency notes were being used to finance corruption and fund terrorism out of their unaccounted wealth. Therefore, the abolition of such notes can go a long way in curbing the black money in India. Hence, on 8 November, 2016, Prime Minister Modi announced that the Rs. 500 and Rs. 1,000 currency notes are no longer legitimate means of payment, and that people were given the opportunity to exchange these old notes for newly-developed Rs. 500 and Rs. 2,000 notes until the end of the year. Trust that the entire process was done with secrecy and the big whales did not get any prior news.

2. Experts' View on Demonetization and its Impact on Indian Economy

Here are the summary views by some eminent economists on the recent move of demonetization of high value notes in India.

Nobel Laureate and eminent economist Prof. Amartya Sen argued that "the demonetization of currency was a despotic act as the government broke the promise of compensation that comes with a promissory note." Professor Amartya Sen said in an interview to NDTV that "Demonetization goes against the trust. It undermines the trust of entire economy." He also

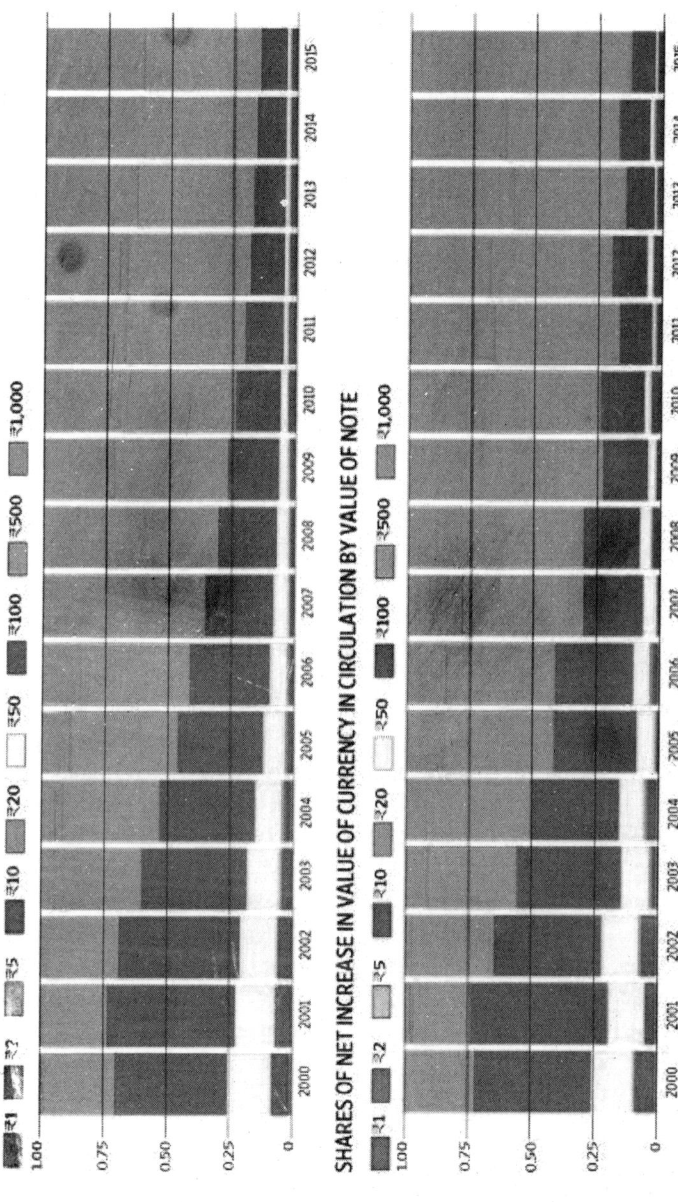

Fig. 2.1: Share of different Currency Notes in Total Value of Currency in Circulation

Source: RBI data.

further said, "Only an authoritarian government can calmly cause such misery to the people—with millions of innocent people being deprived of their money and being subjected to suffering, inconvenience and indignity in trying to get their own money back". Terming the move as authoritarian, the Nobel laureate also said that telling the public suddenly that the promissory notes you have, do not promise anything with certainty, is a more complex manifestation of authoritarianism, allegedly justified—or so the government claims—because some of these notes, held by some crooked people, involve black money. At one stroke the move proclaims that all Indians—indeed all holders of Indian currency—are possibly crooks, unless they can establish they are not.

The other leading Indian economist Kaushik Basu wrote in the *New York Times* and argued in the similar manner that when the government announced demonetization, it justified the measure as a way to control terrorism financing that depends on counterfeit rupee notes, as well as to reduce inflation. These two justifications are blemished. Catching fake notes already in circulation neither helps trap the terrorists who minted them nor check more such money from being injected into the economy. It simply inconveniences the people who use it as legal tender, the majority of whom had no hand in its creation. Thus, he proclaims that the demonetization of currency by the government is likely to fail. Similarly, former Prime Minister and eminent economist Dr. Manmohan Singh also slammed the demonetization of Rs. 500 and Rs. 1,000 notes and called it a "monumental mismanagement" that may bring GDP down by 2 per cent in the current financial year (2016-17). Considering the advantages and disadvantages of demonetization policy by the government, Dr. Maitreesh Ghatak, Professor at Landon School of Economics believed that demonetization of currency may result in huge collateral damage. According to him, the demonetization policy, at best, is a one-time tax on black money that is stowed in the form of cash. But only around 5 to 6 per cent of hidden income is held in cash. Therefore, even if all of it gets targeted by the above measure, it will not be an effective technique to go at the existing stock of black money. Moreover, black money generation is a continuing process that involves tax evasion and regulations, and engaging in corrupt and criminal activities. These cannot be tackled with a one-time measure. They will continue unabated with the new currency notes. Ironically, this reform may even increase the stock of black money held in cash in the future by facilitating hoarding in currency notes of a higher denomination, i.e. Rs. 2,000 notes.

He also said that even if the effectiveness of the policy in controlling black money will be minimal, the cost may be very high. Other than the direct cost of printing new notes, given that the affected currency notes constituted 86 per cent of the total volume of cash in the country, this policy effectively led to a much higher drop in liquidity than even the drip in the money supply (about 30%) that the US Fed is criticised for doing during the Great Depression. The informal sector is largely cash-dependent and alone accounts for 40 per cent of the GDP and employs 80 per cent of the workforce. It, along with the rest of the economy, is suffering perhaps the biggest policy-induced recessionary shock in post-Independence India. Add to it the physical hardship levied on normal citizens in terms of standing in line, and strain on the capacity of the banking sector, which have resulted in deaths.

However, there are other leading Indian economists Arvind Virmani, Surjit Bhalla etc. expressed their views on demonetization of high value currency notes in India in a positive line. Arvind Virmani former India's representative at IMF and Former Chief Economic Adviser, GoI, reportedly said that the demonetization of Rs. 500 and Rs. 1,000 notes by the government is a useful method of flushing out black money, given that a large percentage of cash holding is in these two denominations. On sudden announcement of currency invalidation, he also further added, "the manner in which it was implemented is not surprising—such actions are always secret till announced, so, that insiders do not take advantage of the information at the cost of the outsiders. However, he agreed that it may have a negative impact on the small businesses. According to him, when a country demonetizes such a large proportion of currency, the immediate effect is a collapse of retail trade in goods and services.

Similarly, Dr. Surjit Bhalla, former Professor at Delhi School of Economics, terms the demonetization move a "bold step and bigger than GST." According to him, there should be no question that the demonetization policy taken by the government is bold and courageous. The trading community has long been identified as the BJP's core constituency and Prime Minister Shri Narendra Modi has gone against this powerful support group. So, let us give Modi a considerable amount of credit for taking a bold step for the country—genuinely in the name of the nation. In the same piece, he also argued that the fight against corruption and black money in India has just begun. If successful, this will go down as the biggest reform in India, bigger than the GST (though the two are related) and bigger than the industrial policy reform of 1991. But, while the policy is very effective in its attack on past black money, it is silent on the creation of money.

Thus, there is two way track arguments carried out on the recent historical move by the government. Conceptually speaking, the concept of demonetization may have a positive impact on any economy whose reserved money has been strucked in the hands of few tax evasion people in the long run. But in reality this effect may differ as it depends on so many factors. Therefore, it is important to go through the data on various macroeconomics aggregates after the demonetization.

3. What the Data Says?

It is expected that the demonization may have a detrimental effect on private consumption and housing investment. In response to the demonetization operation, many analysts have revised their growth expectations for the financial year 2016-2017 (see Table 2.1).

Table 2.1

Analyst	*Growth rate*
RBI*	7.1
World Bank*	7.0
IMF*	6.6
Actual**	7.1

Note: * Expected growth rate, ** actual growth rate.
Source: RBI Data.

The latest data released by CSO, shows that the Indian economy grew by 7.1 per cent (year-on-year) during 2016-17 financial year, which is at odds with expectations, particularly, it is in line with the Reserve Bank's assessments, which also has dropped the GDP growth prospects to 7.1 per cent. Thus, so far the economy seems to hold up remarkably well. It might be due to the quality of data. Especially, the informal sector, which borne the brunt of the demonetization operation due to cash-dependency, is understated in the national accounts. Private consumption contributed strongly to growth by 5.7 percentage (Fig. 2.2). If we look at the sector contribution to the macro-growth figure, the real estate sector seems to have taken a hit in the fourth quarter, but this was mostly counterbalanced by a robust contribution of the agricultural sector and manufacturing, were also anticipated to be damaged by demonetization due to heavy cash-dependency and withdrawal of investment, respectively (Fig. 2.2).

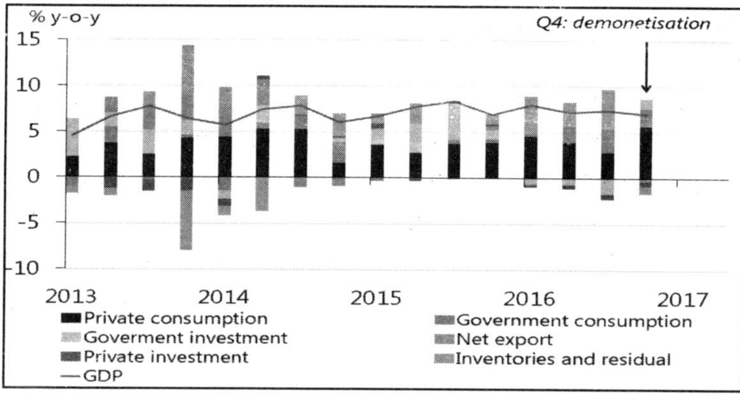

Fig. 2.2: Gross Domestic product Composition.
Source: RBI.

Going further, the purchasing managers' index (PMI) shows a large rebound, indicating the worst of the demonetization may already lie behind (Fig. 2.3). The similar sharp shrinking is also visible in vehicle sales, particularly, two wheelers, the major constituent of total sales, dropped by 12 per cent in November and 20 per cent in December, but also shows a recover in January (+23%) (*see* Fig. 2.4). Certainly, the amount of sales is still far below peak sales in August and September 2016, but this rebound suggests that sales have been delayed rather than cancelled.

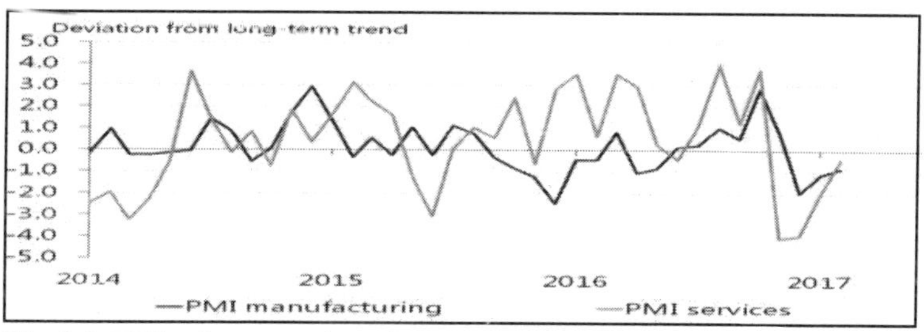

Fig. 2.3: PMI points to a rebound.

Impact on General Price Level

There is a considerable uncertainty as to how vegetables prices will pan out over the coming months. Given that recent vegetables price declines have also been affected by demonetization induced distress sales in addition to seasonal factors, it is possible that with significant

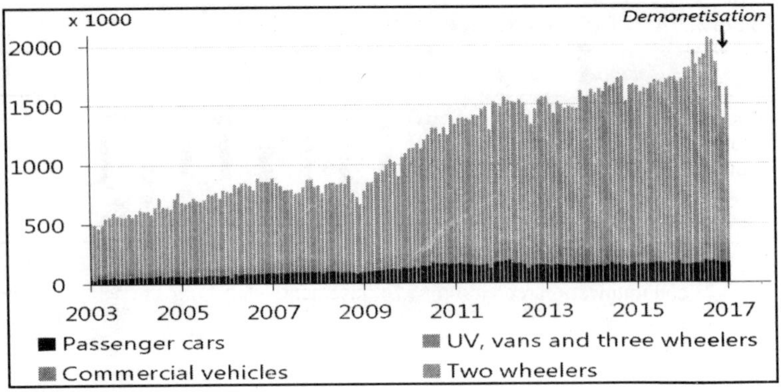

Fig. 2.4: Vehicle sales.

Source: Macrobond, Rabobank.

remonetization having taken place, there could be some reversal in vegetables prices in March and beyond. Thus, with inflation without food and fuel left sticky, the headline inflation outcome in the near term would depend on how food price dynamics progresses. With a weight of 46 per cent, the sharp fall in food inflation by about 240 bps during November 2016ţ January 2017 dragged down the headline Consumer Price Index based inflation by around 100 bps to 3.2 per cent in January 2017, the lowest inflation reading since the publication of the all-India consumer price index based inflation series. Inflation without vegetables, which was at 5.0 per cent in October 2016, moderated marginally to 4.8 per cent in November 2016 and remained unchanged at that level in December 2016 before moderating to 4.5 per cent in January 2017. The softening in CPI without vegetables suggests the larger role of vegetable sub-group in the observed sharp decline in inflation in recent months. Moreover, inflation based on consumer price index excluding food (which is about 54% of CPI basket) edged up to 4.7 per cent in December 2016 from 4.6 per cent in November 2016 and further to 4.9 per cent in January 2017 (see Table 2.2).

Despite optional consumer spending on items such as household goods and services, clothing and footwear, recreation and amusement, and personal care (which constitute 16% of the CPI basket) may have been impacted, the prices of these items weathered the transitory effects of the cash shortage as they are normally revised according to pre-set cycles and showed minimal changes post-demonetization. Prices of housing, health, transport and communication, pan, tobacco and

Table 2.2: CPI Inflation based on CPI of Selected Groups

Category	Jan-2016	Oct-2016	Nov-2016	Dec-16	Jan-17
Fuel and light	5.3	2.9	2.8	3.8	3.4
Clothing and Footwear	5.7	5.2	5.0	5.0	4.7
Housing	5.2	5.1	5.0	5.0	5.0
Miscellaneous*	3.9	4.7	4.8	4.7	5.1
CPI excluding Food and Fuel	4.7	4.9	4.9	4.9	5.1

* Includes household goods and services, health, transport, communication recreation and amusement, education, and personal care and effects.

Source: CSO.

intoxicants, and education—together accounting for 31 per cent of the CPI basket—also remained mostly unchanged. Though the real estate sector was in stress, no correction was seen in rentals. Barring new rental agreements, existing contracts have pre-set annual rental increase clauses of a fixed percentage. Thus, on the whole, inflation excluding food and fuel during November 2016—January 2017 was not impacted due to demonetization (Table 2.2).

Data Measurement Issues

The most key explanation why the cash crunch has not produced a significant dip in the Q4 GDP figures might be found in the quality of the data available in India. Two major issues are at play (Nagaraj and Srinivasan, 2016) methodology to measure gross domestic product (G.D.P.) in India. Before this revision, only a small number of companies actually filed their balance sheets to the firm administrator, owing poor law enforcement. The firms that have not registered their financial metrics were used as a sample and the data were scaled up. However, this method becames unreliable, as the number of registrations increased considerably, but filing of balance sheets data remained low. Many of these new registrations were so-called shell companies, which were used to run black money through the economy. Since 2006, the Ministry of Corporate Affairs (MCA) has increased its effort to persuade companies to file their returns, for instance by threats of de-registration.

In the 2015 revision, the improved database of the MCA has been by the CSO to produce more reliable national accounts data for the private corporate sector. However, the CSO is still using a scale factor to blow up the sample of companies in the database, whereas many question if the number of companies in the database is not the *actual* number of active companies. By using a scale factor, the CSO would be overstating the size of the private corporate sector. Overstating the private sector might be the main cause for the high manufacturing contribution to GDP growth. Indications of industrial production (Industrial Production Index) for manufacturing shows subdued growth or even contraction. And even if we consider the Industrial Production Index for eight key sectors of the Indian economy, we do not arrive at the high growth of manufacturing value added reported by the CSO (Fig. 2.5).

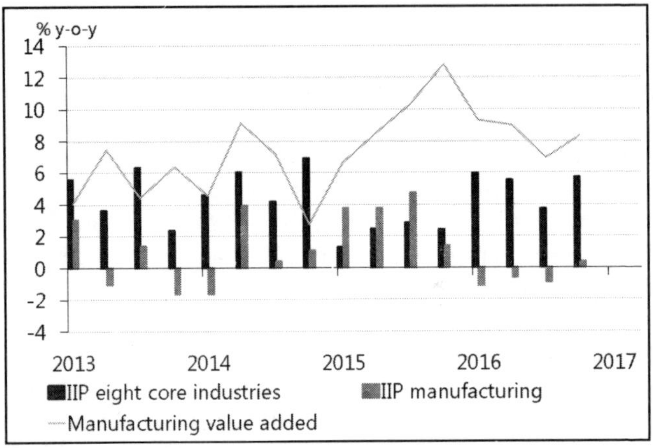

Fig. 2.5: Index of Industrial Product.
Source: RBI.

The second data issue is related to measurement of the informal economy, which is, as stressed, very substantial in India. Although the CSO has revised its proxy of informal sector activity, there are still concerns that the national accounts statistics is biased towards the registered and taxable part of the economy. Srinivasan and Nagaraj (2016) states that there are reasons to suspect that the new methodology for estimating labour input has underestimated the contribution of the unorganized sector to domestic output. This possible underrepresentation is worrying, as the unorganized part of the economy especially has borne the brunt of the demonetization operation.

4. Conclusion

Overall, given the information available so far, it is clear that the impact of demonetization on the real economy has not been significantly visible. The empirical analysis suggests that the impact of demonetization on gross domestic product (GDP) growth was felt modest during 2016-17. The organised sector remained largely robust. The latest CSO estimates suggest that the impact of demonetization on GDP growth during Q3 and Q4 of 2016-17 was felt mostly in construction and real estate, but because of stronger growth in agriculture, mining, manufacturing, and electricity the overall impact on GDP growth was not significantly visible. With remonetisation progressing at a fast pace, the adverse impact is expected to have reversed from the current financial year (2017-18). Although, the effect of demonetization perhaps did not cause the economic hurricane that some analysts expected, we believe the slight puff of headwind that the economy has faced up till now won't be all of it. Eventually, the negative effects are dependent on the time period before liquidity in the economy has returned to pre-demonetization levels. The gap between former and current levels is still large and we believe the negative effects on the Indian economy might expose themselves in upcoming revisions of GDP or when more reliable informal sector data is released in the current year. As of now, we will stick to current predictions and expect the Indian economy to grow by 8.2 per cent in 2017-18. The pick-up in growth later this year may be due to important reforms that Modi has been able to implement, such as the Goods and Service Tax (GST), which brings uniformity in India's complicated and inefficient tax scheme and reduces the cascading effect in the old system. This biggest tax reform is now a reality and will result in lower prices of goods and services, as well higher investment and tax revenues. The empirical analysis also shows that with inflation excluding food and fuel remaining sticky, the headline inflation outcome in the near term will depend on how food price dynamics evolve. Similarly, many indicators, such as economic sentiment and vehicle sales, show a rebound after the demonetization operation, but the initial drop is not visible in the headline GDP figure. The most key explanation why demonetization did not produce a big dip in the GDP figures might be due to the quality of the data available in India. Especially, the informal sector, which borne the brunt of the demonetization operation due to cash-dependency, is understated in the national accounts. The gap between former and current liquidity levels is still substantial and we believe the positive/negative effects might reveal themselves in upcoming revisions of GDP or when more reliable informal sector data is released in current financial year.

References

HDFC Bank Investment Advisory Group, "Demonetization and its Impact", November 2016.

Kaur, Manpreet (2017). "Demonetization and Its Impact on Indian Banking System (With Special Reference to E-Cash)", *International Journal of Business Management and Scientific Research*, Vol. 27, March, ISSN: 2394–6636.

Nagaraj and Srinivasan (2016). "Measuring India's GDP Unpacking the Analytics and Data Issues behind a Controversy that refuses to go away", *India Policy Forum,* July 12–13.

Staff of Monetary Policy Department (MPD). "Macroeconomic Impact of Demonetization—A Preliminary Assessment", March 10, 2017.

https://www.quora.com/What-will-be-the-impact-of-demonetization-in-India

https://en.wikipedia.org/wiki/2016_Indian_banknote_demonetization

3

Indian E-Commerce Industry

In the Post-Demonetization and GST Era

Sarngadharan, M.

Introduction

Indian economy has since emerged to seek its legitimate position in the table of leaders by maintaining the annual GDP growth in a consistently higher rate. The unique demographic feature of the economy with 65 per cent young population at or below 35 years of age and the buoyant market system serving one billion plus internally and many more internationally envisages robust position for business entities in the years to come. Economic liberalization has brought about drastic changes by way of trimming import tariff, removing regulations of markets, mitigating taxes, and attracting large volume of foreign investments. The policy decisions on the demonetization of November 2016 and the reforms in indirect taxes by introducing Goods and Services Tax in July 2017 have opened up wider scope for online business deals removing the barriers of international trade.

The mammoth inflow of foreign investments, goods and services, India must be capable and vigorous enough to provide adequate support and security to the international investors and business houses. The opening up of the Indian legal service profession to the overseas firms is the need of the hour. The success in attracting any form of investment in the economy relies on building investor confidence and investor protection. The improvement of legal professional services of international standards is essential for boosting the confidence of foreign investors. It will offer a good time for the competent and well informed young legal professionals to get themselves associated with overseas business houses in online business deals in specific and all business and financial deals in general. The online business deals, popularly known as e-commerce, demand through knowledge for legal professionals on Taxation Laws, Electronic Payments, Contract Law and Evidence Act, Laws on imposition of Liability, Intellectual Property Rights, Copyright Protection, Consumer Protection, Protection of Minors, Privacy Issues, and International Private Law and so on.

It is in this backdrop, an attempt is made in this chapter to examine how the introduction of digitalization through demonetization and standardization of indirect taxes through the Goods and Services Tax (GST) Act would escalate the e-commerce industry in India in the coming years.

Basics of E-commerce

Electronic Commerce, popularly known as e-commerce, is the process by which business houses and consumers sell and buy goods and services through electronic media. The business deals, which accept credit/debit cards for commercial online sales; generate online advertising revenue; trade stock in an online brokerage account; navigate information through a company *via* its intranet; manage manufacturing and distribution through a value chain with partners on an extranet; and sell to consumers on a pay-per-download basis, through a web site, are covered under the ambit of e-commerce. Of late, in the business world, the terms 'e-commerce' and 'e-business' are used interchangeably, ignoring the differences existing in the procedures to be followed for 'commerce' and 'business'.

The use of electronic commerce, emerged in the early 1990s, has increased at a rapid rate. Today, almost all large and medium companies have an online presence. In fact, having the ability to conduct business through the Internet, e-commerce has become a necessity for people of all walks of life. Everything from food and clothes to entertainment and furniture can be purchased online. The transactions carried out in e-commerce transpire under different models such as, business-to-business (B2B), business-to-consumer (B2C), and consumer-to-consumer (C2C). Of this, the most common is business to consumer, wherein the business sells products/services directly to consumers over the Internet. Another type of electronic commerce is business to business, in which companies sell products or services to other companies using electronic mode. Consumer to consumer e-commerce deals with goods, wherein consumers sell products to other consumers, especially second hand goods and immovable properties.

Relative Merits

The consumers have a much wider recourses available on the cyber market. They get goods and services at lower costs on account of the increased online competition among suppliers. Since wide-range of information is disseminated in the current situation, consumers are able to compare products, features, prices, designs, shapes, and even look up reviews before final selection. They are free to seek advice from experts and peers, besides saving shopping time and money. They also have the convenience of having their orders delivered right to the door step. On the other side, it is possible for the companies/suppliers to minimize inventory cost, since e-commerce ventures need not maintain huge inventories or expensive retail showrooms. The inventory costs are minimized by adopting just-in-time (JIT) system for inventory management. Research studies have found that both consumers and traders could save up to 10 per cent of the operating costs towards providing 'after-sale services'. By putting these services on-line under e-commerce, the costs get reduced and simultaneously, the quality of services also gets ameliorated. High quality customer relationship termed as 'customization' is vital to hold on customers in the e-commerce domain. That is what the essence is underlying in customer relationship management (CRM), which has become the buzzword of business houses globally.

E-commerce provides plenty of openings for CRM solutions and, in turn, in initiating better relationship with the customers. It becomes thoroughly essential for the company to magnify customer loyalty. Otherwise, the customers with wide options would leap from one website to another. The business houses have to arrange for delivering the products or services to customers in accordance with the latters' desires and needs. The studies carried out globally have revealed that the time needed to process an order declined abruptly by a minimum of 50 per cent to a maximum of 96 per cent in e-commerce deals. This helps companies, especially small ones, to make information on its products and services available to all the potential customers globally. The whole product design process online, drawing partners and customers into the process and removing the traditional communication barriers, can bring products and services to market far expeditiously. E-commerce solutions allow customer to reduce the costs of sales and open new markets in terms of speed and simplify order accuracy, approval, and processing, tracking and delivery and improve decision-making, leverage existing investments in infrastructure, business systems and repositions and link manufacturers with suppliers on the same network.

Recent Trends

Electronic commerce industry, all over the world, has been changing very fast and its scope has widened from just buying and selling products online. It also covers the intact online process of product planning, pricing, advertising, sales promotion, delivering, servicing and mode of payment. India has been witnessing drastic headway through e-commerce success stories distinctly in e-retail in consumer electronics, fashion apparels and home furnishing segments. Abundant opportunities for new entrepreneurial start-ups are visualized in India, paving way for generating more employment and escalating overall production in the economy. Adroitness of Internet access, safe and secure payment modes coupled with aggressive marketing by e-commerce giants has revolutionized this segment.

However, India, the third largest user base in the world, has a low penetration of e-commerce, compared to markets like China, the United States, United Kingdom or France. China and the US accounted for more than 55 per cent of global internet retail sales in 2016. It is worth mentioning in this context that Indian e-commerce industry has been enlarging at an impressive rate and by 2018, it is expected to account for 1.61 per cent of the global GDP. Recently, the Asia-Pacific region has evolved as the largest e-commerce market in the world, outshining Europe. Forrester reports outline that India is set to become the sprightly emerging market in the Asia-Pacific region with a growth rate of over 57 per cent during 2012-2016. Conjointly with this breakthrough, Indian e-commerce industry has been growing much faster, adding on an average of six million new entrants every month. It is estimated that volume of sales of Indian e-commerce would be to the tune of $2.489 trillion, marking 8.8 per cent of overall retail sales in 2018, as against retail e-commerce sales stood at $1.316 trillion with 5.9 per cent of overall retail sales in 2016.

Digital-buyer penetration, one of the yardsticks of digital reach, is the key factor that determines the success of retail e-commerce sales. India's digital-buyer penetration was quite low at 24.4 per cent in 2014 as compared to the global average of 41.6 per cent. Cash on delivery has been the most preferred payment method, accumulating 75 per cent of the e-retail activities. However, this has been changing favourably in the post-demonetization era since 2016 and the use of various forms of electronic payment modes such as credit cards, debit cards, net-banking, mobile money and prepaid cards conducive to e-commerce have come into vogue. It is also worth mentioning that demand for international consumer products (including long-tail items) has been growing much faster than in-country supply from authorized distributors and e-commerce offerings.

The Indian e-commerce industry has been confronted with the challenges in various areas such as taxation, logistics, payments, internet penetration and skilled man power. Absence of uniform tax structure on goods and services had resulted in complications like double-taxation and created other hurdles in the free flow of goods across the country. In respect of taxation, a large number of taxes, including VAT, CST, Excise Duty, Service Tax, and TDS, with multiple taxes applicable on any given transaction, were in practice. The complexities of logistics and reverse logistics, advertising and promotion services, software products, music, and e-books make it even harder to differentiate between goods and services in each transaction.

GST Impact on E-commerce Business

In the tax regime existed till June 2017 in India, there was no uniformity in the tax rates among the different states and therefore, every state dictated its own tax rates specific to the products. For example, a particular product in state A was taxed under VAT at five per cent and in state B at 14.5 per cent. As a result, the buyers in state B were not interested to purchase locally but would prefer to buy from state A, resulting in loss of revenue for state B. E-commerce operators had set up distribution centres only in certain locations and collect the VAT applicable on sales made from such centres. In order to compensate for the loss of VAT revenue, many states started imposing entry tax on goods coming from other states, which discouraged sales made from other states. The entry tax acted as a trade barrier, restricted free movement of goods from one state to another and was instrumental in increasing the cost for traders.

However, such trade barriers have been reducing gradually as GST and it is comprehensive of entry tax. The destination state gains the revenue from GST on sales regardless of where the sale was made. Moreover, there is no rate arbitrage under GST in view of the fact that the classification of goods and rate of GST is common across states. E-Commerce for GST comprises the supply or receipt of goods and/or services, or transfer of funds or data, over an electronic network, primarily the internet, by using any of the applications that rely on the internet, like but not limited to e-mail, instant messaging, shopping carts, web services, universal description discovery and integration (UDDI), file transfer protocol (FTP) and electronic data interchange (EDI) whether or not the payment is managed online and whether or not the ultimate delivery of the goods and/or services is effected by the operator. The e-commerce operator is required to collect/deduct an amount out of the consideration paid or payable to the actual supplier of goods or services in respect of supplies of goods and/or services made through such operator. The amount so deducted/collected is called as Tax Collection at Source (TCS). The timings for such collection/deduction are earlier of the two events: (a) the time of credit of any amount to the account of the actual supplier of goods and/or services; and (b) the time of payment of any amount in cash or by any other mode to such supplier. The amount collected by the operator is to be paid to the credit of appropriate government within 10 days after the end of the month in which amount was so collected. Further, in terms of Section 43C(4) of the Model GST Law (MGL), the operator is required to file a statement, electronically, containing details of all amounts collected by him for the outward supplies made through his Portal, within 10 days of the end of the calendar month to which such statement pertains.

The changing regime of electronic commerce in India has also triggered in the genesis of online marketplaces. Marketplace enables third-party vendors to register and sell online on their platform. It levies a subscription fee/commission on value of sales from the listed sellers. Third-party seller under this model gains entry to a larger customer base, registered with marketplace. Customers on the other hand gain access to multiple sellers and competitive prices for befitting products. Items purchased on such marketplaces are either shipped by merchant/third-party seller directly or through the fulfilment centre managed by marketplace operator. It also requires special attention in this regard that the Government has permitted foreign direct investments (FDI), to foster e-commerce marketplace business model in India.

Marketplaces have been contributing retailers with supplementary channel of sales and reach and this setting was incredible for an offline seller. Major marketplaces claim to have thousands of sellers affiliated with their platform with millions of SKUs. While the number of sellers and their business have increased significantly, GST has specifically taken up marketplaces and has come out with rules and regulations specific to this segment.

Introduction of these regulations requirements has compelled the online seller community to embrace GST regime. Some of the compliances are:

Government has specified a threshold limit for all the businesses. A business is liable to register under Goods and Services Tax once such threshold limit is ruptured. However, such limit is not applicable in case of e-commerce sellers. All the business ventures carrying out e-commerce activity are indispensable to get registered under GST irrespective of their turnover. Most of these sellers registered with marketplace operators are small and medium business houses. The Government has introduced composition scheme under GST law. This scheme is fundamentally positioned to diminish the burden of compliance for small and medium business ventures. Under this scheme, business houses are required to file returns quarterly in lieu of monthly and pay taxes at ostensible rates up to 2 per cent. However, GST law has explicitly precluded e-commerce business houses from this scheme.

Marketplace operators are compulsorily required, in the present set up, to subtract a percentage of sum as the GST liability of seller and deposit it with the Government. This mechanism is being termed as "Tax Collection at Source (TCS)" under the GST law. Eventually, the marketplace seller will have to file monthly return under GST to claim the credit of TCS collected by the marketplace operator. This will also impact the liquidity and cash flow of these sellers. While the entire marketplace, operator has already completed the first level analysis of impact of GST on their operations, marketplace sellers are still unaware of these rules. Need of the hour is to keep themselves aware of the changes that are going to come. Also such sellers should now start planning their transition strategy for GST regime.

With the inclusion of retail entrepreneurs in the ambit of GST and the introduction of specific provisions for e-commerce companies, certain areas of GST will impact the e-commerce sector. Every company in India, be it a multinational company or a small/medium enterprise, is gearing up for the implementation of GST. The e-commerce sector would follow suit in its preparation by focusing on provisions specific to this sector in the GST law. The success of the e-commerce sector is largely dependent on the increasing number of retail entrepreneurs, who fall in the unorganised retail sector category. The government has included such players in the ambit of GST with an intention of broadening the tax base and has introduced specific provisions for the e-commerce companies. Here are some of the key areas of GST that impact the e-commerce sector.

Tax Collection at Source (TCS)

This brings in significant compliance challenges to sellers and may discourage sales through marketplace model. However, this may not be applicable for inventory based models, where the e-commerce operator makes the sale from its own inventory. The key purpose of this provision is to encourage compliances under GST and provide a mechanism for the government to track suppliers who sell through e-commerce operators.

Increase in Compliances for E-commerce Operators

The e-commerce operators should report all supplies made by the seller and the TCS collected thereof on a monthly basis. The sales reported by the e-commerce operator will have to match with the sales declared by the supplier himself at the end of every month, and any difference will be added to the turnover of the supplier and consequently be liable to discharge GST on such additional turnover. The e-commerce operator has to report the product/service code and the applicable rates for each item level individually. This requires them to map every sale done by the dealer and ensure TCS is deducted at the right value. The implementation of compliance is cumbersome for both e-commerce operator and the supplier. Additionally, the e-commerce operators will have to register in each state and file the reports separately on a monthly basis. This process increases the challenges in compliance and costs of running the business.

Mandatory Registration of Sellers

GST mandates that all sellers supplying through an e-commerce operator need to be registered under GST irrespective of the threshold limit of Rs. 20 lakh. These sellers cannot opt for composition scheme, where they pay a flat tax at the rate of two per cent and do not maintain details of each product sold. In this scenario, it is not feasible for small businesses to maintain a detailed record of purchases and sales and pay higher rate of tax. Because of this, many small retailers may not prefer to work with an e-commerce company, which impacts the business for e-commerce operators. The GST law has extended the meaning of 'input tax' to cover any goods/services used by the company in the course of business, which has widened the ambit of input GST credits. This has removed the requirement to establish the direct nexus of inputs/input services with the final product/service provided by companies. For e-commerce operators and sellers, the unavailability of credit towards excise duty and VAT on goods and service tax on certain services adds to the cost of running the business, which would be avoided under GST on account of increase in credits.

The Demonetization Impact

There are a few roadblocks blameworthy for slow growth of e-commerce in India. In India, most of the consumers as well as business houses prefer to pay cash on delivery owing to the low trust on electronic payment system. Lesser popularity and use of electronic payment system (EPS) has been acting as one of the real threats for the growth of e-commerce market in India. Moreover, the internet penetration in India is still very low (34.8%) compared to other countries. It was in this backdrop that Indians, as a whole, came to a stop dead when the Prime Minister Shri Narendra Modi announced the demonetization of Rs. 500 and Rs. 1,000 currency notes on 8th November, 2016. Consequent on this surprise declaration 86 per cent of the currency in circulation ceased to become legal tender after midnight of that day of this declaration. Currency demonetization is an act of devastating a unit of currency legally. It is based on the fact that old currency is retired with changes in currency unit. It applies a break on black money and helps in managing corruption. It brings transparency in economy and can stop circulation of fake currency. An enormous change is visible in all spheres in the economy like local market, banking sector, marketing sector, e-commerce business, and even daily life. Online financial transactions and digital payments are not as difficult as they were earlier. This makes it easy to smartly tackle the sudden ban on old currencies and online transactions do come with a lot of benefits. This is the right time to unleash the full potential of online payments, apply for easy loans, pay the bills and do a lot more.

A study carried out by Bloomberg revealed the information that the volume of cash transactions in India was 98 per cent as compared to 55 per cent in the U.S. and 46 per cent in the UK immediately prior to this drastic move. This does urge for an investigation into the impact of demonetization on e-commerce in India.

Financial analysts all-over the world are debating on what the long-term impacts could be while several businesses and people are caught up in the unprecedented cash crunch that has been caused. With the retail businesses taking an all new dimension in respect of the growth of internet users, evolution of new business models and maturing of payment methods. Though, it is true that this can lead to a more positive effect in the long term, articulating the short-term effects, it has been predominantly adverse for the customers and businesses. The components of e-payment system such as credit cards, debit cards, net banking, mobile money, and prepaid cards are used for e-commerce in India. Of this, credit card is the easiest form of electronic money that is available and most widely used today. There are millions of credit cards that are being used to make online payments in India and as such a chunk of the e-commerce deals use credit cards for payments.

The second largest e-commerce payment medium in India debit cards and repeatedly for customers who want to stay within their spending capacity, paying for things online using a debit card proves to be a preferred choice. With the debit card, one can only pay for procured goods with the money that already exists in the current or savings accounts as incompatible to the credit card where the amounts that the buyer spends are accumulated and have to be paid in lump sum at the end of the billing period. Online stores offer other diversified payment options like, net banking, e-wallets and cash on delivery (CoD). Of this, CoD has emerged as one of the most sought after services for e-commerce entities and it is reported that in some cases as high as 50 per cent of orders are placed with various online retailers with this payment option, while the remaining opt for credit card or bank payments.

In India, many customers tend to prefer CoD as the online payment modes are yet to catch up in many parts of the country. Amongst that massive unbanked population, majorities have mobile phones, and for them, mobile money is likely to be hugely beneficial. Even for petty transactions, where credit cards are not accepted, it might be simpler to just hand over cash under this mode. In order to proactively encourage electronic payment systems for ushering in a less-cash society in India, it is exigent to ensure that payment and settlement systems are safe, efficient, interoperable, authorized, accessible, inclusive and compliant with international standards. Integration of various systems through unified solution architecture and current technology would lead to adoption and usage of resilient payment systems. It is in this context that despite the negative expected results in demonetization it is an accepted fact people from all walks of life have started coming under the ambit of digitization. This trend shall bring about favourable impact for e-commerce deals.

Regulation will channelize innovation and competition to meet these demands on par with the international standards and best practices. The overall regulatory policy stance is aligned towards fostering a less cash/ less paper society, as part of the "green" initiative. The increased emphasis on the use of electronic payment products and services that can be accessed anywhere and anytime by all at affordable prices. Grabbing new technology and innovation to disclose a bouquet of easily manageable, low cost, and effortless to use modern payment products and services would be the centrepiece of this venture. The Reserve Bank has recognized that building mastery of payment systems through standardization and a broad consultative process is a continuing agenda.

In light of the above, the Reserve Bank has set out the roadmap to ensure benefits of a structured modern payment and settlement system, inclusive of innovative products, to reach out beyond the currently served target groups thereby facilitating greater financial inclusion. This is to be achieved by stimulating a payment system that satisfactorily serves the national and international transaction needs of customers and business houses of varied sectors and sizes. The e-commerce and m-commerce platforms are poised for a big footstep in coming years. Similarly, electronic bill presentment and payments involving insurance, utility bills, and GST present immense opportunities. As of late, the number of non-cash transactions per person stands has been tremendously increasing since demonetization. If the efforts of demonetization bear fruit and if each person in India undertakes a minimum of one transaction in a month, the total transactions in the country would reach an astronomical 13 billion transactions per annum.

E-Commerce and Demonetization

Demonetization aims at pushing consumers towards making digital payments, thereby contributing to a cashless economy. Niti Aayog published a report on the growth of digital payments in India during the period of post-demonetization. This report indicates that digital payments have seen a screaming outpouring of 271 per cent in the very first month following demonetization. The number of mobile wallet transactions has increased to 6.3 million from 1.7 million. *Paytm,* one among the biggest players in the mobile wallet space disclosed that it could serve 45 million customers within three weeks after demonetization. Transactions *via RuPay* cards have also enlarged proposing that more Jan Dhan account holders have started using debit cards for online transactions.

Demonetization in the long run is expected to bring enormous benefits to the growth of e-commerce in India, although initial days have witnessed lot of confusions throughout the domestic market. One of the long term benefits for the e-commerce industry is predicted as trimming in payments *via* CoD. For online retailers CoD is mixed up with extra cost and the risk of returns or thefts is greater in this form of payment.

It would be interesting to examine how demonetization has affected the main segments of the e-commerce industry.

Retail

Online retailers, like Amazon and Snap, stated that there has been flump in the volume of business. The decline in COD orders is worked out to be 30 per cent to 40 per cent. The final quarter of 2016 was not as gainful as in the previous years for giants in the e-commerce industry. The consumers are not in a low spirit to spend and this situation has been showing favourable signs since the beginning of second quarter of 2017. Most of the online retail stores continue to be dependent on cash payments as it is going to take some time for all customers to switch from CoD to digital payments.

Payment

The digital wallet and payment segments have emerged explicit heroes in post-demonetization. Even local vegetable shops and small vendors have been showcased on social media for displaying signs asking for digital payments. Payment gateways have already shown commendable growth and the number gets enhanced each week. The germination in low-value transactions is of a commendable rate.

Logistics

E-commerce based logistic firms have taken a smash as 20 per cent of CoD orders were cancelled in the beginning of after the demonetization announcement. In the transport industry, earlier most of the transactions were effected through cash and this has started staging positive signals, focusing attention on accepting card payments and other modes of payment like wallets on delivery. There are some other logistic firms that do not offer card payments and ask for some time to scale up their operations.

Hyper-local Delivery

This sector in the e-commerce industry has witnessed massive swelling since post-demonetization. Hyper-local delivery firms supply groceries, household items and food from restaurants to customers. The number of new customers that this segment receives has been increasing day by day and there is a surge in pre-paid orders. Online food-ordering platforms like Swiggy and Zomato have seen a rise in transactions.

Undelivered Orders

Most of the orders that were placed with the cash on delivery option could not be delivered on account of the fact that the online retailers could not accept old notes. All the overheads and the costs incurred in shipping the orders went a waste in case of undelivered orders. This is indeed a significant loss for the e-commerce players. Some of the retailers temporarily were forced to suspend the option of paying with cash on delivery. Buyers had to wait for exchanging the old currencies available with them and few were reservations about online payments. This lead to a notable surge in the number of orders placed on the online shopping sites.

This came as a severe blow to the e-commerce partners. Although the problems on this issue have not been fully resolved, e-commerce retailers could take certain steps to make it easy for the customers to make their payments. Besides payment through internet banking and debit or credit cards, mobile wallet payment, e-commerce players have added more options of payments for overcoming the payment related problems. Online retailers also have introduced impressive discounts for all the cashless payments. This encourages more customers to choose a payment method other than CoD and claim their discounts and in turn helping the e-commerce businesses to retain a reasonable cash flow.

The support of the government has also been in favour of encouraging Unified Payments Interface (UPI) for online payments. This facilitates the freedom to choose an EMI option for bulk purchases. Banks have introduced debit card EMI option for mobile and purchases of costly items. This can also benefit customers making online purchases without a credit card. The micro-loans are paid through the debit cards and this makes it easy for procurement of high-priced products on EMI without a credit card from any of the favourite online retailer. Online payments are quick, convenient and time saving. This avoids causing a financial strain on bulk purchases bearing higher value.

Conclusion

E-commerce sector in India is one of the most rapidly advancing sectors and the government is vigorously promoting digitized economy, the introduction of such cumbersome compliances cringe the growth of this sector. It has become official that the international giant Walmart has acquired around 77 per cent of the Flipkart, a Bengaluru-based company, having valuation of over $20 billion, for $16 billion. It needs special mention in this regard that this has been one of the world's biggest e-commerce deals. It is expected that this deal is going to create commendable changes in the e-commerce industry in India and the fight between Amazon and Flipkart for leadership in the Indian market would swell rapidly. Statutory framework introduced by the government should be towards the advancement of business rather than creating obstacles. The GST law should provide an enabling environment that encourages e-commerce operators and suppliers. The foregoing discussion manifests that demonetization has been showing favourable impact on the e-commerce industry in India. The consumers have started relying on new methods of making payment with a shift from payment by choosing the cash on delivery. The change in consumer behaviour clearly demonstrates colossal openings for the e-commerce industry, paving the way for massive scope for digital payment market. Standardization of taxes such, including VAT, CST, Excise Duty, Service Tax, and TDS, with multiple taxes applicable on business deals has started portraying positive results in online business deals in the country.

Bibliography

E-Commerce in India: Drivers and Challenges a The PwC India Proposition (2015, November 11) Retrieved from https://www.pwc.in/assets/pdfs/technology/ecommerceinindia-drivers-and-challenges.pdf

E-commerce in India (2015, November 10) Retrieved from https://www.en.wikipedia.org/wiki/Ecommerce_ in_India

Goele S., Channa, N., Future of E-Commerce in India, *International Journal of Computing and Business Research*, Proceedings of, I-Society 2012 at GKU, Talwandi Sabo Bathinda, Punjab (Referred from:, 10/11/2012)

Jain, S., Kapoor, B., E-commerce in India: Boom and the Real Challenges, *VSRD International Journal of Business and Management*. 2012; 2(2):47-53.

Mitra, Abhijit (2013). "E-commerce in India: A Review." *International Journal of Marketing, Financial Services and Management Research*, 2.2 (2013): 126-132.

Padmini Sivarajah (2016, November 11). "Demonetization: Madurai Corporation makes record tax collection on a single day. *The Times of India*. Retrieved from http://timesofindia.indiatimes.com/city/ chennai/Demonetization-MaduraiCorporation-makes-recordtaxcollection-on-a-singleday/articleshow/55374378.cms

Prelec, Drazen, and Duncan Simester. "Always leave home without it: A further investigation of the creditcard effect on willingness to pay." *Marketing letters*. 12.1 (2001): 5-12.

Raghubir, P. and Srivastava, J., (2008). "Monopoly money: The effect of payment coupling and form on spending behaviour", *Journal of Experimental Psychology-Applied*, 14(3), 213-225. Special correspondent. (2016, November 13).

Soetevent, A.R. (2011). "Payment choice, image motivation and contributions to charity: evidence from a field experiment", *American Economic Journal: Economic Policy*. 3: 180–205.

Soman, D. (2001). "Effects of payment mechanism on spending behaviour: The role of rehearsal and immediacy of payment", *Journal of Consumer Research*, 27(4): 460-474. http://dx.doi.org/10.1086

4

Global Economic Slowdown and Changes in Employment Pattern in Organized Manufacturing in India

A State-wise Analysis

D. Indrakumar

1. Background

Manufacturing segments went to a multistage phenomenon of reforms over the years. When Second Five Year Plan (1956-61) were thought of heavy industries, there was a huge flow of investment by the public sector. Many ancillary and subsidiaries units were established round the heavy industries of the public sectors mostly in form of tiny and small scale industries. These tiny and small scale industries constituted a major portion in industrial phase of the country late of 1980s. Until then these segments of small scale industries were legally protected from the competition of heavy and big industries mostly from domestic. First time when reforms were introduced at a moderate level in late 1980s, some of these small scale units were de-reserved from the list of protected industries favouring the big domestic industries. When the new economic policy was adopted in 1991 with intention of liberalization, globalization and privatization the small scale units were largely de-reserved from list of protection not only in favour of big domestic industries, but also to global competitors.

Manufacturing sector has started moving towards 'less regulated form' of functioning from the highly controlled and regulated system. Especially, the new economic reforms of 1991 have lifted many formalities of licence and registration checks and simplified the ways for new entrants. This attracted many new players into the sectors and the manufacturing industries reached bloom over the years. The reform has increased the productivity and competitiveness of the manufacturing sectors (Singh, 2012). Indian manufacturing sector is continuously contributing to greater employment and national income. Organized segment of manufacturing is contributing more in terms of output in the overall segment of manufacturing industries. Due to its favourable features, the organized manufacturing industries continuously show significant growth both in terms of output and employment. Relatively larger in size, use of more advanced technology, and locational advantages are some of special features which contribute more output than unorganized manufacturing contribution (Bhalla, 2006).

However, the sectors' contribution to employment was stagnated around 11-12 per cent during 1999-2000 to 2009-10. The share of manufacturing employment in total workforce was 11.10 per cent (44.05 out of 396.76 million) in 1999-2000. Afterwards there was sharp rise in total workforce of the country and it reached 457.46 million in 2004-05 from 396.76 millions in 1999-2000. In the same manner manufacturing employment also increased to 55.77 million in 2004-05. Despite the increase in the total workforce after 2004-05, employment in manufacturing sector has come down to 50.74 million in 2009-10 hence the total workforce was increased to 460.22 million (NSSO Reports of 1999-2000, 2004-05 and 2009-10 on Employment and Unemployment Situations). It highlights a fluctuating trend in the manufacturing employment in the country. This fluctuation was once again proved due to the global financial crisis which happened in 2008 in United States of America and spread to Western countries and made an impact on rest of the world.

However, employment in organized manufacturing shows a fluctuating trend during the post-reform period. While in the year (1990-91) when the reforms were initiated, the employment was 8.23 million in the sector and it has been drastically increased to 9.23 million in 1994-95. Around one million new jobs were generated by the organized manufacturing sector within the period of five years. This positive trend was not continued and the employment in organized manufacturing was declined to 8.17 million for 1999-2000. The sector has lost more than one million jobs within next five years (between 1994-95 to 1999-2000). Since 1999-2000, there is a rise in employment in the sector and it reached to 8.45 million in 2004-05 and further 11.79 million in 2009-10. The recent year (2013-14) data shows the number of employment at 13.54 million. Similar trend was observed for composition of workers among this total employment of the sector. However, there is sharp rise in the proportion of contractual workers in the sector. In the year 1999-2000, the contractual workers were 1.24 million and it increased to 1.75 million for 2004-05. Again the number of contractual workers in the sector increased to 3.04 million in 2009-10 and 3.51 million for 2013-14.

The literatures indicate that, there is decline in the total workforce of the country in recent years especially after the global financial crisis of 2008. Ministry of Labour and Employment Survey during the 2008, indicates a loss of 0.5 million jobs in the manufacturing sector. This survey report also highlights that economic slowdown after the financial crisis, has weakened the new job creation even by the sectors which contributes more to the economy (GoI, 2009). The global economic slowdown which originated from United States of America in August, 2007 has impacted most of the economies in the world. Economic slowdown has also adversely impacted the Indian economy. During the second half of the financial year 2008-09, the economy decelerated resulting in loss of employment (Labour Bureau, 2009). However, the employment in the organzied manufacturing has shown an increasing trend during recent past. The Labour Bureau has made an assessment on the impact of global economic slowdown on Indian employment situation for a period of one year between 2010-2011 and the report points out the increase in employment in the country after 2010. The employment has increased by 0.91 million particularly between 2010 to 2011 (Labour Bureau, 2012).

The chapter has made an attempt to assess the impact of the global economic slowdown due to the financial crisis of US and Europe on the Indian manufacturing sector. As per the various literatures (Labour Bureau, 2009; Rajya Sabha Secretariat, 2009; Shah and Anand, 2013 and UNCTAD, 2013) there was slow down in the employment in the country due to global crisis of 2008. The organized manufacturing sector which has the data on yearly basis has been taken for the assessment. The data from 2003-04 to 2013-14 has been analysed for two periods that is, before (2003-04 to 2007-08) the global economic crisis and after (2009-10 to 2013-14), the crisis. Data was assessed state-wise on few indicators like, number of factories, total employment, workers' components, and extent of contractual workers.

2. Growth of Registered Factories

In order to assess the employment trend, the number of factories data were analysed by state-wise. Factories in the organized manufacturing sector have registered growth around 5 per cent per annum during the period 2000-01 to 2010-11. However, the sector has registered a better growth (7.17% per annum) between 2009-10 to 2013-14, the post-crisis period. In the pre-slowdown period 2003-04 to 2007-08, it was 2.55 per cent of growth in registration of factories. It clearly indicates that, Indian economy has recovered from the global economic slowdown at very faster rate. On an average 2.77 per cent annual growth was observed during the period of global economic crisis that is between 2007-08 to 2009-10. The state-wise analysis highlights the disparities in the performance of the states in registration of factories.

Three Indian states have registered a significant growth rate in both the periods, *viz*. Himachal Pradesh and Uttarakhand and Jammu & Kashmir. During 2003-04 to 2007-08, the pre-slow down period these three states have achieved a double digit growth. Surprisingly, Jammu & Kashmir stands at one of the top by pushing back all the industrially developed states with around 15 per cent of annual growth during the period. Himachal Pradesh and Uttarakhand occupy top two positions with around 17 per cent of annual growth. Worrying fact is that, all the bottom-level states have achieved almost negative growth during the period. Well known states for organized manufacturing like Delhi, West Bengal, and Tamil Nadu have registered very less growth between 2003-04 to 2007-08. Among the bottom five states Goa have lost more factories per annum during the period.

During the period (2007-08 to 2009-10) of global economic slowdown much of the states have posted negative and very little growth in registration of factories. Even state which has achieved a better growth rate during 2003-04 to 2007-08 has also registered a very less growth during the period of global slowdown. Uttarakhand and Himachal Pradesh occupy the top two places 17 and 10 per cent annual growth respectively. Apart from Uttarakhand and Himachal Pradesh, Jharkhand and other North Eastern States have also occupied a place in the top five positions along with Tamil Nadu. All the states which placed under bottom five have registered a negative growth in the registration of factories. Delhi stands at top of the bottom rank with 3.45 per cent of annual loss in growth of registered factories. Similarly, Jammu & Kashmir, other Union Territories, Haryana and Goa also lost many factories during the period of slow down.

Post-slow down period shows a drastic improvement by the sector for registration of more factories. At all-India level, growth rate for registration of factories registered an impressive growth rate of 7.13 per cent per annum between 2009-10 to 2013-14. Surprisingly, Bihar and

Assam take a place at top five positions regarding the growth of factories. Himachal Pradesh and Jammu & Kashmir are again posted a good growth during post-slowdown period also. Almost all states have achieved a better growth trend during the period. The least of growth regarding the registration of factories was registered in Madhya Pradesh around 3 per cent annual growth (Table. 4.1).

Table 4.1: Growth Trend of Registered Factories during 2003-04 to 2013-14

Growth Rate between 2003-04 to 2007-08		*Growth Rate between 2009-10 to 2013-14*		*Growth Rate during 2007-08 to 2009-10*	
Top 5 States					
States	*Growth*	*States*	*Growth*	*States*	*Growth*
Himachal Pradesh	16.96	Himachal Pradesh	12.68	Uttarakhand	16.72
Uttarakhand	16.77	Bihar	12.26	Himachal Pradesh	10.02
Jammu & Kashmir	14.66	Andhra Pradesh	11.70	Tamil Nadu	8.38
Punjab	8.23	Assam	9.38	Jharkhand	7.96
Chhattisgarh	7.44	Jammu & Kashmir	8.54	Other NE States	6.87
Bottom 5 States					
States	*Growth*	*States*	*Growth*	*States*	*Growth*
Goa	(–) 1.25	Madhya Pradesh	2.81	Delhi	(–) 3.45
Delhi	0.01	Goa	3.51	Jammu & Kashmir	(–) 2.34
West Bengal	0.15	Punjab	3.65	Other & UTs	(–) 1.21
Kerala	0.34	Other UTs	3.72	Haryana	(–) 0.48
Tamil Nadu	0.77	Kerala	3.84	Goa	(–) 0.13
National Averages					
Big States	2.64	Big States	7.25	Big States	2.96
Small States	0.45	Small States	6.07	Small States	(-) 1.54
Union Territories	1.62	Union Territories	4.80	Union Territories	0.07
All India	**2.55**	**All India**	**7.17**	**All India**	**2.72**

Source: Computed from Annual Survey of Industries for respective years.

States' Share in Factories

Big states, consisting of 20 states are holding the 95 per cent of the industries of organized manufacturing in the country. Even in big states, top five states (Tamil Nadu, Andhra Pradesh, Maharashtra, Gujarat and Uttar Pradesh) are controlling almost 60 per cent of the industrial units in the segment. In the remaining five per cent units, three per cent of the industrial establishments are locating in small states like Delhi, Goa,

Tripura and other North-Eastern States. Union Territories have two per cent of the country's organized manufacturing industries. Among the UTs, Dadra Nagar Haveli, Daman Diu followed by Puducherry have the maximum units. Tamil Nadu which has the maximum number of industrial units in the country with around 17 per cent of the organized manufacturing units. Andhra Pradesh and Maharashtra stand second and third positions with 13.28 and 12.97 per cent respectively. Gujarat is having 10 per cent of the organized manufacturing industries of the country (Fig. 4.1).

It is clear from the data that, very few states is attracting or promoting more new factories in their respective states. However, there are some new destinations (states) which are also growing at par with these big states. Especially, the North Eastern States like, Himachal Pradesh and Uttarakhand on hill region states, Assam, Tripura and other states (Manipur, Meghalaya, Nagaland) in North Eastern region and Jammu & Kashmir, Bihar has shown a significant growth in registration of factories than the industrially developed states.

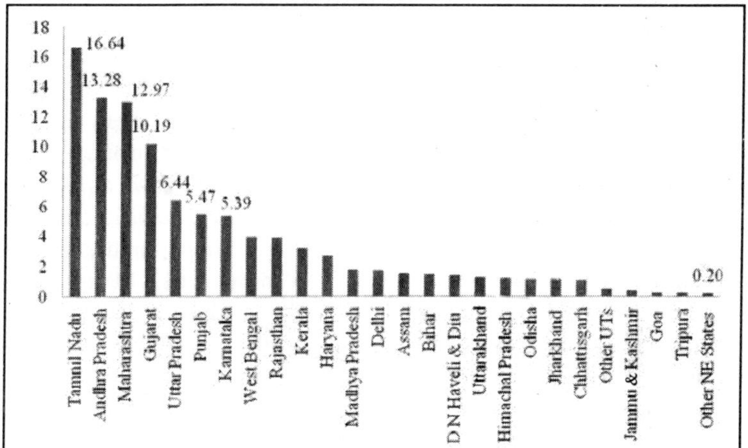

Fig. 4.1: State-wise share of organized manufacturing in industries, 2013-14.

Source: Computed from Annual Survey of Industries data for 2013-14.

3. *Status of Employment*

There is a fluctuating trend in the total organized employment in the country. It is applicable to employment in organized manufacturing sector too. When the new economic reforms were introduced in 1991, the total organized employment in the country was 26.35 millions. The share of employment of the organized manufacturing in the total organized employment was 23.69 per cent. There was slight improvement in the initial five years of reforms and the share has been increased to 24.29 per cent in 1995-96. Total organized employment has been increased to a maximum of 28.24 millions in 1996-97 afterwards there was a continuous fall in the organized employment in the country. Decline in the public sector employment in the organized segment due to privatization was one of the key reasons for fall in organized employment in the country. Simultaneously, there is rise in the organized employment in the private sectors is the proof.

The manufacturing employment in public sector was 1.85 million in 1990-91 and it has declined to 1.4 million in 2001. There was continuous fall in the manufacturing employment in public sector since 1991. However, employment in the private segment of manufacturing was 4.48 million in 1991 and reached to 5.10 million in 2001 and shows an improvement since 1991.

In 1999-2000, there was 44.05 millions of employment in the manufacturing sector and the share of organized manufacturing in overall manufacturing was 18.5 per cent (8.17 million) of total workers. It has increased to 8.45 million out of 55.77 million workers in total manufacturing for the year 2004-05. Again the composition of organized employment in total manufacturing employment has shown an increase in 2009-10. Organized manufacturing sector contributed 11.41 million jobs out of 50.74 million total manufacturing job opportunities (NSSO, 2011, 2006 and 2001) in 2009-10. As of now (data of 2013-14), the sector employs 13.54 million workers of the country directly.

However, there was a decline in growth rate of employment in manufacturing sectors in 1980s particularly fall in number of workers in the registered manufacturing units. Economists identified policy, indeed rigidities in the labour market as the main reasons for the decline in employment. However, new economic reforms of 1991 have liberalized and simplified the registration process which led to increase the industrial units. After the introduction of new economic reforms in 1991, the manufacturing sector especially the organized manufacturing registered a better growth both in terms of output and employment (Hoda and Rai, 2015).

Total Employment (Total Persons Engaged)

The sector employs almost 13.54 million workers in 2013-14. Since the introduction of reforms in 1991, the total employment (total persons engaged) in sector have increased in maximum years. The total employment has increased from 8.28 million in 1990-91 to a maximum of 10.22 million in 1995-96. Afterwards the total employment in the sector has shown a declining trend, it reached lowest level at 7.75 million in 2001-02 (Fig. 4.2).

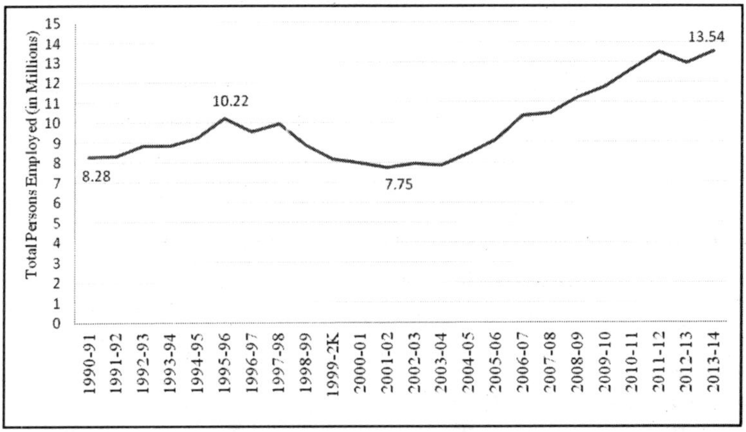

Fig. 4.2: Trend of total employment in Organised Manufacturing.

Source: Computed values from ASI data for respective years.

The growth trend of the total employment at national level stands at 3.84 per cent per annum between 2000-01 to 2013-14. However, if we analyse the employment growth between different breakpoints there is absolute ups and down in the growth trend. The decade before the introduction of new economic reforms there was *vice versa* in the rate of growth that is first five years a loss of 2 per cent employment and second half of 2 per cent increase in employment. The period between 1995-96 to 2000-01 was the worst period for total employment in the organized manufacturing country. There was almost five per cent loss per annum in total employment of the sector in the period and after that there was positive trend in the total employment of the sector (Fig. 4.3).

On the other hand, the state-wise analysis indicates some excellence and poor performances during the reference period pre- and post-slowdown. States which have larger share of employment does not make significant growth for the overall employment opportunities during 2000-01 to 2013-14. Tamil Nadu, Maharashtra, Gujarat, Andhra Pradesh and

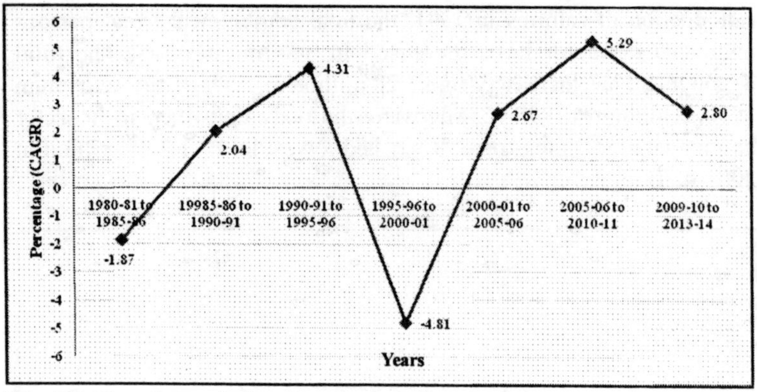

Fig. 4.3: Growth trend of total persons employed.

Source: Computed values from ASI data for respective years.

Uttar Pradesh are the states which have huge share of employment, but none of these stats have entered at top ranks for growth in two period of analysis. Small states and Union Territories have achieved drastic growth in the total employment between 2000-01 to 2013-14.

During the pre-slowdown period (i.e. 2003-04 to 2007-08), hill states like, Uttarakhand, Himachal Pradesh and Jammu & Kashmir in the northern region have registered very significant growth in the total employment in the sector. Especially Uttarakhand, has achieved more than 25 per cent annual growth in the total employment during the pre-slowdown period. Other North Eastern states and Punjab, the only big state with more factories have registered double digit growth in the total employment in the organized segment of manufacturing. During the pre-slowdown period West Bengal achieved the least growth with 0.03 per cent in the total employment in the sector.

Post-slowdown periods' employment growth highlights slow recovery of majority of the states in employment in the sector. Only three states have registered double digit growth in total employment. Uttarakhand has posted almost 23 per cent annual increase in total employment between 2007-08 to 2009-10. Among the industrially developed states Tamil Nadu alone is on the top five for better growth in employment during the slowdown period. Jharkhand, Delhi, Other Union Territories and Chhattisgarh have registered a negative growth in total employment between 2007-08 to 2009-10 (Table 4.2).

Table 4.2: Total Employment (Total Persons Employed) in the Sector since 2003-04

Growth Rate between 2003-04 to 2007-08		*Growth Rate between 2009-10 to 2013-14*		*Growth Rate during 2007-08 to 2009-10*	
		Top 5 States			
States	*Growth*	*States*	*Growth*	*States*	*Growth*
Uttarakhand	25.54	Other NE States	13.33	Uttarakhand	22.60
Himachal Pradesh	21.07	Uttarakhand	10.12	Other NE States	19.35
Jammu & Kashmir	14.34	Himachal Pradesh	8.63	Himachal Pradesh	10.40
Other NE States	12.50	Jharkhand	5.84	DN Haveli & D Diu	8.98
Punjab	10.35	Bihar	5.57	Tamil Nadu	6.84
		Bottom 5 States			
States	*Growth*	*States*	*Growth*	*States*	*Growth*
West Bengal	0.03	Delhi	(–) 1.53	Jharkhand	(–) 2.51
Jharkhand	1.10	Kerala	(–) 0.78	Delhi	(–)1.80
Delhi	2.07	Other UTs	0.45	Other UTs	(–) 0.85
Kerala	2.38	Tripura	0.50	Chhattisgarh	(–) 0.28
Assam	3.33	Karnataka	0.90	Jammu & Kashmir	0.23
		National Averages			
Big States	5.82	Big States	2.84	Big States	4.10
Small States	4.53	Small States	1.19	Small States	1.15
Union Territories	8.04	Union Territories	2.44	Union Territories	6.50
All India	**5.84**	**All India**	**2.80**	**All India**	**4.10**

Source: Computed from Annual Survey of Industries for respective years.

Workers' Composition

As expected, the reforms have not boosted workers' composition in the organized manufacturing industrial sector. Industrial growth between 1991 to 2013-14 is 3.01 per cent per annum whereas it is 2.07 per cent for the workers during the 25 years of new economic reforms. Industries are growing list faster and technology and machineries are replacing the labourers may be the reason for the less growth of workers. In pre-slow period 2003-04 to 2007-08 workers growth rate was stood at 7.73 per cent, it has declined to 3.34 per cent for 2009-10 to 2013-14, the post-slow down period. It is true the slowdown has impacted on the employment in the country. Similarly, some new states have registered remarkable growth than the traditionally industrial stronghold states like, Tamil Nadu, Maharashtra, Gujarat, Andhra Pradesh, West Bengal, Punjab etc. States like Uttarakhand, Himachal Pradesh, North Eastern States, and Jammu & Kashmir have registered better growth for both the periods (Table 4.3).

Table 4.3: Trend of Workers' Composition by States

States	*2003-04 to 2007-08*	*2009-10 to 2013-14*	*2003-04 to 2013-14*
I. Major States	**7.69**	**3.47**	**5.57**
1. Andhra Pradesh	4.52	2.63	3.75
2. Assam	4.21	5.82	5.09
3. Bihar	7.43	6.96	7.47
4. Chhattisgarh	13.36	3.03	6.23
5. Gujarat	10.33	4.20	6.91
6. Haryana	14.31	0.22	7.13
7. Himachal Pradesh	27.09	7.46	16.99
8. Jammu & Kashmir	17.71	4.56	9.17
9. Jharkhand	1.43	5.59	1.62
10. Karnataka	9.97	4.85	6.16
11. Kerala	3.17	–2.07	0.63
12. Madhya Pradesh	4.78	3.39	4.04
13. Maharashtra	5.34	5.75	5.55
14. Odisha	10.22	2.43	7.70
15. Punjab	13.26	1.67	6.26
16. Rajasthan	9.81	3.68	6.39
17. Tamil Nadu	7.88	1.58	5.65
18. Uttar Pradesh	7.64	4.40	4.80
19. Uttarakhand	37.17	13.38	27.45
20. West Bengal	0.75	2.88	2.48
II. Small States	**6.25**	**0.98**	**3.37**
1. Delhi	2.79	–2.82	–0.53
2. Goa	10.74	0.46	4.71
3. Tripura	12.10	0.74	7.31
4. Other NE States	16.06	17.67	18.92
III. Union Territories	**10.75**	**–0.36**	**6.30**
1. D N Haveli & Daman Diu	12.22	–0.54	7.62
2. Other UTs	7.21	0.28	2.66
All India	**7.73**	**3.34**	**5.55**

Source: Computed from Annual Survey of Industries for respective years.

Similarly like total employment states which have the maximum share of workers proportion have posted a least growth in the workers component. States like, Tamil Nadu, Maharashtra, Gujarat and Andhra Pradesh have very good growth in employment of workers for pre- and post-slowdown periods.

Contractual Workers

New economic reforms of 1991 have liberalized many rules and regulations exclusively for the industrial sector. To sustain in domestic market and present at global market quality of the products was emphasized. It forced the manufacturing industries to move towards more sophisticated and technically advanced process in production techniques. Technical cooperation and collaboration led to another stage of outsourcing of specific activities of production process from out of factories. Outsourcing of particular activities to other agencies slowly become inner part of the industries—started using outsourced labourers for particular jobs and responsibilities. These processes become common among the organized sectors either in private or even in public sector.. These kinds of labourers/workers were termed as 'contractual workers'. The globalized economy has forced the Indian manufacturing to opt more contractual workers in order to survive in the market (Rajeev, 2009). Organized manufacturing was started subcontracting its production activities in 1980 itself. Many production processes were given to unorganized segments (Goldar and Aggarwal, 2010).

Policy-makers and planners are arguing for flexible labour laws. It poised out with two types of perceptions—one is favouring the industry and another is for workers. The industry favoured argued the rigid or inflexible labour laws have made negative impact on them. On the other hand, those who oppose the flexible labour laws have argued there was steady increase in the contractual employment in the country (Bhirdikar, Paul and Murthy, 2011). More use of contractual labour is a global phenomenon and Indian labour market is accepted the contractual jobs (Sincavage, Haub and Sharma, 2010). Labour regulation is one of the factors which caused the stagnation of employment in the manufacturing sector in the country. It is argued that it should be to have flexible regulations to increase or downsize the workers as per the demand and market conditions (Hoda and Rai, 2015).

The contractual workers are more prevalent in modern industrial establishments. Data on the prevalence of the contractual labourers in the Indian organized manufacturing industries shows an upward trend over the years. Since in the early 1990s, the employment structure of the organized Industries in the country have undergone a structural changes with steep rise in contractual workers (Sengupta and Ray, 2013). Similarly, Saha and Sen, 2014 and Sharma, 2014 also indicate the rise in contractual employment in the country's manufacturing industries. The liberalization process of 1991 has given the rights to firms to cut the job and wages in manufacturing sector (Verma and Awasthi, 2010). Deregulation of employment and wages become part of industries rights and led to more casualisation of employments. It was observed from the data that, all the years the incidence of contractual workers is increasing in the sector. The share of contractual workers among the total persons engaged was below 20 per cent (16.58%) in 2000-01 to almost 26 per cent in 2013-14. Similar trend was observed in share of contractual workers among the total workers.

The trend of contractual workers since 2000-01 is highlighted in the Figure 4.4. During past decade, there was a sharp increase in engagement of contractual workers in the sector. It was 16.58 per cent of total employment and 21.59 per cent total workers' proportion in 2000-01 and it reached to a maximum of 27 per cent of total employment and 35 per cent in workers' share in 2011-12.

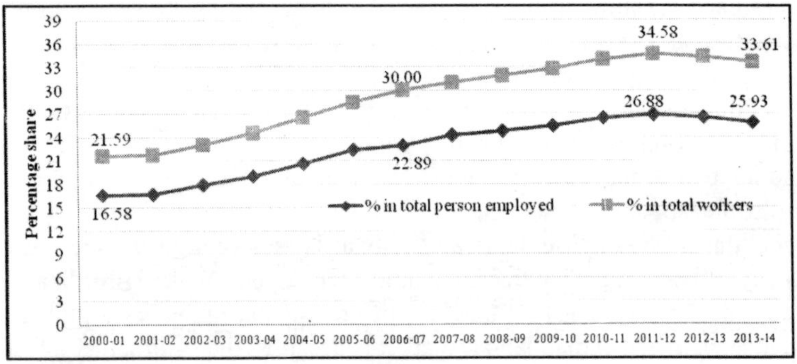

Fig. 4.4: Percentage distribution of contractual workers

Source: Computed from ASI data for respective years.

Contractual Workers and Factories

The data reveals some very interesting findings about the prevalence of contract workers in organized manufacturing sector. Almost top states which have the maximum number of contract workers per factory are from small category states and industrially emerging new states. Tripura stands at first with the average 51 contractual employees per functional factory during 2000-01 to 2013-14. The alarming point is that, the state is under the rule of trade union strong hold Communist Party. It is very clear that the industrial establishments coming up the states are opting more jobs under contractual in nature. States has no control over the labour regulations, nature of employment opportunities generated rather state needs industrial developments for creating more opportunities.

More than 10 states and Union Territories are having more than 20 workers per factory from contractual category. Surprisingly, industrially developed states like, Tamil Nadu and Maharashtra, Punjab, and Karnataka have this average contractual workers per factory is very less compared with other small states which are emerging destinations for industrial developments. Among these states Tamil Nadu has very least proportion of contractual workers per factory (Table 4.4).

Haryana, Jammu & Kashmir, Odisha, Uttarakhand, Goa and Tripura have number of contract workers per factory with more than 30 workers. Small states are having more prevalence of contract worker than the industrially developed and big states. Bihar, Chhattisgarh, and Other North-eastern States, all are emerging states which have more contract workers than the national average of 18 workers per factory. Few industrially developed states have the prevalence of contract workers just around the national average. Andhra Pradesh, Gujarat, Uttar Pradesh and West Bengal have the numbers which are almost equivalent to national average. However, as compared with other small states, the average number of workers in these states very less. Further in the reference period, these big states have registered comparatively less industrial growths than the above mentioned small states.

Delhi followed by Kerala and Tamil Nadu has the least number of contractual workers in the organized manufacturing industrial establishments. An average of 3 persons in Delhi, 8 persons in Kerala and 9 persons in Tamil Nadu are working as contractual workers between 2000-01 to 2013-14. Only these three states have the single digit number of contractual workers in registered factories during the period. Remaining vast majority of the states has more number of contractual workers per factory under function.

Empirical evidence significantly supports the data that, the proportion of contract workers in total workers at oil fields and petroleum refineries are 76.94 and 80.12 percentages respectively. The duration of employment of contract workers in these industries are too short in the length of service. At national level 68.15 per cent of contract workers are having 1-3 years length of service in oil fields. In petroleum refineries, 64.27 per cent oil contract workers are having the less than one year of service (Labour Bureau, 2011). The proportion of contractual workers in top 82 companies in India stands at 34 per cent. Out of 3.2 million total employments in these top companies, 1.08 million workers are contractual in nature. Among these companies, automobile sector has the maximum share of 47 workers in contractual category (Ananthanarayanan, 2014).

Table 4.4: Number of Contractual Workers per Factory by State-wise

States	Number of contractual workers per factory													
	2000-2001	2001-2002	2002-2003	2003-2004	2004-2005	2005-2006	2006-2007	2007-2008	2008-2009	2009-2010	2010-2011	2011-2012	2012-2013	2013-2014
I. Major States	**10**	**10**	**11**	**12**	**13**	**15**	**17**	**18**	**18**	**19**	**16**	**17**	**16**	**16**
1. Andhra Pradesh	24	24	24	24	25	28	28	27	28	27	19	19	17	10
2. Assam	5	9	7	8	8	10	12	12	10	10	10	10	8	9
3. Bihar	12	15	13	16	16	19	19	21	21	25	21	23	21	19
4. Chhattisgarh	13	12	13	17	20	21	21	24	23	21	25	25	23	21
5. Gujarat	11	12	13	14	15	16	18	20	23	22	17	17	17	17
6. Haryana	15	14	17	20	26	32	34	41	41	53	33	36	33	36
7. Himachal Pradesh	9	6	7	9	10	11	14	15	15	18	14	11	15	10
8. Jammu & Kashmir	13	13	15	15	17	19	24	26	31	32	27	31	23	28
9. Jharkhand	11	10	13	10	10	9	13	12	11	8	12	17	17	18
10. Karnataka	16	5	6	6	7	9	11	11	13	12	12	14	11	13
11. Kerala	2	5	5	3	4	5	8	7	10	8	8	7	6	5
12. Madhya Pradesh	14	10	11	11	14	15	16	17	19	19	18	19	18	21
13. Maharashtra	8	8	10	11	12	15	18	19	18	21	17	19	17	19
14. Odisha	17	16	18	22	25	25	24	30	41	45	43	40	44	45
15. Punjab	6	8	9	8	11	12	14	12	13	13	11	11	11	13
16. Rajasthan	8	9	11	11	12	13	13	14	15	16	15	16	14	16
17. Tamil Nadu	4	4	5	5	7	8	8	9	8	10	9	8	8	9
18. Uttar Pradesh	11	10	13	14	14	14	17	20	19	20	17	18	16	19
19. Uttarakhand	8	8	9	9	14	26	26	28	41	38	43	50	48	56
20. West Bengal	8	9	10	10	10	13	15	15	17	18	19	21	21	19

(Contd.)

Table 4.4: (*Contd.*)

States	*Number of contractual workers per factory*													
	2000-2001	2001-2002	2002-2003	2003-2004	2004-2005	2005-2006	2006-2007	2007-2008	2008-2009	2009-2010	2010-2011	2011-2012	2012-2013	2013-2014
II. Small States	**3**	**4**	**0**	**5**	**5**	**7**	**8**	**10**	**13**	**13**	**12**	**12**	**11**	**13**
1. Delhi	1	1	0	1	1	2	2	2	3	4	3	2	2	3
2. Goa	8	9	0	14	21	21	26	33	39	31	29	32	28	31
3. Tripura	20	26	1	24	9	30	40	51	55	55	58	55	28	43
4. Other NE States	7	8	0	10	10	14	20	15	14	21	25	42	36	35
III. Union Territories	**6**	**8**	**11**	**9**	**10**	**11**	**14**	**16**	**15**	**21**	**17**	**14**	**15**	**13**
1. D N Haveli D Diu	5	8	10	10	10	11	16	18	15	23	16	14	16	16
2. Other UTs	8	10	11	8	9	10	12	13	13	15	18	14	11	3
All India	**10**	**10**	**8**	**12**	**13**	**15**	**16**	**17**	**18**	**19**	**16**	**17**	**16**	**16**

Source: Annual Survey of Industries respective years.

Composition of Contractual Workers in Total Persons Employed

As mentioned there is an increase in the overall employment in the sector up since 2000-01 to 2013-14 except for initial two year period. However, total employment in the organized sector has declined in 2012-13 by 0.5 million. A similar trend was observed in the share of contractual workers in the total employment of the sector. It was 16.58 per cent of the contractual employment in the total employment of the sector in 2000-01 and increased to 22.89 per cent in 2006-07. Further the share increased to 25.5 per cent in 2009-10 and 26.90 per cent in 2011-12. Next year (2012-13), the employment composition of contractual labourers in total employment has slightly down to 26.6 per cent. The state-wise interpretation gives very interesting findings from the analysis. All the top five states are from category of industrially emerging new states by pushing back the industrially developed states. Tripura, again stand at top with 81.41 per cent of the share of contractual workers among the total persons employed in the sector. Bihar (57.52%), Odisha (46.7%), Other North Eastern States (44.6%) and Uttarakhand (42.64%) are the other states at the top five positions with Tripura for the year 2013-14. Vast majority of the employment created during this period are contractual in nature. Altogether, 14 states have the maximum number of contractual workers which is higher than the national average of 25.9 per cent.

Other Union Territories consisting of Andaman & Nicobar Islands, Chandigarh and Puducherry have the least percentage of contract workers with just 5.42 per cent among the total persons engaged in the organized manufacturing sector. Most of the southern states like Andhra Pradesh, Kerala, Karnataka and Tamil Nadu also have the less proportion of contract workers which is below to the national average of 25.93 per cent. Madhya Pradesh, Jharkhand, Union Territories of Dadra & Nagar Haveli and Daman & Diu and Himachal Pradesh are other states which have the proportion of contractual workers below to the national average (Fig. 4.5).

Proportion of Contractual Workers among Total Workers

The data clearly brings out the magnitude of contractual workers in the organized manufacturing sector in the country. Half of 32 States/UTs reporting for availability of organized Industrial units have the share of contractual workers which is above to the national average. Again five states have the proportion of more than 50 per cent of contractual workers

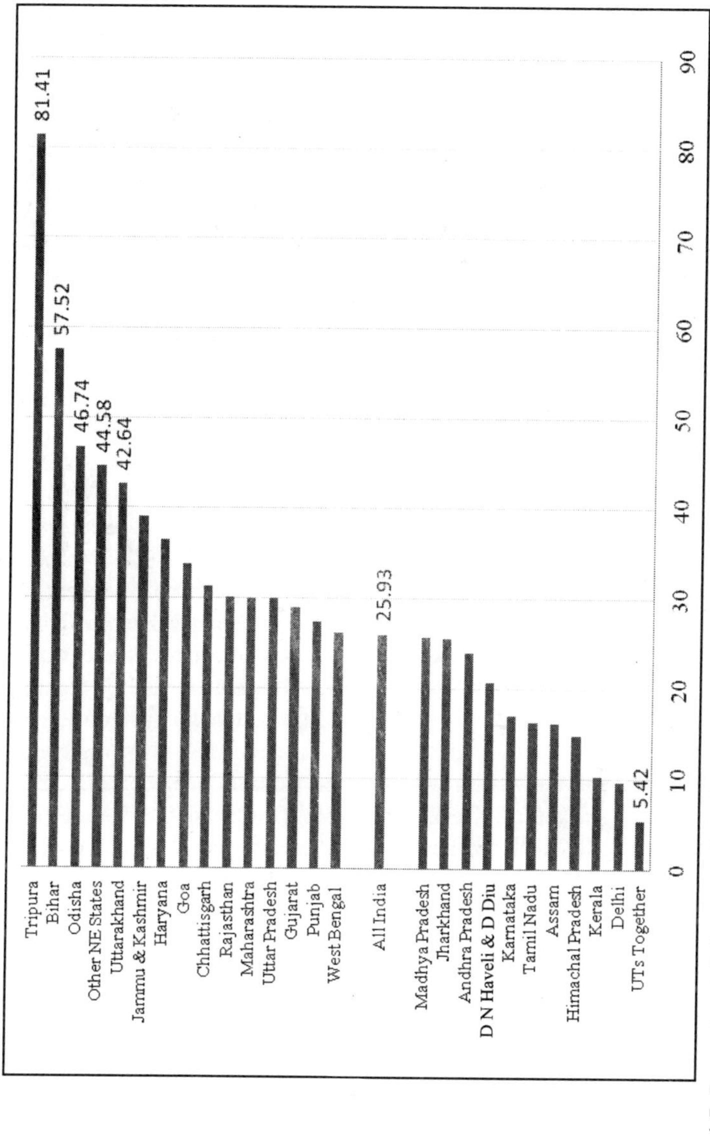

Fig. 4.5: Percentage of Contractual workers in total persons employed.

Source: Annual Survey of Industries, 2013-14.

in 2013-14. Quite surprisingly, almost 90 per cent of the workers in the industries in Tripura are under contract in nature. The state's share of contractual workers in 2000-01 was 62.41 per cent. The percentage is keeping on increase and reached the peak of 90 per cent for the recent year 2013-14. Similarly, among the other top five states, Bihar stands at second position with 67.98 per cent. Odisha have 59 and Other North Eastern States (includes of Manipur, Meghalaya, and Nagaland) and 53 per cent of the contractual workers respectively. However, except Tripura all four states (Bihar, Other North Eastern States, Odisha and Uttarakhand) had little proportion of contractual workers in 2000-01. Only four states have the percentage of contractual workers among total workers at less than 20 per cent in 2013-14. Other Union Territories, Delhi and Kerala are states with least share of contract workers in 2013-14 (Fig. 4.6).

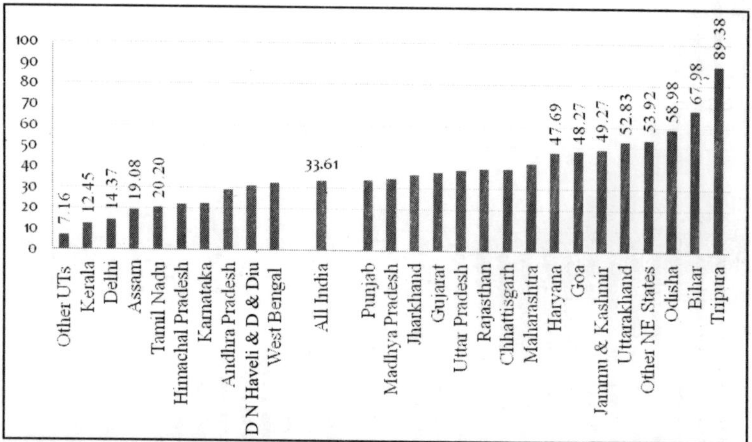

Fig. 4.6: Percentage of contractual workers in total workers, 2013-14

Source: Annual Survey of Industries, 2013-14.

Growth Trend of Contractual Workers

Table 4.5 shows the growth pattern of the contractual workers since 2000-01. It is very clear that only small and new emerging states have occupied the top positions for all the three reference period. Between 2003-04 to 2007-08, Uttarakhand posted a maximum of 45.89 per cent annual growth in the employment of contractual workers. However, these states have registered relatively less growth in the total employment during the period. Uttarakhand has registered 25 per cent annual growth in total employment against this 46 per cent growth of contractual workers during the same period. Similarly, other states which have reached to top five position in growth rate of hiring contractual workers are Himachal Pradesh, Jammu & Kashmir, Tripura and Kerala. Even among bottom five states which have least growth in hiring contractual workers have registered 5 and above percentage as annual growth between 2003-04 to 2007-08. Only two states have reported the negative growth in the use of contractual workers (Table 4.5).

Between 2009-10 to 2013-14, the post-period of global economic slowdown, vast majority of the Indian states have reported little use of contractual workers as in this period there was a slow growth in the total employment generation in the sector. Again small and industrially emerging new states have largely reported higher growth in contractual workers. Only four states (Jharkhand, Other North Eastern States, Uttarakhand and Karnataka) have achieved double digit growth of only two states (Uttarakhand and Other North Eastern States) have registered double digit growth both in total employment and contractual employment. Remaining vast majority of the states has reported very little growth in total employment and higher growth in contractual employment. Karnataka and West Bengal states which have registered around 12 and 9 per cent growth respectively in contractual employment have posted only less than one per cent and 2 per cent growth respectively in total employment per annum. Among the bottom five states regarding the growth rate of contractual employment, all the states have posted the negative growth for the contractual employment during the post-slow down period. All these states have registered very slow growth in total employment also during the post-slow down period (Table 4.5).

Over the period of past ten years (between 2003-04 to 2013-14), Uttarakhand has registered highest of 38.92 per cent of annual growth rate in contractual employment growth. Himachal Pradesh, Tripura and Other North Eastern States have the highest growth in use of contractual employment. Other Union Territories, Andhra Pradesh and Uttar Pradesh along with Rajasthan are positioned at bottom level in the growth chart. The average growth at national level is begged at 8.91 per cent during the period 2003-04 to 2013-14. A maximum of 13.29 per cent by category of Small States and 6.62 per cent by Union Territories has registered the growth during last ten years. During the previous decade (2000-01 to 2010-11) Uttarakhand and Himachal Pradesh along with Other North Eastern States, Tripura and Goa have registered a maximum annual growth rate (CAGR) on use of contractual workers. And these states have also registered a better growth in growth in number of registered factories.

The growth rate achieved by these emerging states is far higher than the rate of growth achieved by any industrially developed state (Annexure Table A1).

One way other this is helping the labour force of the country by providing more number of employment opportunities rather if not focusing on job security or other social security measures. It is observed from the data that more jobs which are generated during the recent years are falling under contract in nature. Further, new industries which are coming up during the reference period have moved towards new destinations. Tripura, Himachal Pradesh, Uttarakhand, Bihar, Assam and Jharkhand, other North Eastern States and Jammu & Kashmir have registered better growth than the industrially developed states.

Table 4.5: Growth of Contractual Workers Since 2000-01

Growth Rate between 2003-04 to 2007-08		*Growth Rate between 2009-10 to 2013-14*		*Growth Rate during 2007-08 to 2009-10*	
Top 5 States					
States	*Growth*	*States*	*Growth*	*States*	*Growth*
Uttarakhand	45.89	Jharkhand	29.09	Uttarakhand	48.48
Himachal Pradesh	30.23	Other NE States	23.75	Delhi	46.51
Jammu & Kashmir	27.25	Uttarakhand	16.41	Odisha	29.82
Tripura	21.84	Karnataka	11.87	Other NE States	29.35
Kerala	20.48	West Bengal	8.68	Himachal Pradesh	25.19
Bottom 5 States					
States	*Growth*	*States*	*Growth*	*States*	*Growth*
Andhra Pradesh	4.55	Other UTs	(-) 29.64	Jharkhand	(-) 7.50
Delhi	5.50	Andhra Pradesh	(-) 9.89	Chhattisgarh	(-) 3.58
Jharkhand	7.37	Kerala	(-) 7.87	Goa	(-) 3.31
Rajasthan	7.47	DN Haveli & D Diu	(-) 2.30	Assam	(-) 0.76
Odisha	7.98	Haryana	(-) 2.23	Uttar Pradesh	(-) 0.09
National Averages					
Big States	11.01	Big States	4.15	Big States	8.63
Small States	16.89	Small States	5.84	Small States	12.80
Union Territories	13.97	Union Territories	(-) 5.95	Union Territories	12.34
All India	**11.16**	**All India**	**3.97**	**All India**	**8.79**

Source: Computed values from ASI data for respective years.

Concluding remarks

While analysing data from 2000-01 to 2013-14 of the organized manufacturing, it is evident that the sector is moving towards new direction. Industries are started opening in small and new states which really need more industries rather than already industrially developed states. Assam, Bihar, Chhattissgarh, Himachal Pradesh, Tripura and Other North Eastern States and Uttarakhand have shown a better growth in number of industries registered, total persons employed and total workers and also in hiring of contractual workers. There is an increase in the total employment (total person employed), and workers' share in total employment over the years. The global economic slowdown does not make a significant impact on the organized manufacturing sector in the country. There was a decline in employment and it has been recovered very fastly. It is clear from the data that industries are opting or following more liberalised process in labour/workers' policy. The higher and an increasing trend in the prevalence of the contractual labour is evident for such process.

Notes: Grouping of States: States are grouped on the basis of geographical area. Assam has been included in big states group and taken away from North Eastern States due to big volume of Industrial indicators. Except Assam all other North Eastern States are placed in Small Category States. Further Tripura has been placed separately because of certain unique features on employment especially the prevalence of contractual employment in the state. Other North Eastern States includes: Manipur, Meghalaya, Nagaland and Sikkim together placed as 'Other North Eastern States' and no data are available for Arunachal Pradesh and Mizoram. Again Union Territories are classified into two separate groups, Dadra Nagar Haveli and Daman Diu placed together as these two UTs are well established in industries. All other UTs including Andaman Nicobar Island, Chandigarh and Puducherry are placed together as 'Other UTs' category.

Contract Worker/Labour: 'Contract Labour' is distinguished from direct labour in terms of employment relationship with the principal establishment and method of wage payment. A person, who is hired, supervised and remunerated by a contractor who in turn compensate by the establishment. In short, contract labour is neither borne in payroll or muster roll or wage paid directly to the labour even though they perform similar duties.

Accordingly to the Contract Labour (Regulation and Abolition) Act, 1970: Contract labour/worker is one who is hired in connection with the work of an establishment by a principal employer through a contractor. A workman shall be deemed to be employed as "contract labour" in or in connection with the work of an establishment when he is hired in or in connection with such work by or through a contractor, with or without the knowledge of the principal employer.

Global Financial Crisis and Economic Slowdown: In United States, the collapse of sky-high home prices (real estate business) in mid-2007 has made a great impact on the financial institutions in the country. In early 2008 many banks and financial institutions in US started collapsing and have had an immense effect on the capital market of the country. Then immediately, this collapse in US has made an impact on European Economy too. Rest of the world and developing countries were affected because of this slowdown due to stop in imports by US and Europe. Largely export oriented manufacturers were affected more.

Annexure Table

Table A. 1: Growth Trend of Contractual Workers

States	Statewise % 2013-14	2003-04 to 2013-14	2003-04 to 2007-08	2009-10 to 2013-14	2000-01 to 2010-11	2000-01 to 2013-14	2007-08 to 2009-10
I. Big States	**96.39**	**8.88**	**11.01**	**4.15**	**9.57**	**7.69**	**8.63**
1. Andhra Pradesh	8.66	-1.68	4.55	-9.89	3.85	-0.92	1.25
2. Assam	0.86	8.70	11.69	7.71	15.37	12.28	-0.76
3. Bihar	1.86	11.15	10.67	8.50	12.01	10.05	11.86
4. Chhattisgarh	1.48	9.04	15.31	5.83	13.49	9.32	-3.58
5. Gujarat	11.33	8.16	10.30	4.02	9.15	7.85	7.06
6. Haryana	6.35	10.02	17.62	-2.23	11.72	9.84	12.42
7. Himachal Pradesh	0.82	20.01	30.23	1.35	21.01	15.00	25.19
8. Jammu & Kashmir	0.74	17.45	27.25	6.82	16.56	14.28	7.24
9. Jharkhand	1.36	12.98	7.37	29.09	6.00	8.46	-7.50
10. Karnataka	4.50	13.25	15.57	11.87	1.39	2.68	3.68
11. Kerala	1.03	8.61	20.48	-7.87	17.19	9.62	11.72
12. Madhya Pradesh	2.36	9.35	10.20	5.29	5.48	4.80	10.65
13. Maharashtra	16.08	11.67	12.90	8.36	12.21	10.51	9.17
14. Odisha	3.47	12.45	7.98	6.92	14.47	11.83	29.82
15. Punjab	4.69	11.62	16.97	5.66	11.68	10.35	4.88
16. Rajasthan	4.02	8.70	7.47	7.32	11.88	10.21	10.04
17. Tamil Nadu	9.45	11.86	12.52	5.67	15.64	12.20	16.79
18. Uttar Pradesh	7.77	7.99	11.54	5.77	8.47	7.92	-0.09
19. Uttarakhand	4.69	38.92	45.89	16.41	34.44	28.88	48.48
20. West Bengal	4.82	11.07	8.04	8.68	12.56	10.20	17.96
II. Small States	**1.98**	**13.29**	**16.89**	**5.84**	**15.07**	**12.27**	**12.80**
1. Delhi	0.31	10.68	5.50	1.69	6.71	5.82	40.51
2. Goa	0.54	9.67	17.74	4.43	15.73	12.87	-3.31
3. Tripura	0.67	13.96	21.84	1.33	18.81	12.91	14.27
4. Other NE States	0.45	22.76	14.65	23.75	19.60	20.42	29.35
III. Union Territories	**1.62**	**6.62**	**13.97**	**-5.95**	**15.67**	**9.33**	**12.34**
1. DN Haveli & Daman Diu	1.52	8.99	14.36	-2.30	17.41	12.76	15.20
2. Other UTs	0.09	-7.32	12.74	-29.64	12.04	-4.89	2.34
All India	**100**	**8.91**	**11.16**	**3.97**	**9.76**	**7.78**	**8.79**

Source: Annual Survey of Industries, various periods.

References

Ananthanarayanan, Ravi (2014). "Contract workers make up 46 per cent of workforce of india's largest industrial companies", *The Live Mint*, March 19, 2014.

CSO, Annual Survey of Industries, different periods, Central Statistical Organisation, Ministry of Statistics and Programme Implementation, Government of India, New Delhi.

Bhalla, Sheila (2006). "Recent Developments in The Unorganised Rural Non-farm Sector", Working Paper No. 28, Institute of Human Development, New Delhi.

Bhirdikar, Kishore, Paul, G.D. Bino and Murthy, Venkatesh (2011). "Understanding labour market flexibility in India: Exploring emerging trends in India", ATLMRI Discussion Paper No. 10, *Tata Institute of Social Sciences*, Mumbai.

GoI (2009). "Global Economic Crisis and Its Impact on India", Occasional Series Paper No. 4, Research Unit, Rajya Sabha Secretariat, New Delhi.

Goldar, Bishwanath and Aggarwal, Suresh Chand (2010). "Informalization of Industrial Labour in India: Are Labour Market Rigidities and Growing Import Competition to Blame?", Paper Presented at the 6th Annual Conference on Economic Growth and Development, held at Indian Statistical Institute during 16-18, December 2010 in New Delhi.

Hoda, Anwarul and Rai, Durgesh K. (2015). "Regulations and Growth of Manufacturing Employment in India: Balancing Protection and Flexibility", Working Paper No. 298, Indian Council for Research on International Economic Relations, New Delhi.

Labour Bureau (2012). "Report on Working Conditions of the Contract Workers in Petroleum Refineries and Oil Fields", Labour Bureau, Government of India, Chandigarh.

Labour Bureau (2011). "Report on Effect of Economic Slowdown on Employment in India (July–September, 2011)", Labour Bureau, Government of India, Chandigarh.

Labour Bureau (2009). "Report on Effect of Economic Slowdown on Employment in India (October–December 2008)", Ministry of Labour and Employment, Labour Bureau, Chandigarh.

NSSO (2011). Report on "Employment and Unemployment Situation in India", Report No. 537 (66/10/1) National Sample Survey Organisation, Ministry of Statistics and Programme Implementation, Government of India, New Delhi.

NSSO (2006). Report on "Employment and Unemployment Situation in India", Report No. 515 (61/10/1) National Sample Survey Organisation, Ministry of Statistics and Programme Implementation, Government of India, New Delhi.

NSSO (2001). Report on "Employment and Unemployment Situation in India", Report No. 458 (55/10/2), National Sample Survey Organisation, Ministry of Statistics and Programme Implementation, Government of India, New Delhi.

Saha, Bibhas and Sen, Kunal (2014). "The rising use of contract workers: Is globalization responsible?" *Live Mint*, October 29, 2014.

Sengputa, Debashish and Titus, Ray (2013). "Evaluating employees welfare through provision and utilisation of employees benefit scheme", *International Journal of Economy, Management and Social Sciences*, New Jersey, USA. 2(8): 544-549.

Shah, Sweety and Aanand, Shubhra (2013). "Global Economic Crisis: Impacts, Challenges and Opportunities for India", *Pacific Business Review International*, Volume 6, No. 5: 29-34.

Sincavage, Jassica R., Haub Carl and Sharma, O.P. (2010). "Labour Costs in India's Organised Manufacturing Sector", *Monthly Labour Review*, Division of International Labour Comparisons, Bureau of Labour Statistics, United States Department of Labour, Washington DC.

Singh, Fulwinder Paul, (2012). "Economic Reforms and Productivity Growth in Indian Manufacturing Sector—An Interstate Analysis", *International Journal of Marketing, Financial Services and Management Research*, ISSN 2277 3622, Vol. 1, No. 12, pp. 1-22.

UNCTAD (2013). "Impact of the Global Slowdown on India's Export and Employment", Publication of United Nations, DITC/TNCD/2009/1, United Nations Conference on Trade and Development, Geneva.

Verma, N.M.P. and Awasthi, I.C. (2010). *Contractual Employment in Indian Labour* Market, Concept Publishing Company Pvt. Ltd., New Delhi.

5

Special Economic Zones (SEZs) and Its Linkage with Land Acquisition and Smart Cities

M.R.B. Anantha Padmanabha and *M.R. Biju*

A Special Economic Zone (SEZ) is a specified, delineated and duty-free geographical region that has different economic laws from those of the country in which it is situated. In some countries, such a region is even treated as a deemed foreign territory. A SEZ is a trade capacity development tool, with the goal to promote rapid economic growth by using tax and business incentives to attract foreign investment and technology. Today, there are approximately 3,000 SEZs operating in 120 countries, which account for over US$ 600 billion in exports and about 50 million jobs. By offering privileged terms, SEZs attract investment and foreign exchange, spur employment and boost the development of improved technologies and infrastructure.

Most developing countries in the world have recognized the importance of facilitating international trade for the sustained growth of the economy and increased contribution to the GDP of the nation. As part of its continuing commitment to liberalization, the Government of India (GoI) has also, since the last decade, adopted a multi-pronged approach to promote foreign investment in India. The Gol has pushed ahead with second-generation reforms and has made several policy changes to achieve this objective.

As of April 27, 2006, there were 13 functional SEZs and about 61 SEZs, which have been approved and are under the process of establishment in India. The total value of the exports from some of the key SEZs in India during the financial year 2003-04 was US$ 3.08 billion, which increased to US$ 4.07 billion in 2004-05. Recently, after the enactment of the Special Economic Zones Act, 2005 ("SEZ Act"), which made several facilities and benefits available, several industrial houses have shown keen interest in setting up SEZs and SEZ Units. In the last six months, over 100 approvals have been granted for setting up SEZs spread over 15 States and 2 Union territories, taking the current tally to 117 SEZS.

The SEZ policy was first introduced in April 2000, as a part of the Export-Import ("EXIM") policy of India. The objective was to provide an internationally competitive environment for exports that would in turn earn precious foreign exchange for India. However, in its initial form the concept was not able to inspire sufficient confidence in the investors. To provide a stable economic environment for the promotion of export-import of goods in a quick, efficient and hassle-free manner, GoI enacted the SEZ Act, which received the assent of the President of India on June 23, 2005. The SEZ Act and the SEZ Rules, 2006 (SEZ Rules) were notified on February 10, 2006. The SEZ Act is expected to give a big push to exports and consequendy to the foreign direct investment (FDI) inflows into India, and is considered to be one of the finest pieces of legislation that may well represent the future of the industrial development strategy in India. The new law is aimed at encouraging public-private partnership to develop world-class infrastructure and attract private investment (domestic and foreign), boosting economic growth, exports and employment.

Special Economic Zones (SEZs) can be compared to their predecessors, Free Trade Zones and Export Processing Zones, in that they are aimed at stimulating foreign direct investment (FDI) and rapid, export-led, industrial growth. The essential characteristic of such schemes is that they allow the by-passing of particular social legislation or tax provisions which are perceived to be an impediment to progress or the competitiveness of an export-oriented activity.

A brainchild of the Ministry of Commerce and Industry (MoCI), the SEZ Act that was passed in 2005 goes much further than previous policies as it seeks to establish a large number of private industrial townships, each covering hundreds or thousands of hectares of land. According to the MoCI, "As of February 2010, formal approval has been accorded by states to 571 proposals out of which 348 SEZs have been notified. A total of 105 SEZs are already exporting. The 571 approved proposals are for SEZs sponsored by State governments and are in addition to seven Central Government SEZs and 12 State/private sector SEZs that were set up prior to the enactment of SEZ Act, 2005 (MoCI, 2010)". These 571 approved SEZs represent a total of 67680 hectares.

SEZs have shown a dramatic rate of growth with total exports of Rs. 996,890 million during the financial year 2008-09, a growth of 50 per cent over the exports for the same period of the previous year. Exports in the first three quarters of 2009-10 financial year registered a growth rate of about 12.7 per cent over the corresponding period of the previous financial year (MoCI, 2010).

The Controversy Surrounding SEZs

Despite the huge rate of approval and establishment of SEZs, and thus their apparent success, the development of SEZs has faced considerable opposition and is stalling in some cases. This resistance has arisen because of various controversial aspects regarding the establishment of SEZs that will be discussed in more detail in the following section.

At the heart of the problem is the fact that the establishment of an SEZ generally requires the forced acquisition of land and the eviction of its previous users. This is possible for Indian states under the Land Acquisition Act of 1894 for "public purposes". The invocation of "public purpose" for what are essentially private commercial ventures has been repeatedly questioned. In particular, the Comptroller & Auditor General (CAG) of India has investigated SEZs and suggested that far from being in the public interest, the net effect is a strong loss of revenue to the state because of foregone tax revenue.

Resistance to SEZs, however, has been most strong from the communities that are directly affected and from popular organisations. In state after state, plans for forcible land acquisition have met with concerted opposition from "below", and in certain cases have been abandoned as a result. At this level, the controversy centres on the grave inadequacy of packages of compensation, resettlement and rehabilitation. While state authorities are required to compensate previous owners for the value of land and dwellings, such compensation, even if paid in full, is woefully inadequate to the loss of land and non-land assets, the loss of livelihood opportunities and the disruption to traditional rural live. Popular resistance to SEZs also contests the whole development model that replaces farming on fertile agricultural land with autonomous, private industrial enclaves that mostly just provide jobs for urban skilled and semi-skilled workers. SEZs are charged with being a sop to corporate, rather than popular interests.

Against this backdrop, the present chapter explores the fundamentals of Indian Policy framework to be followed in establishing an SEZ followed by its linkage with the Land Acquisition and Smart Cities. This chapter has been classified under four heads, *viz.*:

(a) Regulatory framework for SEZ,
(b) Linkage between SEZ Act and Land Acquisition Act,
(c) Smart Cities, and
(d) Advantages and Limitations of SEZs.

PART-I

A. Regulatory Framework for SEZ

The Ministry of Commerce and Industry lays down the regulations that govern the setting up and administering of the SEZs. The Central Government is involved in notifying SEZs and in overseeing their functioning, while the State Governments play a significant lead role in the development of SEZs in their respective States by stipulating the conditions to be adhered to by an SEZ and granting the necessary approvals. The policy framework for SEZs has been enacted in the SEZ Act and the supporting procedures are laid down in SE Rules.

The provisions under the SEZ Act and the SEZ Rules, *inter alia*, cover the following aspects:

I. Constitution of authorities and bodies for regulating the SEZs and SEZ Units,
II. Permissible services and manufacturing activities in SEZs,
III. Criteria and procedure for setting up of SEZs and SEZ Units,
IV. Obligations on the part of SEZs and SEZ Units,
V. Dispute Resolution, and
VI. Facilities and Incentives to the Developer of SEZs and to SEZ Units.

Constitution of Administrative Authorities and Bodies for Regulating the SEZs and SEZ Units

The SEZ Act provides for the constitution of the following authorities and bodies to regulate the SEZs and SEZ Units:

1. Board of Approval ('Board')

2. Development Commissioner
3. Approval Committee
4. SEZ Authority

Permissible Services and Manufacturing Activities in an SEZ

An SEZ could be jointly or severally developed by the Central or State Government or a private party, (a) for manufacturing goods, (b) for rendering services, or (c) as a free trade and warehousing zone.

"Manufacture" means to make, produce, fabricate, assemble, process or bring into existence, by hand or by machine, a new product having a distinctive name, character or use and shall include processes such as refrigeration, cutting, polishing, blending, repair, remaking, re-engineering and includes agriculture, aquaculture, animal husbandry, floriculture, horticulture, pisciculture, poultry, sericulture, viticulture and mining.

"Services" means tradable services which (a) are covered under the General Agreement on Trade in Services, (b) may be prescribed by the Central Government for the purpose of SEZ Act, and (c) earn foreign exchange. The "Services" as prescribed by the Central Government include:

- Trading, warehousing, research and development services;
- Computer software services and ITES, call centres, data processing, engineering and design, insurance claim processing, legal databases, medical transcription, support centres and web site services;
- Off-shore banking services, professional services (excluding legal services and accounting), rental/leasing services without operators; and
- Other business services, courier services, audio-visual services, construction and related services, distribution services (excluding retail), educational services, environmental services, financial services, hospital services, tourism and travel related services, recreational, cultural, entertainment services, transport services and transport auxiliary services.

"Free Trade and Warehousing Zone" means a SEZ wherein mainly trading and warehousing and other activities related thereto are carried on.

The types of SEZs along with their minimum area requirements prescribed under the SEZ Rules have been enclosed in Annexure B.

Criteria and Procedure for Setting Up an SEZ and an SEZ Unit

Procedure to Set up an SEZ

Application

An SEZ can be set up by the Central or State Government, the public or the private sector including a foreign company or jointly in the form of a consortium. A person who wishes to set up a SEZ (Developer) should submit a proposal in the form of an application before the Board or directly to the State Government after identifying the area. The State Government then forwards the application to the Board along with its recommendations within 45 days, or the Board may grant approval subject to the applicant obtaining the concurrence of the State Government. A State Government intending to set up a SEZ may directly forward the application to the Board after identification of the area. Further, the Central Government can directly notify the SEZ, without any application being made to the Board or reference to the State Government.

The application submitted to the Board by the Developer should contain the following details: name, address and status of the Developer (whether individual/private company/State Government/NRIs, etc.), and should be accompanied by a project report covering the following particulars:

- Location of the proposed SEZ with details of existing infrastructure and infrastructure proposed to be established.
- Its area and distance from the nearest seaport/airport/rail/road etc.
- Financial details, including proposed investment, mode of financing and viability of the project.
- Details of foreign equity and repatriation of dividends etc., if any.
- Whether the SEZ will allow only certain specific industries or will be a multi-product SEZ.

Criteria for approval of SEZ

Proposals for setting up SEZ would be governed by the following criteria:

- Generation of additional economic activity.
- Promotion of export of goods and services.
- Promotion of investments from domestic and foreign sources.
- Creation of employment opportunities.
- Development of infrastructural facilities.
- Maintenance of sovereignty and integrity of India and security of the States.

The Board may approve, reject or modify the proposal for the establishment of the SEZ. The Board also has the power to cancel the approval, provided the applicant is given art opportunity to be heard before cancellation.

After the Board of Approval has scrutinized the application, it forwards the application to the Central Government, which reviews it and grants a Letter of Approval (Letter) if the application is found satisfactory.

The Letter has a validity of 3 years within which time the applicant has to effectuate the proposal and start operations. However, the Board may grant a further extension for 2 years on a case-by-case basis. The applicant/Developer has then to submit the documents of the land so acquired for the purpose of setting up the SEZ to the Central Government to declare it as a SEZ.

After the approval has been granted, the Developer is required to submit all details to commence the authorized operations, and to apply for the exemptions, drawbacks and concessions. The SEZ will be demarcated into the processing and non-processing areas. The Developer can allot land in the processing area to individual Units. The Developer is not permitted to sell the non-processing area in a SEZ; however, the Developer may allot such land for business and social purposes. Further, the Developer is required to execute a bond-*cum*-legal undertaking, with regard to the proper utilization of the goods.

The Developer/Co-Developer should hold a minimum of 26 per cent equity in the entity (i.e. special purpose vehicle or separate entity) that is proposing to create business, residential or recreational facilities in the SEZ.

Further, the Developer has to sign an undertaking that it will be governed by the following local laws:

- Area planning
- Sewerage disposal

- Pollution control
- Industrial and labour laws

The SEZ Authority constituted under the SEZ Act is duty-bound to undertake measures for the development, operation and management of the SEZ for which it is constituted, induding the development of infrastructure, and promotion of exports from the SEZ, and to review the functioning and performance etc. of the SEZ.

B. Procedure to set up a SEZ Unit

Application

To set up a SEZ Unit, copies of project proposal are required to be submitted to the Development Commissioner who will forward the proposal to the Approval Committee. The Approval Committee shall consist of Development Commissioners, Officers from State and Central Government and also a representative of the Developer as a Special Invitee.

A consolidated application form is required to be submitted for the following approvals:

- Allotment of Land/Industrial Sheds in SEZ
- Registration-*cum*-Membership certificate
- Annual permission for sub-contracting
- Allotment of Import Exporter Code Number
- Power connection
- Water connection
- Small Scale Industries registration
- Registration with the Central Insecticides Board
- Registration with Central Pollution Control Board
- Building approval
- Sales Tax registration
- Approval from the Inspectorate of Factories
- Pollution control clearance wherever required
- Any other approval as may be required from the State Government, or as prescribed or sought by the State Government.

If an industrial enterprise is operating in both the Domestic Tariff

Area ("DTA") and a SEZ, then both the Units shall have different identities though they do not need to be separate legal entities.

To set up an Offshore Banking Unit ("OBU"), approval from the Reserve Bank of India ("RBI") is required. Further, if the Unit is to be set up in an International Financial Services Centre ("IFSC"), approval from Central Government is also required. However, only one IFSC is permitted per SEZ.

Criteria for Approval of an SEZ Unit

The approval of a proposal for an SEZ Unit is based on the fulfilment of certain conditions which *inter alia* require that:

- the SEZ Unit achieves positive net foreign exchange ("NFE") to be computed cumulatively for a period of 5 years from commencement of production. NFE means excess value of exports and deemed exports over the value of imports/expenses.
- the availability of space and infrastructure support has been applied for and is confirmed by the Developer.

A single point clearance system has been provided to the Units in the SEZ under State laws/rules. Proposals for setting up Units in SEZs other than those requiring an industrial licence may be granted approval by the Development Commissioner within 15 days. Proposals for setting up Units in SEZs requiring an industrial licence may be granted approval by the Development Commissioner after clearance of the proposal by the Board and Department of Industrial Policy and Promotion within 45 days. Once granted, an approval is valid for 5 years.

The Approval Committee, however, has the power to cancel the approval granted to the SEZ Unit. Any challenge to the order of the Approval Committee with respect to the grant of approval to the SEZ Unit should be made before the Board of Approval within 45 days of communication of such order. Further, the concerned Development Commissioner shall give the possession of the space in the SEZ to the entrepreneur only after the issue of the Letter.

Exit Mechanism

The SEZ Unit may opt out of an SEZ with the approval of the Development Commissioner. Such exit is subject to the payment of applicable duties and taxes on the imported or indigenous capital goods, raw materials, components, consumables, spares and finished goods in stock. If the SEZ Unit has not achieved positive NFE, the exit shall be subject to penalty. The SEZ Unit shall continue to be treated as an SEZ Unit till the date of the final exit.

Obligations of a SEZ/SEZ Unit

- SEZ Units shall be required to achieve positive NFE. For this purpose, a legal undertaking is required to be executed by the Unit with the Development Commissioner.
- The Unit is required to provide periodic reports to the Development Commissioner and Zone Customs.
- The Unit is required to maintain proper accounts and furnish details regarding the value of imports, exports etc. to the Development Commissioner on a quarterly basis.
- The Unit is also required to execute a bond with the Zone Customs for its operations in the SEZ.

Dispute Resolution

The SEZ Act provides that designated Courts shall try any suit of civil nature arising in the SEZ and from notified offences committed in an SEZ. Appeals against the Orders of designated Courts shall be filed before the High Court within 60 days from the date of communication of decision. Till such time as the designated Courts are set up, any dispute of civil nature arising between two or more entrepreneurs or two or more Developers or between an entrepreneur of a Unit and a Developer in the SEZ, shall be referred to Arbitration under the provisions of Arbitration and Conciliation Act, 1996.

C. Facilities and Incentives Available to a SEZ/SEZ Unit

Income Tax Benefits

As per the Income-tax Act, 1961 (ITA), the following are the key tax benefits to be provided to SEZs and SEZ Units:

Benefits to SEZ Developers

(a) 100 per cent of the profits of the Developer arising from the business of developing a SEZ, notified after April 1, 2005 under the SEZ Act, shall be deducted from taxable income. This deduction can be claimed at the option of the assessee for any 10 consecutive years out of 15 years beginning from the year in which the SEZ has been notified by the Central Government. If a Developer who sets up an SEZ after April 1, 2005, transfers the operation and maintenance of the SEZ to another Developer, the transferee is entitled to the above deduction of profit for the remaining period.

(b) With regard to a Developer who is entitled to claim an exemption under Section 80-lA4 of the ITA, the Developer can claim an exemption for the remainder unexpired exemption period under Section 80-lA, and thereafter it can claim the 10 year tax exemption available to such Developer under Section 80-lAB.

(c) The Developers of SEZ are not required to pay Minimum Alternate Tax.

(d) No dividend distribution tax shall be paid by a Developer engaged in developing, operating and maintaining an SEZ.

Benefits to SEZ Units

(a) The Units set up in an SEZ which have begun to manufacture/provide services during the financial year beginning April 1, 2005 will get the following exemptions:
   - 100 per cent exemption of profits and gains from business for the first 5 years.
   - 50 per cent exemption on profits and gains from business for the next 5 years.
   - 50 per cent exemption to the extent that such amounts are reinvested in the SEZ Special Reserve Account.

   If the SEZ Unit has already availed benefits for 10 years under Section 10A of the ITA, the above exemptions are not available. Further, when a Free Trade Zone (FTZ) or an Export Processing Zone (EPZ) is converted into an SEZ, the Units, which have already availed of the 10-year tax exemption in an FTZ or EPZ, cannot avail of the Section 10AA exemptions.

(b) Losses falling under the heads "Profits and Gains from Business or Profession" and income from Capital Gains can be carried forward/set off as long as such loss is related to the business of the SEZ Unit.

(c) Capital Gains on transfer of assets in case of shifting of an industrial undertaking from an urban area to an SEZ shall be exempt, provided that 1 year before, or 3 years after the transfer (i) machinery/plant was purchased for the business of the industrial undertaking in the SEZ, (ii) building or land was acquired or building was constructed in the SEZ, (iii) the original asset was shifted and the establishment was transferred to the SEZ, and (iv) the assessee incurred such other expenses as are notified by the Central Government.

(d) Interest income received by a non-resident or a person who is not ordinarily resident in India, on a deposit made in an OBU situated in an SEZ, shall be exempt from total income.

(e) No tax deduction shall be made by the OBU from interest paid:
  (i) on deposits made on or after April 1, 2005 by a non-resident or a person not ordinarily resident in India, or
  (ii) on borrowings on or after April 1, 2005 from a non-resident or a person not ordinarily resident in India.

(f) The gross total income of an assessee having an OBU or an assessee being a Unit of an IFSC shall be deductible to the extent of 100 per cent for 5 consecutive years from the year of grant of permission under the Banking Regulation Act/SEBI/other relevant law and 50 per cent for the next 5 years. It further defines the exempted "income", which is:
  - Income from an OBU in an SEZ.
  - Income from business referred to in the Banking Regulation Act, 1949, or any other Unit which develops, develops and operates, or develops, operates and maintains an SEZ.
  - Income from an approved unit of an IFSC.

(g) Exemption from Securities Transaction Tax available to taxable securities transaction entered into by a non-resident through the IFSC.

(D) Other Benefits

Customs and Excise

- Exemption from Customs Duty SEZ Units may import or procure from the domestic sources, duty free, all their requirements of capital goods, raw materials, consumables, spares, packing materials, office equipment, DG sets etc. for implementation of their projects in the SEZ without requiring any licence or specific approval.

- Goods imported/procured locally which are duty-free could or should be utilized within the approval period of 5 years.
- Domestic sales by SEZ Units will be exempt from Special Additional Duty.
- Domestic sale of finished products, by-products is permitted on payment of applicable Customs duty.
- Domestic sale of rejects, waste and scrap is permitted on payment of applicable customs duty on the transaction value.
- Exemption from applicable excise duty on goods brought in from the DTA to an SEZ.

FDI

- 100 per cent FDI under the automatic route is allowed in the manufacturing sector in SEZ Units, except for arms and ammunition, explosives, atomic substances, narcotics and hazardous chemicals, distillation and brewing of alcoholic drinks and cigarettes, cigars and manufactured tobacco substitutes.
- Exemption from the applicability of Press Note 2 (2005).

Banking/Insurance /External Commercial Borrowings

- Setting up OBUs has been allowed in SEZs. External Commercial Borrowings by SEZ Units up to US$ 500 million a year is allowed without any maturity restrictions.
- Freedom to bring in export proceeds without any time limit.
- Flexibility to keep 100 per cent of export proceeds in an EEFC account and freedom to make overseas investments with it.
- Commodity hedging permitted.
- SEZ units allowed to write-off unrealized export bills.

Central Sales Tax

- Exemption from Central sales tax on inter-state sale or purchase of goods.

Other Central Enactments

- Exemption from other Central enactments, which are specified in Schedule 1 of the SEZ Act.

State Taxes

- The respective State Governments may for the purpose of giving effect to the provisions of the SEZ Act, notify policies for Developers and SEZ Units and take suitable steps for the enactment of any law for granting exemption from state taxes, levies and duties to a Developer or an entrepreneur.

Service Tax

- Exemption from Service Tax to the Developer and the SEZ Units to carry on authorized operations in the SEZ. Service tax exemption granted only to Units in the DTA providing services to a Developer or to a Unit.

Labour Laws

- All labour laws as applicable within the country apply in a SEZ.

PART-II

The Linkage Between SEZ Act and Land Acquisition Act

In the era of liberalization and privatization, the issue of land acquisition has assumed new dimensions with the setting up of the Special Economic Zones. SEZs and land acquisition are interconnected, for in the setting up of SEZs huge amounts of land are required. The Government of India is encouraging the setting up of SEZs in the country for they help in the economic and industrial growth of the nation.

Land acquisition refers to the process by which the government forcibly acquires private property for a public purpose without the consent of the landowner, which is different from a market purchase of land. The law of land acquisition derives its legitimacy from the juridical principle of the power of Eminent Domain of the State—a power by which the state enjoys "sovereign control over all property in a state, with the right of expropriation." The Land Acquisition Act, 1894 confers upon the Central and State governments this power to acquire land "for public purposes and for Companies and for determining the amount of compensation to be made on account of such acquisition." Since this Act finds a place in the Concurrent List of the Constitution, the various State governments have made necessary amendments.

Therefore, a question naturally arises as to why was a need felt for a separate specific legislation on SEZs, when the land for the same could have been acquired under the Land Acquisition Act. Though there is no explanation or answer for this question but it can be found on exploring the similarities and the differences between the procedure followed under the two along with other aspects. It is the hypothesis in this chapter that the concept behind land acquisition for SEZ has emerged from land acquisition under the Land Acquisition Act as is apparent from the similarity of procedure followed under both at the same time SEZ incorporates certain distinguishing features, therefore, SEZ Act appears to be both the baby and the lost and found cousin of the Land Acquisition Act depending on the aspect that is being examined.

Under the Land Acquisition Act, 1894, Appropriate Government can acquire land only for 'public purpose' or for the purpose of a Company. The Act takes a broad definition of 'public purpose' permitting a diverse range of projects. In a number of cases, the Supreme Court (SC) has highlighted concerns relating to fair compensation, valuation of land, definition of public purpose and other issues relating to land acquisition. The court has also held that the constitution permits acquisition by the state of private property only if it is required for a public purpose. In the recent cases of land acquisition, the "public purpose" is being questioned. But, for development to take place, particularly at a time when the agriculture sector is on the decline, land has to be acquired for industrial growth. The question is when, how and in what situations should the state intervene to acquire land. Under the SEZ Act, the only purpose for which land can be acquired is for the establishment, development, and management of SEZs. While the preamble to the SEZ Act, 2005 says that SEZs have been established "for the promotion of exports", Section 5 of the Act says that the Central Government will be guided by the following principles while notifying any area as a SEZ, *viz.*: (a) generation of additional economic activity, (b) promotion of exports of goods and services, (c) promotion of Investment from domestic and foreign sources, (d) creation of employment opportunities, and (e) development of infrastructure facilities. However, the underlying object seems to have been established to have a nexus with the 'public purpose' That is to say that there are several reports which establish that setting up of SEZs has helped the country to prosper in ways more than one thereby serving 'public purpose'.

Procedure Adopted for Acquisition of Land Under LA Act and SEZ Act

Under Land Acquisition Act, two separate procedures have been provided for acquisition of land for 'public purpose' and for 'companies'. For the former, the process commences with publication of preliminary notification of government intention to acquire a particular land, followed by hearing of objections, publication of declaration that it is needed for a public purpose, acquisition by Collector, notice to persons interested, ultimately leading to enquiry and award by the Collector. For the purpose of acquisition for companies, there has to be previous consent of the appropriate government along with an agreement executed by the Company.

Under the SEZ Act, 2005, the person intending to set up SEZ first makes a proposal to the State Government, or to the BOA. Even the State Government, if it intends to set up SEZ can make a proposal to the Board. This is followed by authorization to Developer to operate, and notification of SEZ.

Thus functioning of the SEZ is governed by a three tier administrative set up. The Board of Approval is the apex body and is headed by the Secretary, Department of Commerce. The Approval Committee at the Zone level deals with approval of units in the SEZs and other related issues. Each Zone is headed by a Development Commissioner, who is *ex-officio* chairperson of the Approval Committee.

Once an SEZ has been approved by the Board of Approval and Central Government has notified the area of the SEZ, units are allowed to be set up in the SEZ. All the proposals for setting up of units in the SEZ are approved at the Zone level by the Approval Committee consisting of Development Commissioner, Customs Authorities and representatives of State Government. All post-approval clearances including grant of importer-exporter code number, change in the name of the company or implementing agency, broad banding diversification etc. are given at the Zone level by the Development Commissioner. The performance of the SEZ units are periodically monitored by the Approval Committee and units are liable for penal action under the provision of Foreign Trade (Development and Regulation) Act, in case of violation of the conditions of the approval.

Broadly speaking there is a similarity in the procedure adopted to acquire land under Land Acquisition Act and SEZ Act to the extent that the consent of the landowner is not required under both. However, under Land Acquisition, the final authority is the appropriate government whereas under SEZ it is the Board of Approval.

Advantages and Disadvantages of Land Acquisition Act and SEZ

SEZs and land acquisition often involve in agricultural land and the Central and State governments are acquiring the land from the farmers. The various advantages of the SEZs and land acquisition in India are that it has helped in bringing in huge amounts of foreign currency into the country, increased the number of jobs for the people and to bring technological advances to Indian industry, and make it a cost-effective producer. On the other hand, the disadvantages are that it is estimated that more than ten lakh people, who are dependent upon agricultural land, will be evicted from their lands. It is estimated that the farming families will have to face a loss of around Rs. 212 crore each year in total income, and it will also lead to putting the food security of India to risk. Land acquisition in India has now resulted in dissent, uproar and opposition from farmers for the livelihood has been put to stake. Whether it is Nandigram, Singur, Koodankulam, Jagatsinghpur (POSCO), Kannamangal or Bastar, the issues are the same. In the name of development, land acquisition is being done forcibly without due respect to basic human rights—the right to life and personal liberty. The government promises 'humane' displacement followed by relief and rehabilitation. However, historical records show that an estimated 40 million people have lost their land since 1950 on account of displacement due to large development projects. At least 75 per cent of them still await rehabilitation. Moreover compensation is being discussed only for those who hold titles to land. No compensation had been planned for those who don't till the Narmada Water Disputes Tribunal provided for it. The present system of payment of compensation to the farmers is perceived to be totally unfair. If the land is being acquired for a commercial purpose under the garb of public purpose then let the market decide the price of the land as free markets are not about corporate entities, or even industrialisation, they are about freedom. Then why restrict freedom of the farmers to sell their land at the market price. (Mutual negotiation, with the prospect of reverting to Land Acquisition only after 90 per cent of the Land has been bought by negotiation, may become necessary.)

The Way Ahead

Why does a landowner of agricultural land hesitate to dispose his/her land right to the industrialist/government for SEZ development or for land acquisition even with an offer of lucrative compensation package? The sole answer to this can be found from the sentiments of the landowners who are forced to dispose land for SEZ development. They often complain that they got so much income every year out of their agricultural crop production, which would cease now permanently if disposed for development of SEZ. If a way is found to safeguard the land ownership right of landowner as well as compensating loss of livelihood generated out of land in a sustainable manner, no landowner would perhaps be disinterested to lease out his land. However, with certain pre-conditions such model framework is to be developed. To develop such corporate-private partnerships, Panchayati Raj Institutions (PRIs) can play a dual role.

- During the acquisition of agricultural/private land for SEZ development, ownership right should not be fully sold out rather should be given to the entrepreneur under a lease agreement for 25 years, which means neither the government nor the entrepreneur operating in SEZ would enjoy absolute ownership of land.
  Since land conceptually keeps a minimum importance of 25 per cent of stake in an industrial unit, the land components should be regarded as minimum 25 per cent of the stake of the total value of the industry. This means, in tune of growth of the industry, the value of land would be increasing and with downfall of the industry, the value of land will be coming down to its original price. Hence, an industrial unit coming up in SEZ ideally needs to allocate 25 per cent share of its industrial value to the landowners. An Industry coming up in SEZ often enjoys acquisition right with nominal price over government land. However, private land belongs to farmers or local inhabitants, which consists of a small portion of SEZ need only to be acquired with proper compensation.
- The industry acquiring the agricultural/private land need to employ at least the sole bread earner of the family of landowner from the very day the owner losses its right to earn agricultural livelihood from its land. High priority to be given to local work force for unskilled labour utilization in the industries of SEZ.
- The entrepreneurs should ensure local skill upgradation as per

the requirement of industry through setting up Industrial Training Institutes in the surrounding areas of SEZ.

These suggestions are basically for SEZ. For, land acquisition under Land Acquisition Act, though compensation is paid, there still exists some sort of mysterious cloud as regards the intention of the government. Therefore, it is suggested that every time government acquires a land for "public purpose", it should make an attempt on its part to communicate such intention to the people adequately and if possible to make them a part of such project by engaging them for the same. But these are at best directory guidelines.

In conclusion, though there are several similarities in Land Acquisition Act and SEZ Act which might appear magical, there are ample differences too which might such similarities to mere eyewash. The need of the hour is to maximize the utility of both for the welfare of public and reduce the discontentment caused thereby to whatever extent possible.

PART-III

Smart Cities

A smart city (also smarter city) uses digital technologies to enhance performance and well-being, to reduce costs and resource consumption, and to engage more eflèctively and actively with its citizens. Key 'smart' sectors include transport, energy, health carc, water and waste. A smart city should be able to respond faster to city and global challenges than one with a simple 'transactional' relationship with its citizens. Other terms that have been used Or similar concepts include 'cyberville', 'digital city', 'electronic communities', 'flexicity', 'information city', 'intelligent city', 'knowledge-based city', 'MESH city', 'telecity', 'teletopia', 'Ubiquitous city', 'wired city'.

Interest in smart cities is motivated by major challenges, including climate change, economic restructuring, the move to online retail and entertainment, ageing populations, and pressures on public.

Finances

The European Union (EU) has devoted constant efforts to devising a strategy for achieving 'smart' urban growth for its metropolitan city-regions. The term smart city is still quite a fuzzy concept and is used in ways that are not always consistent. Here are a number of definitions:

- *Giflinger* et al., *2007:* "Regional competitiveness, transport and Information and Communication Technologies economics, natural resources, human and social capital, quality of life, and participation of citizens in the governance of cities."
- *Smart Cities Council:* "A smart city is one that has digital technology embedded across all city functions."
- *Caragliu and Njkamp 2009:* "A city can be defined as 'smart' when Investments in human and social capital and traditional (transport) and modern (ICI) communication infrastructure fuel sustainable economic development and a high quality of life, with a wise management of natural resources, through participatory action and engagement."
- *Frost and Sullivan 2014:* "We identified eight key aspects that define a Smart City: smart governance, smart energy, smart building, smart mobility, smart infrastructure, smart technology, smart healthcare and smart citizen."
- *Institute of Electrical and Electronics Engineers Smart Cities:* "A smart city brings together technology, government and society to enable the following characteristics: smart cities, a smart economy, smart mobility, a smart environment, smart people, smart living, smart governance."
- *Business Dictionary:* "A developed urban area that creates sustainable economic development and high quality of life by excelling in multiple key areas: economy, mobility, environment, people, living and government. Excelling in these key areas can be done so through strong human capital, social capital, and/or ICT infrastructure."
- *Indian Government 2014 :* "Smart City offers sustainability in terms of economic activities and employment opportunities to a wide section of its residents, regardless of their level of education, skills or income levels."
- *Department of Business, Innovation and Skills, UK 2013:* "The concept is not static, there is no absolute definition of a smart city, no end point, but rather a process, or series of steps, by which cities become more 'liveable' and resilient and, hence, able to respond quicker to new challenges."

Characteristics

A smart city use information technology devices to : Make more efficient use of physical infrastructure (roads, built environment and other physical assets) to support a strong and healthy economic, social, cultural development. Engage effectively with local people in local governance and decision by use of open innovation processes and participation with emphasis placed on citizen participation and co-design. Learn, adapt and innovate and thereby respond more eflctively and promptly to changing circumstances.

They evolve towards a strong integration of all dimensions of human intelligence, collective intelligence, and also artificial intelligence within the city. The intelligence of cities "resides in the increasingly effective combination of digital telecommunication networks (the nerves), ubiquitously embedded intelligence (the brains), sensors and tags (the sensory organs), and software (the knowledge and cognitive competence)". Some major fields of intelligent city activation are:

Innovation economy	Urban Infrastructure	Governance
Innovation in industries, clusters, districts of a city	Transport	Administration services to the citizen
Knowledge workforce : Education and employment	Energy/Utilities	Participatory and direct democracy
Creation of knowledge – intensive companies	Protection of the environment/Safety	Services to the citizen: Quality of life

PART-IV

Advantages and Disadvatanges of SEZs

(A) Advantages

A Special Economic Zone (SEZ) is a stipulated and duty-free territorial domain having various economic regulations from those of the country in which it is situated. In certain countries, such a region is taken as an estimated foreign area.

Special Economic Zones in India is also taken as a trade capacity development tool, with the aim to promote quick economic growth using business and other tax incentives to gain foreign investment and technology. Today there are approxinsately 3,000 SEZs functionrng in 120 countries, which account for more than US$ 600 billion in exports and 50 million jobs. By providing privileged terms, SEZs attract lucrative investments and foreign exchanges, generate employment opportunities and also give a boost to technological development and infrastructure.

Today majority of developing nations round the globe have recognized the relevance of encouraging international trade for a sustained economical growth and maximized contribution to the GDP of the nation. As a part of its commitment to liberalization, Government of India (GoI) over the past decade adopted a multipronged approach to enhance foreign investment in India. The GoI further pushed forward the second generation reforms and has made numerous policy modifications to attain this objective.

Benefits of Special Economic Zones

Today numerous engineering services companies have contributed to the development of special economic zone in India. An eminent example is the Precision Engineering and Manufacturing SEZ unit in Belgaum. This unit acts as a base for foundry operations for multiple industrial and automotive facilities. There is presence of more than 100 foundries and 150 machine shops. Simultaneously, there is access to skilled labour force at a competitive price range that adds value to it credibility.

This engineering special economic zone provides an organic, eco-friendly and a sustainable industrial development. Other SEZ benefits and basic incentives are—

- There is international standard landscaping with approximately 15,000 trees.
- There are bicycles for intra-zone mobility.
- A proper landscape with a huge amphitheatre visible and available from total campus.
- Has rain water harvesting.
- Provides a water treatment plant.
- Provides a sewage treatment plant.
- An existing small stream is being converted to a natural water body.

(B) Disadvantages

In all its totality Special Economic Zones in India has helped to increase the international trade volume. Furthermore, a huge amount of foreign investment has been directed not only to export trade but also into infrastructure construction and commerce. There are foreign engineering companies that have been encouraged to set up their units in various regions and the export industry has grown. This apart innovative foreign technology had resulted in the inflow of foreign investment. All these had contributed to the development of the Indian economy.

No policy in recent years has shown up a government in a poorer light than that on the Special Economic Zones not the least because of the difference of opinion it has generated between the Finance and Commerce Ministries. While the former has voiced its concerns, rather belatedly, about possible revenue losses from the tax privileges for the SEZs, the latter is stoutly defending the policy with statistics suggesting minimal losses and highlighting the eventual gains in terms of employment and revenues. Since these are all, at this point in time, notional, one can only marvel at the figures trotted out by both sides.

The battlelines have, as it were, been extended with the Reserve Bank of India joining the Finance Ministry in expressing concern about revenue losses. To its credit the central bank made the more fundamental point that the SEZs may lead to a diversion of resources from the less developed areas without creating the necessary linkages that could benefit them. Part of the reason for the differences among policy-makers lies precisely in the immense popularity of the concept; so far more than 160 applications are with the Commerce Ministry and the number is growing. From the viewpoint of the developer, the SEZ is a sure winner; from the economy's perspective, the gains are doubtful. This dichotomy is embedded in the very notion of the SEZ and in experience.

Inspired by the highly successful Chinese zones, such as Guangdong, the SEZ Act, 2005 morphed the existing Export Processing Zones into SEZs and opened the door to newer developers with more liberal concessions and looser mandates than those enjoyed by the EPZs. Thus, the Act affords tax exemptions, captive infrastructure and minimal transaction costs but expects far less in return. For instance, SEZs will enjoy complete freedom to sub-contract abroad, thus encouraging global rather than domestic linkages. In a word, the SEZ will be "a designated duty free enclave to be treated as foreign territory for trade operations..." Small wonder the Commerce Ministry is inundated with applications.

The economic benefits of the SEZs are debatable. Revenue losses will certainly accrue in the period of the tax holiday and indirect tax exemptions. Studies have shown that the EPZs with all the tax exemptions generated far fewer jobs than expected and there is little to suggest the SEZs will do so given liberal labour laws and the current productivity concerns. The SEZs will encourage the relocation of existing resources and production activity, as did some State-level excise duty exemptions, thus rendering non-SEZ areas that much poorer or disadvantaged. Clearly, tax exemptions for specific locations are perverse incentives and the SEZ Act goes further down that road by the exclusive promise of facilities that should be available for the entire country but are not. Opponents of the SEZ focus on one or other of its aspects. It is time to view them as islands of privilege untenable in an era of competition and fair play.

Summing Up

The establishment of the SEZs has undoubtedly helped to increase the volume of international trade. Further, a large amount of foreign investment has found its way not only into the export trade, but also into infrastructure construction and commerce. Foreign companies have been encouraged to establish their presence in the territories and the export industry has grown. Advanced foreign technology has been brought in with the inflow of foreign investment. All these factors have contributed to the growth of the Indian economy. The enactment of the SEZ Act and its implementation should enable the GoI to fulfil its agenda of economic reforms as the multiplier effect on the economic activities triggered by SEZ materialize. The challenge now is whether India through its SEZs can leverage its cost advantage and huge knowledge base and break the hold of China in manufacturing by making India the preferred destination for doing business.

References

Department of Business (2013). "Smart cities—background paper" (https://www.gov.uk/ government/ uploads /system/uploads/attachment data/file /246019/his-13-1 209-smart-cities-background-paper-digital.pdf). UK Government Department for Business, Innovation and Skills.

"Draft Concept Note on Smart City Scheme" (http://indiansmartcities. in/downloads/CONCEPT NOTE -3 12.201 4_REVISED_AND_LATEST_.pdf). Government of India - Ministry of Urban Development.

Holands, R.G (2008). "Will the real smart city please stand up?". *City*, 12 (3): 303-320. doi:10. 1080/13604810802479126 (https://dx.doi.org/ 10.1080%2F13604810802479126).

Komninos, N. (2008). *Intelligent Cities and Globalisation of Innovation Networks*, Routledge.

Komninos, N. (2009). "Intelligent cities: towards interactive and global innovation environments", *International Journal of Innovation and Regional*

Development (Inderscience Publishers) 1 (4). doi:10. 1 504/ijird.2009.022726 (https://dx.doi.org/10.1504%2Fijird.2009.022726).

Nishith Desai Associates, *Special Economic Zones*, April 2006, Mumbai www.nishithdesai.com

Paskaleva, K. (25 January, 2009). "Enabling the smart cily:The progress of e-city governance in Europe". *International Journal of Innovation and Regional Development,* 1(4):405-422(18).doi:10.1504/gird.2009.022730 (https :// dx.doi.org/10. 1 504%2F jjird.2009. 022730).

"Smart City—Definition" (http://www. businessdictionary. corn/definition/ smart-city. html).BusinessDictionary. com.

Vidya Bhushan Rawat, Mamidi Bharath Bhushan and Sujatha Surepally, *The Impact of Special Economic Zones in India*, Social Development Foundation, New Delhi, 2010.

Wikipaedia encyclopaedia.

6

Examining the Fuel-Finance Nexus in a Macro-economic Framework

Econometric Evidence from India

Aparna Sajeev and *Simrit Kaur*

1. Introduction

India is presently the fastest growing economy of the world with GDP growth rate of 7.3 per cent in fiscal year 2014-15.[1] High growth rate coupled with large population size has made demand for energy increase immensely. With demand for energy requirements outpacing domestic production, dependence on imported crude oil for energy requirements has made India a net importer of crude oil.[2] Further, India's oil import dependence which in recent times has been close to 80 per cent in fiscal year 2014-15 is expected to be pushed to around 90 per cent by 2040. Resultantly, fluctuations in global fuel prices are bound to affect major macro-economic indicators for India, such as inflation, industrial production, stock markets and GDP growth rates itself. In view of these linkages, in the present chapter, we examine the relationship between fuel prices and macro-economic variables with a focus on stock market movements. The relationships are examined in the context of Indian economy over the period 1994 to 2015.

Crude oil prices have witnessed wide fluctuations in the past two decades. From being traded at US dollar 10 per barrel in 1999, it peaked to US dollar 147 per barrel in 2008, before falling again. In 2015, it was being traded at levels close to US dollar 30 per barrel. Empirical evidence states that there is asymmetry in the effects of oil price shocks on the economy. That is, while on the one hand, dramatic rise in oil prices often depress national economies leading to recession, a fall in oil prices on the other hand, does not necessarily nurture economic booms (Hamilton, 1983; Mork, 1989; Mork *et al.*, 1994; Hammoudeh *et al.*, 2013).

Further, in addition to impacting GDP growth rates adversely, a rise in oil price is also expected to affect stock markets negatively. This is because with an increase in oil price, the cost of production is likely to go up, thereby restraining profits, causing a decrease in shareholders' value. Hence, in efficient markets, oil price rise is expected to be accompanied by decrease in stock prices (Fisher, 1930; Williams, 1938).

Fall in oil prices is also expected to influence stock market movements though the impact is expected to be different for oil exporting countries *vis-à-vis* oil importing countries. For oil exporting countries, the reduction in revenue from oil export is expected to adversely affect the economy, including its stock market. Despite the fall in price of oil, oil importing countries may not necessarily gain. This is because even though their cost of production might have reduced, these countries could experience massive petro-dollar[3] flight. With fall in oil prices, oil exporting countries often withdraw their investments from emerging economies to bridge their revenue shortfall. The more the dependence of emerging economies (such as India and China) on stock markets for nurturing their economic growth, more grave will be the implications of petro-dollar flight.

Impact of Oil Price Shocks on stock markets are also expected to differ not only between oil exporting and oil importing countries but also whether oil price shocks are demand induced or supply induced. For instance, a favourable supply shock is expected to have an adverse effect on stock markets of oil exporting countries. However, the effect on oil importing countries is expected to be ambiguous. To substantiate, a favourable supply shock could impact their stock markets favourably on account of enhanced firm profitability (due to lower cost of production). However, the impact on their stock markets could also be adverse in case the petro-dollar flight is substantial. In case of a favourable demand shock, the stock market of an oil exporting country is expected to benefit. This is on account of the increased investments from higher revenues earned by the oil exporting companies. However, the effect on oil importing countries continues to remain ambiguous. Substantiating, if the favourable demand shock is on account of increased GDP growth rate, then this could impact stock market favourably. Also, with increase in petro-dollar investments from oil exporting countries, the stock market of emerging economies may boom. However, with an increase in oil prices on account of positive demand shock, the cost of production may increase which in turn is expected to adversely affect the stock markets of oil importing countries.

Table 6.1: Plausible Relationships between Oil Prices and Stock Markets

Criteria	Favourable Demand Shock	Favourable Supply Shock
Oil Importing Country	Ambiguous Impact *Favourable*: Increase in Petro-dollar investment inflow *Adverse*: Increase in cost of production, thereby expected decrease in profits	Ambiguous *Favourable*: Decrease in cost of production, thereby expected increase in profits *Adverse*: Petro-dollar flight
Oil Exporting Country	In general, favourable impact due to rise in oil prices	In general, adverse impact due to fall in oil prices

Source: Compiled by Authors.

Given the diverse set of relationships that exist between oil price movement and its differential and sometimes ambiguous impact on stock markets, an in-depth country level analysis on how stock markets move on account of fluctuations in oil prices remains important from a policy perspective. The present chapter focuses on the said relationship for India. Relationship between crude oil prices and Indian stock market is hereby provided briefly.

India's Crude Oil Prices and Stock Markets: In India, the pricing of petroleum products until July 1975 were under the Administered Pricing Mechanism (APM). However, with effect from April 2002, the government dismantled APM. Since then, wide fluctuations in crude oil prices have been observed. Given India's major dependence on oil imports, fluctuations in international fuel prices are expected to influence the Indian basket of crude oil price. Around 72 per cent of Indian basket of crude oil is composed of Dubai oil and remaining by Brent oil. The Indian basket of crude oil averaged around US dollar 23 per barrel in March, 2002 at the time of dismantling of prices. During the peak of global fuel prices, Indian basket of crude oil averaged around US dollar 130 per barrel in June 2008. However, following the trend of international crude oil price, Indian basket of crude oil and petroleum product prices started sliding since June 2014. In January 2016, it was below US dollar 30 per barrel.

Ever since the onset of financial reforms in 1990s, volume of investment by domestic and international investors in Indian stock market has grown stupendously. Bombay Stock Exchange (BSE) which was set up in 1875 and the National Stock Exchange (NSE) which was founded in 1992, witness most of the trading activities in India. Since 1992, stock markets of India are regulated mainly by Securities Exchange Board of India (SEBI). BSE accounts for more than 50 per cent of total turnover across all stock exchanges in India. BSE has more than 5,500 companies listed and is worlds No. 1 exchange in terms of listed companies. Total market capitalization of BSE stood at US dollar 1.64 trillion in September 2015. BSE SENSEX is the oldest[4] and most prominent market index in India. It includes shares of 30 firms listed on BSE, which represents about 45 per cent of the indexs—free float market capitalization. SENSEX crossed 20,000 points in December 2007 before falling to around 9,000 points in November 2008. In June 2014, SENSEX peaked at around 25,500 points. The favourable movement continued and in July 2015, the SENSEX was close to 28,000 points.

Figure 6.1 presents the Crude oil price and SENSEX movements for India over the period April 2000 to December, 2015.[5] The graph is analysed in 4 phases. In phase 1, both crude oil prices and stock markets move together. The rising trend in oil prices since the beginning of 2000 is primarily on account of negative supply shocks (due to international events, such as, Twin tower attack, US-invasion in Iraq and Venezuelan war). The rising oil price trend until 2007-08 (until the financial crisis) is also on account of positive demand shocks with stagnating supplies. During the period of Phase 1, SENSEX also continued to increase gradually. In phase 2 (around the time of global financial crisis), both crude oil prices and SENSEX movements witness a fall, though the fall in SENSEX occurred earlier, and was less sharp. The fall in crude oil price witnessed steep decline during this period. In phase 3, the effect of global financial crisis on both crude oil price and stock market movement dissipates and both gradually regain momentum. Though both rise sharply until end of December 2010, thereafter, the two remain more or less stagnant at their respective levels. However, the peaks and dips remain more pronounced for crude oil prices than for SENSEX. In phase 4, on account of positive oil supply shocks, oil prices began to fall steeply around November 2014. However, the SENSEX continues to rise gradually, largely on account of India's growth momentum. This is the only phase over the time period represented wherein the movements of oil prices and SENSEX are not reflective of each other's trend.

For the period analysed, the correlation coefficient between oil price movement and SENSEX is estimated at 0.875. This is significant at the 1 per cent level. The positive relationship between the two does not necessarily contradict theory, as movements in the two are also influenced by parameters other than the two themselves. For instance, macro-economic variables such as GDP growth, industrial growth and inflation are also expected to influence the stock markets. Observing and analysing these relationships remains important for judicious investment decisions by private investors, as well as, appropriate monetary policy decision-making by relevant policy-makers.

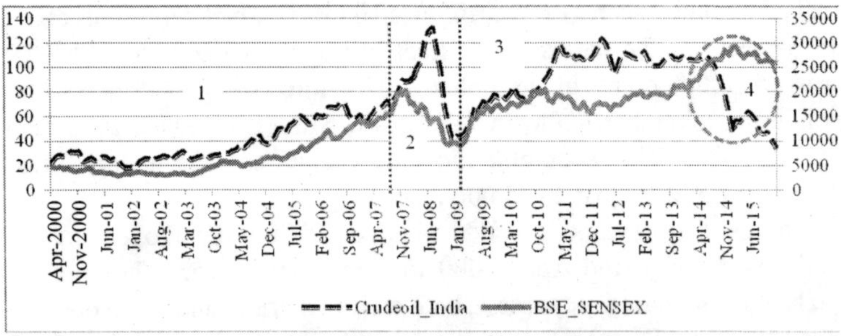

Fig. 6.1: Crude Oil Price (Indian Basket)[6] and BSE SENSEX (April 2000– December 2015).

Source: BSE India, Ministry of Petroleum and Natural Gas.

The remaining of this chapter is structured as follows. A brief literature review is provided in Section 2, followed by data description and methodology in Section 3. Section 4 presents and analyses the empirical results. Finally, Section 5 concludes the study from a broad perspective.

2. Literature Review

Hamilton's work (1983) is the pioneer in the study of oil prices and its macro-economic impact. In his paper, Hamilton provides evidence for statistically significant correlation between oil price shocks and recessions in the United States prior to 1972. His findings reveal that seven out of eight, post-war recessions in the United States have been preceded by dramatic increase in the price of crude. Since then, a vast amount of literature has been published on the relationship between oil prices, stock markets and other macro-economic variables. Few of these papers are hereby reviewed.

Oil Price and Stock Market Movements—International: Using regression analysis, Jones and Kaul (1996) investigate how stock market returns react to oil price fluctuations in four developed countries, *viz.* Canada, Japan, United Kingdom (UK) and the United States (US). They report negative links between oil price changes and stock returns in the US and Canada; however, for Japan and UK the results are inconclusive. Cobos-Reyes and Perez Quiros (2005) use a Markov switching ARCH model to analyse the relationship between oil price shocks (OPS) and the industrial production and between OPSs and stock returns. The study employs monthly data from 1963 to 2004. The results show that an increase in oil price has a negative effect on industrial production and stock markets. Miller and Ratti (2009), analyse the long-run relationship between world oil price and international stock markets using a cointegration Error Correction Model (ECM). A rolling likelihood ratio test, using the procedure of Hansen and Johansen (1993) is used to endogenously determine break points. Monthly stock market prices and crude oil price data from 1971 to 2008 is analysed for 6 OECD countries. The results indicate that stock market indices respond negatively to oil price increases in all the 6 OECD countries. Filis (2010) examines the relationship of the cyclical components of Consumer Price Index (CPI), industrial production and stock market in Greece and the influence of oil prices on these variables using a Vector Auto Regressive (VAR) model. The results, using monthly data for the period 1996 to 2008 indicate that stock market receives negative and significant influence from oil prices and CPI.

Kilian and Park (2009) examine the response of aggregate US real stock returns and stock prices based on the nature of oil price shock and nature of economy. The estimates, using a structural VAR model based on monthly data, indicate that positive shocks to the global demand for industrial commodities cause both higher real oil prices and higher stock prices and that oil supply shocks have no significant effects on returns. According to them, the stock market can respond to rise in oil prices either positively (for oil-exporting countries) or negatively (for oil-importing countries) based on the nature of the economy. Wang *et al.* (2013), compare the effects of OPS on stock market co-movements for oil-importing and oil-exporting countries. Using monthly data from 1999 to 2011 for 9 oil-importing countries and 7 oil-exporting countries, and applying structural VAR, their results indicate that the oil market has a significant negative impact on stock markets for oil importing countries. Further, precautionary demand too depresses stock markets in the long-run, and oil supply uncertainty also impacts stock markets negatively (and significantly) for oil-importing countries. Their results also reveal that the effects of oil demand uncertainty on stock markets in oil-exporting countries are negative and significant, and persist for 7 months, whereas the effects in oil-importing countries are temporary. As such the authors recommend that since OPS tend to induce more market co-movement in oil-exporting countries, a portfolio of stocks in oil-importing countries is better than a portfolio of stocks in oil-exporting countries. Le and Chang (2015), construct a model based on Fama's (1981) hypothesis to examine the extent of change in stock market returns due to changes in oil price fluctuations for three distinct Asian economies, *viz.*, Malaysia (oil-exporting country), Singapore (oil-refining country) and Japan (oil-importing country). They report that the market reacts to hike in oil prices differently across different periods, depending on differences in the oil characteristics of the economy and the nature of oil shock. The threshold cointegration and Toda-Yamamoto (TY) causality results indicate that there is no causality between oil prices and stock markets.

Oil Price and Stock Market Movements—India: Chittedi (2012) investigates the long-run relationship between oil prices and stock prices using an Autoregressive Distributed Lag (ARDL) approach. The ARDL results support the existence of long-run cointegrating relationship between oil prices with SENSEX and NIFTY. Based on the findings, the author concludes that despite India's aggressive economic growth, the volatility of stock prices in India has a significant impact on the oil prices and not *vice versa.* Bhunia and Mukhuti (2012) examine the short-term and long-term relationship between daily indices of Bombay Stock Exchange and crude oil prices using Granger causality and Johansen Cointegration tests. Based on their analysis, the authors observe the presence of a cointegrating long-term relationship between the variables. Further, Granger causality test results reveal that each stock index has one way causality relationship to crude price. Jain and Ghosh (2013) examine the long-term equilibrium relationship between daily global oil prices, precious metal prices and Indian Rupee-US Dollar exchange rate. ARDL bounds test indicates presence of cointegrating relationship among the variables only when exchange rate and gold are dependent variables. The empirical findings of the paper validate economic theory that, shocks in international oil and precious metal prices are transmitted to the Indian economy through fluctuations in the exchange rate (since India is import dependent for both precious metals and crude oil). The results validate the importance of exchange rate in determining the prices of commodities in India. Ghosh and Kanjilal (2014) explore non-causality and non-linear cointegration between daily international crude oil prices and Indian stock market using the Toda-Yamamoto (TY) causality and threshold cointegration tests which determine breaks endogenously. The results indicate presence of threshold cointegration. Authors conclude that the effect of crude oil price increase impacts the Indian stock market *via* the channel of fiscal deficit, inflation and depreciation of rupee. Further, TY causality reveals that there exists unidirectional causality running from oil price to stock market.

Fang and You (2014) adopt the modified Kilian and Park (2009) procedure to investigate how structural shocks in crude oil prices affect the stock-market returns in Newly Industrialized Economies, *viz.*, India, Russia and China. Monthly data from 2000 to 2012 is utilized in a Structural VAR framework. The findings of the study signify that positive oil shocks driven by global oil demand have significant negative impact on Indian stock market in the short-run, i.e. Indian economy is hurt by the pumped up oil price driven by the oil demand of the world instead of reflecting the positive spillover effect from global economic expansion. Zhu *et al.* (2014) use constant and dynamic copula models to explore dependence structures between crude oil prices and stock market returns in ten Asia-Pacific countries. Based on the evidence using daily data from 2000 to 2012, the authors conclude that the influence of crude oil prices were greatly limited till the global financial crisis. Further, the results reveal strong dependencc between crude oil prices and the Asia-Pacific stock returns, especially Indian stock market since the global financial crisis.

3. Data and Methodology

The objective of the present chapter is primarily to understand the relationship between oil price fluctuations and stock market indices for India. As the existing empirical evidence regarding the relationship between oil prices, stock markets and macro-economic variables remains ambiguous, there is a need to explore the same further. Also, very few studies have analysed the relationship between fuel prices and stock market movements in India, while considering structural breaks. The present chapter analyses the relationship between oil prices, stock market movements and macro-economic variables such as inflation and economic growth using a threshold cointegration methodology. To the best of our knowledge, the present chapter is a first that analyses the said relationship in a closed economy model. Further, the chapter is a first that differentiates the response of oil prices and stock market movements, in pre- and post-structural break period in the Indian context, using generalized impulse response functions.

3.1 Data

Data for the period[7] January 1994 (1994:01) to April 2015 (2015:04) is used for the study. Dubai crude oil prices (US$/bbl) is used as a proxy for Indian fuel prices. The data on the same is collected from World Bank Commodity Price Dataset.[8]

BSE SENSEX is used a proxy for stock market movement. Monthly data is downloaded from BSE website.[9] Sensex is an abbreviation for Bombay Stock Exchange Sensitive Index—the benchmark index of BSE.

In the absence of monthly data on Gross Domestic Product (GDP), we use Index of Industrial Production (IIP) as the proxy for output. Also, since in India, inflation based on Wholesale Price Index (WPI) is used for monetary analysis and formulation, we use WPI (all commodities) as the measure of inflation (Gregorio *et al.*, 2007; Mandal *et al.*, 2012). The monthly data for these two variables are taken from the website of the economic advisor, Government of India.[10] The base year for the same is 2004-05.

Dubai crude oil price, BSE SENSEX, index of industrial production and Wholesale Price Index are denoted by Du_Oil, B_Sen, IIP and WPI respectively. Table A1 (Annexure) provides the descriptive statistics of data.

Methodology

To examine the said relationships between the variables, following tests have been conducted:

(1) Unit root Tests: Zivot-Andrews
(2) Granger Causality
(3) Gregory Hansen (1996)
(4) Generalized Impulse Response Functions (GIRF)

A brief on each is provided next.

(1) Unit root Tests (with break)

In the presence of structural changes like economic crises, policy changes (deregulation of crude oil prices in 2010), technological shocks or external shocks (global financial crisis etc.), there may be structural breaks in the time series. We implement the Zivot-Andrews (ZA hereafter) (1992) test to check for unit root. The null hypothesis of ZA test is that the series is integrated without an exogenous structural break. The alternative hypothesis stipulates that the series can be represented by a trend-stationary process with a one-time break occurring at an unknown point in time. Hence, ZA test (allowing for a single break in intercept and both in intercept and trend) is employed to account for an endogenous structural break in the data series.

(2) Granger Causality

The existence of a relationship between variables does not necessarily prove causality or direction of influence (Gujarati and Sangeetha, 2007). Therefore, it is important to test for causality between the variables to know whether there exists any causality among them as also, to understand the direction of causality. We study the causality based on the Granger Causality test (Granger, 1986). Given the following equations:

$$Y_t = \sum_{i=1}^{n} \alpha_i Y_{t-1} + \sum_{j=i}^{n} \beta_i X_{t-j} + u_{1t} \quad \text{.........................} \quad (1)$$

$$X_t = \sum_{i=1}^{n} \omega_i X_{t-1} + \sum_{j=i}^{n} \delta_i Y_{t-j} + u_{2t} \quad \text{.........................} \quad (2)$$

The null hypothesis that X_t does not Granger cause Y_t, against the alternative hypothesis that X_t Granger causes Y_t is tested by checking if $\beta_j = 0$ for all $j = 1$ to n for equation (1) using a standard F test. Similarly, we check the null that Y_t does not Granger cause X_t using equation (2).

(3) Gregory Hansen

In the presence of structural breaks; tests for the null hypothesis of cointegration are rejected despite one with stable cointegrating parameters. The sensitivity of outcome to structural breaks has been documented in several studies (Gregory *et al.*, 1996; Wu, 1998). Gregory and Hansen

(GH hereafter) (1996) have introduced the tests of cointegration, which allow for possibility of structural break. The test is widely known as threshold cointegration test. In this study, we employ the GH test of cointegration to account for the possible presence of structural break.

All the variables in the model are supposed to be I(1). The cointegration procedure consists of two steps. First the Hansen's (1992) instability tests are performed to determine whether the cointegrating relationship has been subject to a structural change. The Hansen's test is employed to verify whether the long-run relationship between oil price and macro-economic variables is subject to a break. Thereafter, in the second step, time period of structural break is estimated to get the exact break point. Structural change can take several forms, of which three models are employed in the study corresponding to three different assumptions concerning the nature of shift in the cointegrating vector.

The three models employed are: the level shift model (C), the level shift with trend model (C/T) and the regime shift model (C/S). They are respectively, represented as follows:

$$Y_t = \mu + \varphi D_t(T_b) + a'x_t + u_t \quad \ldots (3)$$

$$Y_t = \mu + \varphi D_t(T_b) + a'x_t + \beta t + u_t \quad \ldots (4)$$

$$Y_t = \mu + \varphi D_t(T_b) + a'x_t + \gamma' x_t(T_b) + u_t \quad \ldots (5)$$

where the step dummy variable $D_t(T_b)$ is defined as: $D_t(T_b) = 1$ if $t > T_b$ where 1 denotes the indicator function, and $D_t(T_b) = 0$ otherwise. 'Y_t' is a scalar variable, X_t is an m-dimensional vector of explanatory variables, u_t is the disturbance term, parameters μ and φ measure respectively the intercept before the break in T_b and the shift occurring after the break, while α' are the parameters of the cointegrating vector, β is the trend slope before the shift, and γ' is the change in the cointegrating vector after the shift. Residual-based OLS are employed to estimate the equations and modified versions of the cointegration ADF tests of Engle Granger (1987), as well as modified Z_t and Z_a tests of Phillips and Ouliaris (1990) are applied to the regression errors. The test statistics are:

$$\text{ADF}^* = inf_{T_b} ADF(T_b) \quad \ldots (6)$$

$$Z_t^* = inf_{T_b} Z_t(T_b) \quad \ldots (7)$$

$$Z_\alpha^* = inf_{T_b} Z_a(T_b) \quad \ldots (8)$$

The break point corresponds to the minimum of the above test statistics. Next, smallest values of test statistics are used to test the null hypothesis of no cointegration in the presence of possible breaks for all the three models.

(4) Generalized Impulse Response Functions (GIRF)

Vector Auto Regressive (VAR) models capture co-movements that cannot be detected in univariate or bivariate models since they involve current and lagged values of multiple time series. The Impulse Response Function (IRF) traces the effect of a one standard deviation shock to the dependent variable on current and future values of all endogenous variables. A major limitation of the conventional method is that the impulse response analysis is sensitive to the ordering of variables in the VAR (Lutkepohl, 1991). The generalized impulse response functions (GIRFs) are invariant to the reordering of the variables in the VAR (Pesaran and Shin, 1997). The study reports impulse responses using the generalized impulse response method, since it overcomes the dependence on the ordering of the variables in the VAR.

4. Empirical Estimates and Analysis of Results

Unit Root Tests: Zivot-Andrews

In Table 6.2, the test statistic for Zivot-Andrews test is provided. The finding is similar for both models with break in 'intercept' and in 'intercept and trend'. The common suggestion is that the series is non-stationary at level, while in first differencing all the variables are stationary with a structural break. We take Du_Oil, B_Sen, IIP and WPI for application of cointegration with break methodology. We do so since these variables are at I(1), which is a precondition for GH tests.

Granger Causality

Table 6.3 reports significant results of bi-variate granger causality tests. Analysis of Table 6.3 reveals the results as shown.

Gregory Hansen Cointegration Analysis

Following the modelling approach elaborated earlier, we conduct the test

Table 6.2: Unit Root Tests with Endogenous Structural Break: Zivot-Andrews

	Variables	*Lag*	*t-stat*	*Break point*
		At Level		
Intercept	Du_Oil	2	–4.823381	2005M12
	B_Sen	0	–2.785676	2000M03
	IIP	2	–5.194410	2006M11
	WPI	2	–3.605754	2009M04
Intercept & Trend	Du_Oil	2	–4.842699	2010M10
	B_Sen	0	–3.253420	2005M05
	IIP	2	–5.014445	2006M11
	WPI	2	–3.484928	2004M10
		First Differencing		
Intercept	Du_Oil	2	–8.825281***	2008M08
	B_Sen	0	–16.41033***	2008M01
	IIP	2	–9.759513***	2011M04
	WPI	1	–7.658828***	2009M03
Intercept & Trend	Du_Oil	2	–8.913912***	2009M04
	B_Sen	0	–16.52999***	2008M01
	IIP	2	–9.862996***	2011M04
	WPI	1	–8.350450**	2012M01

Note: ***, ** and * denote significance at a 1 per cent, 5 per cent and 10 per cent respectively. The critical values for ZA tests are: With intercept: –5.34, –4.80 and –4.58 and with intercept and trend: –5.57, –5.08 and –4.82 at 1 per cent, 5 per cent and 10 per cent Level of Significances respectively. Maximum number of lags: 2. Results Generated by E-views 8.

Table 6.3: Granger Causality Test Results

Null Hypothesis	*F-Statistic*
IIP does not Granger Cause WPI	27.0642***
DU_OIL does not Granger Cause WPI	25.8535***
WPI does not Granger Cause IIP	15.5501***
IIP does not Granger Cause DU_OIL	11.2303***
B_SEN does not Granger Cause DU_OIL	9.21856***
B_SEN does not Granger Cause IIP	4.70674***
WPI does not Granger Cause DU_OIL	3.87774**
WPI does not Granger Cause B_SEN	3.76919**

Note: ***, ** and * denote significance at a 1 per cent, 5 per cent and 10 per cent respectively. Results Generated by E-views 8.

Bi-Causality: There is a bi-directional causality between Du_Oil and WPI and also between IIP and WPI.

Uni-Causality: B_SEN is caused by WPI. B_SEN causes both Du_Oil and IIP.

for instability of the long-run relationship between oil prices and four macro-economic variables *viz.* B_Sen, IIP, WPI and Du_Oil. The test statistics are reported in Table 6.4.

Table 6.4: Hansen's Instability Test

Dependent Variable	*Test Estimate*
B_Sen	72.01550*** (<0.01)
Du_Oil	1.586685*** (<0.01)
IIP	5.808901*** (<0.01)
WPI	259.5799*** (<0.01)

Note: ***, ** and * denote significance, i.e. rejection of the null hypothesis of stability at 1 per cent, 5 per cent and 10 per cent levels respectively. The Tests are performed on software EViews 8. Numbers in (.) are p-values.

The results show that, at 1 per cent level, there is not enough evidence to accept the null hypothesis of stability in most of the long-run equations, since all test statistics are significant. This supports for the presence for structural change at 1 per cent level.

The next step is to conduct the threshold cointegration tests by Gregory and Hansen (1996). The 3 model representations employed are:

(i) The level shift model (C)

$$B\_SEN_t = \mu + \varphi D_t(T_b) + \beta_0 Du\_Oil + \beta_1 IIP + \beta_2 WPI + u_t \quad ...(9)$$

(ii) The level shift with trend model (C/T)

$$B\_SEN_t = \mu + \varphi D_t(T_b) + \beta_0 Du\_Oil + \beta_1 IIP + \beta_2 WPI + t + u_t \quad ...(10)$$

(iii) The regime shift model (C/S)

$$\begin{aligned} B\_SEN_t = {} & \mu + \varphi D_t(T_b) + \beta_0 Du\_Oil + \delta_0 D_t(T_b) Du\_Oil + \\ & \beta_1 IIP + \delta_1 D_t(T_b) IIP + \beta_2 WPI + \\ & \delta_2 D_t(T_b) WPI + u_t \end{aligned} \quad ...(11)$$

where, u_t = error term;

μ = intercept before the break in T_b;

φ = shift occurring after the break in T_b;
β = parameters of the cointegrating vector;
δ = change in the cointegrating vector after the shift;
= trend slope before the shift.

Similar models are used for Du_Oil, IIP and WPI.

The null hypothesis of no cointegration is tested first by running regression equations (9), (10) and (11) for each possible structural break and then applying (6), (7) and (8) for regression errors of each possible break.

Results of GH threshold cointegration tests are reported in Table 6.5. It indicates rejection of the H_0 of no cointegration for most of the equations in regime shift model. The results are invariant across C, C/T and C/S models only for IIP. The existence of cointegrating relationship among

Table 6.5: Estimates of Gregory and Hansen Cointegration Test

Dependent Variable	*B_SEN*	*Du_Oil*	*IIP*	*WPI*
Level shift C				
ADF*	–3.08 (0)	–5.45(2)**	–5.91(1)***	–4.97(2)
	2006M04	2005M12	2011M11	2011M12
Zt*	–3.26	–5.56**	–8.88***	–6.13***
	2000M11	2005M10	2012M12	2012M12
Za*	–24.87	–36.23	–125.76***	–74.82***
	2000M11	2005M10	2012M12	2012M12
Level shift with trend C/T				
ADF*	–6.21(0)*	–6.85(2)***	–8.02(1)***	–6.27(2)*
	2008M02	2008M11	2009M02	2007M12
Zt*	–6.48**	–7.15***	–13.62***	–6.31*
	2009M05	2005M04	2010M01	2009M05
Za*	–80.35**	91.15***	–218.70***	–79.26**
	2009M05	2005M04	2010M01	2009M05
Regime Shift C/S				
ADF*	–5.85(0)*	–7.06(2)***	–7.42(1)***	–5.39(2)
	2008M05	2008M04	2008M10	2011M06
Zt*	–6.52***	–6.95***	–11.84***	–8.34***
	2009M05	2008M07	2008M10	2011M06
Za*	–79.99**	–52.50	–183.54***	–114.64***
	2009M05	2008M07	2008M10	2011M06

Note: ***, ** and * denote significance, i.e. rejection of the H_0 of no cointegration at 1 per cent, 5 per cent and 10 per cent levels respectively. Numbers in (.) are lag orders to include in the equations. Results generated by Stata 12.

IIP, Du_Oil, B_Sen and WPI indicates that allowing for structural change in the cointegrating relationship, the series moves together in the long-run, though in the short-run they may diverge from each other. Hansen's instability test results also support the presence of structural change at the 1 per cent level of significance.

The threshold cointegration for stock market indicates that the cointegrating relationship has witnessed level shift with trend and regime shift and has changed during 2008-09 period. The global fuel-financial crisis that occurred during the period has probably changed the empirical relationship of Indian stock market, domestic fuel price and other macro-economic variables. Similarly, shift in cointegrating relationship is also observed in case of Du_Oil and IIP. This is also around the same period. Further significant shift in WPI is witnessed much later, around 2011. This is closer to the period of global food price inflation.

Amongst the three models (C, C/T and C/S) for our purpose, the level shift with trend (C/T) seems to be better model for three reasons: firstly, it accounts for both intercept and trend shift; secondly, no regime shift was noticed during the period. Thirdly, in C/T model, amongst the ADF*, Z_t* and Z_a*, the structural breaks based on ADF* have been preferred since these breaks corroborate substantially with the evidence of global financial crisis of 2007-08.

Our result is similar to that by Chittedi (2012) that found a cointegrating relationship between BSE and fuel price. Our result is also consistent with the study of Ghosh and Kanjilal (2014). Using monthly data, they found that there is cointegration with a structural break between oil price, exchange rate and stock market for India.

Generalized Impulse Response Analysis

In order to get an in-depth understanding of the relationship between stock index and other endogenous variables in the system, the study estimated the generalized impulse response functions (GIRFs) based on the unrestricted VAR models of the variables.

A lag length[11] of 2 has been selected as per Schwarz information criterion (SC) and Hannan-Quinn information criterion (HQ). The sample period is sub-divided further into pre-and post-structural break period, based on the results under the C/T Model (ADF* results as reported in Table 6.5). Correspondingly, the pre-structural break period is from 1994M01 to 2007M11. The post-structural break period is from 2009M03 to 2015M04. The period from 2007M12 to 2009M02 is omitted, as it includes the structural break points in the long-run relationship. It may also be noted that this period largely corresponds with the turbulence associated with the global financial crisis, repercussions of which also trickled into the Indian economy.

In Figure 6.2 and Figure 6.3, select IRFs have been represented. The impulse responses generated in our study show the response to one standard deviation shock in the error terms of other variables. The X axis represents the time period, while the Y axis represents the shock in the movement trend. Figure 6.2 provides IRFs for stock markets when innovations are given to oil prices, industrial production and inflation (6.2a,6.2d; 6.2b, 6.2e; and 6.2c, 6.2f respectively). Figure 6.3 provides IRFs for stock markets, industrial production and inflation when innovations are given to oil prices (6.3a,6.3d; 6.3b,6.3e; and 6.3c,6.3f respectively). A brief of each of the IRFs is hereby provided. Annexure Figures A1, A2 and A3 represent the IRFs for all variables of the study, for the Pre- and Post-structural break period.

A positive shock to Du_Oil causes two very contrasting movements in B_SEN in the pre (Fig. 6.2a) and post (Fig. 6.2d) structural break period. Though initially in the pre-structural break period (until the 4th month), there is no effect of Du_Oil on sensex, by the 4th month Du_Oil starts having a positive effect on B_Sen. Further, the positive impact gets stronger over time. However, for the post-structural break period, there is an immediate and sharp negative effect on B_Sen, which by the 4th month stagnates at the lower level.

Further, with one standard deviation shock to IIP, B_Sen movements in pre (Fig. 6.2b) and post (Fig. 6.2e) structural break periods are also very different. Before the structural break, there is a very slight positive change in B_Sen from the original level which continues throughout the 10 month period. However, for the post-structural break period there is an immediate negative effect on stock prices until about the 5th month. Thereafter, the negative effect stabilizes at its lower level.

Finally, with shock given to WPI, in the pre-break period (Fig. 6.2c), there is an immediate negative impact until the 2nd month, which stabilizes at the lower level thereafter. In post-break period (Fig. 2f), there is a sudden negative effect until the 2nd month. However, the negative effect dissipates so much so that Sensex comes back to its original level by 5th month. Thereafter, B_Sen goes above the original level and continues to do so until the end of 10th month.

To conclude, there is a striking difference in the effect of oil prices, industrial production and inflation on the Sensex during the pre- and

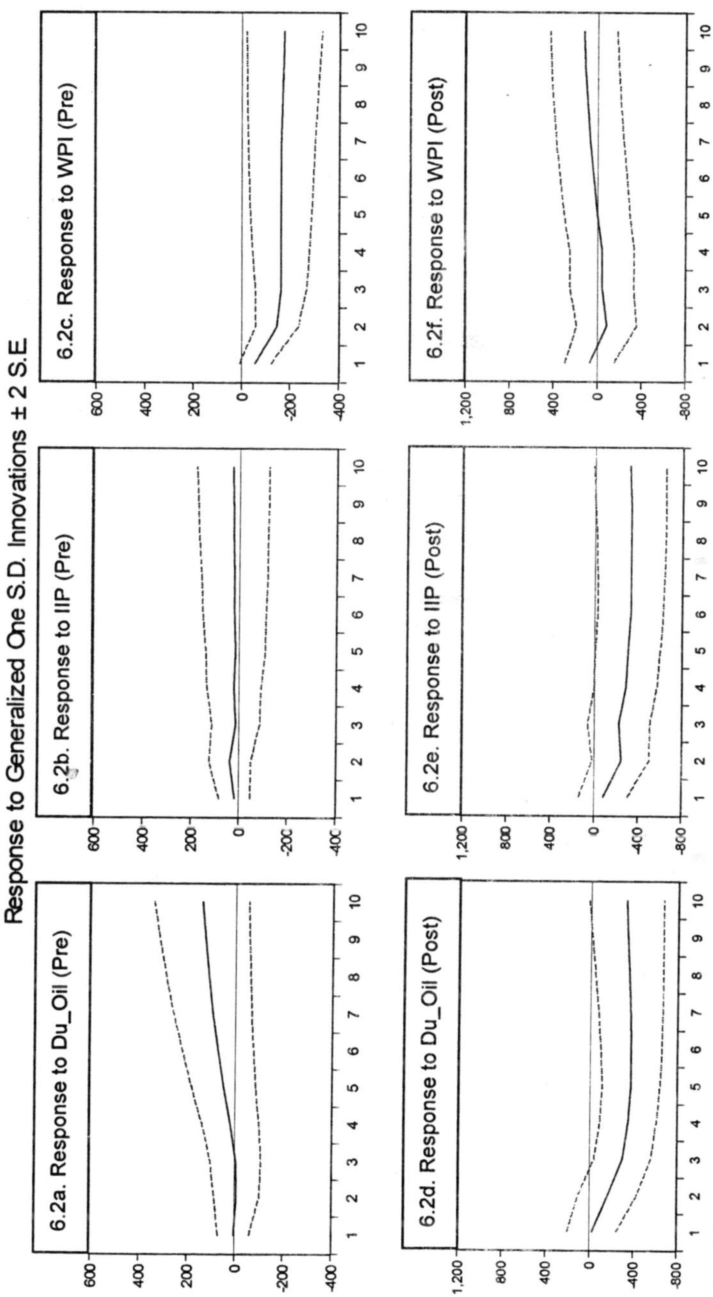

Fig. 6.2: Impulse Response Functions of B_SEN to Other Variables (Pre- and Post-structural break period).

Source: Generated by Authors, using Eviews 8.

post-structural break period. While positive shocks to Du_Oil and IIP have negative effect on B_Sen in the post-break period, shock to WPI has a positive effect on B_Sen for the same period. Further, in general, macro-economic variables that cause a favourable effect in the pre structural break period have an adverse effect in the post-break period. The reverse is also true, i.e. variables that have an adverse effect on Sensex in the pre-structural break period, have a favourable effect in the post-break period. Additionally, the magnitude of response is stronger for the post-break period.

In Figure 6.3, with shock given to B_Sen in the pre-break period (Fig. 6.3a), there is a sharp positive effect on Du_Oil prices. By 3rd month, the magnitude of effect reduces, though the gap from original level continues to widen until the 10th month. However, in post-break period (Fig. 6.3d), there is a sudden positive effect, which transforms into negative effect soon thereafter (by the end of 2nd month). The negative effect continues until the 5th month. Thereafter, it stagnates at the lower level until the end of the 10th month.

In the pre-break period with a one S.D. shock on IIP (Fig. 6.3b), there is a slight positive effect on Du_Oil, which remains throughout the 10 month period. Similarly, in the post-break period, there is a sharp positive effect on Du_Oil which continues until the 4th month (Fig. 6.3e). Thereafter, the effect stabilizes and remains positive until the end of the 10th month. Further, while the directional movements remain same in the pre- and post-break period, the magnitudes are more pronounced for the latter period.

Finally, with a shock given to WPI, there is a constant negative impact on Du_Oil in pre-break period (Fig. 3c) which stabilizes post the 4th month. In the post-break period, with innovation to WPI, there is a sudden peak in Du_Oil price in the 2nd month. Thereafter, the effect gradually dissipates and comes back to its original level by the end of 10th period.

To conclude, oil prices respond differently depending on which macro-economic variable is given a shock, as well as, whether the time period is pre or post the structural break. In the post-break period, both sensex and industrial production have a negative effect on oil prices, whereas inflation based on wholesale prices does not impact oil prices substantially. Also, while the effect of sensex on oil prices varies between the two time periods, the impact of industrial production on oil prices remains positive in both the periods. However, the magnitude of the response remains stronger for the post-structural break period.

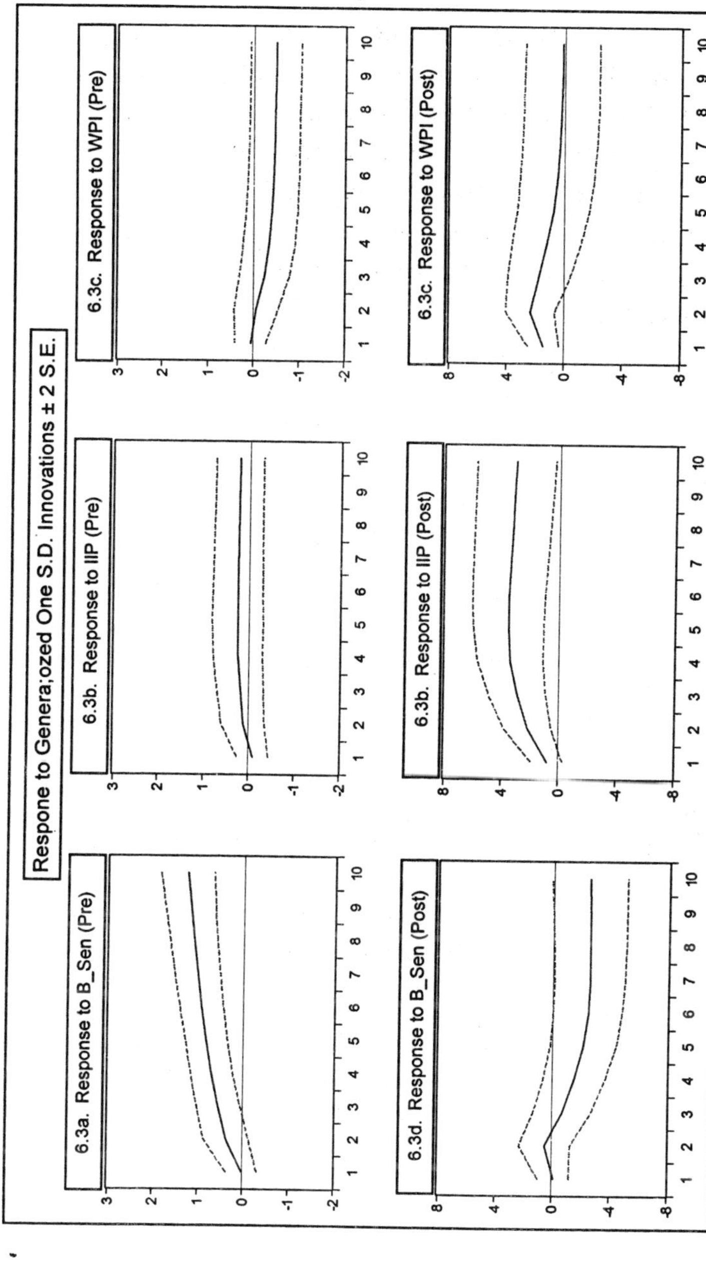

Fig. 6.3: Impulse Response Functions of Du_Oil to Other Variables (Pre- and Post-structural break period)

Source: Generated by Authors, using Eviews 8.

5. Conclusion

Fuel prices have substantial linkages with the financial and economic sectors of an economy. Findings of existing literature reveal that crude oil prices have differential effect on macro-economic variables, depending upon the nature of economy (net exporter or net importer of oil), time period considered and the variables under consideration. Further, very few studies have analysed the relationship for India while considering structural breaks in datasets. Therefore, in this study, an attempt is made to understand the relationship between fuel price fluctuations and stock market movements for India, after analysing structural breaks in the variables. The study specifically aims to understand the interrelationship between oil prices, stock market movements, prices and economic growth as proxied by Index of Industrial Production. Various time series econometric tests such as Zivot-Andrews, Granger Causality, Gregory-Hansen cointegration and Generalised Impulse Response Functions (GRIFs) are deployed on monthly data over the period January 1994 to April 2015.

The main findings of the study are:

- The series is stationary at first difference with the presence of a structural break.
- With respect to stock market, Granger Causality results indicate that there is a uni-directional causality:
  (i) from stock market to domestic fuel prices and economic growth, and
  (ii) from inflation to stock market.
- Hansen's test of stability supports the presence of structural break at 1 per cent level. Further, the threshold cointegration results indicate that there is a long-run cointegrating relationship with a structural break between the stock market movements, fuel prices, growth and inflation. The presence of threshold cointegration reveals that there is a cointegrating relationship that changes somewhere around 2008-09. This seems to be on account of the global financial crisis of 2008-09. These findings are in line with Ghosh and Kanjilal (2014) and Pradhan *et al.* (2015).
- Based on results under the "level shift with trend" model (ADF* statistics), and having divided the sample period into sub-periods

representing pre- and post-structural break period. GIRFs have been generated. The pre-structural break period corresponds to January 1994 to November 2007 and the post-structural break period from March 2009 to April 2015. The period from December 2007 to February 2009 is omitted, as it includes the structural break points in the long-run relationship. Analysis of impulse response functions for the pre- and post-structural break period reveals the following:

- *Impact on stock market on account of innovations to fuel prices, inflation and economic growth:* The four main findings are: first, positive shocks to oil prices and economic growth have negative effect on stock market in the post-break period; second, shock to inflation has a positive effect on stock market for the same period; third, in general, macro-economic variables that cause a favourable effect in the pre-structural break period have an adverse effect in the post-break period and finally, the magnitude of response is stronger in the post-break period.
- *Impact on fuel prices on account of innovations to stock market, inflation and economic growth:* Oil prices respond differently to shocks depending on the macro-economic variable and the time period considered. The two main findings are: first, positive shocks to stock market and economic growth have a negative effect on oil prices in the post-break period; and second, shock to inflation does not have a significant impact on oil prices for the same period.

Our chapter has important implications for investors and policy-makers. For instance, portfolio investors often work towards creating a portfolio which is expected to give best returns depending on their risk preference. In view of this, our study helps to understand the relationship between oil prices and stock market for portfolio investment. In the past decade, our evidence suggests that a hike in fuel prices adversely impacts the stock market. Therefore, in view of the present low structure of oil prices, an important implication is that investors should invest in the stock market for better returns. Further, for India, despite lower global oil prices, the stock market returns have risen. This is indicative of the fact that petro-dollar flight may not have been substantial.

Though on the face of it our results indicate that shocks to GDP growth are not conducive for stock market, the inherent reason for the same may not necessarily be as pessimistic. This is because there could be a possibility of diversion of funds (by public and/or institutions) towards physical investments as against financial investments. Such a behavioural response is expected to further promote economic growth.

Our evidence also suggests a positive relationship between inflation and stock markets. A plausible reason for the same could be diversion of funds towards shares and stocks to hedge against inflation. Therefore, it is important for monetary policy-makers to contain inflation at levels which do not lead to diversion of funds from fixed and savings deposits into stock market. This is so because economic theory states that growth and its sustainability depends on the fundamentals of economic development (such as production and prices) rather than on the momentum of stock markets, which may have elements of speculation as well.

Annexure

Table A1: Descriptive Statistics

Sample: 1994M01 2015M04

	B_SEN	DU_OIL	IIP	WPI
Mean	10012.00	50.48901	110.7069	108.5248
Median	5683.970	34.68007	98.42419	100.9464
Maximum	29361.50	131.2248	198.1000	185.9000
Minimum	2810.660	10.05000	47.06834	55.46195
Std. Dev.	7351.431	35.21328	44.53711	37.66155
Skewness	0.727751	0.603022	0.293444	0.591701
Kurtosis	2.262157	1.900831	1.576119	2.142199
Jarque-Bera	28.40428	28.40229	25.29999	22.78682
Probability	0.000001	0.000001	0.000003	0.000011
Sum	2563071.	12925.19	28340.96	27782.34
Sum Sq. Dev.	1.38E+10	316193.6	505806.3	361690.1
Observations	256	256	256	256

Table A2: Lag Length Selection

VAR Lag Order Selection Criteria
Endogenous variables: B_SEN DU_OIL IIP WPI
Exogenous variables: C
Sample: 1994M01 2015M04
Included observations: 248

Lag	LogL	LR	FPE	AIC	SC	HQ
0	–5487.796	NA	2.02e+14	44.28868	44.34535	44.31149
1	–3785.105	3336.724	2.49e+08	30.68633	30.96968	30.80040
2	–3667.177	227.2972	1.10e+08	29.86433	**30.37435***	**30.06964***
3	–3647.203	37.85425	1.06e+08	29.83228	30.56897	30.12884
4	–3627.483	36.73573	1.03e+08*	29.80229*	30.76564	30.19010
5	–3615.770	21.44268	1.07e+08	29.83686	31.02689	30.31592
6	–3599.236	29.73442	1.07e+08	29.83255	31.24926	30.40286
7	–3580.997	32.21356*	1.05e+08	29.81449	31.45787	30.47605
8	–3571.199	16.98801	1.10e+08	29.86451	31.73456	30.61732

* indicates lag order selected by the criterion
LR: sequential modified LR test statistic (each test at 5% level)
FPE: Final prediction error
AIC: Akaike information criterion
SC: Schwarz information criterion
HQ: Hannan-Quinn information criterion

Results generated by Eviews-8.

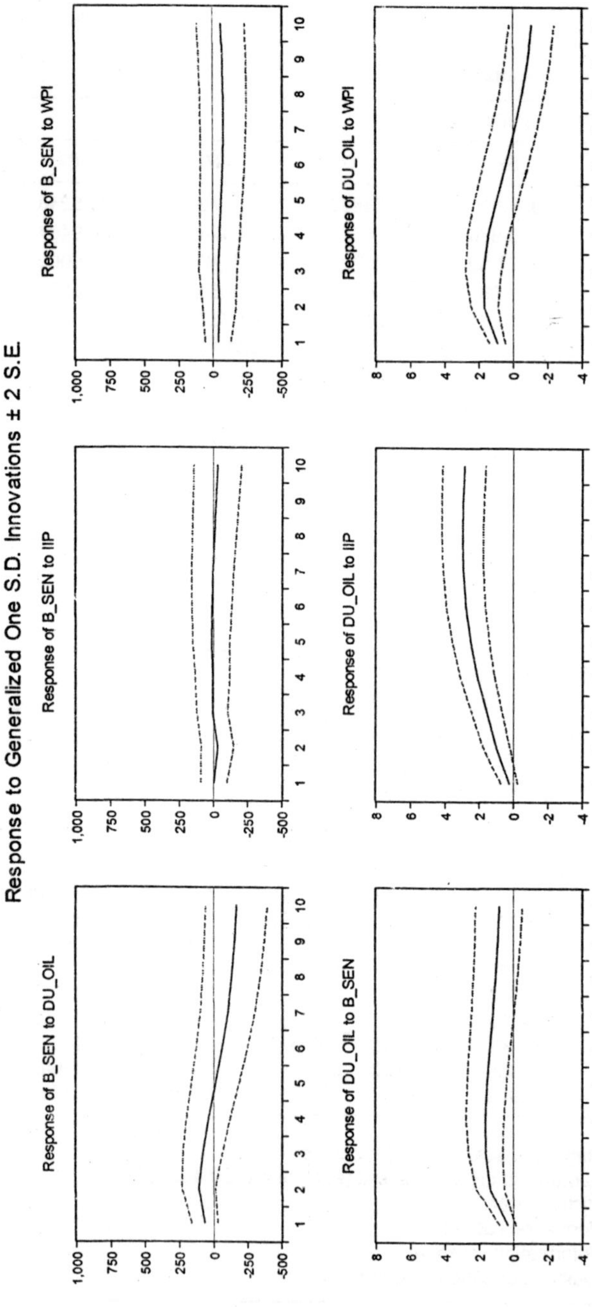
Response to Generalized One S.D. Innovations ± 2 S.E.
Response of B_SEN to DU_OIL
Response of B_SEN to IIP
Response of B_SEN to WPI
Response of DU_OIL to B_SEN
Response of DU_OIL to IIP
Response of DU_OIL to WPI

(Contd.)

Fig. A1: *(Cond.)*

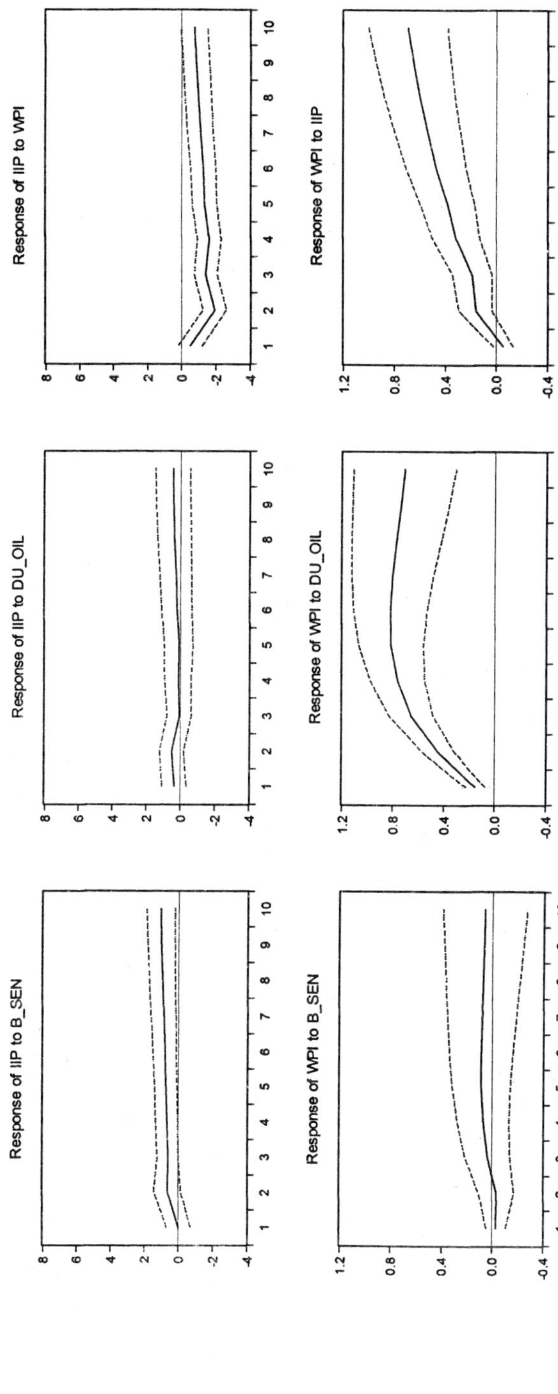

Fig. A1: Generalized Impulse Response Functions (1994M01 to 2015M04)

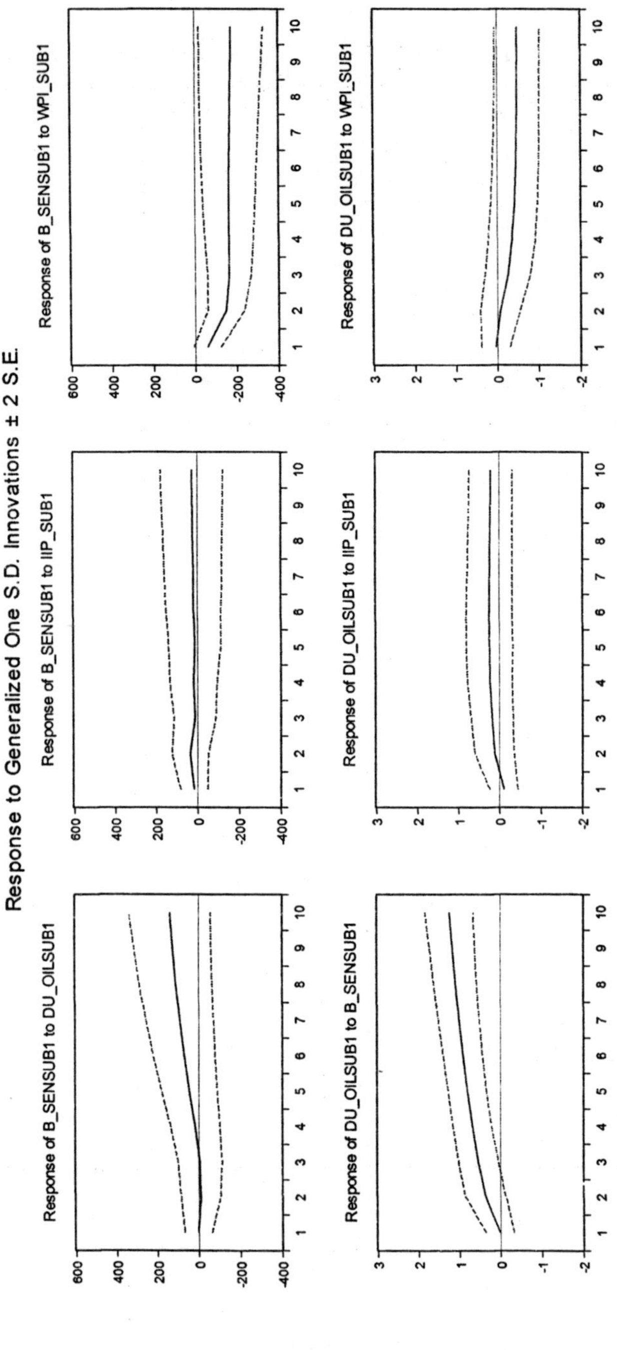
Response to Generalized One S.D. Innovations ± 2 S.E.
Response of B_SENSUB1 to DU_OILSUB1
Response of B_SENSUB1 to IIP_SUB1
Response of B_SENSUB1 to WPI_SUB1
Response of DU_OILSUB1 to B_SENSUB1
Response of DU_OILSUB1 to IIP_SUB1
Response of DU_OILSUB1 to WPI_SUB1

(Contd.)

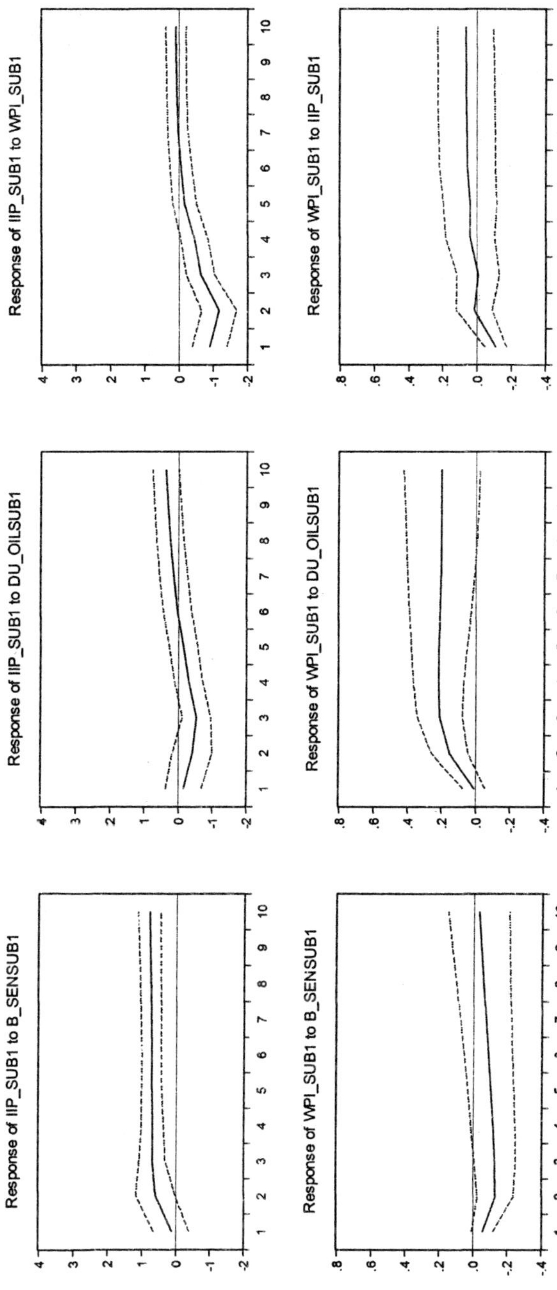

Fig. A2: Generalized Impulse Response Functions (Pre Break Period)

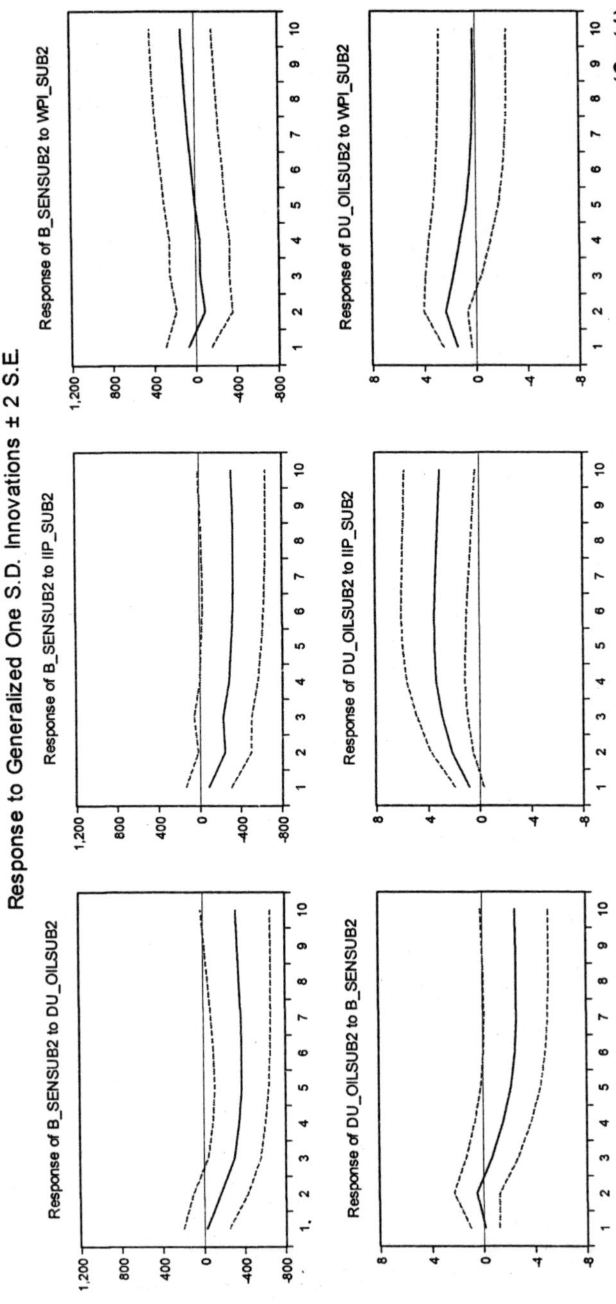
Response to Generalized One S.D. Innovations ± 2 S.E.
Response of B_SENSUB2 to DU_OILSUB2
Response of B_SENSUB2 to IIP_SUB2
Response of B_SENSUB2 to WPI_SUB2
Response of DU_OILSUB2 to B_SENSUB2
Response of DU_OILSUB2 to IIP_SUB2
Response of DU_OILSUB2 to WPI_SUB2

(Contd.)

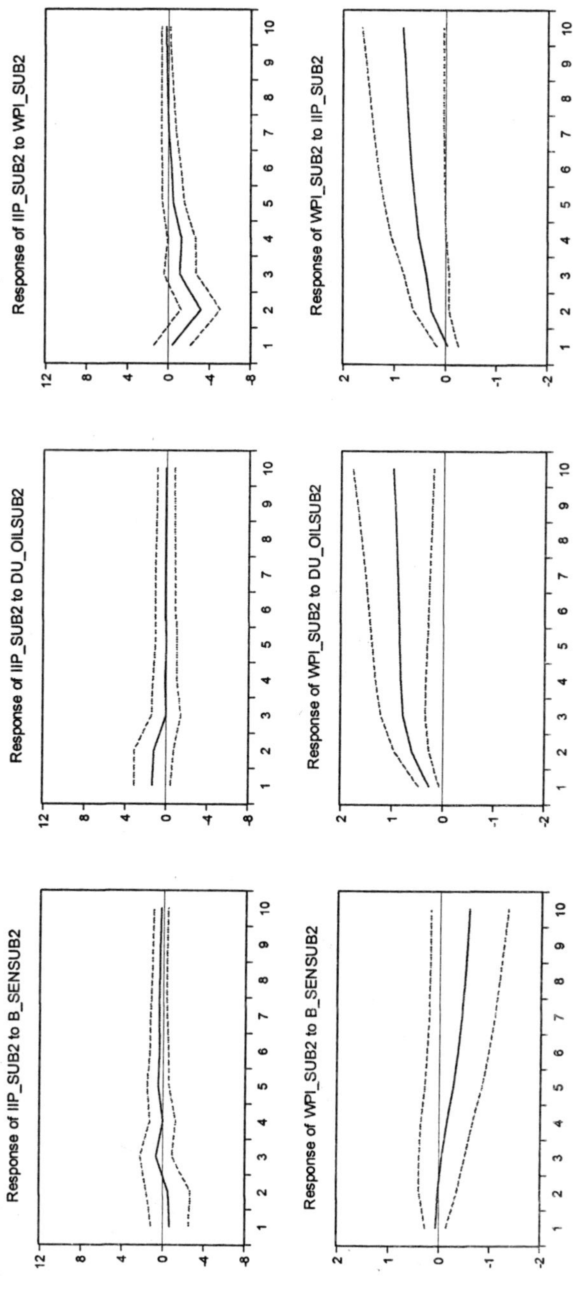

Fig. A3: Generalized Impulse Response Functions (Post Break Period)

Notes

1. International Monetary Fund estimates, for fiscal year 2014-15.
2. India imports around 80 per cent of its oil and gas requirements; this constitutes around 37 per cent of total imports.
3. Petro-dollar investments are generally made by the oil exporting economies in government bonds, corporate bonds and real-estates in emerging economies with higher growth rates. These are excess earnings they have from export of oil during periods of higher oil prices globally.
4. Launched in 1986.
5. The figure is divided into four phases.
6. The composition of Indian Basket of Crude represents Average of Oman and Dubai for sour grades and Brent (Dated) for sweet grade in the ratio of 72.28:27.72 for 2015-16; 72.04:27.96 for 2014-15; 69.9:30.1 for 2013-14; 68.2:31.8 for 2012-13; 65.2:34.8 for 2011-12, 67.6:32.4 for 2010-11, 63.5:36.5 for 2009-10, 62.3:37.7 for 2008-09; 61.4:38.6 for 2007-08, 59.8:40.2 for the year 2006-07 and 58:42 for the year 2005-06.
7. The period of study is restricted based on the availability of data.
8. https://blogs.worldbank.org/prospects/files/prospects/pink_data_0.xls (accessed on:17/3/2015)
9. http://www.bseindia.com/sensexview/indexview_new.aspx?index_Code=16 & iname=BSE30#. SENSEX was initially complied in 1986; it is the oldest in India. It is composed of the largest and most actively traded stocks of BSE. (accessed on: 12/3/2015)
10. www.eaindustry.nic
11. Refer to Table A2 for Lag length selection.

REFERENCES

Apergis, N., and Miller, S.M. (2009). "Do structural oil-market shocks affect stock prices?" *Energy Economics*, *31:* 569-575.

Arouri, M.E. (2011). "Does Crude oil move stock markets in Europe? A sector investigation", *Economic Modelling*, *28*: 1716-1725.

Basher, S.A., Haug, A.A., and Sadorsky, P. (2012). "Oil prices, exchange rates and emerging stock markets", *Energy Economics*, *34* (1): 227-240.

Bhattacharya, K., and Bhattacharya, I. (2001). "Impact of increase in Oil Prices on Inflation and Output in India", *Economic and Political Weekly*, *36:* 4735-4741.

Bhunia, A., and Mukhuti, S.S. (2012). "An Empirical Association between Crude Price and Indian Stock Market", *International Journal of Business and Management Tomorrow*.

Bloomberg, S.B., and Harris, E.S. (1995). "The commodity-consumer price connection: Fact or fable?" *Economic Policy Review*, *1* (3).

Cheung, Y.W., and Ng, L.K. (1998). "International evidence on the stock market and aggregate economic activity", *Journal of Empirical Finance, 5* (3): 281-296.

Chittedi, K.R. (2012). "Do oil price matter for Indian stock markets? An empirical analysis", *Journal of Applied Economics and Business Research*, 2-10.

Cobo-Reyes, R., and Perez Quiros, G. (2005). "The effect of oil price on industrial production and on stock returns", *Departamento de Teoria e Historia Economica*, Universidad de Granada.

Cong, R.G., Wei, Y.M., Jiao, J.L., and Fan, Y. (2008). "Relationships between oil price shocks and stock market: An empirical analysis from China", *Economic Policy, 36*: 3544-3553.

Deb, K., and Appleby, P. (2015, July 14-15). *India's Primary Energy Evolution: Past Trends and Future Prospects.* Retrieved February 28, 2016, from NCAER: http://www.ncaer.org/uploads/photo-gallery/files/1436715601 IPF%202015%20Kaushik%20Deb%20Conference%20Version%20 Draft.pdf

Engle, R.F., and Granger, C.W. (1987). "Co-integration and error correction: representation, estimation, and testing", *Econometrica: Journal of Econometric Society*, 251-276.

Fang, C.R., and You, S.Y. (2014). "The impact of oil price shocks on the large emerging countries' stock prices: Evidence from China, India and Russia", *International Review of Economics and Finance*, pp. 330-338.

Filis, G. (2010). "Macro-economy, stock market and oil prices: Do meaningful relationships exist among their cyclical fluctuations?", *Energy Economics*, pp. 877-886.

Fisher, I. (1930). *The Theory of Interest,* New York: MacMillan.

Ghosh, S., and Kanjilal, K. (2014). "Co-movement of international crude oil price and Indian stock market: Evidences from non-linear cointegration tests", *Energy Economics*.

Goswami, G., and Jung, S. (1998). "Stock Market and Economic Forces: Evidence from Korea", *Global Finance Conference.* Mexico.

Greene, W.H. (2003). *Econometric Analysis* (Fifth ed.), Pearson Education.

Gregory, A.W., and Hansen, B.E. (1996). "Residual-based tests for cointegration in models with regime shifts", *Journal of Econometrics, 70:* 99-126.

Gregory, A.W., and Hansen, B.E. (1996). "Tests for cointegration in models with regime and trend shifts", *Oxford Bulletin of Economics and Statistics, 58* (3): 555-560.

Gregory, A.W., Nason, J.M., and Watt, D.G. (1996). "Testing for structural breaks in cointegrated relationships", *Journal of Econometrics, 71*: 321-341.

Gujarati, D.N., Porter, D., and Sangeetha, G. (2012). *Basic Econometrics* (Fifth ed.). Tata McGraw Hill Education Private Limited.

Hamilton, J.D. (1983). "Oil and the Macroeconomy since World War II", *Journal of Political Economy*, pp. 228-248.

Hamilton, J.D. (2000). "What is an Oil Shock?", *NBER working paper no. 7755.*

Hammoudeh, S., and Li, H. (2005). "Oil sensitivity and systematic risk in oil-sensitive stock indices. *Journal of Economics and Business*, *57* (1): 1-21.

Hammoudeh, S., Santos, P.A., and Al-Hasan, A. (2013). "Downside risk management and VAR-based optimal portfolios for precious metals, oil and stocks", *The North American Journal of Economics and Finance*, *25*: 318-339.

Jain, A., and Ghosh, S. (2013). "Dynamics of global oil prices, exchange rate and precious metal prices in India". *Resources Policy*, *38*: 88-93.

Johansen, S. (1988). "Statistical analysis of cointegrating vectors", *Journal of economic dynamics and control*, pp. 231-254.

Johansen, S., and Juselius, K. (1990). "Maximum likelihood estimation and inference on co-integraion with applications to the demand for money", *Oxford Bulletin of Economics and Statistics*, *52* (2): 169-210.

Jones, C.M., and Kaul, G. (1996). "Oil and the stock markets", *The Journal of Finance*, *51* (2): 463-491.

Kazi, U.A. (1988, April 16). An exploratory stochastic framework to analyse the relationship between macro-oil price shocks and economic development.

Kilian, L., and Park, C. (2009). "The impact of oil price shocks on the US stock market", *International Economic Review*, *50* (4): 1267-1287.

Kustepeli, Y., and Önel, G. "Fiscal deficit sustainability with a strutural break: An application to Turkey", *Review of Social, Economic and Business Studies*, *5* (6): 189-208.

Le, T.H., and Chang, Y. (2015). "Effects of oil price shocks on the stock performance: Do nature of shocks and economies matter?", *Energy Economics*, *51*: 261-274.

Le, V.T., and Vinh, N.T. (2011, September). The impact of oil prices, real effective exchange rate and inflation on economic activity: Novel evidence from Vietnam. Discussion Paper Series.

Lee, K., and Ni, S. (2002). "On the dynamic effects of oil price shocks: A study using industry level data", *Journal of Monetary Economics*, pp. 823-852.

Levine, R., and Zervos, S. (1996). "Stock market development and long-run growth", *The World Bank Economic Review*, *10* (2): 323-339.

Lütkepohl, H., and Don S. P. (1991). "Estimating orthogonal impulse responses *via* vector autoregressive models", *Econometric Theory*, *7* (4): 487-496.

Mandal, K., Bhattacharyya, I., and Bhoi, B.B. (2012). "Is the oil price pass-through in India any different?" *Journal of Policy Modelling*, *34* (6): 832-848.

Miller, J., and Ratti, R.A. (2009). "Crude oil and stock markets: Stability, instability, and bubbles", *Energy Economics*, *31*: 559-568.

Mork, K.A. (1989). "Oil and the macroeconomy when prices go up and down: an extension of Hamilton's results", *Journal of Political Economy*, *97* (3), 740-744.

Mork, K.A., Olsen, O., and Mysen, H.T. (1994). "Macroeconomic responses to oil price increases and decreases in seven OECD countries", *The Energy Journal*, 19-35.

Nandha, M., and Hammoudeh, S. (2007). "Systematic risk, and oil price and exchange rate sensitivities in Asia-Pacific stock markets", *Research in International Business and Finance, 21* (2): 326-341.

Park, J., and Ratti, R.A. (2008). "Oil price shocks and stock markets in the U.S. and 13 European countries", *Energy Economics, 30*: 2587-2608.

Perron, P. (1989). "The great crash, the oil price shock, and the unit root hypothesis", *Econometrica: Journal of the Econometric Society*: 1361-1401.

Pesaran, H.H., and Shin, Y. (1998). "Generalised impulse response analysis in linear multivariate models", *Economic letters, 58* (1): 17-29.

Philips, P.B., and Perron, P. (1988). "Testing for a unit root in time series regression", *Biometrika*, pp. 335-346.

Philips, P.C., and Ouliaris, S. (1990). "Asymptotic properties of residual based tests for cointegration", *Econometrica: Journal of the Econometric Society*, pp. 165-193.

Phillips, P.C. and Pierre, P. (1988). "Testing for a unit root in time series regression", *Biometrika, 75* (2): 335-346.

Pradhan, R.P., Arvin, M.B., and Ghoshray, A. (2015). "The dynamics of economic growth, oil prices, stock market depth, and other macroeconomic variables: Evidence from the G-20 countries", *International Review of Financial Analysis, 39*: 84-95.

Sajeev, A. (Forthcoming). "Macroeconomic Effects of Crude Oil Prices in India". Doctoral Research Work undertaken at the University of Delhi under completion. India.

Sardosky, P., Huag, A.A., and Basher, S.A. (2010). "Oil Prices, Exchnage Rates and Emerging Stock Markets". *University of Ontago Economics Discussion Papers No. 1014*. New Zealand.

Turhan, M., Sensoy, A., and Hachihasanoglu, E. (2014). "A comparative analysis of the dynamic relationship between oil prices and exchange rates". *Journal of International Financial Markets, Institutions and Money, 32*, 397-414.

Wang, Y., Wu, C., and Yang, L. (2013). "Oil price shocks and stock market activities: Evidence from oil-importing and oil-exporting countries". *Journal of Comparative Economics, 41*: 1220-1239.

Williams, J.B. (1938). *The Theory of Investment Value. Cambridge: Harvard University Press*, p. 36.

Zivot, E., and Donald W.K., A. (1992). "Further Evidence on the great crash, the oil-price shock, and the unit-root hypothesis", *Journal of Business and Economic Statistics, 10* (3): 251-270.

7

The Energy Future of India

An Alternative Approach

Raj Kishor Pradhan

Introduction

Now, we are facing different type of problems. Important among them is the increasing energy crisis. Day by day industries are progressing. People are more dependent on energy than ever. But our chief sources of energy are fossil fuels like petroleum and coal. These sources have their limitation in terms of their availability. These sources are the root cause of different geopolitical problem like Middle East War etc. and Global Warming. But we cannot altogether abandon these sources unless or until we get other viable sources of energy.

India is the third largest economy in Asia. Therefore, her energy need is also insatiable. But as far as fossil fuels are concerned India has its own limitations. It has to depend on import of petroleum and coal for her economic development. India imports more than 80 per cent of crude oil for her annual consumptions. Although India has fourth largest coal reserve in the world but the quality of coal is also not good. Therefore, we have to spend huge foreign exchange for the import of the item. It is also one of the reasons for the huge current account deficit in BOP and fiscal deficit in the budget.

As economists have pointed out that petroleum and coal have already passed their peak. It means the days of cheaper crude oil and coals are already over. In recent past, the price of crude petroleum in the international market was more than $100 per barrel. So was the price of coal in international market. Now, the prices of crude oil and coal are near record low. It is temporary phenomenon. It is due to newly discovered inventory in USA and slow down of China. But in near future prices of crude oil and coal will touch the new height very soon. As we already know that the minerals are exhaustible. Therefore, we cannot use them for ever. So, we have to use it judiciously. This is what we call as "sustainable development".[1] It is the development model which we should aim at. But unfortunately free market economy advocate endless use of natural resources. Although, it adds to our national GDP but indirectly increases our environment degradation. Now, every environmental economist agrees about the possibility of global warming and its negative repercussion on environment as a whole. Therefore, the need of the hour is to use environment friendly energy resources or Green Energy. Now, we shall briefly discuss about the state of energy use in India and the possibility of phasing out of fossil fuels and gradually switching over to green energy.

India as an economy basically depends on coal for its energy needs. Thermal power plants generally generate 80 per cent of our electricity. Rest of the energy is generated by Hydel project, Nuclear reactor and other unconventional energy sources. India does not have a sustainable energy model as we have to depend more and more on conventional energy resources. Therefore, the Prime Minister of India has also declared India's energy road map. In Twelfth Five Year Plan approach one chapter is devoted to securing energy future in India. Adequate availability of energy is one of the basic requirements for faster economic growth.

To make growth truly inclusive, access to energy in rural areas and in urban area has to be ensured. Ensuring certain minimum level of energy consumption for everyone is a critical requirement for providing basic amenities required for everyone. The overall availability of energy would need to be increased substantially to meet these twin objectives and to enable a sharp reduction in energy demand and supply gap. It implies that the pace of addition of power generation capacities would need to be stepped up. The addition of new capacities in earlier five year Plans has been quite inadequate. The position will improve in Eleventh Five Year Plan. These initiatives will need further support with substantially large investments from the private sector. Specific measures to incentivize them to step up the pace of investment and provide competition in the power sector will need to be taken up. Development of energy markets will be promoted as part of this overall policy to help this process. This will ultimately lead to greater competition and better prices for consumers. With limited fuel resources, development of energy-efficient supercritical thermal capacities would be given a very high priority. The Plan will aim to develop at least half the thermal capacity through such energy efficient measures. Simultaneously, policies on setting up new nuclear power capacities and development of fast breeder reactor technologies would be continued.

Fuel subsidies are unsustainable for long periods. Given the large step-up in fuel needs, pricing of coal and other fuel sources would move towards market-based pricing. Accordingly, price of oil products, coal, gas and other energy sources will gradually converge towards international market price. While support to below poverty line families would be provided through a regime of direct subsidy, the overall pricing structure would be market-based.

Although, the Planning Commission has set right assessment and target the real problem is the implementation of the policy. In Eleventh Five Year Plan government has aimed at high capacity addition in power generation. But, it was not possible due to lack of coal and other problems. The hydro-electricity projects are struck due to delaying of clearance by Ministry of Environment (MoEF). Therefore, a number of private players have opted out of these ventures due to cost escalation and non cooperation from respective state governments. Consequently, these hydel projects are not sustainable.

Therefore, we have to think beyond the present scenario, so that we can get alternative energy sources. There are other conventional energy sources, i.e. nuclear energy apart from fossil fuel, which can solve our energy problems. Although India has technology to produce nuclear energy, she lacks uranium reserves. Therefore, we have to depend on other countries for uranium and other high end technology. Till 2008, India was considered pariah in nuclear trade in international arena due to non-commitment for non-proliferation treaty. But after signing the nuclear treaty with the USA in 2008 India became regular member of G-44. But the tragic incident of Fukushima has cast a shadow on the future of nuclear energy. In Kudunakulam large scale protest has also created doubt over future of nuclear energy.

In this light India has to adopt a long term plan to adopt clean and green non-conventional energy sources. Wind energy, solar energy, geo-thermal energy, bio-fuels are the few examples of non-conventional energy sources. We will discuss about these each and every source separately and their economic viability in Indian context and also in terms of Government's energy policy.

Wind Power in India

The development of wind power in India began in 1990s, and has significantly increased in the last few years. Although relative newcomer to the wind industry compared with Denmark or the USA, India has the fifth largest installed wind power capacity in the world. In 2009-10, India's growth rate was highest among the other top four countries. As of 31 January, 2013, the installed capacity of wind power in India was 1966.1 MW. It is estimated that 6000 MW of additional wind power capacity will be installed in India by 2014. Wind power accounts for 8.5 per cent of India's total installed power capacity, and it generates 1.6 per cent of the country's power.

But the main problem with wind power is that its initial cost for wind turbines is greater than that of conventional fossil fuel generators per MW installed. And also noise is produced by the rotor blades.

Solar Power in India

India is densely populated and has high solar insolation, an ideal combination for using solar power in India. India is already a leader in wind power generation. With about 300 clear, sunny days in a year, India's theoretical solar power reception, on only its land area, is about 5,000 per watt-hours per year (PWh/yr)(i.e. 5,000 trillion kWh/yr). The daily average solar energy incident over India varies from 4 to 7 kWh/m^2 with about 1500-2000 sunshine hours per year, which is far more than current total energy consumption.

The Government of India is promoting the use of solar energy through various strategies. In the latest budget for 2010-11, the government has announced an allocation of Rs. 1000 crore towards the Jawaharlal Nehru National Solar Mission. The Jawaharlal Nehru National Solar Mission also known as the National Solar Mission is a major initiative of the Government of India and State Governments to promote ecologically sustainable growth while addressing India's energy security challenges. It will also constitute a major contribution by India to the global effort to meet the challenges of climate change. Named after Jawaharlal Nehru, the Mission is one of the several initiatives that are part of National Action Plan on Climate Change. The amount of solar energy produced in India in 2007 was less than 1 per cent of the total energy demand.

Challenges—Land is scarce in India and per capita land availability is low. Dedication of land area for exclusive installation of solar arrays might have to compete with other necessities that require land. Also another is cost effect. In India, cost of solar electricity produced on grid is Rs. 18.44/unit. This high cost is mainly due to dependence on imports for silicon and solar wafers used for the manufacture of solar cells about 80 per cent of which comes through imports. Solar projects are capital intensive and the lack of an effective financing infrastructure of these projects is another major factor impending growth in impending in this sector.

Geo-thermal Energy in India

Geo-thermal energy is quite new in India. In India exploration and study of geo-thermal fields started in 1970. The GSI (Geological Survey of India) has identified 350 geo-thermal energy locations in the country. The most promising of these is in Puga Valley of Ladakh. The estimated potential for geothermal energy in India is about 10,000 MW.

Potential Applications:

Power generation
Cooking
Space heating
Use in greenhouse cultivation
Crop drying

Unlike traditional power plants that run on fuel, geo-thermal power plants use a renewable resource that need not be imported. However, the initial costs will be on the higher side because of exploration costs and the possibility of only in many explorations resulting in a sustainable and useful reservoir.

Tidal Energy in India

Among the various forms of energy contained in the seas and oceans, tidal energy, has been developed on a commercial scale. India has a long coastline with the estuaries and gulfs where tides are strong enough to move turbines for electrical power generation. The Gulf of Cambay and the Gulf of Kutch in Gujarat on the west coast have the maximum tidal range of 11m and 8m with average tidal range of 6.77m and 5.23m respectively. The Ganges Delta in the Sundarbans is approximately 5m with an average tidal range of 2.7m. The identified economic power potential is the order of 8000 MW with about 7000 MW in the Gulf of Cambay, about 1200 MW in the Gulf of Kutch in the State of Gujarat and about 100 MW in the Gangetic Delta in the Sunderban region in the State of West Bengal.

These sources of energy are more or less discussed in mainstream. But the main problem is that apart from solar and wind power another sources are not being used in prominent way. Therefore, the main problem with the non-traditional source is the cost aspect. The solar panel and wind turbine are costly. So, more the people use it, the cost will be decreased gradually.

Government is giving subsidies in solar panel and wind turbine to encourage their use. Still it is nascent in use. So, the use of these non-traditional energies sources is not that popular in various parts of India. But the Ministry of New and Renewable Energy (MNRE) is giving priority to non-traditional energy sources to be used in remote parts of India where traditional energy sources are not available. The broad aim of the Ministry is to develop and deploy new and renewable energy source to supplement the energy requirement of India. The Ministry is giving priority to solar energy. The Jawaharlal Nehru National Solar Mission was launched on the 11th January, 2010 by the Prime Minister. The mission has set the ambitious target of deploying 20,000 MW of grid connected solar power by 2022, thereby aiming at reducing the cost of solar power generation in the country through (i) long term policy; (ii) large scale deployment goals; (iii) aggressive R & D; and (iv) domestic production of critical raw materials, components and products, in order to achieve grid tariff parity by 2022. The mission will create an enabling policy framework to achieve this objective and make India a global leader in solar energy. Although, the ambitious plan of Government is highly praiseworthy but in reality the achievement is not near perfect till date. The main problem is the cost effect and also the change of behavioural pattern of common people. The economies of scale gradually look after the cost effect. But the behavioural pattern depends on many factors. In India where thousands of remote habitats and hamlets are devoid of any source of electricity, it will be a huge challenge to the authority to put them into renewable energy map. But plainly speaking these challenges are conducive to adoption of new technology. When the traditional sources have its limitations, the push for new energy will create new vistas.

Another facet of the current energy policy is the huge subsidy given by the Government on different petroleum products. As a result fiscal deficit has been touching record high. Now, it has become fiscally unstable for Indian economy. And also the subsidy is unable to capture the negative externalities from energy consumption, including the effects on climate change, local pollution, and traffic congestion. Energy subsidies aggravate fiscal imbalances, depress growth, damage the environment, and reinforce inequality. A country experience suggests that well-designed energy subsidy reform strategies can win public support. A far-reaching communications strategy, appropriately phased energy price increases, and targeted mitigating measures to protect the poor are among the most important elements of these strategies. These subsidies can be diverted to purchasing of solar panel or wind turbines. So, that current scenario will be improved dramatically.

The present government has taken right step towards energy conservation by freed petrol and diesel price from administrative control. Now, the price of both commodities will be determined by market. This step was long overdue. Now, the LPG subsidy is also targeted to right beneficiaries. But we should not forget the present energy scenario in the world. For last one year, the international crude oil price has been historical low of around $50 per barrel. This is due to various reasons. One is increasing inventory in the USA and another reason is slowing down of Chinese economy. It is also result in slowing down of coal and other commodities market in the world. But it is a temporary phenomenon. So, sooner or later, the price of these commodities will be catching up. So, we have to better prepare for alternative energy sources. We can say that present scenario has given us the opportunity to try for renewable energy source in the wide scale. No other major change can be initiated in the rural India by adopting traditional but environmentally safe method of energy consumption. In rural area people basically use energy for cooking purpose and in agricultural activities. For cooking they still depend on firewood. For that they depend on forests. For other purpose they depend on animal or other traditional energy source. Transport is major purpose. In this case public transport is very viable solution. In India, public transport is still in nascent stage. Therefore, major investment should be done in road and public transport. This will save huge expenditure on petroleum products, for cooking purpose use of bio-gas is a very good option in rural India. The Government is giving huge subsidy for bio-gas plant. It has a huge potential to solve the energy problem in near future. The poorest of poor depend on jungle for firewood. But existing law prohibited them to use this forest produce easily. Another problem is that as forest is public goods so nobody take care of the forests. Here, the Tragedy of commons[2] arises. This can be solved by social forestry. It has provision for forest management by the people of that village jointly by the government. Here government is acting as facilitator. Till today thousands of villages in remote areas are deprived of electricity. This can be solved by the use of solar power.

As the effect of climate change have been directly experienced in extending summer and delaying monsoon, the demand for power has been at the all time high. But the main problem is in generation of adequate electricity. As we have discussed earlier traditional energy source cannot fulfil the present peak demand. So, alternative approach should be adopted as early as possible. Otherwise public outrage cannot be overlooked. Change may be painful. But it is better in the long run.

Notes

1. Sustainable development—"Development that meets the need of the present without compromising the ability of future generations to meet their own needs."
2. The tragedy of the commons is an economic theory by Garrett Hardin, according to which individuals, acting independently and rationally according to each one's self-interest, behave contrary to the whole group's long term best interests by depleting some common resources.

References

1. Ganesh N. Prabhu (2012). "Evaluating the future of Indian solar industry", tejas@iimb
2. The Planning Commission.
   Approach to the 12th Five Year Plan.
   Securing the Energy Future for India.
3. India energy portal.
4. Puskar—Geothermal energy and its potential in India, 2013.
5. GoI, Ministry of New and Renewable Energy, "*Tidal Energy*" 2013-9-29.
6. Ministry of New and Renewable Energy website.
7. Benedict Clements, David Coady, Stefania Fabrizio, Sanjeev Gupta and Baoping Shang (2014) *Economics of Energy and Environmental Policy*, Volume 3, Issue Number 1.

8

Changing Structure of Manufacturing Industry in India

Issues, Challenges and Opportunities

Swami Prakash Srivastava

> "India needs to shift about half of its workforce from agriculture to manufacturing and services sectors for economic transformation. In longer run, you do need that (farm) workers come out of agriculture into manufacturing and services jobs. About 49 per cent of workforce in agriculture (as per 2011-12 NSSO Survey) produces only 14 per cent of the GDP."
>
> *Arvind Panagariya*,
> Vice Chairman Niti Aayog

1. Introduction

The ability of the manufacturing sector to absorb excess labour from the agriculture sector and shift the same to services renders it the driving force in the development process of an economy. While, the Indian manufacturing sector has witnessed remarkable growth in recent years; its contribution to GDP and employment is well below its true potential. Manufacturing holds a key position in the Indian economy, accounting for nearly 16 per cent of the real GDP in FY15. With launch of the "Make in India" initiative, Mr. Narendra Modi, the Prime Minister of India, aims to give global recognition to the Indian economy and also place India on the world map as a manufacturing hub. As per the United Nations Industrial Development Organisation (UNIDO), after China, the country is currently the largest producer of textiles, chemical products, pharmaceuticals, basic metals, general machinery and equipment, and electrical machinery. The sector's prominence in the domestic and global economies is set to rise in FY15 as a combination of supply-side advantages, policy initiatives and private sector efforts set India on the path to becoming a global manufacturing hub.

2. Review of Literature

Cyrus Mistry (2014): The hygiene factors should include infrastructure build up, competitive and transparent duty structure, stable policies, cost effective and reliable energy—we need to reform our labour laws.

Kumar Mangalam Birla (2014): Manufacturing has to become the next big wave for us. This "Make in India" campaign is a clarion call that will galvanize India's economy to reach greater heights.

Mukesh Ambani (2014): It is important to be open to capital and expertise from all across the world. Our investments of over Rs. 1.8 lakh crore are coming into fruition in the next 12-15 months. We would be creating over 1.2 lakh jobs in India in the next 12-15 months.

PWC (2013): Manufacturing companies appear to have battened down their hatches and are preparing for a period of uncertainty. New investments seem to have been put on hold, with half of the companies surveyed indicating that they do no plans for major investments in FY 14.

Bhat (2014): The shrinkage in manufacturing employment is on account of increased capital intensity in all manufacturing firms. The path to revive manufacturing growth requires development of infrastructure, better access to land and application of new technology, education, skill development and festering innovation in frontier technologies.

UNIDO (2005): The liberalization of the economy has opened new windows of opportunity for manufacturing sector. Increasingly the success of manufacturing industries is dependent on innovations, research and development. It is critical not only to remain competitive but also, significant advantages can be gained by developing and commercialization new technologies.

Chakraborti (2014): The government has realized the importance of this sector to the country's industrial development and has taken a number of steps to further enhance the industry. Today, the country's attractiveness as a manufacturing centre for foreign companies is clear.

Saurabh Patel (Finance Minister), Gujarat (2015): We are making labour laws more industry friendly and at the same time we want to ensure that labour is also looked after by the industrialists. We believe that workers should also be given the due share while giving certain freedom to industries too. The amendments to the Act are still to be approved by the Cabinet.

McKinsey and Company (2015): The Indian manufacturing industry is expected to touch US $ 1 trillion by 2025. Industry experts accredit the increasing demand of manufacturing units and the penchant for setting up low-cost plants in India by multinational firms for this possible development.

D.K. Pant, Chief Economist, India Ratings (2015): Economist believe that the data must also be seen in the context of domestic and international developments. The demand for automobiles in the world is going down. If one of India's states has a heavy automobile industry base, the exports for the state will go down. The effect on its economy will be very evident. But it will only be clear if you place the state in context of the larger picture globally you can't just say that the state is performing poorly.

Nirmala Sitharaman (Commerce and Industry Minister) (2015): The new Foreign Trade Policy will be for 2015-2020. This time, the policy is going to be different. We have taken a calibrated and open-ended approach to strengthen our exports.

Arun Jaitley, Finance Minister (2015): India is one of the youngest nations in the world with more than 54 per cent of the total population below 25 years of age. Yet, today less than 5 per cent of our potential workforce gets formal skill training to be employable and stay employable. A sum of Rs. 1500 crore has been allocated for this scheme, for which disbursement will be through a digital voucher directly into qualified student's bank account.

RBI Annual Report (2014-15): India's growth outlook is improving gradually and the real activity indicators are backing its 7.6 per cent gross domestic product (GDP) projection.

NSDC Website: The government plans to skill more than 150 million youth by 2022 which means skilling about 45,000 youth each year for next ten years. This ambitious target can be achieved only if the industry, academia and government come together and form a golden triangle.

Mc-Kinsey, 2014: Most people focus on flow—the one million young people joining the labour force every month for the next 20 years—but a bigger opportunity is stock-retooling the 200 million who are already in the labour force, but stuck at low productivity in farms and elsewhere. In 2011, India's 1,200 employment exchanges run by the government provided only 3,00,000 jobs against the 40 million people who are registered in these employment exchanges.

3. Present Status of Manufacturing Sector in India

Manufacturing is the process of production of merchandise, i.e. goods for use or for the purpose of sale. It uses labour, machines and tools and chemical and processing formulas. The term may refer to a range of human activity, from handicraft to high tech, but is most commonly applied to industrial production, in which raw materials are transformed into finished goods on a large scale.

Manufacturing Industry in India has gone through various phases of development over the period of time. Since Independence in 1947, the Indian manufacturing sector has travelled from the initial phase of building the industrial foundation in 1950s and early 1960s, to the Licence-permit Raj in the period of 1965–1980, to a phase of liberalization of 1990s, emerged competitiveness.

The reforms that then Prime Ministers, Narsimha Rao began and Prime Minister Atal Behari Vajpayee carried forward had focused mainly on liberalization of products markets. Removal of investment and import licensing, price and distribution controls, high tariffs on industrial goods, restrictions on foreign investment and small-scale industries reservation all related to product markets. While the liberalization successfully placed India on a high growth trajectory, impediments to sustained rapid growth over several decades remain. Indeed, the total absence of follow up reforms during the last decade has returned India to the 1980s growth rate. Moreover, even while the economy grew 8 per cent a year, unlike in South Korea and Taiwan in 1960s and 1970s and China more recently, manufacturing failed to emerge as the leading sector in India.

The government's push for manufacturing comes at a time when many big companies are seeking an alternative to China as costs and risks there rise. The objective is also to ensure solid growth and employment creation. During 2005-2012, India added only 15 million jobs, a quarter of the figure added in the previous six years. During 2011-12, industrial growth in terms of the Index of Industrial Production (IIP), released by the Central Statistics Office (CSO), showed a low growth of 2.9 per cent compared to 8.2 per cent growth registered in 2010-11. The moderation in the industrial growth, however, had started in 2008-09. The IIP growth rate was 2.5 per cent in 2008-09 which improved slightly to 5.3 per cent in 2009-10 compared to the peak growth rate of 15.5 per cent achieved in the year 2007-08. Rapid growth in the manufacturing sector has been accompanied by higher productivity and profitability of Indian manufacturing companies. As per a study by the Reserve Bank of India (RBI), productivity of companies was 24 per cent higher in 2005 *vis-à-vis* 2000. The study also identified that Indian companies achieved higher growth in profits during the same period. A vast labour force notwithstanding, employment-intensive manufacturing in the organized sector has performed poorly in India.

Potential of Manufacturing Sector in the Country's Real GDP Growth

Manufacturing holds a key position in the Indian economy, accounting for nearly 16 per cent of the real GDP in FY15 and employing about 12 per cent of the country's labour force. Growth in the sector has been strong, outpacing overall GDP growth since the past few years. India's manufacturing sector could touch US $ 1 trillion by 2025, according to a report by Mckinsey & Company. There is potential for the sector to account for 25-30 per cent of the country's GDP and create up to 90 million domestic jobs by 2025. In a major boost to the "Make in India" initiative, the Government has received confirmation from top technology firms such as GE, Bosch, Tejas etc. The contribution of manufacturing sector in the country's Gross Domestic Product (GDP) may fall below 15 per cent in 2013-14 owing to demand slowdown, leading to un utilised excess capacity. During 2012-13, the share of manufacturing sector in the GDP declined to 15.2 per cent, compared to 15.7 per cent in the previous financial year. The government has introduced the National Manufacturing Policy in October 2011, which seeks to raise the share of manufacturing to GDP from 16-25 per cent within a decade and create 100 million jobs.

Global Manufacturing Competitiveness Index (GMCI)

The rising competitiveness of India's manufacturing companies is reflected in the country's second position in the world in terms of competitiveness as per the 2010 Global Manufacturing Competitiveness Index (GMCI) prepared by the US Council on Competitiveness and Deloitte. The index considers market dynamics and policy issues that influence the sector. India is ahead of several developed and emerging economies such as the US, South Korea, Brazil and Japan. GMCI expects the country's competitiveness score to improve to 9.01 (out of 10) by 2015 from 8.15 in 2010, as shown in Table 8.1. Rapid growth in the manufacturing sector has been accompanied by higher productivity and profitability of Indian manufacturing companies.

Table 8.1: 2010 Global Manufacturing Competitiveness Index

Current Ranks	*Country*	*Index Score*	*Rank in 2015*
1	China	10.00	1
2	India	8.13	2
3	Republic of Korea	6.79	3
4	United States of America	5.84	5
5	Brazil	5.41	4
6	Japan	5.11	7
7	Mexico	4.84	6
8	Germany	4.80	8
9	Singapore	4.69	11
10	Poland	4.49	9
New Add*	Thailand	—	12

* New Addition among the top 10 countries, currently, Thailand ranks 12th with an index score of 4.17

Source: Deloitte and US Council on Competitiveness.

4. India Competitive Edge Existing

A study by the Boston Consulting Group reveals that the world is expected to encounter a shortage of 47 million working people by 2020. On the other hand, India is on a growth trajectory and its potential demographic dividend is making headlines all over the world. Today, it is one of the youngest nations in the world with more than 62 per cent of the population in the working age group of 15-59 years, and more than 54 per cent of the total population below 25 years of age. By 2022, India will have a surplus of 56 million working people. Even as on today, around 12 million youth enter the workforce each year, which, if skilled and educated properly, can become a great human resource pool, capable of serving not only the booming Indian market, but also feed the global economy (Planning Commission Policy Document, Twelfth Five Year Plan). India, like many other Asian countries, is going through five labour market transitions: farm to non-farm, rural to urban, unorganized to organized, subsistence self-employment to decent wage employment and school to work. India's population, long considered a curse, has turned into a desirable demographic dividend. But a demographic dividend does not mean just people; it means skilled, educated or employed people. Low labour cost and a rich talent pool are distinct advantages available to India, clearly powering its global competitiveness as a knowledge-based society. (Sabarwal, 2013).

5. Significance of Manufacturing in Employment Generation in India

The manufacturing sector is widely regarded as the transformational sector, for agricultural labourers moving from low skilled to more value added jobs. This is because, historically, economic development has followed a pattern of pulling people out of agriculture, moving them into non-farm activities such as manufacturing and services. The importance of the role of manufacturing (industrial sector) in absorbing surplus labour from agriculture sector has also been proved by the development experience of many developed countries and lately in various South East Asian countries. This makes manufacturing extremely important for India, where agriculture constitutes a minor share of GDP, but accounts for a disproportionately large share in employment. For India—where provision of gainful high-quality employment has been a key element of goals under successive Five-Year Plans—including the Twelfth Five Year Plan (2012–17), robust growth in the manufacturing sector can be a potential panacea for providing employment to a vast majority of the population.

Present Employment Trends in Manufacturing Sector

In 2013-14, manufacturing sector contracted 0.7 per cent and pulled down the GDP growth rate to less than five per cent. While the manufacturing sector at present contributes 14 per cent to the GDP, the Government aims to take it up to around 25 per cent in the next 10 years. Forecasting a revival in industrial activities from next fiscal, a recent report by Dun and Bradstreet has said that measures taken by the centre and states to develop infrastructure and the industrial sector could take some time to yield results. Most of the State Governments have been emphasizing on the need to develop their industrial sector and infrastructural facilities to drive the growth of their respective states. Table 8.2 and 8.3 shows the Manufacturing growth in value terms given in GDP data (%) and per cent change in manufacturing in volume terms given in the index of industrial production (IIP).

Table 8.2: Manufacturing Growth in Value Terms Given in GDP data (%)

Year	*GDP data (%)*
2010-11	8.9
2011-12	7.4
2012-13	6.2
2013-14	5.3
2014-15*	6.8

Base Year–changes to 2011-12 from 2004-05 from 2012-13 onwards.
Definition of GDP (gross domestic product) also undergoes a change.
* Advance estimates which is a mix of actual data and projections.
Source: Ministry of Statistics and Programme Implementation.

Table 8.3: Per cent Change in Manufacturing in Volume Terms Given in the Index of Industrial Production (IIP)

Year	*% change in manufacturing in volume terms*
2010-11	8.9
2011-12	3.01
2012-13	1.3
2013-14	–0.8
2014-15*	1.2

Note: * for April-December 2014-15.
Source: Ministry of Statistics and Programme Implementation and RBI data.

6. Role of MSMEs in Employment Generation of Manufacturing Sector

MSMEs are critical for the country's economic and social development. They significantly contribute to the GDP, manufacturing output, exports and employment. In India, Micro, Small and Medium Enterprises (MSMEs) account for eight per cent of GDP, 45 per cent of manufacturing output and 40 per cent of exports. Also, the labour-capital ratio is much higher in MSMEs than larger industries. The MSMEs have witnessed the highest growth rate in manufacturing sector employment in recent years. As per the Annual Report—FY11 of the Ministry of MSME, Government of India, the sector is estimated to employ about 73 million workers in over 31 million units throughout the country. MSMEs have consistently registered a higher growth rate *vis-à-vis* the industrial sector. There are over 6,000 products ranging from traditional to high-tech items, which are being manufactured by the MSMEs in India. The sector also offers maximum opportunities for both self-employment and jobs in India, after the agriculture sector.

It is also important to increase the availability of bank credit for the MSMEs sector. Even though the sector falls in the category of priority sector lending, only 8 per cent of the total bank credit finds its way into the sector. Apart from encouraging bank lending to the sector, it is also important to look at other ways of financing in the sector. One way could be the venture capitalist funding for SME-MSME sector, which is practiced in developed countries. Other option can be better regulation and monitoring of micro-finance institutions. Currently, most of the micro-finance institutions operating in India are either too small to make an impact or are operating with welfare motive. Encourage growth in labour-intensive industries: Wood, paper products and textile industries tend to be more labour-intensive and require a large workforce, mostly unskilled with no special qualifications. By focusing on growth in these industries, it is possible to absorb the rising surplus of unskilled workers, particularly in less developed states (such as Uttar Pradesh and Bihar), where population is projected to grow 8–11 per cent by 2015.

7. Contribution of Manufacturing in Exports

Apart from domestic consumption, manufacturing also contributes significantly to India's international trade. Over the past five years, manufacturing exports increased at a CAGR of 20 per cent, outpacing the corresponding growth in merchandise exports. During FY11, the total manufacturing exports stood at US 168.1 billion, higher than the FY10 figure of USD 115.2 billion. Of the total value, engineering goods accounted for the highest share (40.4%) followed by gems and jewellery (24.3%) and chemical and related products (17.2%). Another notable contributor is textiles with a share of 13.9 per cent. The US and Western Europe are the main export market. The Middle East also finds mention with UAE in particular a key market for Indian manufactured goods.

8. Skill India to Complement Make in India

Success does not come through magic. It needs necessary skills to succeed. This universal truth is equally applicable for the young generation. Youth energy can be the driving force for social and economic development of any country provided it is channelized effectively. Skill development and employment are the best means to mobilize his force. Skill multiplied by effort equal success. With recent initiatives of the government, the skill development programme has taken the shape of a 'movement'. These efforts of the government may take some time to bear fruits, however, in the long run, the skilled Indians (*Kaushal Bharat*) will lead the country towards being a happy, healthy and prosperous nation (Kushal Bharat) thus justifying the slogan "Kushal Bharat, Kaushal Bharat".

India has a population of over 1.267 billion and a workforce of 474.1 million out of which 336.9 million are rural workers and 137.2 million are urbon workers as per the last survey of NSSO conducted in 2011-12. The unemployment register had 40.17 millions registered in 2010. Providing meaningful employment to all with unemployment rate at 8.8 per cent and a population growing at approximately 1.5 per cent every year is a daunting task indeed. In terms of demographics, almost 35 per cent of Indians are younger than 15 years of age, and almost 50 per cent falling below 25 years of age. The median age of India is 24 years, which makes it one of the youngest population in the world.

India's informal sector constituting 90 per cent, though some experts peg even larger, is both a boom and a bane for the economy. Boon since it meets the aspirations of a population where disparity between 'haves' and 'have not's' in education is massive and a bane since it hits the formal economy where it hurts the most. The above two scenarios would need the academics and the education administrators to seriously rethink the supply chain for education as a necessary indigence to address various incongruencies that have crept in the system. Lack of education and lack of skills is a pestilence that we need to overcome in our current system and the faster we do this, the better for all concerned. Education certainly opens the doors to lead life of liberty but skills makes that liberty meaningful by allowing one to achieve prosperity. We need to map the available job opportunity in various sectors at disparate levels and make a conscious effort at improving the job markets in all the three employment markets. This improves the economy and growth in GDP and has a cascading effect on employment opportunity.

Opportunity

An abundant supply of people in the working-age group has the potential to boost manufacturing growth. However, to absorb much of this labour force, there is a need to lay larger emphasis on building strong human capital. This is important considering that certain manufacturing industries, such as transport equipment, petroleum and electrical machinery, require specialized training, which can be met only by skilled labour force. On a positive note, the government has set up the National Skills Development Council to encourage private participation/management of industrial training institutes (ITIs). Among its objectives, NSDC seeks to contribute significantly (about 30%) to the overall target of skilling/up skilling 500 million people in India by 2022. If the government goes ahead with plans to support the 'Make in India' programme, it could lead to significant demand for various skills. The need to train fresh graduates in new skills and ensure that they remain employable is important since the US $ 118 billion Indian information technology (IT) industry added about 1,80,000 new employees in 2013-14, 70 per cent of which were fresh hires (NASSCOM).

Government Initiative in Union Budget 2015-16

The Government of India in its Union Budget 2014-15, has provided investment allowance at the rate of 15 per cent to a manufacturing company that invests more than US$ 4.17 million in any year in new plant and machinery. The government has also taken steps to improve the quality of technical education in the engineering sector by allocating a sum of Rs. 500 crore (US$ 79.92 million) for setting up five more IITs in the states of Jammu & Kashmir, Chhattisgarh, Goa, Andhra Pradesh and Kerala.

Government Initiative—Skills for Inclusive Growth

Skill human resource at all levels is essential for inclusive growth. Skill development cannot be seen in isolation. It has to be an integral process of linking the skill training with education and employment at the same time. The government agencies and system cannot accomplish this task alone. Private sector, NGOs, Educational institutions with experience in skills training need to be involved in the process of skilling. All sections need to be given equal importance. Vocationalisation of education is of cardinal importance for skilling youth. At the same time, the other section of the society, *viz.* women, marginalized, tribals etc. need tailor made training programme to suite their diverse and specific needs. While being illiterate may be an issue in providing skill training to most marginalized sections, one may have to deal with family issues and social restrictions in case of providing skill training to women. These factors need to be taken into account for any programme to be successful.

India has already started moving on the path of high economic growth.

To put this wave of motion into the next gear we need to focus on advancement of skills which are pertinent to global economic environment. The challenges lies not only in expansion of facilities for skill training, but also in raising the quality of skills to be able to compete at international forum.

The National policy for skill development and entrepreneurship 2015 proposes to meet the challenge of skilling at scale with speed, standard and sustainability. It aims to provide an umbrella framework to all a killing activities being carried out within the country. It also seeks to standardize the process of skilling and link it with demand centres both at national as well as international level.

Government of India has nurtured the skills ecosystem in close partnership with the private sector, international agencies like ILO, World Bank, OECD, EU among others. Through various skill development schemes, 20 plus departments have launched programmes which are outcome driven, now steered by the Ministry of Skills Development and Entrepreneurship (MSDE). They have invested significantly in nurturing the skills ecosystem, such that those in the remotest parts of the country get an opportunity to join mainstreams employment. The largest of the government initiatives being DDU Grameen Kaushalya Yojana (GKY) under Ministry of Rural Development and Integrated Skill Development Scheme (ISDS) by Ministry of Textiles that have reached out to youth from Bottom of Pyramid (BoP) groups in rural and urban areas, backward regions and hilly areas, economies under stress of civil conflict and extremism, minority commitments. Their initiatives have focused on women and Persons with Disabilities (PwD) such that all segments can participate.

Private Sector Role

Several noteworthy private sector initiatives have also played their role. The NSDC, now part of MSDE, is playing a pivotal role in aggregating the industry by way of incubating training initiatives, setting up sector skills councils and promoting skills of Indian youths at international fora etc. Corporates from more than 35 sectors are working closely with the Sector Skills Councils to define the National Occupational Standards (NOS) as per the National Skills Qualification Framework (NSQF), which is the young person's passport to the world of work. These bodies have collectively launched a mechanism for deeper engagement of all stakeholders, including the learner, towards Skill India. The skills ecosystem has hyper-accelerated in the past few years, but the sheer scale and complexities, facing it calls for interventions that keep the learning needs of the trainee in mind whilst preparing him/her for a job.

Skill Development and Economic Progress

Skill development can be defined as proficiency that is acquired or developed through training or experience. Global leaders have acknowledged the role and impact of skill development *via* their national policies. This strengthens the ability of individuals to adopt to changing market demands and benefit from innovation and entrepreneurial activities. Apart from primary determinants of skills development, it is also essential to address the opportunities and challenges to meet new demands of changing economies in the context of competitiveness.

The future prosperity of countries depends ultimately on the number of persons in employment and how productive they are at work. It is a dynamic scenario where the most successful or progressive nations shall be one that can counter VUCA (Volatility, Uncertainty, Complexity, Ambiguity) (Abidi & Joshi, 2015). Hence skill development can be connected to a broader growth, employment and development mandating government intervention.

Skill India is daunting task of keeping sight on the manpower requirements of the industry and the infrastructure needed for achieving the targets of skilling. With many new players entering the skills space, focus has to be on the 3 Is of skills—Investment, Innovations and Institutions—to improve the quality of training, assessment and jobs. Many successful industry led models of training have emerged ensuring that the training is competency based and improves work readiness of trainees. On its part, technology has played an integral role as an anchor to the programmes being delivered at scale.

Ultimately, skilling has the potential to socially transform young people. For individuals, who are most often school drop-outs seeking to join the workforce, skills training is the critical bridge of information, training, soft skills, and experience that will lead them to gainful employment.

Government Initiative to Boost Manufacturing Sector in India

The Government of India has taken several initiatives to promote a healthy environment for the growth of manufacturing sector in the country. Some of the notable initiatives and developments are:

1. Make In India—A Transition Formula

This campaign will help in achieving objectives of National Manufacturing Policy, i.e. to increase the share of manufacturing sector in GDP from current 15-16 per cent to 25 per cent till 2022 and creating 100 million jobs in this sector by 2022. India has also set for itself an ambitious target of increasing the contribution of manufacturing output to 25 per cent of gross domestic product (GDP) by 2025, from 16 per cent currently. India's economy is expected to grow at 7.4 per cent in 2014-15 as per a Government forecast. According to a new formula which uses 2011-12 as the new 'base year', the revised statistics showed inflation-adjusted economic growth rate for October-December 2014 at 7.5 per cent, making India the fastest growing major economy in the world.

2. National Skills Mission of Government of India

The mission will work through the Skill Development and Entrepreneurship Ministry and aims to consolidate skill initiatives spread across several ministries. It will allow the government to standardise procedures and outcomes across 31 Sector Skill Councils. The idea of providing at least one job for every family is also a noble one and again we think "at least one skilled person per family" will be a desirable and essential starting point for this dream to be realised. Rs. 1,500 crore allocated under the Deen Dayal Upadhyay Gramin Kaushal Yojana for skilling rural youth is also a welcome move that will help skill development penetrate deeper into the country's landscape. Finally, Rs. 1,350 crore allocated for National Skill Certification and Monetary Reward Schemc (STAR Scheme) will go a long way in helping those who wish to acquire a skill but need financial support. A further Rs. 150 crore allocated under Kaushal Vikas Yojana will also provide essential fillip to the Skill Development initiatives in the country.

3. National Investment and Manufacturing Zones (NIMZs)

The government has also unveiled the National Manufacturing Policy 2011, which aims create to 100 million jobs in the manufacturing sector and increase the share of manufacturing in GDP to 25 per cent by 2022. To achieve this objective, the policy proposes to develop National Investment and Manufacturing Zones (NIMZs), which will be integrated industrial townships, with world class infrastructure. In line with China's policy of building up large economic zones, these NIMZs will be built on minimum size of 5,000 hectares. Further, to improve the business environment in the country, these NIMZs will enjoy single window clearance and a liberal exit policy. This apart, the policy also provides incentives for units in NIMZs such as exemptions from capital gains tax, and incentives for green manufacturing and technology acquisitions.

4. National Manufacturing Policy (NMP) 2011

The National Manufacturing Policy (NMP) was approved by the Government in October 2011. The major objectives of the policy are for enhancing the share of manufacturing in GDP to 25 per cent and creating additional 100 million over a decade or so. Other quantitative and qualitative changes that are envisaged by the policy include creation of appropriate skill sets among the rural migrant and urban poor to make growth inclusive; increasing domestic value addition and technological depth in manufacturing; enhancing global competitiveness of Indian manufacturing through appropriate policy support; ensuring sustainability of growth, particularly with regard to the environment including energy efficiency, optimal utilization of natural resources and restoration of damaged/degraded eco-systems, simplification of business regulations; simple and expeditious exit mechanism for closure of sick units while protecting labour interests; financial and institutional mechanisms for technology development, including green technologies; industrial training and skill upgradation measures; incentives for SMEs, clustering and aggregation support through National Investment and Manufacturing Zones (NIMZs), trade policy etc. The Policy also provides special focus to the industries that are employment intensive, those producing capital goods, those having strategic significance, small and medium enterprises, and public sector enterprises besides industries where India enjoys a competitive advantage etc.

5. The Delhi-Mumbai Industrial Corridor (DMIC) Project

The Delhi-Mumbai Industrial Corridor (DMIC) Project is being implemented on both sides of the 1483 km long Western Dedicated Rail Freight Corridor between Dadri (UP) and JNPT (Navi Mumbai). The project seeks to create a strong economic base with a globally competitive environment and state-of-the-art infrastructure to activate local commerce, enhance investments and attain sustainable development. The DMIC Project covers the six States—Uttar Pradesh, Haryana, Madhya Pradesh,

Rajasthan, Gujarat and Maharashtra. The Japanese Government has also announced their financial support for DMIC project to an extent of US $ 4.5 billion in the first phase for the projects with Japanese participation.

6. Government Extends Validity of Industrial Licences for 7 years from 3 years

The government further extended the validity of industrial licences to as much as seven years from three to encourage domestic manufacturing. As a measure of 'ease of doing business', henceforth, two extensions of two years each in the initial validity of three years of (an) industrial licence shall be allowed up to seven years, the department of industrial policy and promotion (DIPP) said in a notification. In July 2014, DIPP had extended the validity of an industrial licence to three years from two, as part of measures to cut red tape.

Manufacturing Activity in Big States under Make in India Scheme

The centre's plan to push through the 'make in India' scheme to transform India into a global manufacturing hub may face an uphill challenge as some of the country's largest states including Madhya Pradesh, Uttar Predesh and Maharashtra have seen a decline in their manufacturing sector growth despite witnessing healthy economic expansion. Data available with the RBI shows that contribution of the manufacturing sector in each of these states as declined while services and agriculture and allied activities are the main contributors to the net domestic product. For six consecutive years since 2008-09, the largest contribution from agriculture and allied activities in absolute numbers has been to Uttar Pradesh, with the state generating Rs. 92,163 crore or 22.8 per cent of its Net State Domestic Product (NSDP) from agriculture in 2013-14, registering a 2.5 per cent growth in the sector. In 2014-15, the contributions from the sector, after greatest in Andhra Pradesh, Madhya Pradesh, Maharashtra and West Bengal. In comparison, manufacturing contributed 10.46 per cent to Uttar Pradesh's net state domestic product in 2013-14 from a share of 11.03 per cent in 2008-09. Madhya Pradesh's growth rate of about 11 per cent last year—the highest across India—was a result of improvements in agriculture sector that contributed 30.7 per cent of the NSDP, with the service sector pitching in about 57.2 per cent to its economy. However, manufacturing contributed just 8.11 per cent to the state economy last fiscal, down from 12.84 per cent in 2008-09 as shown in Table 8.5.

Table 8.5: Manufacturing as Percentage of NSDP

State	Parameter	2008-09	2009-10	2010-11	2011-12	2012-13	2013-14
Uttar Pradesh	NSDP	3021.92	3209.89	3466.21	3646.84	3836.44	4035.23
	Manufacturing	11.03%	12.61%	12.81%	11.79%	11.08%	10.46%
Andhra Pradesh	NSDP	2922.58	3036.68	3381.64	3628.08	3826.33	4054.82
	Manufacturing	10.29%	9.98%	10.42%	11.34%	10.14%	9.87%
Madhya Pradesh	NSDP	1351.24	1479.33	1557.01	1708.79	1884.8	2098.06.
	Manufacturing	12.84%	12.69%	11.03%	10.34%	9.56%	8.11%
Maharastra	NSDP	5465.33	5993.38	6676.25	6980.86	7390.4	8112.68
	Manufacturing	19.36%	19.17%	19.74%	17.83%	16.64%	16.46%
West Bengal	NSDP	2442.62	2632.2	2791.91	2894.34	3077.2	3345.69
	Manufacturing	8.91%	8.94%	9.29%	8.26%	8.08%	7.87%

Note: NSDP in Billion Rupees.
Source: RBI.

In order to attract investments into the state and boost the manufacturing sector, Madhya Pradesh also held the Global Investor's Summit recently where according to the state government, maximum expressions of interest for investment were into energy and infrastructure sectors. Even in the context of Maharashtra, which has the most number of factories in the country, the share of manufacturing has seen a steady decline from a high of 19.36 per cent in 2008-09 to 16.46 per cent last fiscal (2014-15). Low demand from global markets along with high interest rates and policy uncertainty in the domestic economy slowed down the industrial activities at the national level as well.

Make in India *vs.* Made in China

China will encourage high tech imports, research and development (R & D) to upgrade 'Made in China'. Under the new campaign, China will use tax breaks to encourage enterprises to upgrade their equipment and increase research and development (R & D) efforts to improve the manufacturing industry. Imported high tech equipment will also enjoy tax deduction in aviation, bio medicine production, manufacturing of railway and ships, electronics production, including computer and telecommunication, instrument production and those used in making IT products and software etc. For India's neighbour the focus is on moving up the value chain—from low cost manufacturing of skirts, hand-bags and electronic goods to more sophisticated products and equipment.

In contrast, the Indian Government is targeting all manufacturing sectors, besides the mass-job creators such as tourism and hospitality to create employment. Several government officials have suggested that a key element of India's manufacturing plan should be to target sectors such as garments and engineering goods, where China is giving up space as it looks at higher end goods. In several sectors such as aerospace and defence, where high-end production is involved, the government has only recently opened the door and the volume are much lower to justify a full-fledged presence for international majors. In addition, India still suffers from several infrastructure handicaps, while China has rapidly ramped up capacity at ports and has added significant power generation capacity.

Investment Proposals Received after 'Make in India' Campaign

India has become one of the most attractive destinations for investments in the manufacturing sector. Some of the major investments and developments in this sector in the recent past are:

1. US-based First Solar Inc and China's Trina Solar have plans to set up manufacturing facilities in India. Clean energy investments in India increased to US$ 7.9 billion in 2014, helping the country maintain its position as the seventh largest clean energy investor in the world.
2. Samsung Electronics Co. Ltd. has invested Rs. 517 crore (US$ 83.11 million) towards the expansion of its manufacturing plant in Noida, Uttar Pradesh (UP) under the UP Mega Policy. Samsung India Electronics is committed to strengthen its manufacturing infrastructure and will gradually expand capacity at this plant to meet the growing domestic demand for mobile handsets.
3. India is currently among the top 10 sourcing countries for IKEA. The plan is to double sourcing from India to €630 million (US$ 688.61 million) by 2020.
4. Shantha Biotechnics Pvt. Ltd. has started building a facility to manufacture Insuman, an insulin product to treat diabetes. Sanofi SA, which acquired Shantha Biotechnics, will invest Rs. 460 crore (US$ 73.93 million) to build the facility.
5. BMW and Mercedes-Benz have intensified their localisation efforts to be part of 'Make in India' initiative. The localisation

efforts will reduce the waiting period and accelerate the servicing process of our cars as we had to (previously) depend on our plants overseas for supply and will help us on the pricing front.

6. Suzuki Motor Corp plans to make automobiles for Africa, the company's next big bet, as well as for India at its upcoming factory in Hansalpur, near Ahmedabad, Gujarat, as per Mr. Toshihiro Suzuki, Executive Vice-President, Suzuki.
7. The Government of India has received investment proposals for electronics manufacturing worth Rs. 18,000 crore (US$ 2.89 billion) for 2015-16 and expects the figure to double in another two years. Electronics goods production in India is expected to touch US $ 104 billion by 2020. The country's electronics market is anticipated to grow to US $ 400 billion by 2020 and expand at a CAGR of 24.4 per cent during the period 2012-2020.
8. In a major boost to the 'Make in India' initiative, the Government has received confirmation from top technology firms such as GE, Bosch, Tejas and Panasonic regarding their decision to invest in the electronic, medical, automotive and telecom manufacturing clusters in India.

Suggestions for Improvement in Manufacturing Sector in India

1. A healthy and business-friendly environment will only be created if India can signal easier approval of projects and set up hassle-free clearance mechanism.
2. India should also be ready to tackle elements that adversely affect competitiveness of manufacturing.
3. To make the country a manufacturing hub the unfavourable factors must be removed. India should also be ready to give tax concessions to companies who come and set up unit in the country.
4. India's micro small and medium-sized industries can play a big role in making the country take the next big leap in manufacturing. India should be more focused towards novelty and innovation for these sectors. The government has to chart out plans to give special SOPs and privileges to these sectors.
5. India's 'Make in India' campaign will be constantly compared with China's 'Made in China' campaign. The China launched the campaign at the same day as India seeking to retain its manufacturing prowess. India should constantly keep up its strength so as to outpace China's supremacy in the manufacturing sector.

6. India must also encourage high-tech imports, research and development (R & D) to upgrade 'Make in India' give edge-to-edge competition to the Chinese counterpart's campaign. To do so, India has to be better prepared and motivated to do world class R & D. The government must ensure that it provides platform for such research and development.
7. A continuous culture of innovation induced products and process will then propel the country towards inclusive growth. Learning is one of the main pillars of innovation but transforming both what the young people need to learn and also how they can learn will be key determining factors to realize the success of initiatives such as 'Make in India'. An ecosystem which fosters creation of value-added technologies and products is vital to build a knowledge-based economy. Towards this end, Government and Industry will need to collaborate and capitalize on each other's strength more effectively.
8. According to Confederation of Indian Industry (CII), the rates of service tax, central excise and customs duties should be maintained at the current levels in the Budget in order to aid the success of the government's 'Make in India' initiative. At present, the rate of service tax and excise duty is 12 per cent each, while the customs duty stands at 10 per cent. For the success of 'Make in India', Budget 2015-16 should avoid the temptation of raising excise duties. Moreover, manufacturing sector continues to be vulnerable. Under these circumstances, it would be prudent to allow excise duties to remain at current 12 per cent.
9. Finally, Applied science, technology and innovation should focus on faster, sustainable and inclusive development for India's 1.25 billion citizens. Encouraging and facilitating enterprises to invest in innovation to accelerate the pace of discovery, diffusion and delivery of science and technology-led solutions, is, therefore, the right way forward.

SWOT Analysis of Manufacturing Sector in India

Strength

The strengths of the Indian Manufacturing sector are as follows:

- India has already marked its presence as one of the fastest growing economies of the world. The country is expected to rank amongst the world's top three growth economies and amongst the top three manufacturing destinations by 2020.

- Favourable demographic dividends for the next 2-3 decades. Sustained availability of quality workforce.
- The cost of manpower is relatively low as compared to other countries.
- Responsible business houses operating with creditability and professionalism.
- Strong consumerism in the domestic market.
- Strong technical and engineering capabilities backed by top-notch scientific and technical institutes.
- Well-regulated and stable financial markets open to foreign investors.

Weaknesses

Indian manufacturing sector still suffer from bottlenecks, like—

- Use of primitive technology or underutilization of technology.
- Poor infrastructure.
- Overstaffed operations.
- Expensive financing and bureaucracy.
- Ineffective Paradigms of Industrial Policy.
- Ineffective Models Centrally Planned Economy.
- Seven major manufacturing sectors suffered an estimated loss of Rs. 1,05,381 crore during 2013-14 due to illicit trade, according to a FICCI report. The study on 'illicit markets' focused on seven major manufacturing sectors—auto components, alcoholic beverages, computer hardware, FMCG personal goods, FMCG packaged foods, mobile phones and tobacco.

Opportunities

The opportunity for the Indian manufacturing sector are as follows:

1. Gaining competitiveness against Chinese manufacturers due to currency fluctuations and soaring operational cost in China are offering growth opportunities for the Indian manufacturing sector.

2. Manufacturing activities have gradually risen due to new export orders and increased domestic demand in the recent past.
3. The interim Indian Budget 2014-15 proposed changes in indirect taxes, which includes factory gate tax to be reduced to 10 per cent from 12 per cent on some capital goods and consumer durables as well as excise duty cut on small cars, two wheelers, and commercial vehicles to 8 per cent from 12 per cent. Such tax amendments would boost manufacturing activities.
4. The Indian government has agreed to form five NIMZs outside the Delhi-Mumbai Industrial Corridor (DMIC) region. This would enable to increase manufacturing activities in a balanced approach across the country. The selected zones are Nagpur, Maharashtra; Tumkur, Karnataka; and Chittoor, Medak, and Prakasam in Andhra Pradesh.
5. The Reliance Group, headed by billionaire Anil Ambani, is foraying into the defence manufacturing sector, joining the likes of Reliance Industries, the Tata Group, L & T and Mahindra Group to tap into what could be a $100-billion market in 10 years.
6. Around 90 million domestic jobs are waiting to be created by that timeframe with the manufacturing segment contributing about 25-30 per cent of India's Gross Domestic Product (GDP). India's rapidly expanding economy is giving both international entrepreneurs and home players an array of opportunities to venture out and grow.
7. Indian defence sector is set to embark on a significant growth path in the near future as the new initiatives announced by the government in promoting defence equipment's manufacturing has begun to gain traction among global investors.
8. Medical device makers welcomed the government's decision to allow up to 100 per cent foreign direct investment or FDI in the sector under automatic route, saying the move would boost technology inflow and manufacturing. This would bring technology to India and we need new technology to make the devices. This will also lead to co-investments in brown field projects and import substitution.

Threats

Indian manufacturing sector still suffers from certain threats, like—

1. Increase in energy and raw material prices is the key challenge faced by the companies in the Indian manufacturing sector.
2. Foreign manufacturing companies are less keen to come to India due to its complex regulatory framework. India ranks 132nd among 185 countries classified as easiest place for doing business.
3. Low confidence due to delay in approvals: A number of projects are halted due to delay in approvals for land acquisition and initiating a project. This has led to low confidence among investors.
4. Consumer buying as well as cost of capital for corporations is adversely impacted due to higher interest rates. Despite RBI measures, the interest rate is higher and is hampering the demand and business operations in the manufacturing sector.

Conclusion

It can be concluded that the Indian manufacturing sector had faced a lot of problems like government initiatives, high input prices, cheap labour and its exploitation due to which this sector could not grow up to its actual potential. There is a need for strong commitment from the government as well as the industry for the sector to enter the next orbit of high growth and employment generation. Also, there is a need for a robust labour policy, which strikes the right balance between workers' rights and competitive needs of the manufacturing sector. Furthermore, it is important to enhance the productivity of the labour force by enhancing the quality of training. If the National Manufacturing Policy achieves its objectives, it has the potential to render the manufacturing sector a driving force in India's economic development.

In a globalised world, India needs system drive reform and innovation to sustain fast paced economic growth. Initiatives such as 'Make in India' will improve innovations, but to go beyond 'Make in India', it is imperative to research, design, develop, produce and thus truly 'Create in India'. The emphasis will be on right skill levels of human resources, capital and incubation, technology infusion, building infrastructural ecosystem and leveraging our vast domestic consumer base to become the major pillars of 'Create in India'.

Government leaders, experts, and researchers focusing towards making Indian manufacturing globally competitive and to have a sustained growth, which contributes significantly to GDP growth, employment generation and overall economic development. It also aims to identify factors hampering industrial growth and seeks to redress these factors.

References

The Times of India, April 5, 2014, p. 12.
The Times of India, September 27, 2014, p. 15.
The Hindustan Times, October 18, 2014.
The Sunday Express, October 26, 2014, p. 21.
Sunday Business Standard, March 1, 2015, p. 2.
Indian Express, March 1, 2015, p. 13.
Danik Jagran, May 27, 2015, p. 10.
Economy India, March 2015, p. 43.
Yojana, October 2015, pp. 15-16.

Web-Sites

www.makeinindia.com
www.zeenews.india.com
www.wikipedia.com
www.rbi.org.in
https://www.google.co.in/#q=manufacturing+sector
https://www.google.co.in/#q=contribution+of+manufacturing+sector+in+todays+economy-india
https://www.google.co.in/#q=manufacturing+sector+in+india
https://www.google.co.in/#q=+role+of+manufacturing+sector+in+indian+economy-research+papers
http://reports.weforum.org/manufacturing-growth/india/

9

A Micro-level Analysis of Socio-Economic Implication on Farmers' Death in India

Ashutosh Mohanty

Introduction

India is an agrarian country with around one half of its population depending directly or indirectly upon agriculture. Agriculture sector providing raw materials to a large number of industries; absorbs major chunk of rural work force (58%) shares good per cent of GDP of country (22%) and forms a hub of India's economy (Behera & Behera, 2008). But now-a-days the spate of farmer suicides cases in a number of Indian states is one of the vital concern to indicate multiple crises affecting rural economy and rural society (Das, 2011 & Schurman, 2013). As per Census of India, the farmers include those who own and work on field as well as those who employ/hire workers for fieldwork/farming activities. It excludes agricultural labourers. Despite portrayal of farming as healthy and happy way of life and happy farmers means a prosperous nation as popularly statement, agriculture sector in India records one of the highest number of suicides than any sector of economy categorically in last two decades (Gruère & Sengupta, 2011 and ADSI Annual Report, 2014). For farmers in India; agriculture already becomes a risky venture due to increasing climatic variability, uncertainty in production and cost of cultivation and bottleneck in marketing. This is one of the vital problems needs effective addresses by Government, economists and planner for sustenance of agro-economy and to reduce life risk of farmers in India. There is also great need to stabilize farm income to reduce crisis.

History of Farmer Suicide in Post-Independence India

Perhaps the farmers' suicides reached almost epidemic proportion in certain pockets of the country were first picked up and reported by press around mid-1990. The first state where suicides were reported was Maharashtra. In 2000, this issue gained international attention and for a variety of Indian Government initiatives. Several studies undertaken in India have revealed that farm suicides have kept up steady increase at a compound growth rate of 2.5 per cent per annum over period of 1997-2006 (Nagaraj, 2008). In 2014, a total of 5,650 farmers have committed suicides, accounted 4.3 per cent of total suicide victims of India (NCRB Report, 2014). To the extent agriculture in India has been transformed in Post-Independence period can be illustrated by introduction of Green revolution, mechanization of agriculture with crop diversification, expansion of net sown area under cash crop and crop production. The state policies and promotion to adopt new varieties consequently increased the production cost and demand of capital for agriculture. As a consequence, these were establishment of co-operative societies operated at district level for farmers. But agriculture of India being gamble of monsoon with low percentage of ensured irrigated area suffered from climatic extremities. For these reasons crop losses still remains a major problem faced by resource poor marginal and small farmers at large. This economic setback along with debt trap automatically increases the incidence of farmers' suicides in rural India.

With the introduction of neo-liberal economic policies during 1990, majority of farmers were inspired to adopt policies with an aspiration to improve their socio-economic positions particularly among small farmers. Some of these had overextended themselves financially without awareness and training not only had farmers agricultural income declined but their cost of cultivation and indebtness to informal agencies had increased. These small and marginal farmers experienced an increasing trend towards individualization of market consequently, making them vulnerable. The debt pattern found among farmers in India, that large farmers generally borrow from formal lending agencies like co-operative bank for credits while small holders depend mainly on informal sources like moneylenders, traders and better of which are non institutional ready to deliver credit at farmers' need but at high interest rate. The big farmers generally borrow from these informal sources when required and only for non-agricultural purposes. The small farmers are compelled to mortgage land, jewelleries, as surety to loan and the debt ratio to assets of farmers is very high. In case of large farmers, this debt ratio to assets is generally low or medium. Therefore, any crop loss in season affects the small farmers at large scale increasing the farmers suicide cases. The incidence of farmers suicide in

India did not appear to vary simply according to weather or not agricultural production is in crisis, that suggest in terms that other causes as social, family and health are as important as economic one as factors explaining incidence and variation of farmers suicides in India. Realizing the need for crop insurance as a safety net to farmers, Government of India has implemented various crop insurance schemes to reduce life risk of farmers, since 1999 National Agricultural Insurance Scheme (NAIS) has been implemented as an area based crop yield insurance scheme. Since 2007, Weather Based Crop Insurance Scheme (WBCIS) has been launched on pilot basis in several states to help farmers economically for crop loss by insuring the cropping land and transfer the risk to insures.

Methodology of the Study

The methodology adopted in this study is based on statistical data analysis, Data collected from both primary and secondary sources which is based on spatio-temporal analysis of farmer suicide in India, published Research Reports, Discussion with Farmers Communities, Leaders, Newspaper, FAO findings, ICAR report, Reports of the findings of various GoI committees, besides a detailed survey and analysis of plethora of university research team. We also studied the Reports as available in the form of Books, Journals, Manuals, Periodicals, Articles and public opinion on farmers' suicide which is based on field visits to number of places which is prone to farmers' suicide and related issues.

Temporal Change of Farmers' Suicides in India 2011-14

The NCRE of India reported in its 2011annual report that out of total 1,35,585 suicides cases 14,207 were farmers (14.08%). In 2012, a total of 1,35,445 people committed suicides of which 13,755 were farmers (11.2%). In 2013, the NCRB recorded 11,772 cases of suicides by farmers and farm labourers which increased to 12,360 in number in 2014. It was 9.38 per cent to total suicides cases in India. Out of these, 5,650 number of suicides cases were registered as farmers' suicides accounting 4.3 per cent of total suicides. There is a declining trend in farmers' suicides rate in period from 2011-14.

A decade back between 2001-2005, the situation was too worse for farmers in India. The recorded farmers' suicides cases in India in above period outnumber the present reported farmers' suicides in number as well as in percentage. In 2001, farmers' suicides per cent was 15.1 to total suicides reported in country which increased above 16 per cent in year 2002 and 2004 and registered above 15 per cent in year 2003-05. The number of farmers' suicides cases remained more or less around 17,000 to 18,000 per year in this period (2001-2005). The situation assessment survey of farmers of the National Sample Survey done in its 59th round during 2003 reported that 40 per cent of farmers did not like farming and 'were of the opinion that, given a choice, they would take up some other career'. Further, 27 per cent found it not profitable, another 8 per cent reported that it is 'risky' and another 5 per cent did not like it for other reasons. As per government report due to reported adverse climatic condition, crop lost registered in five states in 2013 affecting 0.35 million hectors of land with estimated loss of 500 crore rupees. In 2014, 6 states in India were badly affected due to similar situation affecting 5.5 million hectors of land and estimated loss of Rs. 5,000 crore respectively. Ultimate stress of agricultural loss bearded by farmer community increased the incidence of farmers' suicides from 2013 to 2014.

Age and Sex Composition of Farmer Suicides in Country—2014

Farmer suicides, according to official data, taken place overwhelmingly by male farmers in the country. In 2014, out of reported 5,650 farmer suicides, 91.6 per cent were male farmers and 8.4 per cent were female farmers. As per different age groups, majority of victims belonged to 30 years and above–below 60 years of age groups accounting for 65.7 per cent of total farmers' suicides. Incidence of farmers' suicides in age group of 18-30 years had registered second largest concentration, 23 per cent to total. The senior citizen farmer (60 years and above age) suicides rate was 10.2 per cent to total farmers' suicides; emerged as third largest group. In young age group (below 30 years age), female farmers suicides incidents was 40.9 per cent and male farmers suicides was 22.52 per cent to their respective gender suicides. In this age group suicides percentage of female farmers outnumbered male farmers mainly because of socio-economic problems. But overall dominance of male farmers' suicides in other age groups with high casualty do not underestimate the role of agriculture in rural economy and acute agricultural crisis in the country would be the basis for this distress.

Table 9.1: Incident of Age Group Wise Farmer's Suicide—2014

Sex/Age	*Below 18 years*	*18 years–30 years*	*30–60 years*	*60 years and above*	*Total*
Male	35 (6.68%)	1131 (21.84%)	3480 (67.20%)	532 (10.28%)	5178 (100%)
Female	24 (5.08%)	169 (35.81%)	232 (49.15%)	47 (9.96%)	472 (100%)
Total	59 (1.0%)	1300 (23.0%)	3712 (65.7%)	579 (10.2%)	5650 (100%)

Landholding Status of Farmers' Suicides in 2014

In India farmers are classified into four categories as marginal, small, medium and large on basis of landholding status of having less than 1 hectare, 1 hectare to below 2 hectares, 2 hectares to below 10 hectares and more than 10 hectares of land respectively. So far farmers' suicide was concerned in 2014; 44.5 per cent farmers were small farmers and 27.95 per cent were marginal farmers. In together these groups shared 72.4 per cent of total suicidal cases in India. As per this statistical figure stated, both small and marginal landholding farmers were highly vulnerable groups in agriculture sector of India and in two sensitive condition to commit suicide in hazards as economic bases were fragile. In case of medium landholding farmers, 25.2 per cent of farmers suicides fall in this category covering one quarter of suicide. The small marginal and medium landholding farmers' suicides covered in total 97.6 per cent of total in 2014. The large farmers' suicides cases was limited to 2.34 per cent showing lesser vulnerable group in farming community.

In the state of Maharashtra, 53.1 per cent of small farmers' suicides, 21.18 per cent of medium farmers' suicides and 2.4 per cent of large farmers' suicides cases were reported which was highest among all states and Union Territories of India in 2014. So far farmers suicides cases for marginal and small farmers in together. Reported by individual states in India, it was found that 10 states registered more than 70 per cent suicides cases. This category followed by 3 states between 50 to 70 per cent registered cases. On regional basis, majority of states registered high percentage of farmers' suicides in small and marginal landholdings. Gujarat and Haryana were the two states where farmers' suicides cases were high among medium farmers community registered above 65 per cent to respective state cases. Andaman & Nicobar Island was the single Union territory where seven marginal farmers and one small farmer committed suicide in above period.

Causes of Farmers' Suicides—2014

Bankruptcy or indebtedness and family problems were two major causes of farmers suicides in India accounted 20.6 per cent and 20.1 per cent respectively to total cases. Crop loans emerged as major causes of indebtedness and for farmers suicides. The other prominent causes of farmers suicides in the year where farming related issues (17.15%) and illness (13.18%). Crop failure was the main concern for farmers related to farming issues that caused loss of life. Suffering from prolonged illness, mental illness/insanity were prominent health troubles causing farmers suicides in the year. Drug abuse and alcoholic addiction emerged as farmer suicides incidence by 4.2 per cent limited to male farmers only. In the year 2014, major causes driving male farmers for suicides accounted to bankruptcy or indebtedness, facing problems and farm related issues 21.5 per cent and 20.0 per cent respectively. The female farmers suicides were related to farming related issues, farming problems, marriage related issues and bankruptcy/indebtedness accounting 21.4 per cent, 20.6 per cent, 12.3 per cent and 10.8 per cent respectively. No female farmer suicide case was registered for drug abuse, alcoholic addiction and property dispute.

Regional Incidence of Farmer Suicides—2014

There is high degree of variation in terms of number and suicide percentage of farmers in different states in country. In the year 2014, the high incidence of farmers' suicides in the country registered in five states—Maharashtra (45.5%), Telengana (15.9%), Madhya Pradesh (14.6%), Chhattisgarh (5.7%), and Karnataka (5.7%), respectively. The incidence of farmers' suicides reached 81.7 per cent in total in these five states on epidemic form being located in Deccan Plateau, Central India. These states often face dry spell of monsoon in growing seasons of crops. Thus, magnitude of problem was felt high in farming sector. In 2001, these five states including present Andhra Pradesh registered 63 per cent of farmers' suicides in country which was highest. It implies that this geographical region is in high risk zone for agriculture sector as well as farmers suicides prone zone of India. In 2014, three southern states—Tamil Nadu, Kerala and Andhra Pradesh—together shared 5.92 per cent of total farmers' suicides in India and emerged as second highest suicides prone region. In 2001, these states accounted high rates of farmers' suicides and relentless increased in number of incidence since 1997. This is the region of country where farmers' suicides are largely concentrated. There was sharp increase of farmers' suicides in previous years in number in this region.

In the highly populous Indo-Gangetic Plain, some states like Bihar, West Bengal, and Jharkhand in east were at other extreme registering zero causalties in 2014. The large state Uttar Pradesh with Punjab and Haryana registered 1.78 per cent of total farmer suicides in India. The farmer suicide rate was not alarming as compared to south. In 2001, these states registered with incidence of farmer suicides in India. Going by farmers' suicides percentage to country, the entire north-eastern hilly states except Assam (0.37%) all registered nil case. But some of the Himalayan states registered cases of farmer suicides in low percentage—Sikkim (0.62%), Himachal Pradesh (0.56%), and Jammu & Kashmir (0.21%) respectively. In western states of India, Rajasthan registered no farmer suicide case and by Gujarat (0.8%) showing low casualty rate in 2014. In 2001, state of Rajasthan registered 505 cases of farmer suicides and in Gujarat it was 594. It referred to a declining trend of farmer suicide percentage in this region. Among seven Union territories of India, Andaman & Nicobar Islands was the only region suffered from farmer suicides (No. 8) in 2014. In 2001, Puducherry had a horrendously high rate—835 farmer suicides per 1,00,000 in the state which dropped to zero in 2014.

Table 9.2: Percentage of Share Group of State in Total Farmer Suicides

Year	*% of share group of state in total farmers suicide*
2000	59.2
2001	63.2
2002	58.5
2003	63.1
2004	64.7
2005	64.0
2006	68.2
2014	84.5

Findings

In farming sector in India, 99 per cent of farmer suicide cases in 2014 were registered for above 18 years age group. This suicide rate was acute among young farmers (18 years below 30 years age) and more severe among middle aged farmers (30 up to 60 years boys). Incidence of senior citizen farmer suicide shared one-tenth of total cases. High concentration of farm suicide among male farmers in fact represents an objective reality that male head being considered as bread winner of household. These phenomena pointed towards economic distress of motivation factor underlying large member of male suicide among farmers. Similarly, rate of suicide casualty was high among small and marginal farmers than other communities accounting 72.4 per cent to total farmer suicide in 2014. Thus, increasing incidences of drought, cyclones, unseasonal heavy rainfall with hail stones cost farming with great loss as a consequence of global warming. The climatologists indicate towards the rising temperature of Tibetan Plateau, rising disturbances in Bay of Bengal, set stream, periodic temperature else of Pacific ocean and other man induced disturbances of factors for erratic behaviour of seasonal climatic condition in India and putting agriculture sector as major economic victim so also rising farmers suicides. The farmer suicide incidences are high in drought prone states as 79.5 per cent of India's farmland lie on flooding during monsoon season. So inadequate rainfall can cause drought, crop failure, and declined crop yield as well as fodder scarcity for cattles in no assured irrigation facilities. Any variability of rainfall lower to normal rainfall generally increases the incidence of small and marginal farmers' suicides rate in growing and harvesting seasons.

The states of India where farmers' suicide are becoming a chronic proportion; the reason in order of importance behind suicides are found to be debt, insufficient or risky credit systems, failure in farming, low produce price, adverse environment, increased cost of cultivation, private moneylenders, poor irrigation, stress and family responsibilities. The incidence of farmer suicides among small farmers are mostly related to agricultural loss, indebtedness, unable to recover production cost in most dry and rain fed agricultural regions and other climatic induced farm problems. But for medium and large farmers agriculture is highly diversified and subsequent income generates from trade and non-agricultural sources. Adverse climatic impacts are less on these farmers. The major causes of farmers suicides are due to a combination of family problem, business failure, social esteem and diminished political influences; a more of a socio-psycho-political problem than economic. While small farmers suicides coincide with harvest period showing economic importance of crop failure; the incidence of farmers suicide in other categories fall in different print of agriculture cycle combine the element of economic distress along with social, political, health and other linkages. The high incidence of suicide in southern states than north has been explained "as a combination of social issues such as interpersonal and family problems, financial difficulties and pre-existing mental illness. Suicidal ideation is as culturally accepted in south India as a method to deal with difficulties." (Patel *et al.*). In 2013, Government of India launched a "special livestock sector and fisheries package" of Rs. 912 million for farmers suicide prone region. Andhra Pradesh, Karnataka, Kerala and Maharashtra aimed to diversify farmers' economy.

The survey of farmers by NSS revealed a huge disaffection by farmers to agriculture as occupation as farm crisis a major factor and switch over to other safe occupation for livelihood. Similarly, a downturn in urban economy in India forced many non-farmers into farming because of alternative economic opportunities. In the absence of suitable counselling services these farmers when ventured for new crops, cash crops and in conditions of failure to reach goal, due to difficulties in farming in semi-arid condition, market fluctuation; they become easy victims to all these range of constrains and debt trap. This is the result of inefficient all location of resources and suboptimal output. These lacks of information, training as well as failure in both traditional and modern knowledge of farming bring desperate condition to farmers and increase the farmer suicide cases in India. The study of agriculture in 2014 found three specific characteristics associated with high risk to farmers; those who grow cash crops, like cotton and coffee, those with marginal landholding below one hectare and minimum debt rupees three hundred or more. It also found that highest farmer suicide cases in Indian states where these three characteristics are more common almost 75 per cent of variability in state level suicide. The status of crop insurance in India is not healthy and encouraging litmus of insurance coverage. There are ten insurance companies working associated with three major projects of governor for interest of farmer and farming in India at present. But these companies failed to reach a broad base covering the majority of small and marginal farmers. According to National Sample Survey (70th round) only 4.8 per cent farm holding under rice and wheat out of 9.02 crore in India covered by insurance between July 2012-June 2013. According to government report, in 2014, only 19.81 per cent farmers availed insurance for Kharif crops and 10.31 per cent farmers insured for Rabi crops. NSS in 70th round also revealed that 51.9 per cent of families related to farming in India were under debt and in the state of Andhra Pradesh 92.9 per cent of farming families were under debt trap. It is a common complaint from farmer holding Kisan Credit Card that banks often deduct the premium amount from loan in advance before distribution to farmers when they need it damming cropping season. It forces them to lend from other informal sectors at high interest rates not only for farming but for other social needs. The chronic indebtedness and inability to pay interest accumulated over years affected family life, depression, alcoholism etc. among farmers. To recover from economic decline; farmers follow suicide so that compensation following helps family to repay debt.

Concluding Remarks

Looking into large population of India pursing agriculture, which is becoming high risk sector due to climatic hazards; some effective steps should be taken on pilot basis to reduce farmers suicide rate. The use of remote sensing for assessing crop status and production in advance are need of time. It can help farmers with necessary intervention beforehand for precaution as well as government to adopt suitable measures for sustenance of agro-economy in India. Further, there is a need to increase the insurance base in rural India and to provide priority insurance services to farmers as well as lending to agriculture sectors. For the catastrophic risk in agriculture sector, public sector should increase its bases on basis of multiple insurances for farmers that may reduce farmer suicide rate among farmers. The economy farmers should be diversified for sustenance, if farmers are given opportunities to use total resources as alternative sources of income through self-help group at block level. Besides the employment generation programmes by government working at rural area; farmers of India must be trained to adopt small scale farm business like apiculture, horticulture, agriculture, and processed food product along with agriculture. These alternative livelihood opportunities will lessen the economic burden of farmers in distress and psychologically boost to save their lives.

References

Behera, P.B. and Behera, A.P. (2008). "Farmers suicides in Vidarbha region of Maharashtra state: A myth or reality", *Indian Journal of Psychiatry*, April-June; 50(2): 124-127.

Das, A. (2011). "Farmers' suicide in India: Implications for public mental health", *International Journal of Social Psychiatry*, 57(1): 21–29.

Gruère, G. and Sengupta, D. (2011). "Bt cotton and farmer suicides in India: An evidence-based assessment", *The Journal of Development Studies*, 47(2): 316–337.

Mohanty, B.B. (2011). "We are like the living Dead: Farmers' suicides in Maharashtra, Western India", *The Journal of Present Suicides*, 32(2): 243-276.

Nagaraja, K. (2008). *Farmers suicides in India: Magnitudes, trends and spatial patterns*.

National Crime Record Bureau: Accidental Death and Suicides in India, Annual Publication 2001-2006, 2014, Ministry of Home Affairs, Government of India.

National Crime Reports Bureau, *ADSI Report Annual–2014*, Government of India, p. 242, Table 2.11.

Schurman, R. (2013). "Shadow space: Suicides and the predicament of rural India", *Journal of Peasant Studies*, 40(3): 597–601.

Swain, M. (2008). "Agricultural risk and crop insurance in a globalized economy", *Man and Development*, 30(3): 107-28.

The Hindu, Kadapa, Tuesday, March 17, 2009.

Mohanty, B.B. and Sangeetha Shroff (2004). "Farmers suicides in Maharashtra", *Economic and Political Weekly*, 32(54): 5591-5598.

Section II

Displaced Identity, Multiculturalism and Social Capital

10

Migration, Ethnicity and Displaced Identity

Implications of India's Open Border Policy with the Himalayan States on Indian Nepalis

Rana Sonia Tez Bahadur

Migration of population among the countries of Bhutan, Nepal and India reflects a natural movement guided by socio-cultural affinity and a kinship factor. It is not political in character rather is more historical. Darjeeling and its areas was part of the dominions of the Monarch of Sikkim till 1835. In 1706, the Bhutanese took what is now the Kalimpong sub-division of the District from Sikkim. Sikkim later became engaged in unsuccessful struggles with the Gorkhas who had seized power in Nepal and invaded Sikkim in 1780. During the next 30 years, the Gorkhas ruled the District. Disagreement over the frontier policy of the Gorkhas, led to Anglo-Nepal war in 1813 in which the British Army led by General Octerlony defeated the Gorkhas. By the Treaty signed at Segoulie (1816) the Gorkhas ceded Darjeeling to the British, which in turn by Treaty of Titaliya (1817) was handed over to the Monarch of Sikkim. However, Darjeeling was "granted" away by Sikkim to the British as per a "deed of agreement" in 1835. The present Siliguri subdivision was annexed by the British in 1850 rather forcefully, as a punitive measure for having got Campbell and Hooker imprisoned by Namgyal Dewan, brother-in-law of the Monarch of Sikkim. And the Kalimpong sub-division was finally annexed in 1885 following the Anglo-Bhutanese War of 1864 and included in Darjeeling district in 1866. The Dooars, which too was a part of Sikkim conquered by Bhutan in 1706, was annexed to the British India in 1865. It is thus clearly understood that it was only when borders were redrawn following the independence of India that various solidarities were fragmented and the legality or otherwise of the movement of people across borders came into question.

Indo-Nepal Peace and Friendship Treaty, 1950

India-Nepal migration is a social interrelationship since peoples on both the sides of the border share a common language, religion and ethnic identity; their relations transcend political considerations. The commonalities are more evident between the Terai (Plain) people of Nepal and Indians across the border reflected in linguistic commonality and practice of Hinduism. The migration was further promoted by the Indo-Nepal Peace and Friendship Treaty of 1950 which allows Nepalis to freely reside, own property, find employment and carry on business in India. Article VI of the 1950 treaty states: "Each Government undertakes, in token of the neighbourly friendship between India and Nepal, to give to the nationals of the other, in its territory, national treatment with regard to participation in industrial and economic development of such territory and to the grant of concessions and contracts relating to such development." Article VII further adds: "The Governments of India and Nepal agree to grant, on a reciprocal basis, to the nationals of one country in the territories of the other the same privileges in the matter of residence, ownership of property, participation in trade and commerce, movement and other privileges of a similar nature."

India thus generally does not treat Nepali immigrants as "illegal". They have become just like other Indian nationals within the broad framework of the Indian Federation. There is sizeable Indian migration to Nepal from the adjoining districts in India, particularly to its Terai region and that of the Nepalese of Nepal to the adjoining districts in India, particularly Darjeeling and Siliguri in West Bengal. Marriage is also an important reason for migration. The immigrant Nepalese marry into local Indian families as do Indians settled in Terai townships in Nepal as traders and moneylenders. This has resulted in the cross-fertilisation of cultures, reinforcing commonalities between Indians and Nepalese. Accordingly, Nepalese migration to India and *vice versa* has been on a permanent and seasonal basis.

Eruption of the Madhesi Movement in Nepal

Nepal has three topographic regions: mountains (the Himalayan range), hills (the Shivalik range) and the Terai or Madhes (the southern plains). The Tarai region consists of 20 districts, with shared borders with India. Consequently, a considerable population in Tarai consists of Nepalis of Indian origin (often called *Indian Madhesis*) that migrated to Nepal from the adjoining districts of India. Indian Nepalis face discrimination owing to their strong social, cultural and ethnic linkages across the border. Apart from the ethnic factor and proximity to the Indian border, the Terai remained the hub of the pro-democratic movement during the 1950s and 1960s.

The ruling elites perceived India as being anti-establishment and the Indian Nepalis as India's agents. Fearing the influx of Indian immigrants into the Terai, which might prompt India to claim the Terai as Indian Territory, the Nepali elite in 1951, displaced Terai residents to control Terai land in the name of population distribution. The Nepal Resettlement Company, established in 1964, distributed 77,000 hectares of forest land in the Terai to those who were loyal to the Palace or the then Panchayat system. Land was distributed to the migrant population from the hills partly by clearing the forest and partly by uprooting many of the indigenous people, including the Indian Nepalis.

The ruling elites of Nepal have given the impression that Madhesis are mostly people of Indian origin and speak Hindi. They disregard the fact that the Terai consist of not only recent Nepali immigrants from India but also Indo-Nepalese who migrated to Nepal from India when there was Hindu/Muslim conflict and settled in more fertile lower hills, river valleys, and later on in Terai plains prior to 1950. The similarities between the Indian Nepalis and the Nepalese of Nepal settled in the Terai region of Nepal reflected in linguistic commonality and practice of Hinduism, have given rise to misgivings in the minds of Nepalese authorities about the loyalty and leanings of the Terai people. They are referred to as '*Madhesis*' implying 'outsiders' by the Nepalese of Nepal. This led to the emergence of an identity-based Madhesi movement in Nepal with the formation of the Nepal Terai Congress under Vedanada Jha in 1951 and Madhesi Mukti Andolan by Raghunath Thakur in 1956. Both the organisations raised their voice against discrimination and the exploitation of the Madhesis by the ruling elite. Autonomy of the Terai region and equal representation for Madhesis in state agencies were demanded under Article 73 of the UN Charter. The movement could not be sustained for long. However, it certainly sowed the seeds of the identity movement in Nepal.

The Pahadis in Nepal believe that India has been encouraging the 'One Madhes One Pradesh' demand. There is a suspicion amongst the Pahadis and major political leaders in Nepal that India is out to balkanise Nepal. There is still no visible change even after the formation of the democratic, secular republic of Nepal. The Pahadi narrative that portrays

Madhesis as Indian agents still continues. The Madhesis, on the other hand, believe that India's policy towards Nepal is Kathmandu-centric. They accuse India of neglecting the Madhesi movement. Lately, India has been blamed—both by the UCPN-Maoist party after Prachanda's resignation on May 2009, and by the common people—for its perceived excessive intervention in the internal affairs of Nepal and encouraging encroachment of Nepalese territory along the borders. Thus, India is faced with difficult choices. Any constructive attempt by India to salvage the Terai situation through proactive involvement is likely to be interpreted as unnecessary intervention in the internal affairs of Nepal and upset the *Pahadis* and even the Nepal army. At another level, passive indifference to developments in Terai will be misconstrued as a shirking of responsibility by observers at home and the Madhesis as well.

To date India has treated the Madhesi issue as an internal matter of Nepal, as people of Indian origin are citizens of Nepal. India has also officially expressed the view that the problem can be resolved by accommodating minority rights in the new constitution. Moreover, India held that identification of the Madhesis with India is likely to provoke Nepalese suspicions and hence they should try to become 'full citizens of Nepal'. Indian leaders, however, expressed their concern over the injustice, and its possible fallout, meted out to the Madhesis. In fact, on 29 June, 1971, the Indian Parliament discussed the anti-India riots in south Nepal. However, given the cultural and emotional linkages between the Madhesis and the people from India, the lack of clarity over India's role in the context of the suffering of Madhesis would only complicate the situation further making the anti-Indianism flowing from the Madhesi Movement stronger.

Eruption of Anti-Foreigners Movement in North East India

The real immigration of the Nepalis to North East India began when the British encountered the Nepalis in an adversary situation during the Anglo-Nepal war of 1814-15. They found their adversary not only brave warriors, but also effective in wild, difficult and mountainous tract. Moreover, they found them inexpensive, obedient and efficient even in trying circumstances. So much so that the British adopted many clandestine measures to have them encouraging the Nepalis to settle in places like Shillong, Darjeeling and Dehradun and dispatching *gallawallas* (local appellation for recruiting agents) to collect young boys for their army. The British proved to be a catalyst for an organized migration from the Nepal hills to the Indian Frontiers.

The pre-British economy being a subsistence economy, the British tried to generate more revenue by bringing more wastelands under production. It encouraged cash crop production such as cinchona, rubber, pepper and other herbal plantations. Commercial activities like timber extraction and tea plantation required strong muscle power for jungle clearance. The British, thus, encouraged immigration, and this was done by giving land on favourable terms to Nepalis, who as soon as knew about it, came freely in. Besides, the British also encouraged the Nepalis to settle in the vast wastelands of Sikkim and Bhutan so as to avoid the Chinese and Tibetan infiltration.

The internal situation within Nepal also served as a positive pull factors encouraging Nepalis migration to the North-east India. The classical Nepalis regime was notoriously a repressive one that considered some of the communities as enslavable. The Nepal Government had no system of paying its soldiers in cash: they fought for their nation in lieu of daily food or in case of officers, revenue-free land. The life in the hills was really difficult because there was very limited arable land in the forested and snow-bound mountain region. Under such circumstances, the conscious patronage extended by the colonial state to such migration in the form of good salary, pension disbursement centres and medical facilities for the soldiers made it very attractive for the Nepalis to enlist for the jobs in the establishments as they could even save some surplus for their kinsfolk left behind in the hills. Moreover, the abundance of land in the North-east Region for grazing and cultivation as well as the faster mode of transport by the British made both life and migration relatively comfortable for the Nepalis. The British Indian Government had created a situation in which the Nepalis were not only welcomed but also preferred as more useful compared to the 'natives'. Thus, more than natural migration, it was sponsored immigration and settlement by the colonial administrations.

Indian Nepalis today have their own institutions, socio-cultural practices and have contributed substantively to the making of modern India. Currently, Indian Nepalis are settled around the old Gorkha regimental centres such as Dharmsala, Bakloh in Himachal Pradesh, Dehradun, Darjeeling, Shillong, Assam and other north-eastern states. The constant effort of Nepali-speaking Indians ensured the inclusion of Nepali in the Eighth Schedule to the Constitution as one of India's national languages. It can, therefore, be argued that the Nepali identity already exists as a sub-stratum of the Indian identity.

However, Article VII of the Indo-Nepal Peace and Friendship Treaty,

1950 provided for two-way migration of the nationals of one country in the territories of the other. It nullified the requirement of a visa or passport for entry into either country. Nepal being one of the poorest and underdeveloped country in the world, by the end of 1950, one in every ten Nepalis had immigrated to India. The 1971 Census of India reported that there were 1.3 million Nepal-born Nepalis living in India. Thus, once link between the families of these hills and Nepal was established the initial trickle of Nepalese from Nepal became a surging stream. The fact is that the earlier trends of migration found formal manifestation particularly in the Article VII of the Treaty of 1950.

In the late 1970s, the record 82 per cent increase in the total population of Assam during the twenty-year period from 1951 to 1971 led to an unprecedented anti-outsider upsurge, i.e. the Assam or Anti-foreigners Movement in Assam from 1979 to 1983. The leadership of the Assam Movement began to target not only the illegal immigrants from Bangladesh but also the Nepalese immigrants to Assam. The presence of the Indian Nepalis, well-integrated into the Assamese community and the continuing immigration began to evoke feelings of doubt in the minds of the Assamese, creating a sense of injury to the Assamese nationality caused by the fear of losing their identity in their own homeland. The provisions of the Indo-Nepal Friendship Treaty (1950) were deliberately ignored and it was suggested that those who came after 1951 were 'foreigners' in Assam. The targets were the refugees from Bangladesh, but the Indian Nepalis were also included. Eviction notices were served in Assam against the Nepalis and were deported from Assam while the names of a large number of Nepalis were excluded from the voter's list on the ground that they were foreigners. The Nepalis irrespective of their length of stay in Assam, virtually became 'dangerous', 'unwanted foreigners' in Assam, who were alleged to have been "threatening the socio-cultural and political identity of the Assamese" in their traditional homeland. The Assamese-Nepalis nexus was soon torn apart.

Repercussions of the anti-foreigners agitation in Assam were also felt in the other states of North East India. In Manipur, the movement manifested itself in direct attacks on the Nepalis in 1980, compelling many who were domiciled in 1947 to shift houses and flee to safer areas. The fall-out has been particularly noticeable in Meghalaya where the Nepalis became a special target of attack immediately after the signing of the Assam Accord. The question of Nepali identity cropped in Mizoram too when the influx of people from Nepal increased in the early part of 1980s. The Anti-foreigners Movement caused the Nepalis, although long domiciled, suffer from violence and indiscriminate eviction. These attacks on the Nepalis reflected the growing apathy of State Governments and the local people towards the Nepalis in the region. Even where they were declared as a domiciled community, such as in Mizoram, they were targets of attacks by local population. The local administration, meanwhile, stood silent witness to the full spate of attacks on Nepalis. As a result, the more educated began to reassess their political status and democratic rights in the region. This led to the assertion of Indian Nepalis identity in India. Indian Nepalis maintained their Indian identity and demanded abrogation of the 1950 Treaty with Nepal. They felt that migrants under this Treaty tended to displace their Indian identity.

Eruption of the Gorkhaland Movement in West Bengal

The deplorable plight of the Nepalis in the North-eastern Region led to the formation of Pranta Parishad in North Bengal (April 1980). The Pranta Parishad as per its Constitution was not a political party. It was just a political platform to press the demand for statehood of Darjeeling. It viewed the 'state' as a panacea for all linguistic, cultural and economic grievances of the Nepali people. During the 1982 State Assembly elections, it made a vote boycott campaign to draw the attention of the Government to the plight of the Gorkhas. The vote boycott call was largely ineffective except in the Kalimpong sub-division where a meagre 32 per cent polling was recorded. However, it is important to note that the term 'Gorkhaland' was first used, though not very emphatically during the vote-boycott campaign of Pranta Parishad. Indian Nepalis prefer to call themselves 'Gorkha' instead of Nepali mainly to demarcate their identity from the Nepalese of Nepal.

In the twenty first century, memories of the 1980s incidents have been pushed to the back-burner. Things have limped back to normal. However, due to the similarity in appearance and language, the Indian Nepalis are still mistaken as the Nepalis of Nepal origin. As a result, the Indian Nepalis do not enjoy privileges equivalent to the Indian nationals. For instance, the Nepali people living in Assam for generations are not issued the 'Permanent Residence Certificate' (PRC) by the District authorities and thus they are deprived of citizenship rights. Similarly, the Government of Mizoram, without giving any reasons, has stopped the issuance of the Other Backward Classes Certificates (OBC) to the *bona fide* children of Indian Nepali permanent settlers as a result of which the young Indian Nepalis are facing problems in various fields. Indian Nepalis also not eligible for state services as the 'sons of the soil' policy in the job avenues is prevalent in most areas.

They are continually treated as encroachers from Nepal and have become victims of humiliation and discrimination in India. They faced eviction as seen during the time of anti-foreigners movement in Assam and other North-eastern states by the dominant ethnic group in those regions. The identity of the Indian Nepalis as a distinct ethnic community in India has been disputed time and again. Often labelled as 'Foreigners', 'encroachers' and 'migrators' from Nepal, the identity of the Indian Nepalis as Indian citizens is hardly recognized at the national level. Such an attitude by the dominant community and the policy-makers gave impetus to the 'Gorkhaland' movement by the Indian Nepalis for a separate state of 'Gorkhaland' within the Indian Union. The Indian Nepalis believe that such a state would not only put an end to their identity crisis but would also enable them to be recognized as Indian citizens as distinct from citizens of Nepal. They would no longer be treated as foreigners amidst the immigrants from Nepal as well as be able to maintain their distinctive ethnic identity outside the dogma of the dominant Bengali culture in West Bengal. The issue of ethnic identity as such has largely contributed to the generation of the demand for a separate state of Gorkhaland by Gorkha National Liberation Front of Subhash Ghising that resorted to violence in the 1980s and at present by Gorkha Janmukti Morcha led by Bimal Gurung.

Indo-Bhutan Friendship Treaty, 1949

The influx of Indian Nepali migrants into Bhutan happened in 2 major phases: The first major influx of Nepali migrants began at the beginning of the twentieth century when the Bhutanese Government employed Nepalis from India as contract labour to extract timber from the dense tropical forests in Bhutan's southern foothills. The Nepalis, the trained manpower that they were helped Bhutan to organise its administration and army and provided assistance to improve its agriculture, livestock, trade and commerce. Formally they were, by contract, prohibited to establish permanent residence in Bhutan. However, as control was weak, they illegally stayed on as tenant farmers in the areas where the forests were cleared. They gradually settled in the southern districts and encouraged relatives and friends from India to join them.

Subsequently, the Bhutanese Government made efforts to integrate ethnic eligible Nepalis living in Bhutan. The Bhutan Citizenship Act of 1958 aimed at integrating those who had legally lived in Bhutan for at least 10 years, into the Bhutanese nation and to draw the line to foreigners temporarily working in the Kingdom. Many Nepalis were recognized as citizen and admitted as civil servants; the Nepali speaking Bhutanese were given representation in the National Assembly; Nepali was introduced as second official language and taught in the Primary Schools in Southern Bhutan where most of them lived.

The second major influx of ethnic Nepali migrants into Bhutan began after 1950 when an open border between India and Bhutan was provided by Indo-Bhutan Friendship Treaty updated in February 2007. Since 1949, Bhutanese citizens have been permitted to move freely across the Indian border. A reciprocal arrangement between India and Bhutan grants its citizens equal treatment and privileges. Article V states, "The Government of Bhutan and the Government of India agree that Bhutanese subjects residing in Indian territories shall have equal justice with Indian subjects, and that Indian subjects residing in Bhutan shall have equal justice with the subjects of the Government of Bhutan."

The right to residence, study, and work guaranteed without the need for identity papers encouraged many Indian Nepalis in the adjoining districts of Indo-Bhutan border to migrate to Bhutan. Moreover, the modernisation of the Bhutan's economy, created new job and business opportunities encouraging massive immigration through the long and porous border in the south. In many cases, the new immigrants were again closely related, by family ties with Bhutanese of Indian origin.

Eruption of the Lhotshampa Movement in Bhutan

The King, as well as the prevailing power structure of Bhutan, became apprehensive of the growing Nepalis clout in Bhutanese politics and economy which to their mind, posed a danger to Bhutan's identity, its monarchy as well as the traditional Buddhist values and ethos of Bhutan. Consequently, Bhutanese Government, for the preservation of the national identity adopted the principles of "Dringlam Namzha" (traditional values and etiquette). Accordingly civil servants for their work, citizen at all public functions and visiting public offices, children at school, had to wear the Bhutanese national dress Kho for men and Khira for women. The Nepali language was withdrawn from teaching in primary schools.

This was followed by the implementation of the 1985 Citizenship Act which adopted 1958 as the cut-off year. The Royal Government made it mandatory for every Bhutanese of Indian origin to produce 1958 land tax receipts to qualify for Bhutanese citizenship disregarding that no villagers could preserve such records for thirty years. This provision of the 1958 Citizenship Act was amended in 1977 increasing five of satisfactory service to fifteen years of service and at least ten years of residence in Bhutan to twenty years. Making language as one of the mandatory conditions, the 1977 Citizenship Act demanded allegiance to the King, country and people. Even the marriage clause could be valid if marriage between a woman and a man or *vice versa* took place before 1985.

The coercive measures applied by the Bhutanese seemed was guided by an extreme sense of insecurity for both national identity and state security. It originated from the fears that the Drukpa traditions and customs which are of Tibetan origin would be subordinated to the culture and religion (Hindu) of ethnic Nepalis—known in Bhutan as 'Lhotshampas' dominated society. Thus threatened with the influence of the culture of the Lhotshampa and the increase of a minority Nepalis population that eventually turned out to be majority, the Bhutanese authorities adopted a "well planned programme of depopulation.' In 1991, explaining the *raison d'etre* of the official policy of regularising citizenship for the promotion of national identity, the Royal Government of Bhutan declared:

> "...The Royal Government cannot afford to discontinue the policy of national integration and the concept of 'one nation and one people'. These policies are vital for ensuring Bhutan's long term security and well-being as a united and cohesive nation. That is why the Royal Government considers it so crucial for all citizens to look upon themselves as Bhutanese regardless of their race or religion, and why it is so important for all citizens to take pride in being fraternal members of the United Bhutanese family."

According to an Amnesty International Report, during 1988 several thousand non-nationals were reportedly ordered to leave the country as landless or unemployed illegal immigrants or for overstaying initial permits following the citizenship policy was "apparently implemented" vigorously. The Bhutanese government claimed that most of people fleeing the country were illegal immigrants whose presence was detected by a Census operation in 1988. However, a government census not only showed that the population was much smaller than the 1.2 million hitherto claimed, but that 50 per cent were Nepali who came to Bhutan post the Indo-Bhutan Friendship Treaty as well as ethnic Nepalis whose families were living in Bhutan for generations but failed to produce papers proving they were resident in 1958. The combined Acts made thousands stateless overnight. Yet another measure which had an adverse impact on the Lhotshampas was the 'Green Belt Policy', which sought to transform the rice-growing foothills of southern Bhutan on which depended the livelihood of the ethnic Nepalis into forest land to maintain ecological balance.

Thus, the alleged discriminatory policy-implementation of the Bhutanese State against the "southern Bhutanese" or the people of Nepali origin led to the developing of ethnic conflict between the Southern Bhutanese (Nepalis) and the Drukpa (Bhutanese elite group). In 1989, a group of ethnic Nepalis formed the People's Forum for Human Rights. The Forum accused the government of infringing basic human rights and petitioned for these rights to be restored. Civil unrest ensued, and was put down by the army and Policy. According to the Lhotshampas, their public call for a restoration of human rights triggered a wave of government repression and violence, culminating in the mass exodus of the early 1990s. It was reported that whole villages in southern Bhutan were burned to the ground. After several raids and bombings, the Bhutanese authority ordered the closure of local Nepalese schools, clinics, and development programmes.

Many ethnic Nepalese were forcibly evicted and forced to cross the Indian borders into Assam and West Bengal. The Indian states did not accept the expelled Bhutanese and they were forced to move on. Most went through Nepal to go back into India at different entry points, while approximately 1,00,000 stayed in UNHCR refugee camps in Nepal. Under its reciprocal arrangement with Bhutan, the Indian Government affords the Bhutanese more freedom of movement and residence than to recognized refugee groups. Despite being officially treated as equals to Indian citizens, the refugees experience difficulties in securing driving and business licences, travel documents, cooking gas and school and university admission. This is because the provision of Indo-Bhutan Friendship is provided to nationals and they are denied the acknowledgement of Bhutanese nationals both by the Bhutanese as well as Indian Governments. India, in order to avoid allegation of interference refuses to involve itself in the status determination of the Bhutanese nationals. Thus India, the major power in the region, has so far refused the search for a solution of the status of the Indian Nepalis in Bhutan. While Bhutan continues to undermine provisions of the Article V which was to ensure to the Indian subjects residing in Bhutan equal justice with the subjects of the Government of Bhutan.

Conclusion

Migration has played a vital role in the structural transformation of societies. Unlike in the past when migration involved establishment of new habitations in fertile and virgin lands, migration today is characterised by movement of populations to other countries with people and cultures of their own. It, therefore, raises issues regarding ethnicity and identity. Ethnicity is a relational concept that sets one group of people apart from another—a process of constructing differences. When migrants integrate more and diffuse to a great degree within their adopted homeland, which in turn becomes more diverse, they have a better chance of being valued as enriching society and introducing complementary cultural traits. Ground realities, however, indicate that it posits a "national self" facing one or more threatening "others" within a dichotomous framework. The identity of the host population is seen as being fragmented by the migrant population resulting into crisis of displaced identity and consequent assertion of ethnicity.

Geographical contiguity, socio-cultural affinity, kinship factor and historical reasons together with rapid growing economy have left India vulnerable to migration from Himalayan states of Nepal and Bhutan. Unlike migration elsewhere, ethnic commonalities of Indians with Bhutanese and Nepali migrants imbue migration with an ethnic dimension, both as "push" and "pull" factors. The dynamics of Nepali migration to India is same as that of the Bhutanese migration. With open borders to Nepal and Bhutan, people move back and forth with ease for marriage, family occasions, work and even education. Thus, the artificially made border becomes irrelevant and cross-border identity, together with social networks, transcends political considerations in migration from both Bhutan and Nepal. The implication of the India's open border policy with the Himalayan states of Nepal and Bhutan had an adverse effect on the Indian Nepalis living in India, Bhutan and Nepal. While in India they are looked upon as foreigners having their identity being mistaken for Nepalese in Nepal, in Nepal they are looked upon as Madhesis and in Bhutan as Lhotshampas. Open border policy promoting free migration has displaced their identity as Indian Nationals that each of the three countries is not willing to recognise and acknowledge.

Select Bibliography

Baral, Lok Raj, (1993), "Bilateralism under the shadow: The problems of refugees in Nepal-Bhutan relations", *Contributions to Nepalese Studies*, Volume 20, No. 2, Centre for Nepal and Asian Studies, Tribhuvan University, Nepal, July.

Behera, Shubhakanta, (2011). "Trans-Border identities: A study of the impact of Bangladeshi and Nepali migration to India", *ICRIER Policy Series*, Volume No. 1, New Delhi, May.

Brass Paul (1991), *Ethnicity and Nationalism—Theory and Comparison,* New Delhi: Sage Publication.

Chakraborthi, Dyutish, (1988), "Gorkhaland: Evolution of politics of segregation", *Special Lecture,* Center for Himalayan Studies, University of North Bengal, April.

Nath, Lopita, (2006), "Migration, insecurity and identity: The Nepali dairymen in India's Northeast", *Asian Ethnicity,* Volume 7, No. 2, June.

Pokharel, Ramesh, (2011). "Politics and Problematics of the definition and categorization of ethnicity in Nepal", *Bodhi: An Interdisciplinary Journal,* Volume 5, Kathmandu University, Nepal.

Roy, Sanjay K., (2005), "Conflicting Nations in North-East India", *Economic and Political Weekly*, Volume 40, No. 21, May 21.

Sinha, A.C. and T.B. Subba (Eds.) (2002), *The Nepalis in North-east India: A Community in Search of Indian Identity*, New Delhi: Indus Publishing Company.

11

New Narratology of Women Domestic Workers in Tamil Nadu

A Micro Analysis

G. Palanithurai

Introduction

In Indian society much of the women's labour is informalised, unvalued and unrecognized. It is being done unconsciously and intentionally as it warrants establishing control over women by men. Women and girls involved in domestic work remain unorganized and unnoticed as poor are involved in such activities in order to meet the challenges of poverty. Since they are under the clutches of the middle class, upper middle class and the rich, the policy community paid poor attention on the issues faced by domestic women workers. As a result, studies are scarce, lack of data base and poor attention of the media on the issues of the domestic workers. In general domestic work never gets primacy among the policy-makers as house is not considered as workplace. But finally the conditions of the domestic workers have been captured through a study by the Government of India (GoI, 2011). Yet there are attempts to organize them as groups or unions and they are also not large in numbers (Bhagyashree and Hilaria, 2016:1-8). Even though the activities are lesser intensive, the state responded to the plight of the domestic workers through a new mechanism. It is nothing but inclusion of the domestic work in the list of scheduled employment under Minimum Wages Act of 1948 that too in a few states (ILO, 2012). Even states which are progressive and known for gender activities have not sufficiently paid attention on the issues of the women domestic workers (Neetha, 2008: 26-28). Individual attempts had been taken to ameliorate their conditions through legislation in vain (Sonia,

2013:69-76). The media which are active both, print and electronic, have not covered the stories of the women domestic workers as they have gained neither orientation nor sufficiently conscious of the plight of the women domestic workers. The issues and problems of the women domestic workers vary from state to state and district to district within the state.

A "domestic worker" is a person who works in or for a household and where there is an employment relationship. These workers can be local, migrants, working in one or many homes on a daily basis or only for certain days in a week, but regularly for their livelihood. It is the definition given by ILO Convention 189. The Convention recognizes the rights as other workers such as right to collective bargain, security, minimum wage. A domestic worker performs variety of household services for an individual or a family, by providing care for children and elderly dependent to housekeeping, and in addition to this they use to clean the house and the households, washing, cooking, other than this laundry and ironing, shopping for food and so on.

Problems of the Domestic Workers in General

Most of the domestic workers are women. In India, there are about 16.8 lakh domestic workers and out of them 6.2 lakh are males (Bhatt, 1989). Each woman has different pathetic stories, which may explain the reason behind the field they choose. In India, 45 per cent of women are illiterate, so definitely, they have to work in unorganized sector for their livelihood without the awareness of their rights and entitlements.

Legal Protections

The United Kingdom's Master and Servant Act, 1823 was the first of its kind and influenced the creation of domestic service laws in other nations, although legislation favoured employers more than servants. However, before the passing of such Acts servants and workers in general, had no protection in law. The only real advantage that domestic service providers was got meals, accommodation, and sometimes clothes in addition to a modest wage. Service was normally an apprentice system with a provision for advancement through the ranks.

At its 301st Session (March 2008), the ILO Governing Body agreed to place an item on decent work for domestic workers on the agenda of the 99th Session of the International Labour Conference (2010) with a view to the setting of labour standards. The problems faced by domestic workers varied considerably throughout history and in the contemporary world. In the course of twentieth century movements for labour rights, women's rights and immigrant rights, the conditions faced by domestic workers and the problems specific to their class of employment have come to the fore.

In 2011, the International Labour Organization adopted the convention concerning decent work for domestic workers. In July 2011, at the annual International Labour Conference, held by the ILO, Conference delegates adopted the resolution on domestic workers by a vote of 396 to 16, with 63 abstentions. The convention recognized domestic workers as workers with the same rights as other workers. On 26 April, 2012, Uruguay was the first country to ratify the Convention.

In India, National Domestic Workers Movement was started and mobilized the domestic workers and it gained visibility only after regional groups formed in different places such as Mumbai, Patna, Chennai, Varanasi, Andhra Pradesh, Kerala, Karnataka, Madhya Pradesh and Jharkhand. Though they formed groups and started mobilizing the domestic workers, formally they put up demands to state governments to enact legislations to protect them only after 1990, because they did not get adequate data for policy advocacy. Despite all such small mobilization, it is a pity that "Unorganized Sector Workers Social Security Bill, 2005" did not find any mention of the domestic workers issue. Karnataka is the first state to fix minimum living wage for domestic workers in 2004. Subsequently, many states took efforts to enact legislation (Neetha, 2013:77-84). Yet, conditions are appalling and deplorable (Hamid, 2016).

The issues are much complicated as they are in the clutches of the female family head. Even though, there are legal frameworks to protect them and safeguard the interest of women, their intricate working conditions made them on the job as half slaves in a free society. In the above backdrop an attempt is made to study the life and livelihood conditions of the domestic female workers in rural setting in Tamil Nadu. It is part of a larger study. The study is undertaken with the following objectives:

(a) Under what family background the women are driven towards such domestic works in the families?
(b) What are all the activities carried out by them regularly?
(c) What are the economic and other benefits they gain for the work they do in the families?

(d) What impact the domestic works create in the families in terms of transformation?
(e) What are the problems faced by the domestic women workers in the families they work?
(f) What are the enabling conditions needed to improve the working conditions of the women domestic workers?

Methodology

In order to investigate the problem case study method is being administered. Within the case study method, narratology, a nuanced tool is being adopted to get full details of their family stories, working conditions and the problems they have faced in their families and the families they work as servants, and the intensity of issues arising out of the men folk in the families where they work as domestic workers. By adopting the nuances of narratology, data pertinent to their personal problems are being collected. To complete a case study, the scholar has to devote a few days. The scholar has to create a setting for data collection by working hours and days together with the respondents. Data have to be collected from the full personal story of the domestic workers. With a promise given to the respondent to maintain the secrecy data are being collected from them. One case study is almost one full story about one individual.

Researchers have to create a rapport with the domestic workers and build a confidence in them that the data shared with the researchers will not create any problem either in their families or in the families where they work. Their integrity and name should not be tarnished with the data drawn from them. In such a way, rapport was created with the respondents to collect data from them. Data have been collected from the respondents in different spells in a week time. Even to collect data from one respondent, the investigator has to visit her many times in a week. The researchers involved in data collection have been trained and oriented by the author of the article. Data collection process by using narratology itself becomes a subject for deeper analysis. From the data collected, they are being analysed quantitatively. From the narration of the stories certain main points have been taken and they have been presented in quantitative table form for easy understanding. They are being supplemented with full narration of few cases. All the tables are in Appendix.

Data Analysis

From first ten tables in the Appendix, one can easily infer that however poor they are, they got basic facilities to lead a decent human life. Further, through the development schemes and institutions meant for delivering goods and services to the people, they got their entitlements and services properly without much difficulty. Since Tamil Nadu is a pro-poor state and it has got many pro-poor schemes, the poorest can also lead a decent human life if their life is organised properly and avail the schemes and programmes periodically and properly. Tamil Nadu is known for its infrastructure facilities and hence they are being used profitably by the poor for their livelihood. In Tamil Nadu, poor are highly empowered.

From Tables 11 to 19, one can infer the rising revolution of aspiration to educate their children. They strongly feel education is the only instrument through which one can uplift the social and economic status of the family. Everyone believes that education is a powerful instrument to achieve transformation in the family and society and more particularly in the financial conditions of the family. It is considered as transformative engine. Their handling of money, use of the banking system, developing savings culture, investing the saved money in education of their children have lot of stories to tell about their vision, hope and aspiration. Not even a single maid servant wants her children to work in the sector as they work. They never considered it as a profession to remain in the work as other works. They opted to do this work as there is no alternative to them. They are trying hard to educate their children. They are courageous to spend huge hard earned money in their children's education. Apart from their savings they borrow money and spend it on their children's education. It is to be noted here that majority of the respondents never indulged in borrowing money for interest. Equally, it is interesting that the respondents follow small family norm.

Tables 20 to 23 give the picture about the nature of work the respondents do in the houses, how they do the work, timing of their works and how much earn through the works. The nature and type of works and the amount they earn from their works have been projected. It all vary from individual to individual. There is no uniform wage for the nature and type of work in every family. In the same way, there is no uniform wage for the quantum of work they do. It all depends on the bargain between the worker and the household and in the same way it depends on the relationship between the worker and the household. No way the act meant for the workers has helped them in fixing their wage and the conditions.

Tables 24 to 31 explain the nature of relationship between the workers and the households. As long as, both maintain a cordial relationship, the workers are not treated badly and shabbily. Majority informed that the household had concern for their domestic workers. It means they value the work of the workers. They know the importance of their work also. Yet there are abuses in the houses and it depends on the nature of relationship developed between the workers and the households. They are pushed to this work by poverty and thereby their aspiration to earn more money for their future and for their children. It is a pity that they are all in SHG and yet they are not aware of their entitlements. Majority expressed that they are so tired of their work. They work because of the conditions compelled them. It is unequivocally clear that they are not happy with this job. They are in this job out of compulsion. Their poverty pushed them to this work and their aspiration made them to continue in this work. But their health conditions make them to be free from this job. They are unable to get out from this job as they need money.

Tables 32 to 36 give glimpse of the family conditions with which they perform their work. They do not have their own association. They found uneasy relationship in their families despite their hard work and earnings. They face lot of problems in their families either because of their husbands or because of their in laws. Mostly their husbands are irresponsible and they are the main source of trouble. On most of the occasions their hard earned money is being wasted only by their husbands. Being women they are moving with all age groups in the families they work. Sometimes, they get instruction from the male members and act accordingly. Their movements with men in the families where they work is a source of conflict in families of the domestic workers. Since they are not able to perform their family work they have to face the wrath of many in their families. Everyone wants money of the domestic workers but at the same time they have to work in their families also as domestic worker. This is the pitiable part of the patriarchy in our society. Most of the problems in their families are raised by their husbands. The domestic workers bargain with the house owners to fix their wages and the service conditions. It is not done in the backdrop of the laws or policies. But through their strategies and they settle their problems with house owners very smoothly.

While going through Tables 37 to 39, one would find that the living conditions of the domestic workers are not so bad as government has provided needed facilities to lead a decent human life. But the working conditions are not conducive to lead a dignified life as we find in other places (Kundu, 2007:853-866). Apart from the above salary, working conditions, nature of work, intensity of work, health conditions, gender related problems vary from place to place and house to house as we see in other states (Coelho and Chandira, 2013:39-46). At one point of time, there was no adequate data but now there are macro studies (GoI, 1988) and micro studies (Kiran, 2013:63-68) to portray the conditions of the domestic workers. Yet, there is no comprehensive law for domestic workers in India (Kamala, 2013:85-89). When it is woman domestic worker, the conditions are appalling and vary from city to city and province to province.

Narratology

Case No. 1

Mahalakshmi (name changed) is 72 years old lady still engaging herself as a maid servant for her survival. She was born in Thiruthani, and she belongs to BC Yadav community. Her husband worked as the fitter in Thiruthani. She gave birth to eleven children. Her husband migrated from Thiruthani to Dindigul for want of job. At the age of 44, Mahalakshmi lost her husband. At the time of her husband's death only one son was with her and all others have got married and settled in different places. The son who was with her became a drunkard. All her children are illiterate and they are all going for daily wage in different places. Absolutely, they are not in a position to take care of their mother. Hence, her sons are not in a position to help her for her livelihood. She has no other option excepting to work as domestic worker for her livelihood. She started the work out of her family condition. Her poverty only pushed her to domestic work.

When she started the work as a maid servant she worked with four different houses. In the beginning she received Rs. 300 as her wage per month. In two houses she used to clean the floors, washing vessels and cloths, in the remaining houses she used to cook along with the above mentioned works. She never had the habit of taking breakfast in the work places, but sometimes if she felt tired then she used to take food from her owners houses. They never insist her to take food. If there is any food remains in the houses where she worked she used to take that to her home to give the food to her grandchildren. She said that "I have to work at this age as my sons neither they have needed capacity to look after me nor they have concern for me. Even at this age, I have to work and take care of their children also."

For the past 16 years Mahalakshmi has been working in different houses and of them one house is regularly giving this opportunity and paying Rs. 3,000 per month. Only from that house she used to get Rs. 5,000 as bonus for Deepawali and in all other houses, she could not get it. She was saying that there is no problem in working in the houses but she has not been treated as a dignified human being. The women folk used to ask her family conditions and this made her to feel awkward. In the houses from young siblings to old men and women never use dignified words. One cannot expect any respect from them and that is why changing the houses frequently. Behaviour of men in the houses where she works is always different which is unacceptable to any women. "Since we rely on their salary for our livelihood, we have to tolerate to a point. If they cross the limit we have to move from that house" she said. "When I was in the fifties, I listened many comments about me by the men folk in the families where I worked. I never responded and reacted simply because of poverty. But I never allowed them to cross certain boundaries to save my modesty", she observed. Despite her 27 years of her work she could not save any money. She spends everything for her grandchildren. She has lot of physical ailments but she cannot take any leave. She has no money in her saving account. If she takes leave she will be scolded by the house owners and their siblings next day. She never had the habit of taking three meals a day and with only two meals, she is managing herself. She is not aware of the Minimum Wage Act and she confessed that she used to get all the provisions meant for the poor in the schemes of the Government of Tamil Nadu. She openly admitted that her conditions would be much worsened if the Government of Tamil Nadu has not implemented this much of schemes meant for the poor. She told that she has a plan to join in free old age home when she is not able to work and move freely.

Case No. 2

Mrs. Baby is (name changed) (54) a domestic worker working for a period of eight years. She is married and having two sons and got married. She belonged to B.C. Vaduga Nayakar community. Her native is Dindigul itself. Her husband never goes for a proper stable job, because he is addict to alcohol and he used to drink daily and quarrel with Baby and beat her too sometimes. At once her hand was fractured because of her husband's beating. She managed her family with the income of her two sons, but when her sons got married her daughter-in-laws have not cooperated with her and they wished to lead a nuclear family and hence they went out. Her sons stopped giving any money to Baby and her husband. She could not be able to manage herself without any income. Her husband is also a irresponsible person and he never goes for any job but he want money for liquor and he had been in the habit of harassing his wife. He took all her Jewels including her *Mangalsudru (thali)* for taking arrack. Her life became miserable. To overcome the problems, she has decided to go for domestic works within the radius of three kilometres of her residence.

In her working place, the house owner keeps three domestic servants. One servant meant for cooking and another one for cleaning outside the house, sweeping and taking care of the cattles and Baby is for washing clothes and cleaning the vessels. She used to take all the three times food from her owner's house itself. Sometimes, she used to take food for home also. Now for the past three years she did not go to her home. She is staying in the owner's house itself because her husband keeps on fighting with her and beating her and taking all her salary for drinking liquor. She cannot keep money in her house as her husband takes that money for drinking liquor. When she refuses to give money, he beats her. Her sons are away and they also did not respond to her. Since she has no other alternative, she has decided to stay with the house lord once and for all by abandoning her husband. She is working for her stomach not for money or wealth so she is saying that she does not want to work in many houses for financial purpose. Baby is saying that till her death she wants to work for survival and hence, she needs a safer place for stay. Now her house lord gave her a separate small room to stay. Now Baby is having a bank account and also uses to save money. She spends money from her savings if she is unwell. She never had the habit of borrowing money from her owner. The past three years Baby is not attending any social functions and visiting her relatives. Her house lord is taking care of her and she does not want to see her husband and her sons too, she is summarizing all this and said she will work till her death and her saving money will help for her funeral and she does not want anything from her family members.

Case No. 3

Mrs. Mariammal (name changed) aged 46, belonging to SC community. She studied up to fifth standard, and her husband working as a coolie and her son is studying in twelfth standard. Her native place is Anna Nagar, a village near Gandhigram and now she is residing in the same village. Mariammal is working as a servant for the past 20 years and her nature of work is cleaning. She is doing cleaning work for daily wage and for monthly salary with a bonus during Deepavali festival. She gets allowance also. The house owner fixed the payment and monthly four days she gets leave. She did not avail any Medical Insurance, but she has Aadhaar Card, Ration Card and Bank Account also.

She is working in two houses. Sometimes she takes food in the house where she is working but they are not allowed to take food to her home. Mariammal has some amount of saving. She saves Rs. 500 for social function per month and she saves Rs. 1000 for cultural and religious functions. She spends Rs. 200 for medical expenses every month. She faces problems only in financial front. She did not experience any abuse by the house lord at the workplace besides she did not find any risk in the activities during working in the house. She borrowed some money as advance from the house lords and she borrowed loan also from the house owner. She has been working more than ten years in the present house. She is a member of Self-Help Group (SHG) organised and promoted by a non-profit organisation located very near to her residence. Besides she is availing all the government benefits like TV, Mixie, Grinder, and Fan from the Government of Tamil Nadu by using her ration card.

She has no own house and she is living in a thatched house. She has some household articles in her house such as TV, Grinder, Mixie, Chair and Cell phone. Regularly three times she takes food (Morning, Afternoon and Night) and sometimes she takes snacks in the evening. She has not undergone any training and she is not willing to undergo any training also. If any institution renders such trainings, she has no time and not interested to participate on Sundays also. She has bank account, ATM card besides she has also debt at present. She borrowed money for her son's education.

She demands for wage hike by request, telling the reason that in fact she is not aware of Minimum Wage Act. The house owner is highly satisfied by her performance that is why she is working more than ten years in the same house. Her house owner is a good individual. For the past ten years, she does not have any problem with the house owner, and hereafter also. There is no rift between her and her house owner with regard to payment and fixation of wages. She has no idea about when she is going to pay back her debts. Sometimes, she felt that she is a slave in the hands of the house lords.

Case No. 4

Jayalakshmi (26) (name changed) with fourth standard educational background got married at the age of 19. Her husband is working in a small company which is manufacturing steel cots for smaller hospitals with a salary of Rs. 6,000 per month. They are living in a rented house. Now through her effort the house has been taken for lease for ten years by paying one lakh rupees. She has one daughter and one son and they are in elementary school. Both are studying in a private Christian school by paying fees regularly. She is working in five houses and earning Rs. 9000 per month. She gets food from the houses where she works and feeds her husband, son and daughter in the evening. During night, she is ironing dresses collected from different houses. Since, she belongs to washer man family she knows how to wash cloths and how to press them. Apart from the above job, she used to stitch old clothes. Totally every month she earns around Rs. 12,000. She saves money and looks after the family and educates her children. Her husband is always drink after his work everyday. When he crosses the limit, he used to torture her. She has been abused verbally and physically. Rarely he used to give money for the family. She is tolerating all his tortures only because of her children. Since they are studying well getting high score in their studies she enjoys life and she is able to manage the family. She availed all the schemes of the state government. She has 40 grams of gold chain purchased out of her savings. Since she is working in five houses during day time and do other works in her house during night to earn more, she is tired and hence she has to take leave. She has to face lot of verbal abuses from the houses where she is working. She used to tolerate all the verbal scolds because they are paying regularly. In all the houses, the house owners have evinced keen interest in the studies of her children. Her only problem is her husband and in-laws. When she refuses to give money for her husband to purchase drinks, she is beaten up by him. Till he sleeps, she used to work otherwise he will give all kinds of torture to her in the house. She gets support only from her SHG members and the women folk from the houses where she is working.

Case No. 5

Mrs. Vasanthi (name changed) (54) a repatriate from Sri Lanka settled in a village. She nurtured hope that she is going to live with her kith and kid. She was married to her close relative at the age of 20. After delivering a male baby she has decided to undergo sterilization as it is the only way by which she can escape from his husband's tortures. Later she came to know that her husband will be of no use as he wants money through her. She has decided to go for domestic work and earn her livelihood. Since she was brought up in Sri Lanka, she has been well oriented in cleanliness, sanitation and hygiene. She started working with two houses initially. A small plot was given by the government for constructing a house. She nurtured an ambition in life that she has to lead a dignified decent life by educating her son. She worked hard and learnt cooking practices in the initial stages in the houses where she worked. Quickly she learnt the skill and increased her earning through cooking food. Since her husband troubled her and abused her by suspicion she made it very clear that she do not want to live with him. Her husband went to Chennai. Thereafter, no link between her and her husband. She joined a SHG and availed loan to construct her house. Wthin five years she has constructed a small house and purchased jewels worth about one lakh rupees. Her son got a post graduate degree. She has availed all the government schemes. Her house is electrified. She has all household equipments. She is a model for many domestic workers. She cooks, clean the house, and washes the dishes in the houses where she works. She earns Rs. 20,000 per month. Her saving culture is a model for many. But her only problem is her husband. She used to help many to fix maid servants and help to settle dispute between domestic workers and house owners. She helped both. By this kind of activities she has earned a good name. She is also not aware of the Minimum Wages Act. But she strongly feels that by professionally working in the houses, one can make herself inevitable maid servant. If any maid servant is having capacity and skill, she can easily bargain with the house owners. This is the strategy she followed to enhance her salary.

Case No. 6

Eswari (62) (name changed) is working in two houses and earning Rs. 4,000 per month, she belongs to SC community working in caste Hindu houses. She does all the works from toilet cleaning to dish washing including cleaning inside the house and washing clothes. She has been working in two houses for a long. She did that work in five houses before. Now she is not able to do that job as she is old. She divorced her husband ten years ago as her daughter and son advised her to do so. She was a habitual drunkard and disturbed her throughout life by abusing her physically, mentally and sexually. Hence, she divorced. She is living in a small house purchased from her salary. Her daughter was educated up to 12th standard and got married to a caste Hindu boy working as a driver in a private company in the same town. Her son studied up to 12th standard working in a company along with her son-in-law. Since my son is also earning, with the salary he earns from the company, her house has been expanded with more facilities and amenities. Both her son and daughter are supporting her morally, she leads a peaceful life now. For about thirty years she led a life without peace. All her earnings have been wasted by her husband. Only after her son and daughter went for a job, she was able to lead a decent life. She nurtured them in a better environment. Both of them strongly advised their mother to send their father out from their house. In such a way, he has tortured her and the family. No relative or neighbour helped her when she faced problems because of her husband. She never faced any problem in the families she worked. Everyone was concerned about her and family. She worked hard and not aware of any Minimum Wages Act and she bargained with the house owners to fix her wage by telling her conditions. Everyone was cooperative towards her. They are all sympathetic to her and the kids. Now she has a house owned by her. It has all facilities including toilet and electricity. She is arranging marriage for her son. Once it is over she feels that her life responsibility is over. Since there is a demand for domestic workers, no one will disturb the domestic workers. She never faced problems from the families where she worked. She remembered the nature of help they have rendered to her family and especially for her son and daughter. She availed all the government schemes and they are very helpful to save money from her earnings.

Case No. 7

Nayaki (name changed) (63), working in three houses. Since she belonged to washer man community she used to help her husband in washing clothes collected from number of families in the place where she lives. Both she and her husband through their hard work earned some amount and saved it for future. They have one son and one daughter. Both have been educated up to 12th standard. Her daughter got married. Her son also got married. Her son is working as driver in a private soda factory. Her daughter-in-law is working as a domestic worker in five families. With the help of the family where she works she got the government assistance to build her house in her plot. Under Green House scheme of J. Jayalalitha she constructed the house. Since she and her husband has got savings, she was able to complete the house constructing with extended facilities. She has got two granddaughters and two grandsons. Both she and her husband developed an aspiration to educate all their grandchildren. Hence, all the grandchildren are studying in private schools. They spent money for their education. It is a joint family. She is managing the entire house. Her son is earning Rs. 7,000 per month. Her daughter-in-law is earning Rs. 5,000 per month and she earns Rs. 2,000 per month. Her husband earns

Rs. 10,000 by washing clothes and pressing the washed clothes. They save money through chit funds. They have bank account to get subsidy money from the government schemes. She is regularly purchasing gold for her granddaughter. She informed that she availed all government schemes that helped her to save more money. The families where she and her daughter-in-law work are good families. They provide food for both apart from the salary. Whenever they need money she used to get it from the families where she works. The problem she faces today is not from the families where she works. She faces problem because of her son. He son is a drunkard. She takes lot of efforts to correct him. Yet, he is not able to come up fully from the habit. The entire family faces problem because of his behaviour. Beyond it, it is a model family for the poor to learn how to come up in life one can learn a lot from this family. She used to argue that she developed her family only by availing all the pro-poor government schemes and through savings. Savings helped her family to come out from poverty and to achieve prosperity. She and her husband maintained good relationship with the families where they worked and got all benefits and support apart from wages. She said that their hard work richly helped the family to achieve this much development.

Conclusion

It is obvious that the domestic workers have been pushed to this job only by poverty but because of the pro-poor policies and programmes of the state government, their living conditions are far better than poor living in many other states. Though these workers are in SHG, they are not aware of the Minimum Wage Act that regulates their working conditions and wages. Their works are not professionalised. No one has got any formal training to do this work. But their conditions, nature of work, wage are depending on the nature of relationship between them and house owners. They continue their jobs now not because of the poverty alone. It prompted them to work continuously because they nurtured development aspirations and more particularly to invest in the education of their children or their grandchildren. Everyone has got determination and commitment towards a goal and mostly educating their wards. They are not free from problems. They also face problems in the work front but that number is not so high. They enhance their wages not through organisational agitations and negotiations. By using the labour market demand they bargain with the house owners and increase their salary. Only a few are getting frequent advance from the house owners. Others get monthly salary and save money mostly through chit funds. They spent huge money to educate their children through private schools. Not even a single respondent keep her wards in the house. All the respondents are having high development aspirations. They avail all the schemes and programmes of the government meant for the poor. They have bank accounts and they never keep money in the bank account as it will not fetch interest. Their living conditions are improving and they tried to lead a decent and dignified life. They are neither aware of the Act nor interested in organizing themselves as they do not have time. They have their own political affiliations. Yet, a small number of respondents have problems in the work front and in their own families. Mostly the respondents faced problems because of their husbands and in-laws and sometimes because of their sons. Two things are very clear from their narrations. One that they have strong saving culture. Second, they have strong development aspiration. Mindlessly they invest in their children's education with a hope that their life will be better and bright.

What Comes Out from Narratology?

The poor women have worked hard and earned money by facing lot of problems. But they are not able to lead life happily and peacefully. Government of Tamil Nadu has been implementing an array of pro-poor schemes and by using them all poor can come out from poverty. It is unfortunate the males in the family, whether they are husbands or sons, they are the problems for the women. Most of their earnings are wasted only by them. These women continue to work hard to educate their children. They realize the value of education. But it becomes costly as they are educating their kids in private schools. Since public schools are not functioning efficiently to educate the kids well they prefer private schools. If public schools are maintained and worked well they will save more money. Almost all have unanimously said that they need more information about the Acts related to their wages and working conditions. If they get small training from organizations and institutions on housekeeping, cooking, old age care, their capacity to earn will be enhanced. They want such organizations.

Appendix

Table 1: Social Status

Sl. No.	*Category*	*No. of Respondents*	*Percentage (%)*
1.	OBC	25	52
2.	SC	23	48
3.	FC	0	0
	Total	**48**	**100**

Source: Computed.

Table 2: House Details

Sl. No.	*Details*	*No. of Respondents*	*Percentage (%)*
1.	Own house	20	42
2.	Rented house	28	58
	Total	**48**	**100**

Source: Computed.

Table 3: Type of House

Sl. No.	*Type of house*	*No. of Respondents*	*Percentage (%)*
1.	RCC	15	31
2.	Tiled	20	42
3.	Hut	13	27
	Total	**48**	**100**

Source: Computed.

Table 4: Sanitation Toilet Facility

Sl. No.	*Facility*	*No. of Respondents*	*Percentage (%)*
1.	Individual	15	31
2.	Group	15	31
3.	None	18	38
	Total	**48**	**100**

Source: Computed.

Table 5: Water Supply

Sl. No.	*Water supply*	*No. of Respondents*	*Percentage (%)*
1.	Individual	15	31
2.	Common	33	69
	Total	**48**	**100**

Source: Computed.

Table 6: Drinking Water Supply

Sl. No.	*Drinking water*	*No. of Respondents*	*Percentage (%)*
1.	Payment basis	15	31
2.	Public tape	33	69
	Total	**48**	**100**

Source: Computed.

Table 7: Electricity Connection

Sl. No.	*Electricity*	*No. of Respondents*	*Percentage (%)*
1	Available	48	100
2	Not available	0	0
	Total	**48**	**100**

Source: Computed.

Table 8: Paying for Electricity

Sl. No.	*Payment for electricity*	*No. of Respondents*	*Percentage (%)*
1.	Paying	25	52
2.	Free current	23	48
	Total	**48**	**100**

Source: Computed.

Table 9: Provisions from Public Distribution

Sl. No.	*Provision of PDF*	*No. of Respondents*	*Percentage (%)*
1	Getting	48	100
2	Not Getting	0	0
	Total	**48**	**100**

Source: Computed.

Table 10: All the Materials from the PDS Shop

Sl. No.	*Materials*	*No. of Respondents*	*Percentage (%)*
1.	Yes	48	100
2.	No	0	0
	Total	**48**	**100**

Source: Computed.

Table 11: Bank Account

Sl. No.	*Bank account*	*No. of Respondents*	*Percentage (%)*
1.	Maintained	48	100
2.	No account	0	0
	Total	**48**	**100**

Source: Computed.

Table 12: On your Name

Sl. No.	*Name on account*	*No. of Respondents*	*Percentage (%)*
1.	Yes	48	100
2.	No	0	0
	Total	**48**	**100**

Source: Computed.

Table 13: Money in the Bank

Sl. No.	*Money in the bank*	*No. of Respondents*	*Percentage (%)*
1.	Yes available	30	63
2.	Minimum balance	18	37
	Total	**48**	**100**

Source: Computed.

Table 14: How to Save Money

Sl. No.	*Save money*	*No. of respondents*	*Percentage (%)*
1.	Through Bank	0	0
2.	Local chit fund	48	100
	Total	**48**	**100**

Source: Computed.

Table 15: Borrowed Money for Interest

Sl. No.	*Interest*	*No. of Respondents*	*Percentage (%)*
1.	Yes	17	35
2.	No	31	65
	Total	**48**	**100**

Source: Computed.

Table 16: Children in the Family

Sl. No.	*Children in the family*	*No. of Respondents*	*Percentage (%)*
1.	1–2	43	89
2.	Above	5	11
	Total	**48**	**100**

Source: Computed.

Table 17: Education of Their Children

Sl. No.	*Children's education*	*No. of Respondents*	*Percentage (%)*
1.	School	34	71
2.	College	14	29
	Total	**48**	**100**

Source: Computed.

Table 18: Do you have Gold?

Sl. No.	*Gold details*	*No. of Respondents*	*Percentage (%)*
1.	Nil	15	31
2.	Up to 2 grams	25	52
3.	Above 2.1 grams	8	17
	Total	**48**	**100**

Source: Computed.

Table 19: Do you have Any Other Asset?

Sl. No.	*Asset details*	*No. of Respondents*	*Percentage (%)*
1.	Milch animals	7	15
2.	Bike	4	8
3.	Bi-cycle	37	77
	Total	**48**	**100**

Source: Computed.

Table 20: Nature of Work

Sl. No.	*Nature of work*	*No. of Respondents*	*Percentage (%)*
1.	House cleaning—washing dishes	25	52
2.	House cleaning—washing clothes—washing dishes	12	25
3.	House cleaning—washing clothes—washing dishes—washing toilets	8	17
4.	Cooking with house cleaning	3	6
	Total	**48**	**100**

Source: Computed.

Table 21: Wage Range

Sl. No.	Wage rate	No. of Respondents	Percentage (%)
1.	Rs. 500-1000	5	10
2.	Rs. 1001-2000	8	17
3.	Rs. 2001-4000	12	25
4.	Rs. 4000 and above	23	48
	Total	**48**	**100**

Source: Computed.

Table 22: Working Details

Sl. No.	Working details	No. of Respondents	Percentage (%)
1.	Working in single house	10	21
2.	Working in two houses	15	31
3.	Working in three houses	15	31
4.	Four houses	8	17
	Total	**48**	**100**

Source: Computed.

Table 23: Working Hours

Sl. No.	Working hours	No. of Respondents	Percentage (%)
1.	2 to 5 hours	14	29
2.	5 to 8 hours	25	52
3.	8 to 10 hours	9	19
	Total	**48**	**100**

Source: Computed.

Table 24: Leave Facilities

Sl. No.	Leave details	No. of Respondents	Percentage (%)
1.	Two days in a month	30	63
2.	Three days in a month	14	29
3.	Four days in a month	4	8
	Total	**48**	**100**

Source: Computed.

Table 25: Verbal Abuse

Sl. No.	Verbal abuse	No. of Respondents	Percentage (%)
1.	Yes	22	46
2.	No	26	54
	Total	**48**	**100**

Source: Computed.

Table 26: House Owners Concern for Maid Servants

Sl. No.	*Concern for maid servants*	*No. of Respondents*	*Percentage (%)*
1.	Yes	34	71
2.	No	14	29
	Total	**48**	**100**

Source: Computed.

Table 27: Motivation for Domestic Work

Sl. No.	*Motivation for work*	*No. of Respondents*	*Percentage (%)*
1.	Poverty	32	66
2.	Works for children	10	21
3.	Development aspiration	6	13
	Total	**48**	**100**

Source: Computed.

Table 28: Health Conditions

Sl. No.	*Health condition*	*No. of Respondents*	*Percentage (%)*
1.	Normal	12	25
2.	Tired	36	75
	Total	**48**	**100**

Source: Computed.

Table 29: Age Profile

Sl. No.	*Age profile*	*No. of Respondents*	*Percentage (%)*
1.	20-30	15	31
2.	31-40	19	40
3.	41-50	10	21
4.	50 and above	4	8
	Total	**48**	**100**

Source: Computed.

Table 30: Are you in SHG?

Sl. No.	*SHG*	*No. of Respondents*	*Percentage (%)*
1.	Yes	48	100
2.	No	0	0
	Total	**48**	**100**

Source: Computed.

Table 31: Are you Aware of the Act?

Sl. No.	*Aware of the Act*	*No. of Respondents*	*Percentage (%)*
1.	Yes	0	0
2.	No	48	100
	Total	**48**	**100**

Source: Computed.

Table 32: Do You have Any Association?

Sl. No.	*Aware of association*	*No. of Respondents*	*Percentage (%)*
1.	Yes	0	0
2.	No	48	100
	Total	**48**	**100**

Source: Computed.

Table 33: Do You Find Uneasy Relations in the Family?

Sl. No.	*Relation in the family*	*No. of Respondents*	*Percentage (%)*
1.	Yes	41	85
2.	No	7	15
	Total	**48**	**100**

Source: Computed.

Table 34: Who is Responsible for the Uneasy Relations?

Sl. No.	*Reason for uneasy relation*	*No. of Respondents*	*Percentage (%)*
1.	Husband	28	58
2.	In-laws	13	27
3.	None	7	15
	Total	**48**	**100**

Source: Computed.

Table 35: Do You Bargain with the House Owners?

Sl. No.	*Bargain with owners*	*No. of Respondents*	*Percentage (%)*
1.	Yes	45	94
2.	No	3	6
	Total	**48**	**100**

Source: Computed.

Table 36: Do You Get Advance?

Sl. No.	*Advance*	*No. of respondents*	*Percentage (%)*
1.	Yes	7	15
2.	No	41	85
	Total	**48**	**100**

Source: Computed.

Table 37: Do You Find Discrimination in the House?

Sl. No.	*Discrimination in the house*	*No. of Respondents*	*Percentage (%)*
1.	Yes	15	31
2.	No	33	69
	Total	**48**	**100**

Source: Computed.

Table 38: Are You Getting All the Benefits from the Government?

Sl. No.	*Benefits from the Govt.*	*No. of Respondents*	*Percentage (%)*
1.	Yes	48	100
2.	No	0	0
	Total	**48**	**100**

Source: Computed.

Table 39: Did You Get Any Training for These Works?

Sl. No.	*Training undergone*	*No. of Respondents*	*Percentage (%)*
1.	Yes	0	0
2.	No	48	100
	Total	**48**	**100**

Source: Computed.

References

Amit Kundu (2007). "Conditions of Work and Rights of Female Domestic Workers of Kolkata", *The Indian Journal of Labour Economics*, 50 (4).

Bhatt, Ela (1989). *Shramshakti: Report of the National Commission on Self-Employed Woman and Women in the Informal Sector.*

Coelho, Karen, Venkat, T. and Chandira, K. (2013). "Housing, Homes and Domestic Work: A Study of Paid Domestic Workers from a Resettlement Colony in Chennai", *Economic and Political Weekly*, Vol. XLVIII: No. 43.

George, Sonia (2013). "Towards Recognition Through Professionalization: Organising Domestic Workers in Kerala", *Economic and Political Weekly*, Vol. XLVIII: No. 43.

Government of India (2011). *Final Report of the Task Force on Domestic Workers Realizing Decent Work*, New Delhi: Ministry of Labour and Employment.

Government of India (1988). *Shram Shakti: Report of the National Commission for Self-Employed and Informal Sector workers*, New Delhi: Ministry of Labour.

Hamid, Areeba (2006). "Domestic Workers: Harsh, Everyday Realities", *Economic and Political Weekly*, April 1st.

ILO (2012). *Domestic Workers across the World: Global and regional Statistics and the Extent of Legal Protection*, Geneva, ILO Publications.

Moghc, Kivan (2013). "Organising Domestic Workers in Pave City", *Economic and Political Weekly*, Vol. XLVIII: No. 43.

Neetha, N. (2008). "Regulating Domestic Work", *Economic and Political Weekly*, 43(37).

Neetha, N. (2013). "Minimum Wage of Domestic Workers: Mirroring Devalued House Work", *Economic and Political Weekly*, 48(43).

Sankaran, Kamala (2013). "Domestic Work, Unpaid Work and Wage Rates", *Economic and Political Weekly*, Vol. XLVIII: No. 43.

Vadageri, Bhagyashree S. and Soundari M. Hilaria (2016). "Socio-economic Problems of Domestic Labourers in Karnataka", *Indian Journal of Economics and Development* 4(4).

12

Promoting Women Empowerment and Protecting the Social Capital

Two Priorities of South Asia in General and India in Particular in the Era of Globalization

Shantilin Lazarus

Introduction

South Asia is beset with almost all forms of evils of the world even in the era of information explosion and technological innovations. For instance, our region is well known for all types of terrorism, poverty, illiteracy, ignorance, income disparity, child labour, women trafficking and above all gender inequality. In spite of these negative features, South Asians are proud of their family and moral values, joint family system, community life and social harmony. However, at one side the forces of globalization are attacking the core values of the Social capital and the other side in the name of traditional culture and blind faith the male dominated opinionated society is continuously denying gender equality to women allowing the social evils like female infanticide, dowry etc. In this context, the first part of the present chapter intends to analyse the social evils against women in the forms of infanticide and dowry system and their consequences, and suggests measures to overcome the evils. The second part focuses on the negative impacts of globalization on the Indian social capital. It cautions that if we fail to protect the social capital, the future of South Asia will be bleak. The chapter also gives some problem solving mechanisms to save the social capital of India.

Female Infanticide

Female infanticide is a major assault on women by both men and women of traditional societies. "Female infanticide is the intentionally killing of baby girls due to the preference for male babies and from the low value associated with the birth of females."[1] According to Geneva Centre for the Democratic Control of Armed Forces, infanticide is "a secret genocide being carried out against women."[2] According to Ms. Maneka Gandhi, Union Minister for Women and Child Development, "Two thousand girls are 'killed' everyday due to a preference for sons in India with most aborted or murdered just after birth."[3] If we analyse the factors for the evil, it is easy to find remedies. One of the first causes of this evil is the negative mindset of the rural community. Most of the rural women are ignorant of the ability of the girls and available opportunities in the society to develop themselves. Even before birth, the parents and the relatives prefer male children to girls. They consider boys as assets—bread winners—who will provide for the family, carry on the family name, and perform the last rites for their parents, an important ritual in many faiths in India.[4] Further, girls are considered as liabilities, because of the prevailing notorious dowry system. Secondly, having more girl children is degrading the status of the family, for they consider men as superior to girls in all walks of life. Thirdly, securing the girls from the unsecured village environment, from their own kith and kin itself is a herculean task. Fourthly, providing quality education for both boys and girls involves a lot of financial commitments. When the question of choice and priority comes, the rural, lower middle class and even parents prefer educating boys to girls. Fifthly, most of the Indian mothers give priority to the boys than girls. Sixthly, the society itself allows the disparity. Finally, there are no guaranteed empowerment measures initiated by the government. Consequently, the number of girl children in India shows a sharper decline than that of the male children.[5] The report says that now there are 948 female girls per 1000 boys and more than 3 million girls have lost their lives in India because of infanticide.

The authorities in the state of Gujarat say that female infanticide may be the main cause for the declining number of girls in the villages in the state. In one village, the officials discovered that the boys under eighteen outnumbered girls by four to one. In 3600 villages of the state, there are fewer than 800 girls for every thousand boys under six years of age. In the Amreli District of Gujarat, there are 50 girls under eighteen compared with two hundred boys.[6] Obviously, though female infanticide is rural India's shame, it is a reality. History reveals that it is impossible to eradicate this evil using law.[7] Ms. Maneka Gandhi said that the Union government has taken the initiative to protect the girls from infanticide.

that Union government's "Beti Bachao Beti Padhao" (Save the Daughter, Educate the Daughter) campaign, which aims to reverse the declining number of girls, had already shown results since its launch in January 2015.[8] Therefore, it is necessary to initiate other problem solving measures.

Dowry

Dowry refers to "the property, money, ornaments, any other form of wealth which a man or his family receives from his wife or her family at the time of marriage. Dowry is both a practice and a problem with Indian marriages.[9] In Indian society, "Dowry is the payment in cash or some kind of properties given to the bridegroom's family on their demand as a condition for marrying a girl. Generally, it includes cash, jewelry, furniture, car, household materials, properties, houses etc., all depending upon the demand of the bridegroom's family or the ability of the bride's family."[10] However, the customs differ from religion to religion and nation to nation. In some of the Islamic and Hebrew civilizations, the groom's father has to pay the gift to the bride depending upon the levels of their status. In Islam, a *Mahr* is mandatory payment in the form of money or possessions paid by the groom or by the groom's father to the bride at the time of marriage that legally becomes her property.[11] This custom creates lot of inconvenience among the poor, unemployed Muslim youth, for they are not able to get married according to their wish. This has generated a debate among the Islamic scholars and they have requested for their reduction of dowry so that unemployed men from poor families can get married.[12] Similarly, in Jewish tradition the young man's father is expected to give some gifts to the bride during the time of marriage.[13] However, as in India, Pakistan society also is severely affected by the Indian type of dowry system which is deeply affecting the unmarried women and their families.[14]

Almost all the educated, semi-educated and illiterate families are explicitly condemning and criticizing the dowry system but secretly accepting and practicing the evil when the marriage is arranged for their sons. Obviously, marriage plays an important role in human life as it is a turning point of life. Dowry leads to many problems in life after marriage and it is sprawling its tentacles far and wide in the society distressing almost every segment of the society and it is especially prevalent in Indian culture in spite of the positive factors of information explosion and awareness.

The Main Disadvantages of Dowry System are:

1. People from very poor families suffer a lot when arranging marriage for their daughters.
2. Women become mentally affected as they cannot meet the amount of dowry and they are continually tortured by the in-laws.
3. Many girls who are not getting married due to dowry problem commit suicide to avoid the misfortune and grief.
4. Some lower and middle class parents and the girls try to earn money by evil and unethical ways to meet the demand of dowry.
5. In the name of saving for dowry, the bride's parents meticulously save wealth at the cost of their other comforts.
6. Moreover, dowry creates a lot of intra-family disputes in a family of more than one girl-child. Parents should be very cautious while paying the dowry to the eldest, for the other two may also expect the same or more than that of the elder. In some families, with a lot of enthusiasm the parents arrange the marriage of their elder daughter with generous budget exhausting the scarcely available resources. However, they find it very difficult to arrange the marriage of the other younger daughters due to their inability to make more money or because of ill health. In this situation, the plight of the younger daughters are very pitiable.

Understandably, the negative impacts of dowry system are evidently effective. For instance, the National Crime Record Bureau (NCRB) figures state that 8,233 dowry deaths were reported in 2012 from various states. The statistics workout to the death per hour, but the overall conviction rate was 35.8 per cent. The most worrisome is that the number of dowry deaths has seen a steady growth between the period 2007 to 2011. While in 2007, 8093 such deaths were reported, the number rose to 8172 and 8383 in 2008 and 2009 respectively. According to Suman Nalwa, Additional Deputy Commissioner of Delhi Police (Special Unit for Women and Children), the problem is not only limited to the lower and middle class. She said that "Higher socio-economic strata are equally involved in such practices. Even the highly educated class of our society does not say 'no' to dowry. It runs deep into our social system."[15]

According to Family Counselling Centres (FCCS) in Chandigarh, dowry is a significant factor for marital discord. 36.2 per cent of the married women who approached the FCCS complain of dowry related violence. This violence is manifested in physical, emotional and economic forms. Most women turned to their parental families for help against this violence (23.3%). Only 12.1 per cent approached the police and even fewer 10.3 per cent approached NGOs. The research report reveals that in an overwhelming majority of cases 44.8 per cent, the parents submitted to the dowry demands; only one percentage filed a complaint with the police and just 15 per cent sought separation and divorce. Divorce is painful, expensive as well as destructive.[16] So many reports show that the demand for dowry exists in all religions and regions in all types of marriages (Love/arranged/love-*cum*-arranged), in all types of families (Nuclear, Joint or Joint extended). Moreover, people of economic status and educational background have demanded dowry and indulged in domestic violence when their demand had not been fulfilled. The persons indulged in domestic violence against them are husbands, followed by mother-in-law and father-in-law or all of them. The research reports also reveal that the existing laws relating to dowry prohibition have failed to curb the giving and taking of dowry and thereby reduce violence against brides.[17] Moreover, it reveals that as the dowry system is a deep-rooted social custom, it is very difficult to change the mindset of the people easily, for it is practiced traditionally generation together.

Suggestions to Overcome the Social Evils of Female Infanticide and Dowry System

As discussed above, female infanticide and dowry are notorious and secret evil practices prevailing in India. The first one intends to annihilate the girl children even before their birth (foeticide) or immediately after birth and the second evil is designed to deny the happiness and peace of young girls to enjoy their family life. Marriage plays an important role in every human life, and the success and happiness of a person depends mainly upon his happy married life. However, dowry system is systematically destroying the family system and converting the same into a hell. In this context, it is necessary to initiate multifaceted problem solving programmes. Indian experience of more than 70 years reveals that the legal means have failed to eradicate both the evils. For instance, Indian Parliament in the 12th year of Republic of India passed the Dowry Prohibition Act, 1961 (Act No. 28 of 1961) which extends to the whole of India except the state of Jammu and Kashmir which brands demanding the dowry as a punishable act.[18] Moreover, the Act suggests the state government to appoint many dowry prohibition officials and also to modify the laws according to the ground reality. The Dowry Prohibition Rules 1985 further modify the Act of 1961.[19]

It has been clearly demonstrated that the successive laws or modification of laws, punishments or severe punishments have failed to put an end to the two evils targeting the women folk.[20] Hence, it is necessary to go for a paradigm shift, restructuring the strategies, targeting the roots to the top. To address the above menace, the following problem solving measures may be imitated by the State as well as the Central governments. Firstly, free and quality education for girls from primary to higher level should be implemented. Most of the rural parents do not send their girl children to schools mainly for reasons such as, financial commitments, insecurity and lack of job opportunities and many illiterate parents consider girl children as liabilities. To address the problem, the Central and State governments can implement universal literacy programmes creating competitions at the panchayat levels. The government can give a target period to each and every panchayat giving special incentives for achieving cent per cent literacy for the girl children. To achieve the dream target, the government can take special initiative involving MNCs and other corporates to adopt a few villages mainly for building the school infrastructure. As mentioned above, this evil practice is century old and cannot be wiped out instantly. However, with the help of the local panchayat and the active involvement of the committed NGOs along with the participation of local educational institutions, we can put an end to female infanticide.

Further, the Higher Educational institutions can organize periodical leadership camps and awareness programmes for the village leaders. The governments may announce some financial incentives to the panchayats which achieve the target of cent per cent women literacy. One of main hurdles of girls' education in rural areas in India is lack of proper infrastructure in the educational institutions. For instance, many single teacher schools are functioning without any school buildings or toilets to the girls. Prime Minister Narendra Modi underlined the importance of women education and the importance of providing toilet facilities to all the schools.[21] However, it involves huge monetary commitment and dedication from the government side. To build the necessary infrastructure in the villages, Modi government can pass a law directing the MNCs and other Indian corporates to divert the social responsibility funds exclusively for the cause of building school related buildings for the next ten years,. The plan to achieve the target should be meticulously prepared and implemented with the help of the State governments. If the schools in the villages of India are blessed with modern infrastructure, automatically it will motivate the parents and the girl children towards the schools. Moreover, all the necessary facilities including financial assistance can be given to the girls who are attending schools. Mode of communication is another challenge in rural and tribal areas. In some of the states like Puducherry, the government is providing free transport facilities to all school and college going children and it motivates so many rural girls towards Higher Educational institutions. Further, the government agencies and NGOs may initiate awareness programmes about girls' education through the Women Self Help groups and the local worshipping places. If the state and local government representatives successfully utilize the worshipping places of the people to propagate the importance of women education and anti-infanticide movement, it will give a good dividend in the long run.

The second most important part of the social based initiative is to promote awareness about the importance of women property rights. At present, the Puducherry government has passed the law to reduce the property registration fee for the women, which encourages many parents and husbands to register their properties in the name of their girl children or wives. It is an encouraging sign. This model can be adopted in other parts of India. Similarly, the registration office should be modified with new laws for registration of properties, especially the common properties of the parents. It should be made mandatory to divide the properties between male and female children equally. To implement the law, the registrar office should verify the properties of every parent and should not allow any dealing without fare sharing. At present, the registration offices of all the Districts and Talukas are working as separate units having no knowledge of the holdings of the people. To create transparency, to monitor the ownership of lands and to share their properties equally between male and female children, it is necessary to create computer networking of all the property owners of India. The best answer is to prepare a centralized data bank of all the property owners of every state. It will help not only the income tax department but also the government to know the status of the people's wealth possessions to initiate adequate reforms. Any reform without ground work will not succeed. Without having sufficient data about the ownership of the properties, it is not possible to initiate any reform for equal sharing of the properties.

The third important initiative is to empower girl children with necessary job guarantee immediately after their education. At present, there are job reservations available in the name of caste—SCs, STs, OBCs and Physically Challenged. It is necessary to initiate necessary amendments in the reservation to accommodate the girl children belonging to the first generation. The best means is initiating reservation within reservation under each category of reservation. Under every reservation there should be 5 to 10 per cent reserved only for the girl children belonging to the first generation families. If this reservation is introduced, there will be a possibility for all the first generation families to send their girl children to the higher educational institutions. If the girls are assured of their job immediately after their education, they may face the world with more self-confidence.

Fourthly, teaching job up to middle school level should be reserved only for women teachers at the all India level. Some states like Tamil Nadu have introduced this scheme with some success. However, there is no reservation for the first generation girls in jobs. Fifthly, self-employment and small entrepreneurial training should be giving to the rural girl children who are studying in high school, in order to strengthen the hands of the rural women. Sixthly, periodical leadership training may be conducted for the rural girl children to build their leadership qualities, self-confidence, oratorical capacity, computer training, communication skills and language trainings. Seventhly, rural women should be encouraged to participate in sports and other cultural activities. At present, the former one day Cricket captain M.S. Doni, a tribe from Jharkhand is well known for his leadership qualities and winning abilities. Similarly, the Orissa tribal girls are making a mark in the national sports and games. There are so many untapped and hidden talents available in rural and tribal India. To explore and utilize their talents, the local and state governments should conduct periodical sports and games competitions at the rural levels creating opportunists for the girl children to reach the next levels.

Negative Impacts of Globalization on the Social Capital of Traditional Societies

Liberalization, materialism, individualism, information technology and above all freedom of choice to enjoy the life at the cost of moral values and social responsibilities are creating a society of indifference and no care attitude. Consequently, the forces of globalization are creating more and more negative impacts in the transitional societies than before. The main casualties of the negative impacts of globalization are the women and children. The author strongly believes that women can play an important role in safeguarding the social capital.

Disintegration of Family

Family which is the backbone of any society is one of the main victims of materialism and globalization. In the Western societies, most of the families are divided and disintegrated as the newly married couples do not know the art of living together. According to a report released on 11th August 2011, one in four children in the U.S. is being raised by a single parent—a percentage that has been on the rise and is higher than the other developed countries.[22] Research shows that U.S. has 25.8 per cent of children being raised by a single parent, compared to an average of 14.9 percentage across the other countries. The U.K. is the second followed by New Zealand and Greece. Spain, Italy and Luxemburg have the lowest percentages of single parent children. There are a variety of factors which account for this high percentage of single parent in the U.S., including a cultural shift towards greater acceptance of single parent child rearing. Moreover, U.S. is in lack of policies to support childcare in families, including national paid maternity leave which are common in other countries.

Most of the Western societies are facing social disorder as the family systems are disintegrated and the children being directionless and involved in different types of crimes. It has been reported that in England, 90 children are sent home every day for attacking classmates or teachers and the teachers blame the parents for failing to equip the children with good behaviour and social skills they need to cope in the classroom. Further, watching pornography has its own influence on the children that they are removed from the schools for sexual misconduct.[23] The London Riot Report reveals that most of the youth involved in violence are from broken families.[24] Children reared by both the parents rarely involve in such activities. It is observed that alienated and frustrated children who have no proper counselling are directionless and become easy prey to all forms of social evils. This shows that there is a correlation between social disorder and family system.

The disintegration of family system is clearly revealed through the growing rate of divorce. Of course, at present the divorce rate is low in India among all the countries of the world. Statistics shows that only 1 out of 100 Indian marriages end up to a divorce which is quite low when compared to America's 50 percentages of marriages turning into break-ups. The rate of divorce in India was even low in the previous decades, where only 740 marriages out of 1000 were annulled. The divorce rate in rural India is even lower when compared to that of urban areas.

The following figures reveal the divorce rate in India with respect to global divorce rate:

Sweden	54.9%	United States	54.8%
Russia	43.3%	United Kingdom	42.6%
Germany	39.4%	Israel	14.8%
Singapore	17.2%	Japan	1.9%
Sri Lanka	1.5%	India	1.1%

Although India has one of the lowest rates in the world, at about 1.1 per cent, this rate is slowly rising more so in the major cities than in the rural areas. According to marriage counsellor, Geetanjali Sharma speaking in 2011, "there's been a 100 per cent increase in divorce rates in the past five years alone."[25]

In spite of the fact that nearly hundred percentage of the marriages in India are a success, rapid urbanization and awareness of various rights instigate the divorce rate to shoot up. Empowerment of women, in one way, initiates dissolution of marriage in urban areas, as financially empowered women are now open to the option of ending the relationship rather than bearing the lifelong abuses and tortures. Moreover, the campaigns on gender equality give rise to ego clashes between the husband and the wife, especially if the wife too is the bread winner of the family.[26]

It is also observed that, according to a survey, over the past four years, the divorce rate in Delhi has almost doubled. It was also recorded that in Bangalore, 1246 cases of divorce were filed in the court that pertain to the IT sector exclusively in 2006. Bangalore has another tag to its name that India's IT city is also the divorce capital of South India. It has been reported that at least 25 divorce cases are filed everyday. Between January and June 2010, 1400 couples decided to part ways. Many of those who are filing for divorce are young typically in their late 20s and30s and work in the city's burgeoning corporate sectors.[27] In 2012, 800 divorce suits were filed in the family court. It is estimated that on an average, 7500 cases are filed in Mumbai, 9000 in Delhi and 3000 in Chennai every year. It has been estimated that Mumbai has shot up to 4138 in 2007, while cities that are acknowledged for their cultural richness are no less behind. Agro-based states like Punjab and Haryana are now witnessing an increase of 150 per cent of divorce rate since the last decade. Kerala, known to be the most literate state has experienced an increase of divorce rate by 350 per cent during the last 10 years. Around 20 years back India had a negligible divorce rate of around 5 per cent. But based on the increasing number of divorce being filed today, the divorce rate in India is expected to rise up at a faster rate by the ensuing years.[28]

Under these circumstances, the matured people all over the world should have real concern about these negative trends. The youth are directionless and it is the responsibility of the intelligentsia to show them the right path and direction. And hence the higher educational institutions should take initiatives to educate them the importance of family, art of adjustment with mutual respect, respecting and taking care of the aged and the parents, parental responsibilities, impact of divided families on the children etc. Indian family system with deep rooted traditions and values can be a model to the Western society, which will show them the importance of leading a disciplined life to save the future generation.

Growing Domestic Violence

The exploding problem of violence within our homes is termed as Domestic violence. This violence is towards someone whom we are in relationship with, be it wife, husband, son, daughter, mother, father, grand parent or any other family member. According to 'United Nation Population Fund Report' around two-third of married women are victims of domestic violence attacks and as many as 70 per cent of married women in India between the age group of 15–49 are victims of beating, rape or forced sex. In India more than 55 per cent of women suffer from domestic violence especially in the states of Bihar, Uttar Pradesh and other northern states.[29]

Domestic violence in India is endemic. Around 70 per cent of women in India are victims of domestic violence, according to Renuka Chowdhry, former Union Minister for Women and Child Development. National Crime Records Bureau reveals that a crime against a woman is committed every 3 minutes, a woman is raped every 29 minutes, a dowry death occurs every 17 minutes and one case of cruelty committed by either husband or relative of the husband occurs every 9 minutes. All these occur despite the fact that women in India are legally protected from domestic abuse under the Protection of Women from Domestic Violence Act.[30] Further, a recent data show that from 50,703, in 2003, the number of reported cases of domestic violence has gone up to 1,18,866 in 2013—an increase of 134 per cent over 10 years, far outstripping the rise in population over the same period.[31]

Mr. Bob Herbert a celebrated columnist, in his article entitled 'Everyday Crisis of Gun Violence Grips US' reveals the dark but true picture of America. He has said that since 11th September, 2001, when the country's attention understandably turned to terrorism, nearly 1,20,000 Americans have been killed in non-terror homicides, most of them committed with guns. Think about it—1,20,000 dead. That is, nearly 23 times the number of Americans killed in Iraq and Afghanistan. According to him eight kids are shot to death everyday in America and someone is killed by gun every 17 minutes.

Despite tough controls on weapons, Indians own about 40 million guns, the second highest number in the world. India remains a far less violent society than the US, at 2.78 homicides per 1,00,000 people, compared with 4.96 Americans per 1,00,000. Another interesting revelation is that India's wealthy women are increasingly buying guns to protect themselves, as reports of rapes and other violent attacks on women grow more common in the local media. The whole world is talking about waging an all-out war against terrorism though without defining it. But the worst form of terrorism is domestic terrorism or individual terrorism which cannot be won either with ultra-modern military or other modern weapon system. War against domestic terrorism or individual terrorism can be won by the educational institutions and also by each and every family. At present, in the name of education most of the institutions are producing degrees without inculcating the necessary values or moral education. The real purpose of education is human building. Human building means nation building. In this aspect, the present day curriculum fails to educate the young ones the importance of life and art of living together with a lot adjustment in the world of diversity, respecting the sentiments of others, art of running the family life, and taking care of the elders and the needy with a lot of concern. Plato said that the purpose of education is to help the students to face pain and pleasure together. Now the reports from India also give a negative picture of more and more suicides, growing number of divorces, and alarming number of deserted parents. Providing thought provoking and systematic moral education is the only cure for these ills of the present society. It is high time for the academia to go for a paradigm shift for restructuring the course curriculum to address the need of the society to save it from the social disaster.

Drug Addicts

The disintegration of family and the individualistic tendency are forcing the teenage and adolescent children of the West to find new relationship and new habits to overcome their frustration. According to statistics, 100 people die everyday as a result of drug overdose and another 6,748 people are treated in emergency departments for the misuse or abuse of drugs.[32] Moreover, the young people are the most affected by alcohol and drugs throughout the world. In America alone, more than 23 million people over the age of 12 are addicted to alcohol and other drugs. The statistics further says that most of the young people start drinking alcohol before the age of 15.[33] It further reveals that most of the drug addict teens are from the failed families who are depressed with low self-esteem and stress and complex.[34] According to UN report more than 2.5 million are dying because of alcohol abuse.[35] The World Health Organization also warns that "If current trend continues 250 million children alive today will be killed by tobacco". In India, an NGO survey reveals that 63.3 per cent parents coming for treatment were introduced to drugs at the age below 15 years. According to another report, 13.1 per cent of the people involved in drug and substance abuse in India are below 20 years. Heroin, Opium, Alcohol, Cannabis and Propoxyphene are the five most common drugs being used by children in India. A survey also shows that of all, alcohol, cannabis and opium users are 21 per cent, 3 per cent, and 0.1 per cent respectively of below the age of 18. An emerging trend about child drug abusers is the use of a cocktail of drugs through injection and often sharing the same needle, which increases the risk of HIV infection. Overall 0.4 per cent and 4.6 per cent of total treatment seekers in various states were children.[36]

As per the available statistics, the youth affected by drug addicts in India are alarmingly increasing day by day. One of the reasons for the growing number of drug addicts is the failure of family life. Therefore, it is the urgent necessity to take policy initiatives with implementable programmes to rescue the future generation from disaster. Now-a-days, throughout the world, there is awareness to create problem solving mechanisms in the form of behavioural treatment, medication, residential treatment and legal means so on and so forth.[37]

Illegitimate Children

Another negative impact of the Western materialistic life is the growing number of children born out-of-wedlock. According to *The Telegraph News*, dated 10th July, 2013[38], the proportion of children born to unmarried mothers hit a record of 47.5 per cent in 2012 in the Western countries. The figure has risen from 25 per cent in 1988 and just 11 per cent in 1979. If the trend continues at the current rate, in England alone, majority of children will be born to parents who are not married, by 2016.

In 2013, a total of 3,46,595 babies were born outside marriage in England and Wales, equivalent to 47.5 per cent.[39] Similarly, in America 75 per cent of the non-Hispanic black children were born out of wedlock in 2013. Understandably, children born out-of-wedlock is a universal problem. Though the Indian society is not seriously affected by this phenomenon, the growing number of sexual abuses, moral degradation, drug addicts, divorces and domestic violence may result into pre-marital illegitimate relationship among the youth of India. In this context, it is necessary to take preventive measures to safeguard our society from future disaster.

Growing Number of Old Age Homes

One of the negative social impacts of extreme materialistic lifestyle which is the product of globalization and liberalization is the growing number of deserted parents and the old age homes. Indian society is known for its joint family system and respecting and worshipping the elders. But the competitive world of the fittest is making the youth to lead a self-centred, no care life in most of the Western countries. Normally, Indian society does not accept its parents to live in old age homes. But the trend is changing that maintaining old age homes is becoming a business. If this trend continues, it will be a great liability for the government to open old age homes in each and every village. It involves a lot of financial commitments and human resources apart from the infrastructure which India cannot afford. The Western problem solving mechanism of establishing age old homes cannot be a solution to the Indian problem. India should find solution within its cultural framework.

According to *The New Indian Express* dated 3rd October, 2012, the number of old age homes doubled in three years. It shows the social reality in India.[40] Encouraging old age homes is not a permanent solution for the social problem of India.

Solutions for the Ills of the Society: Educating Women about their Home Building Responsibilities

The solutions for the above mentioned problems lie within the family. As mentioned earlier, women are the home builders. A virtuous woman alone can build her home. Building a home needs special training and education. The chapter suggests the following measures to protect the social capital of India:

1. School and College curriculum may be modified incorporating the importance of Women rights and sensitivity.
2. Outreach programmes can be organized in the villages by the educational institutions creating awareness about women rights in general and the property rights in particular and other privileges.
3. Special scholarships and benefits can be introduced for first generation girl children.
4. Government can take initiatives to guarantee jobs for girl graduates who belong to the first generation.
5. Moral education emphasizing the negative impacts of drugs, pre-marital relationship, and gender sensitivity, honouring and caring their parents can be part of the curriculum of school and college education.
6. Family building education like mutual respect, trust, transparency, investing the time with the children and aged should be part of High School and higher education.
7. Women should be given two week end holidays for they have more responsibility than men in home building. Similarly, there should not be any night shift work for women even in IT related companies which is destroying the essence of family foundations.

Conclusion

From the dawn of history women have been discriminated by almost all cultures and civilization and denied their social, political, cultural and economic rights. Even in the twenty first century, the traditional social evils against women like infanticide, and dowry system have been silently practiced against women folk. As suggested in this chapter, it is necessary to take holistic problem solving initiatives to put an end to the evils against women by empowering them in all walks of life. Similarly, the onslaught of the negative forces of globalization against the Indian social capital can be prevented by taking positive initiatives. As discussed, the ills of the society can be cured by building a strong family foundation and nurturing moral and ethical values.

Notes

1. Marina Porras, *Female Infanticide and Feticide.*

2. Mashru, Ram (18th January, 2012). "It's a girl: The three deadliest words in the world", *The Independent* and also see, Geneva Centre for the Democratic Control of Armed Forces, 2005 Report.
3. *Huffington Post*, 23 April, 2015.
4. *Ibid.*
5. *The Hindu*, 9th October, 2012.
6. *The Telegraph*, (London), "Infanticide May be Behind Boys outnumbering Girls in Indian Village", February 3, 2014.
7. Female Infanticide, another form of eliminating the girl child has been the practice of female infanticide. It is a deliberate and intentional act of killing a female child within one year of its birth either directly by using poisonous organic and inorganic chemicals or indirectly by deliberate neglect to feed the infant by either one of the parents or other family members or neighbours or by the midwife. Kolloor (1990) defines infanticide as, "Killing of an entirely dependent child under 'one year of age' who is killed by mother, parents or others in whose care the child is entrusted". It is unfortunate that the parents also view her as a liability. This attitude is rooted in a complex set of social, cultural, and economic factors.
8. *Huffington Post, op.cit.*
9. Haveripeth (2013). "Causes and consequences of Dowry menace in India—A Criminological Perspective", *Rijs*, Vol. II (2) www.riere.org.
10. Definition by the author of the article.
11. http://www.islamswomen.com/marriage/fiqh_of_marriage_6.php.
12. For details see; *Yemen Times*, "Scholars Call for Cut-Price Dowries, 9 February, 2012.
13. *Genesis,* 24:22.
14. Shazia Gulzar *et al.* "Dowry System in Pakistan", *Asian Economic and Financial Review*, 2 (7): 784-794.
15. *The Times of India*, September 1, 2013.
16. Ms. Mahek Singh (2013), "Dowry as a factor of violence in marriage: A study of women seeking help family counselling centers in Chandigarh", *International Journal of Advancement in Research and Technology*, Vol. II, Issue 6, June.
17. *Ibid.*
18. Dowry Prohibition Act, 20th May, 1961 bans demanding of dowry, advertisement for dowry and acceptance of dowry.
19. For details see: G.S.R.664(E), dated 19th August, 1985.
20. There are alarming reports of the baby girls being murdered even in areas where this practice did not exist earlier. *International Journal of Criminal Justice Sciences*, Vol. 1, Issue 1, January 2006. Poverty, ignorance of family planning, cost of dowry etc. have been reported as the possible causes for this crime (Tandon, 1999: 46-57). Prevalence of female infanticide, in the post-Independence period, has been reported from Madurai district of Tamil Nadu (southern India), Bihar, Orissa, Rajasthan and Maharashtra. According to Chunkath and Athreya (1997) there is a contagious 'female infanticide

belt' that starts from Madurai, extends across the districts of Dindigul, Karur, Erode, Salem, Dharmapuri to North Arcot districts of Tamil Nadu.

21. In rural areas the girls are quitting education as schools lacks toilets, The School Education Minister of Madhya Pradesh said, *Times of India*, December 9, 2014.
22. Kirsten Andersen, "The Number of US Children living single-parent homes has nearly doubled in 50 years", *Economics*, January 4, 2013.
23. For details see "Figures reveal scale of 'sexual misconduct' in schools by children as young as five", *The Independent*, 16 March, 2015.
24. David Lammy, "Riots: Where are the Fathers?" *The Christian Institute*, 12 August, 2011.
25. www.indialink.com.au/whats-responsible-for rising-divorce-rates/
26. www.indidivorce.com/divorce-rate-in-india html
27. *Ibid.*
28. *Ibid.*
29. www.legalindia.in/domestic-vilence-against-women-in-india/
30. En.wikipedia.org/wiki/*Domestic_violence_in_India*
31. www.bbc.com/news/world-asia-india-29708612
32. Centers for Disease Control and Prevention. Web-Based Injury Statistics Query and Reporting System (WISQARS) (2014) Available from URL:http://www.cdc.gov/injury/wisqars/fatal.html.
33. For details see: National Council of Alcoholism and Drug Dependence Inc.
34. American Academy of Child and Adolescent Psychiatry Report dated July 2013.
35. *Indian J. Med Res.* 137, June 2013, pp. 1021-1023.
36. www.childlineindia.org.in vulnerable Children's Issues, ChildLine 1098 day and night
37. However, the best means to address the drug related problems is family preventive measures.
38. *The Telegraph News*, 10th July, 2013.
39. *Ibid.*
40. *The New Indian Express*, 3rd October, 2012.

13

Liberalism in Dilemma

The Future of Multiculturalism and Identity

Bushra Beegom R.K. and *Samseer R.H.*

Introduction

Culture, as Aijas Ahmad notes, rather than being identified with the romantic conceptions that the term evokes has proven to be a sphere of "contention and conflict". That is, he suggests that the systems of meanings that a culture disseminate through its actors is at conflict both internally and externally. The one fundamental assumption that made possible the rise of liberalism as a political phenomenon in Europe was the possibility of developing a common system of meaning that could function above the cultural level. It essentially means the displacement of the cultural meaning systems, thus, radically re-orienting the actors into a new meaning system.

The discourses on multiculturalism are aimed at facilitating the thoughts on liberalism in new perspectives. It critcises certain blind notions propounded by classical liberalism. But, they uphold the essences of the ideology, especially, individual rights. Liberalism is a product of Western rationalism. Its progress was simultaneous with the growth of science. The technological revolutions that the progress of science gave rise to, provide impetus to the backlash that liberalism now suffer. With the technological revolution, the abstract relations became the order of the day. As the natural human emotions are increasingly replaced by the 'simulations' that the technologies offer, the demand of conceding to this distorted psycho-social reality of modernity threatens the existence of many culturally bounded communities. The communities, like species facing extinction, are striving for survival. Thanks to the post-modern theorists who revealed the real power of discourses (the discourses that organically integrate the epistemic, social and political world through the power of articulation). The possibility of a fruitful culmination of the debate depends on the discourses that can direct the debate into its own history and analyse the cause of this pivotal discontinuity (whereby multiculturalism emerged as a subject that is well equipped to confront the powerful liberalism).

At first, liberalism's trajectory feigned being a force that may weaken the cultural diversities as such and thereby act as an impetus to the democracy's progress to the 'promised' egalitarian condition. Thus, when the 'communitarians' brought out the phenomenon of 'liberalism confronting multiculturalism' in the modern societies, for the traditional liberals, it looked nothing more than "veiled forms of propaganda for a return to tribalism" or a coincidental aberration that took place in the otherwise predictable course of liberalism. The traditional Liberals who have been considering individualism the cornerstone of their discourses, views this aberration with perplexity. They are gradually grasping the fallibility of viewing individuals as mere 'utility maximiser' coldly detached from the influences of collectives that he is part of. A spate of new works in political science that deals exclusively with this confrontation evince that the modern man's fervour to regain the collective intimacies cannot to be subsided by labelling it as one among "the postmodernism's unfounded anxieties".

This chapter attempts to perceive multiculturalism as a historical phenomena. It aims to comprehensively grasp the basic tenets of the multiculturalism debate that is in vogue through analysing the discourses by Habermas, Kymlicka, and Chandran Kukathas, and tries to explore the significance of the debate in ferreting out the dynamics of the politics of difference including identity.

Multiculturalism as a Historical Phenomenon

The emergence of multiculturalism is rather a historical phenomenon. As Benedetto Croce explores, history is constructed and reconstructed by our present interest. The present interest that gives a somewhat comprehensive pattern of this return itself is a subject of history. So what really invokes this present interest in the existence of multiculturalism? It is indeed the powerful discourses on politics of difference and the consequent redefinition of the traditional notion of equality and freedom that invoked the existence of multiculturalism as a dynamic phenomenon having much say in this post-modern scenario. The earlier proponents of liberalism like Hobhouse were far-sighted as they unambiguously emphasised the fundamental role of 'organic interdependence' in an individual's quest for self-development.

If democracy is considered as a dialogue between dissenters (that seldom reaches consensus), then liberalism is that body of highly enlightened principles that directs the course of this never ending dialogue through proper rational channel. The two founding principles of liberalism are the 'primacy of reason' and the centrality of individualism. For Chandran Kukathas, Liberalism is one of the modern world's responses—indeed its most plausible response—to the fact of moral, religious and cultural diversity (Kukathas, 2004). What he implies by giving out this specific feature of liberalism is that it can still respond meaningfully and constructively to the modern world politics that is deeply entangled in the question of cultural diversity.

Liberalism once was a fountain of utopias. For a long time it could elude the challenges posed by cultural pluralism, because its defenders could opiate the masses and intellectuals by the egalitarian ends that it proclaimed to achieve. The cultural memories of the masses were either pushed off from the gaze of intellects or degraded by Western historiography. Colonial masters could successfully inculcate in their colonised subjects a deep sense of the supremacy of liberal ideas. Later, nationalism although appealed to a state culture could not get rid of the liberal ideas of the colonial masters. Instead, the founders of nation states, made it there basic principle while designing legal and political institutions. They altogether forgot the culturally diverse masses and the long-term impact that the policies and programmes produced from these liberal institutions can have on their cultural diversity. The strains of the incompatibility between the liberal ideas of the state and the cultural pluralism of the subjects sprang up as gradually intellectuals began to point out that liberal ideas of the state act in favour of the majority culture. As a reaction, the cultural critiques of liberalism strengthened. The intellectuals aimed at nothing less than what Gayatri Chakraborty Spivak upholds as one among the two great contributions of French post-structuralism, "to disclose and know the discourse of society's other" (Spivak, 1988).

In the late 1990s, the idea of the peaceful coexistence of cultures was reckoned a shattered dream with the violent emergence of the fault-lines and fissures between cultures. The conflicts ensued between cultures became an irrefutable trend in the world politics. The events were often powerful enough to influence even international relations. The increased scope and rate of international migrations and the consequent attempts to establish cultural identities in the migrated regions made multiculturalism politically more dynamic than secularism. The immigrants' attitudinal change has given fresh impetus to the rights of culture. The 'inner exclusion' [Inner Exclusion is the creation of a common identity based upon a rigid formula of politics and citizenship, one that refuses to accommodate any alternatives and imperiously demands the subordination of other aspects of citizen's identities (Taylor, 1998)] strategies which was a key instrument of nation states in pressing down the immigrant cultures from entering and influencing the mainstream culture is no longer effective or practical. The trend reveals the fragility of the global belongingness on which the sentiment of cosmopolitanism is founded.

The major argument put forward by those who condemn multiculturalism's role in determining the policies of modern nation states was that, liberal neutrality gives everybody their due, and considering the rights of particular cultural communities in deciding the policies of state apparatus would corrupt the justice and fairness that liberal neutrality promoted. In the multiculturalism war, it was soon found out that this argument is implausible as liberal neutrality in practice is not as culturally neutral as its defenders claim it to be. Now, a clear assertion can be made regarding the significance of multicultralism's: there is no going back into the conception of a state that runs on that type of liberalism that had as its prime principle culture neutrality. At this juncture, Homi K. Bhabha's remark about the culturally blind liberalism, deserves special attention:

> History has taught us, however, to be distrustful of things that run on time, like trains. It is not that liberalism does not recognise racial or sexual discrimination—it has been in the forefront of those struggles. But there is a recurrent problem with its notion of equality: liberalism contains a non-differential concept of cultural time (Bhabha, 1998).

Difference: A Prognosis

After Terry Eagleton, it can be rightly asserted that doing away with binary oppositions is the prime function of a genuine concept of equality (between identity and non-identity, sameness and difference, the individual and the universal) (Eagleton, 1998). In other words, the subjectivity and objectivity regarding liberalism must be allowed to have its own course rather than reducing them to binary oppositions. But the political feasibility of the call for the deconstruction of liberalism needs to be scrutinised in the context where liberalism itself allows identity politics to flourish by constructing 'authoritative frameworks' through discourses that necessitates the existence of the binary oppositions, especially that of sameness and difference.

The generalization of the economic and technological methods is a historical condition that defines advanced industrial societies from any other forms that existed prior to it. The dialogues on difference and identity gets critical insights when it addresses the notion of multiculturalism *vis-à-vis* this pivotal historical development. In fact, the future of multiculturalism depends on how the ideology confront the powerful abstraction that the forces of these generalizations pose in the sphere of culture. At this juncture, Touraine's notion of "combining cultural differences and economic participation" deserves critical attention. The process of 'combining' can be attempted only by those cultural groups whose values serve or are closer to the global economic systems. In other words, Touraine's principle of 'combining' blatantly ignores the rights of the least disadvantaged cultural groups who could resist to a great extent the translations of values of global economic systems into their culture. In the light of this insight, it can be asserted that the real confrontation happens not between 'liberals' and 'communitarians', but between the cultural groups who gain from the economic and technological generalizations and the cultural groups who suffer the pains of these generalizations. The generalization further alienates the latter from political and legal order. Thus, what is defined as difference conceals the expression of a complete social domination (Touraine, 2003).

Liberalism's major proponents usually set their theoretical perspectives trans-cultural. Its prime consequences are that it failed to recognise the equality of diversities and declared uniformity as its foundation. The equality of people at the level of their shared human nature is emphasised while their equality at the cultural level is not. Marion Young gives a clearer picture of what happens when cultural difference as a political paradigm is intentionally valued down. He enlists three major consequences of ignoring cultural difference in general political discourse:

> Firstly, Blindness to difference disadvantages groups whose experience, culture, and socialized capacities differ from those of privileged groups.... Secondly, blindness to difference perpetuates cultural imperialism by allowing norms expressing

> the point of view and experience of privileged groups to appear neutral and universal.... Third, this denigration of groups that deviate from an allegedly neutral standard often produces an internalized devaluation by members of those groups themselves (Young, 1990).

On Sacrificing the 'Freedom of Ancients': Habermas Responds to the Dilemma

For Habermas, classic liberalism delimited the 'meaning of equal ethical liberties' by confining it to individualist interpretations. Consequently, the most pivotal point of equal ethical liberties—'intuitions about forms of solidarity'—which gets materialised in both private and public spheres was missed out. To point out the critical need of addressing this issue Habermas relies on the Rawlsian argument regarding the existence of the normative contents in constitutional principles of a society. Rawls asserts that, even if the constitutional principles of a society could incorporate and strive towards "neutrality of aims" which is based on the contents derived from the ethics and worldviews of civil society, the neutrality cannot be maintained at a cultural level, since, no uniformity of influence that such strivings have on various cultural groups can be guaranteed. Following Rawls' contention, Habermas poses serious doubts regarding the non-existence of normative contents that favours dominant values of society in the constitutional principles. He further argues that what seems universal at the grammatical level discloses its particularistic interests at the semantic level. A normative burden, Habermas continues, imposed on various cultural groups must be subjected to assessment that takes into account "its non-neutral effects by the totality of those who have to bear the consequences". Habermas reaches the conjuncture that until the political mobilisations in relation to group rights (politics of recognition) getting prominent space along with the individual and civil rights, a political culture cannot be declared liberal. He identifies the critical gaps that exists in the realm of equality. The failure to address these critical gaps can have decisive impact on "multiculturalism" *per se*.

> The discussion of "multiculturalism" necessitates a more careful differentiation in the concept of civic equality. Discrimination or disrespect, non-presence in the public arenas of society or a collective lack of self-respect: all these are indicators of an incomplete and unequal inclusion of citizens, to whom the full

> status as members of the political community is denied.... The degree of inclusion refers to the horizontal relations among members of the political community, while the spread of the status-system concerns the vertical relations among citizens of a stratified society (Habermas, 2005).

Multiculturalism as a Context of Choice

Will Kymlicka argues for a radical revision of liberalism to include in it the preferences on which individual have only instrumental control and that largely stems from the culture he represents. Will Kymlicka retains this hope besides the fact that, liberal discourses on multiculturalism still experience the fragility of their principles of 'tolerance' when they attempt to withstand the pressure of revision (Bhabha, 1998).

The term 'minority group rights' recurs in Kymlicka`s now classic work, *Liberalism, Culture, and Community*, that deals with the confrontation between liberalism and multiculturalism. The term invariably represents the culturally diverse groups within larger societies and express their plea for recognition which is completely ignored or is given a narrower acceptance by the liberal state. His primary thesis is that liberal political theory has erred in assuming that political institutions should primarily (or only) to protecting individual rights when it was evident that how well people fared depended not only on whether they enjoyed individual protection under the law but also on whether cultural communities of which they were part were similarly protected (Kukathas, 2013). He takes issue with the false hope that the prevailing mode of liberalism could meaningfully incorporate multiculturalism as a "context of choice". One major hindrance that he finds in successfully designing such a framework is the inability to decide on the appropriate allegiance of the individual. That is whether his rights and entitlements should be legitimized on the basis of his cultural allegiance or on the basis of his citizenship in the common political community. A liberalism that allowed groups to claim rights that conflict with basic individual rights would appear to treat "respect for groups" as more important than "respect for individuals" (Tomasi, 1995). He further justifies his argument that group rights is an essential part of liberalism. To this end he invokes Rawls' conception that the idea of self-respect as the pre-condition to exercises moral power. Self-respect in turn indicates the individual's ability to freely choose from his desired 'life-plans'. The life plan an individual choose depends upon his value judgements. Now, Kymlicka asserts that people's beliefs about values are rooted in the structure of cultural communities in which people find themselves. Thus, for Kymlicka, societal cultures are important because it provide the people with "the context of choice" (Kymlicka and Marin, 1999).

On Defending the Sociological Notion of Community

Culture provides its members with options of life plans that are wanting in an exclusively liberal regime. It is wanting because outside the culture the life plans cannot be meaningful. It is the realization of this important aspect that insinuated the Indian diaspora of many European countries to stress the preservation of their culture an inalienable part of their rights. At this juncture, it is important to examine Kukathas' argument: "the basis of the community's authority is not any right of the culture to perpetuation, or even existence, but the acquiescence of its members" (Kukathas, 1992). Here, Kukathas attempts to debase the authority of communities by acceding to its members an unlimited freedom to chose whether they should remain in the community or not. Kukathas is ignoring the fact that most of the communities that are ascriptive (e.g. caste in the Indian scenario) cannot be expected to provide its members with such freedoms. It is precisely the blindness of liberalism to such pivotal characteristics of the cultural aspects of communities that gives significance to the whole multiculturalism war. Moreover, from a psycho-social point of view, the term acquiescence apart from pointing out an unfounded argument in the multiculturalism war, is diametrically opposed to the characteristics of a cultural community. Moreover, it is impossible to ferret out from the consciousness of its members the sense of acceptance of the community life which has been the driving force of their socialization process. From the perspective of the individual within the culture, however, the affordance, constraints, expectations, possibilities, and patterns may not be overtly apparent or easily verbalized, since culture is lived, and only sometimes scrutinized or described by those who live it (Lott, 1993).

Yet another argument put forward by Kukathas with the intention of reducing the significance of culture in the multiculturalism debate is that:

> Individuals invariably find themselves members of groups or associations which not only influence their conducts but also shape their loyalties and their sense of identity. Group formation is the product of environmental influences, and among these

> environmental factors are political institutions. It is not to say that culture is unimportant, but it is not fundamental, even for the constitution of group identity. Legal rights themselves be important determinants (Kukathas, 1992).

The formation of a cultural group has as its prerequisite, the making out and recognizing of its difference from other cultural groups. A group can hardly recognize its difference from other groups without relying on the particularity of the culture to which it belongs. Thus, by making this assertion, Kukathas deviate from the very logic of identity.

Open Societies and the Mutability of Culture: Whither Identity?

One of the most prominent criticism to the 'ethnic revival' comes from none other than Karl Popper. His conception of open society bear the core attributes of liberal theories, namely, 'individualism', and rationality and is deeply inspired by these theories. In Popperian terms, the enemies of an open society are those who hail community as the essential component of human lives or as he says the ones who cannot conceive of a society that runs entirely on abstract relations. Popper does criticize the organic theory of society because of its questionable universality when it comes to applying the principles to analyse the characteristics of an open society. The criticism is based on the consideration that class struggle that gives visibility to the human beings' inherent tendency to compete for social position does not correspond at any level to the features of an organism. And thereby asserts that organic theory is based on a false analogy.

Although it needs to be acknowledged that open societies resist theorising based on the principles of organic theory, the resistance cannot be seen as capable enough to sideline the relevance of the theory since Popper himself acknowledges that there can never be a society which is purely founded on abstract relations. Thus, at some point of analysis open society too will succumb to the organic theory, thus hailing the persistence of concrete relations manifested in groups:

> For although (modern) society has become abstract, the biological make-up of man has not changed much; men have social needs which they cannot satisfy in an abstract society....There never will be or can be a completely abstract or even a predominantly abstract society—no more than a

> completely rational or even a predominantly rational society. Men still form real groups and enter into real social contacts of all kinds, and try to satisfy their emotional social needs as well as they can (Popper, 1977).

He asserts that we are at a stage of transition from closed society to open society. Anthropologists have long abandoned the notion of purity of cultures. When they say, "culture must be regarded as the product of social interaction" (Cohen, 1993), it signifies the interaction between different cultures too. Thus, new ways evolve that replaces older ones. In this globalized age, where abstract social relations are rule rather than exception, the high mutability of cultural entities is a fact worth considering and it would render the impasse of liberalism a more complex one. Because the mutability will pose the question whether the members of a particular culture can retain their identity to a considerable period.

> The principle problem for multiculturalism is that any notion of group based rights stands in direct contrast to much postmodernist theorizing on identity which—with its related concepts of hybridity, syncretism, creolization and new ethnicities—highlights the "undecidability" and fluidity of much of the identity formation (May, 2003).

When Margalit and Halbertal upholds the view that, "The state is obligated to abjure its neutrality in our view not for the sake of the good of the majority, but in order to make it possible for the minority groups to retain their identity" (Margalit & Halbertal, 2004), she hopefully looks to the emerging debate on multiculturalism for a solution to the high mutability of culture and its impact on the identity of its members. As Zygmunt Bauman rightly comments:

> The moment people say "how nice it is to have an identity"—one can be pretty sure that they are no more certain that they have one, nor do they know exactly what to do to get it. One has an identity if one has no need to think of it. One becomes aware of having an identity, or of a need of having an identity, when there is something not really clear and straightforward about answering the questions "who am I" or "where to I belong"—the two questions which, for all practical intents and purposes, blend into one (Bauman, 1998).

Conclusion

The post-Cartesian subject is performative in essence (which implies that it is impossible to situate the subject's essence in definite frameworks). Thus, the individual rights of man—which has been staunchly defended by liberalism—undergoes a historical rupture. The 'freedom of the moderns' was founded on a slippery ontological condition which is positivist in nature. Multiculturalism thrives on this uncertain ontological condition. It challenges liberalism to delineate the range of individual rights that does not contradict with the cultural meaning system of which the individual is an active agent.

Liberalism that prescribed the freedom of the subject from its commitment to traditional network of relationships absolutely ignores the basic notion of social interaction—that the subject constantly represents its 'other', however, partial the representation be. In the disenchanted world of modernity, the individuals who have well-developed rational value orientations represent the people who live in traditional cultural meaning system. Such representations become highly influential when the former have access to relatively stable structures of historical narratives about the latter. These conditions are in the due course of time translated into political realm. The individual attracted to the possibility of the culture—to which he belongs—entering into the power structure of the society, try to identify himself with its meaning system. The end result is the emergence of multiculturalism. Thus, it is at this level of representation that the solution for the dilemma of liberalism be sought.

References

Bauman, Zygmunt (1998). "Identity—Then, now, what for?", *Polish Sociological Review*, No. 123, p. 205.

Bhabha, Homi K. (1998). "Culture's in between", In: *Multicultural State: Rethinking Difference and Identity* eds. David Bennett, Routledge, London, p. 30.

Cohen, Anthony P. (1993). "Culture as Identity: An Anthropologist's View", *New Literary History*, Vol. 24, No. 1, p. 196.

Habermas, Jurgen (2005). "Equal Treatment of Cultures and the Limits of Postmodern Liberalism", *The Journal of Political Philosophy*, Vol. 13, No. 1, p. 16.

Kukathas, Chandran (1992). "Are There Any Cultural Rights?", *Political Theory*, Vol. 20, No. 1, p. 118.

Kukathas, Chandran (2004). "Liberalism and Multiculturalism", In: *Contemporary Political Theory: A Reader* eds. Colin Farelly, London: Sage Publications Ltd., p. 289.

Kukathas, Chandran (2013). "Multiculturalism", In: *The Routledge Companion to Social and Political Philosophy* eds. Gerald Gaus and Fred D' Agostino, Routledge, New York, p. 506.

Kymlicka, Will, Marin, Ruth Rubio (1999). "Liberalism, Minority Rights: An Interview", *Ratio Juris*, Vol. 12, No. 2, p. 138.

Lott, Bernice E. (1993). *Multiculturalism: A Social Psychological Perspective*, UK: John Wiley & Sons Ltd., p. 12.

Margalit, A. and Halbertal, M. (2004). "Liberalism and the Right to Culture". *Social Research*, Vol. 71, No. 3, p. 530.

May, Stephen (2003). "Critical Multiculturalism", *Counterpoints*, Vol. 168, p. 204.

Popper, Karl (1977). *The Open Society and Its Enemies, Volume I: The Spell of Plato*, London: Routledge & Keagan Paul, p. 178.

Spivak, Gayatri Chakraborty (1988). "Can Subalterns Speak?", In: *Marxism and the Interpretation of Culture*, eds. C. Nelson, L. Grossberg, MacMillan Education, Basingstoke, p. 271.

Taylor, Charles (1998). "The Dynamics of Democratic Exclusion", *Journal of Democracy*, 19(4): 148-50.

Tomasi, John (1995). "Kymlicka, Liberalism, and Respect for Cultural Minorities", *Ethics*, Vol. 105, No. 3, p. 583.

Young, Iris Marion (1990). *Justice and the Politics of Difference*, Princeton University Press, Princeton, pp. 164-165.

14

Consumer Protection Rights in India

Emerging Issues and Challenges

Ashwani Kumar Dubey and *Ashutosh Pandey*

Introduction

In the early times, consumer was considered as King of the market but in the contemporary society, consumers are no longer safe against the mal-practices, such as substandard goods and unsatisfactory services. The consumer has every right to reject any product or services rendered by any manufacturer in the market and can mould them to produce goods of their choice. Indian consumers are ignorant, illiterate and do not know the role of consumption *vis-à-vis* economic system as well as quality of life. When they are ignorant of their rights, they cannot know their responsibility as consumers. Consumers in the market find themselves deceived by wrong weights and measures, adulterated and substandard products causing great damages to health. Neelkanta and Anand[1] found that people prefer to absorb and endure the wrong done to them rather than fight against injustice. This is because consumers do not know the ways and means of facing them confidently.

The Consumer Protection Act, 1986 (Act 68 of 1986) (for short, "the Act") is an innovation in the Indian context for the better protection of the consumers. The Act is a modern legislation containing substantive, procedural and limitation aspects. In pith and substance, the Act is a complete code in itself. It also contains machinery provisions for the execution of the orders passed by the various fora constituted under the Act. The enforcement provision, contained in Section 27, is the heart, soul and life of the Act.[2]

The laudable objective of the enactment of the Act was to provide cheap and quick justice without any delay whatever to the affected consuming public in the fora constituted therein. Decrees or orders obtained after a decade or two in other courts have to be executed in the manner contemplated by law under the relevant provisions of the procedural code. The fruits of such decrees or orders to be realised by resorting to execution proceedings also takes decades and decades, and by the time such orders or decrees are realised by way of execution, what comes to the litigant public is a Pyrrhic victory and nothing more. In order to make sure that that sort of a thing should not happen in the case of the execution of the orders of the various fora created under the Act, statutory provisions in the shape of Section 27 were incorporated.

The constitutional validity of Section 27 had been challenged in the writ jurisdiction of the Karnataka High Court in the case of Parmjit Singh *vs.* Union of India by its Secretary of Law and Parliamentary Affairs, New Delhi & Ors. [1999 CTJ (Karnataka High Court) (CP) 570].[3] Chief Justice R.P. Sethi, as he then was, speaking for the Bench, had struck down the proviso to Section 27 as null and void despite upholding the validity of the main provision of the said Section as being violative of Article 20(1) and Article 21 of the Constitution.

Parameshvar[4] analysed that unless consumer awareness is created, the effort of the government and voluntary organization cannot achieve the desired results. Thus, the consumer education should be given the top priority. Awareness Regarding Consumer Protection Laws can exercise more effectively towards rights and responsibility of consumers.

Findings by Heggade[5] reported that consumer cooperatives and organizations are concentrated to a large extent in urban areas. The consumer co-operatives provide the necessary protection against the exploitation of the leading community.

Consumer Protection—Whose Responsibility?

The issue of consumer protection is closely related to ethics and values. In all philosophies, Eastern or Western and in all religions, great emphasis has been laid on individual as well as social values. Even the founding fathers of the Science of Economics like Adam Smith was of the opinion that it should not teach people to be selfish. Greek philosophers like Aristotle are known for propagating the idea of good conduct for good society and good government. Multinational Companies like Coca-cola and other reputed manufacturing companies are charged with the heinous act of adulteration and selling of spurious drugs. In all walks of life, whether it is in business or services or even in noble professions of education, judiciary and medicine, the race to become rich overnight is the end and by what means has become irrelevant. Is it not a matter of shame for a human society which claims to be highly advanced and knowledgeable that an Act has to be passed to protect the consumers?[6]

In a civilized society of twenty first century, is it not a slur on our individual, social and national character that several legislations are passed which testify how unethical and characterless we are. The MRTP Act, the Consumer Protection Act, the food and drug control order, The Right to Information Act and several other provisions like that of Banking Ombudsman Scheme indicate two important aspects of social and national character of the modern times—that we are either ignorant of what is good or tolerant of whatever happens. It is obvious that these two social weaknesses of ours as a nation are no doubt responsible for erosion of ethical values and promotion of many evils including that of hypocrisy for which we are infamous in many foreign countries. What is Consumer Protection and Why? It is needless to narrate why and against what the consumers need protection. The experience of the common man as a consumer of goods or services makes him well aware of its need. The newspapers, the T.V. channels and other news media probably devote 50 per cent of their space and time narrating what is happening allaround us.

What we really need is to remove our ignorance and know our rights as citizens of a free country.

Every citizen—whether he is a labourer, industrialist, employer, employee or unemployed—is a consumer. It is, therefore, rightly said that consumer protection is citizen protection. The prevailing all-round corruption in the country has not spared any one. Consumers in the country are the worst sufferers. We have producers, manufacturers and sellers (which include Government, Corporations, Companies etc.) of various items needed everyday by citizens, on the one side, and on the other side the customers or the buyers. The relationship between the buyer and seller, their liabilities and disabilities etc. are, by and large, regulated by Law of Contract (1872) and Sale of Goods Act. But, in the proper distribution of consumable goods and when the consumer is having some grievances, these Acts are of no avail. So with a view to protect consumers, Government has enacted number of laws[7] and the latest one is the Consumer Protection Act, 1986. Law of Torts and provisions of Indian Penal Code[8] are also applied to protect the consumers.

In spite of all these Acts and various efforts made by the Government, the consumer are badly suffering. Problems of price, quality weight and measures are age-old problems. Food adulteration is rampant these days rather it is on peak. Sale of narcotic drugs and other psychotropic substances which are very harmful to the health of consumers has added fuel to the fire. Thus, today the customer is most unsecured and also the most undefended victim. Truly speaking there is no shortage of laws to safeguard customer interests in the country; in fact there are adequate, but their implementation is so poor that there is least protection available to the consumers.[9]

The problems with which the customers are suffering are almost common throughout the world. There are many countries which have come forward with some special legislation and have appointed Customers Ombudsman, Health Commissioner Ombudsman, Business Ombudsman, Commerce Ombudsman, Antitrust Ombudsman etc. to deal with such problems. Especially since Government or legislatures in many countries have been active in recognizing the need to evolve effective measures designed to protect consumers in there day-to-day transaction in the market place.[10]

Consumers' Problems in India

So, the basic problem in our country is the lack of strong will to see things done in right perspective. Even of a law is made by Parliament, the enforcement of the law is either delayed or if enforced it is enforced very lightly. No serious efforts are made for the real enforcement of the Act, say for example.[11] Broadly speaking, problems in India which affect consumers more are of three kinds, *viz.*:

1. Health Problems,
2. Drugs Problems, and
3. Food Problems.

In some countries (such as U.K., U.S.A.), with a view to deal with the health problems a special Ombudsman has been appointed. In U.K. he is known as Health Service Commissioner and in U.S.A. as Nursing Home Ombudsman. In other countries Ombudsman for Civil Affairs takes care of health problems, which includes drugs and food problems as well.

Indian Parliament passed an Act—the Consumer Protection Act, 1986[12], provides for the better protection of the interests of the consumers. It has provided for the establishment of consumer councils[13] and other authorities.[14] Through this Act, Government is trying to bring into operation an effective forum in the shape of the Central Consumer Protection Council; Consumer Redressal Forum to be known as District Forum (established by the State Government, with the prior approval of Central Government in the State by notification) and National Consumer Dispute Redressal Commission established by the Central Government by notification.

The Objective of the Central Council is to promote and protect the rights of the consumer, such as:

(i) the right to be protected against the marketing of goods which are hazardous to life and property;
(ii) the right to be informed about the quality, quantity, patency, purity, standard and price of goods so as to protect the consumer against unfair trade practice;
(iii) the right to be assured, wherever possible access to a variety of goods at comprehensive prices;
(iv) the right to be heard and to be assured that consumers interests will receive due consideration at appropriate forums;
(v) the right to seek redressal against unfair trade practices or unscrupulous exploitation of consumer; and
(iv) the right to consumer education.[15]

Besides Central Council, the District Forum, State Commission and National Commission are required to work for the redressal of the grievances of the consumers within their jurisdiction. There is also provision for appeal from District Forum to State Commission[16], from State Commission to National Commission[17] and from National Commission to the Supreme Court.[18] However, every order of a District Forum, State Commission or National Commission, shall, if no appeal has been preferred against such order under the provisions of this Act be final.[19]

Consumer Rights and Their Manifestations

Each of one of us is a consumer. Everyday we buy goods or services. While buying goods or services, we are concerned with our money, health, safety, environment etc. However, generally we feel that we are always in a sellers' market, it is because the sellers' attitude towards the consumer is take it or leave it. We, thus, feel at the receiving end. To a great extent it is true also. Consumer being the weaker party in the commercial dealing is either taken for granted or taken for a ride. Fleecing the customer has become so widespread that no share remains untouched by this malady. False or misleading advertisements or representation, bargain price, offering of gifts, prizes, contest etc., non-compliance of product safety standards, hoarding of goods etc. make us victims in one way or the other knowingly or unknowingly.

But, there is other side of the picture also, that is lack of awareness, lack of a sense of responsibility and undue feeling of helplessness on our part.

Most of us believe that we act rationally. We see ourselves as being well informed by social trends or commercial tactics. But in reality it is not so. Our buying behaviour is often irrational, influenced by social trends, sales pressure, salesmanship and advertisements. As a result, we often purchase goods or services without paying sufficient attention to price and quality. Many of us do not realize the environmental consequences of our consumption.

The anonymity of urban living has been responsible for large scale unfair trade practices on the part of the unscrupulous manufacturers and traders. As a consequence, ill-informed and unorganized consumers have to bear the brunt of exploitation by the manufacturers and traders. India is a seller's paradise being a country of shortages. Exploitation of consumers is Manifestations, therefore, more conspicuous. Legislations protecting the interests of consumers, therefore, were much too warranted.

Manifestations of Consumers' Rights

Rights of consumers manifest themselves in remedies and reliefs made available to them. Since the passing of the Consumer Protection Act, a large number of cases have been reported to the Consumer Courts and other parallel fora like MRTP Commission. In many cases, relief was made available to the consumer. Reliefs provided include replacement of defective goods, refund of excess price charged, compensation for deficiency in service, compensation for loss due to unfair practices etc.

A few exemplary cases are being presented hereunder to give you an ideal of the malpractices:

(1) A courier agreed to deliver consignment on a particular day. The goods reached there, but were quarantined for inspection there. The courier failed to inform consignor about it. It was held that this is deficiency in service. Compensation was awarded

even though the standard condition mentioned 'limited liability' up to US $ 100 only. It was held that liability clause is printed in very small print and not necessarily read by party. In any case, courier is liable for negligence and deficiency in performance of service irrespective of any clause in the contract, Sudhir Deshpande *vs.* Elbee Services Ltd. (1993) 12 CLA 68 (NCDRC).[20]

(2) Again, in Airpack Couriers (India)(P) Ltd. *vs.* Suresh, (decided on 11.03.1993)[21], NCDRC awarded compensation of Rs. 1,000, a sum mentioned as per term incorporated in the consignment note as maximum liability of courier, for loss of important papers, as nature of contents were not disclosed to the courier.

(3) In Tele-Communication Dept. *vs.* Shanmugham Chemical Industries—(1995-CS Sept. 95)[22] telephone department accepted application for telephone connection. However, after three years, the department replied that the application should be signed by working partner or all partners and not by an attorney holder. These were the internal instructions to department and outsiders cannot be aware of such instructions. It was held that rejection of application after three years creates a suspicion that the objection is not *bona fide*, but only to defeat the priority claim of applicant. In this case, departmental officers were personally asked to pay compensation of Rs. 10,000.

Certain Problems Relating to Consumers' Rights

The discussion on consumers' rights is suggestive that consumer today enjoys a good amount of statutory protection. But, even today, a large number of us remain exploited. Some of the reasons for continued exploitation are:

1. Lack of Awareness

There is an utter lack of awareness especially among rural populations of their rights and particularly the way of putting them into practice. Therefore, there is a need for spreading consumer awareness among various sections of society, particularly the illiterates and more so the helpless and unorganized sections among them. As mentioned earlier even some of the well educated consumers are neither aware of their rights as consumers nor of the existence of consumer dispute Redressal Fora. The

Government, both at the Centre and the States and voluntary organizations, in both urban and rural areas, are doing a lot and spending good amount of money for spreading this awareness. These efforts need to be strengthened by informed citizens, teachers, students and journalists in particular.

2. Responsibilities

Apart from lack of awareness there is also lack of sense of responsibility. This responsibility is of two types. One responsibility to enforce our rights and second responsibility to do our duties related to rights. It is well known fact that laws by themselves do not serve any purpose. Therefore, unless we make ourselves aware of laws, make the traders know of our awareness, have the necessary ability to lodge complaints against violation of rights and continue to follow the complaints lodged; these rights will remain only on paper.

Duties of Consumers as a Corollary to Consumers' Right

It is also a fact of social life that rights and duties are two sides of the same coin. As consumers we have two types of duties. For instance, for meaningful enforcement of rights to safety and healthy environment it is our duty to by only ISI marked goods particularly where safety is most important, for example electric/electronic items, helmets etc. similarly, for eatables, particularly, spices, oils, ghee, *atta*, our duty to buy packed foods with an AGMARK certification. The AGMARK products ensure the four rights:

(i) the right to safety;
(ii) the right to be informed;
(iii) the right to choose; and
(iv) the right to be heard. It is also our duty to check out the batch number and date of manufacturing etc. when buying packed items.

Two duties towards others, these can be called our social and ecological responsibility. It means that as consumers we should make responsible choices about our purchases and, consumption in relation to society and the environment. Pollution, exhaustion of resources, and energy the proliferation and hazardous wastes are all problems associated with irresponsible consumption. Purchase of a sub-standard vehicle emitting too much smoke affects others right for healthy environment. Overpurchasing of goods which are in short then rights to availability and fair price etc., therefore, let us not forget that the choices we make as consumers affect others and in particular the environment.

Liberalization and globalization have two key components:

(a) The effective and competitive operation of markets, and
(b) Improvement in infrastructure, environment and quality of goods and services and thus ultimately in quality of life.

Nearly two decades have passed but the impact of this Act is negligible. The non-vegetarian chocolates having worms were discovered by the consumer who went to the media, but not the Act enforcement agency. Similarly pesticides in reputed soft drinks were discovered by an NGO, not by the government.

The worst case of government in action (connivance?) is in the case of drugs, medicine and hospital instrument purchases. The Government has created food and drug authority (FDA) but the menace of spurious drugs has reached such massive proportions that it might be better not to treat an illness than to treat it. Take the case of meat and poultry industry. Both use slaughtering techniques that the extremely unhygienic. A chicken can be slaughtered any where, any time, any how; no one cares. We have dangerous levels of pesticides in our food items. Hospitals use X-rays cleaned. LPG cylinders leakages and explosion is not uncommon. Electrical wiring and gadgets are not safe. The most glaring negligence is that of bait advertising. There are advertisements in newspapers, T.V. and the latest SMS on mobiles where people are allured and duped.

If the government will not be on the consumer's side and the consumer himself shows apathy, who will help?

Of late some agencies and NGOs are coming forward to help the consumer. The government has pitched in with necessary legislations and formation of consumer forums and consumer courts at the District, State and National level. The National Consumer Disputes Redressal Commission, New Delhi, which is the apex consumer court, has launched a Legal Aid Programme in the interest of the common man, with the active cooperation of NCDRC Bar Association.

The RBI has enforced the Banking Ombudsman Scheme for redressal of grievances against deficiency of banking services. Citizen charters put up on websites provide the consumers the necessary information to make a more informed choice about various products and services with the objective of improving the quality of services. Government departments, organizations and ministries have also put up Information and Facilitation Counters/Enquiry Counters. NGOs like Centre for Science and Environment and a highly active media are furthering the crusade of quality for consumers.

The Federal Trade Commission is USA's consumer protection agency which works for the consumer to prevent fraud, deception and unfair business practices. It enhances consumer confidence by enforcing federal laws that protect consumers, empowers them with free information to help them exercise their rights and encourages them to interact. Its Bureau of Consumer Protection has seven divisions which cover the entire field of consumer protection: Advertising Practices, Consumer and Business Education, Enforcement, Financial Practices, Marketing Practices, Planning and Information, and Privacy and Identity Protection. We can surely borrow a few of these systems from the FTC to strengthen our consumers. It is true that Consumer Protection Act, 1986 is an excellent comprehensive legislation which covers all types of consumers of goods and services and protects their interests but in a country whose majority of the people live in villages, where 40 per cent of the population is illiterate as well as below poverty line, a question arises as to whom does the Act seek to protect? Even if the people are aware of the Act and its provisions, what are the means to know what is good and what is spurious and bad. In these circumstances what appears to be most important and necessary is to awake the conscience of the law enforcement authorities and agencies. All our efforts should be to bring about a change in the functioning of the law enforcing agencies and the government.

In the Writ Petition filed in the Supreme Court with regard to genetically modified food and crops, the statement of the Hon. Court is worth noting. It says "This is a scientific revolution with enormous, social, economics, environment and ethical impacts that transcend science and must be addressed. Personally, I have a hard time coping with the fact that governments mostly are the promoters of genetic engineering technology, but the point is they are also the regulators."

Let Us Sum Up

India is a country of shortages thus a sellers market. Many a times, sellers take consumers for a ride. A large number of unfair practices prevail. The Consumer Protection Act, 1986 confers six rights upon consumers, *viz.*

right to safety, right to be informed, right to choose, right to be heard, right to seek redressal and right to consumer education. Besides these statutory rights, consumers also have certain other rights including right to healthy environment, right arising out of trade codes. These rights of the consumer manifest themselves in remedies and reliefs made available to them.

In spite of certain rights having been made to consumers, exploitation of consumers continues unabated because of lack of awareness of these rights and the lack of sense of responsibility to seek enforcement of these rights.

Consumers do have certain duties also which are necessary for enforcement of their own rights. These include duty to buy ISI or AGMARK products and also not to buy polluting items.

Thus, we can say that the Consumer Protection Act, 1986 is a very important development making provisions for the establishment of Central and State Consumer Protection Councils charged with promotion and protection of the rights of consumers and creating a national network of consumer disputes redressal agency. This law also recognizes the role of consumer organizations in solving consumer's problems.

Notes

1. Neelkanta, B.C. and H.B. Anand (1992). "Educating the Consumer", *Social Welfares*, 37(11-12):5-6.
2. *The Hindu*, New Delhi, dated February 1, 2000.
3. *Parmjit Singh* vs. *Union of India* by its Secretary of Law and Parliamentary Affairs, New Delhi and Ors. [1999 CTJ (Karnataka High Court) (CP) 570].
4. Parmeshvar, K.R. (1988). "Protect Consumer against quality trichsters", *Yojana*, 32(5):29-31.
5. Heggade, O.D. (1983). "Consumer co-operatives in urban areas", *Indian Cooperative Review*, 21(2): 165-185.
6. Dr. Madhulika Agrawal, "Shodh, Samiksha aur Mulyankan", *International Research Journal*, Vol. II, Issue-5 (Nov. 08-Jan. 09).
7. Some important Laws are: The Monopolies and Restrictive Trade Practices Act, 1959; Prevention of Food Adulteration Act; the Essential Commodities Act, 1955; Indian Standard Institution Act, 1952—now the Bureau of Indian Standards Act, 1986; Drugs Control Act, 1950; The Narcotic and Psychotropic Substance Act, 1985; The Prevention of Black Marketing and Maintenance of Supply of Essential Commodities Act, 1980; Prevention of Corruption Act etc.

8. See Chapter XIII, Offences relating to Weights and Measures, Chapter XIV Offences affecting Public Health; Chapter XVII, Chapter etc.
9. See also Section 2(b) of the MP Consumer Protection Act, 1984.
10. D.J. Harland. *Some International Dimensions of the Consumer Law and Policy*, 29 July,1987, p. 454.
11. *Indian Express*, New Delhi, dated January 7, 1989.
12. Received the proceedings of the President on 24-12-1986, and published in Gazette of India, 26-12-1986.
13. The Consumer Protection Act, 1986, Section 4.
14. *Ibid.*, Section 9.
15. *Ibid.*, Section 13.
16. *Ibid.*, Section 15.
17. *Ibid.*, Section 19.
18. *Ibid.*, Section 23.
19. *Ibid.*, Section 24.
20. *Sudhir Deshpande* v. *Elbee Services Ltd.* (1993) 12 CLA, 68, (NCDRC).
21. *Airpack Couriers (India) (P) Ltd.* vs. *Suresh*, 1993.
22. *Tele-Communication Dept.* v. *Shanmugham Chemical Industries*, 1995.

15

An Evaluation of the Scheme Meant for Excluded Rural Habitations

G. Palanithurai

Introduction

Tamil Nadu is known for its pro-poor policies, schemes and programmes. From the time of Independence, the political parties in Tamil Nadu which had been in power have developed a pro-poor perspective. Schemes designed and implemented by Government of Tamil Nadu, often, serve as model for other states to follow. Pro-poor focus and intensity of reaching the people at the bottommost rung has been increasing over the years. For instance, it may be mid-day meal scheme or reservation for backward class or most backward class, Tamil Nadu is a frontrunner. The concern for the poor has deepened among the regimes on quite a competitive mode after 1967.[1]

Pro-poor schemes have been a plenty in Tamil Nadu[2] and of these 'THAI' (Tamil Nadu Village Habitations Improvement) is the one with most significant intent and impact. The State Government under the AIADMK regime launched 'THAI scheme' five years ago. Even after implementing plethora of schemes for rural upliftment, there are small hamlets and habitations which have never seen proper roads, adequate water supply for drinking purposes, street lights, and electricity in the houses. People, especially the poorest and mostly *Dalit* women, have to walk for miles to fetch drinking water from the main village. There are villages where the school going boys and girls never saw electricity either in their homes or in the street. Impoverished and aged *Dalit* men and women expose themselves to all sorts of risks if they have to go out in the nights for attending to nature's calls.

In a multi-caste society, *Dalit* women going to the main village to fetch drinking water is [socio-culturally] an unkind task to perform. Communities in the rural areas have not come up to the level of maintaining equality and equity. When a person from the side-line goes to the main village to use the commons, the dignity and self-respect of the person performing that task is always compromised. Commons in the villages are always a bone of contention. However, perhaps, the general impression about Tamil Nadu, especially outside the state is that in every village adequate resources are available; and the resources available are being used equitably by all communities. These kinds of impressions are based on short, cursory visits made by experts who do not have time to get off their cars in order to interact with the rural people. But the reality is different and shocking. Studies have proved time and again[3] that main settlement in most Gram Panchayats gets all facilities. The empirical truth underneath this statement can be laid bare, if we probe the question a little deeper: "who reside in the main villages, and where do the *dalits* and other poorer sections live?" Those in the main village are well-heeled families whose voice has played a significant role in local decision making; or dominant caste groups who capture the scheme/programme/facility as their right, as it always has been.[4] The poorer sections remain distanced and away from the visible mains.

Successive governments have made attempts to provide basic facilities to all the hamlets or villages or habitations but they could not reach out to all the habitations due to reasons, *inter alia*, the varying size of the gram panchayats ranging from 3 to 37 habitations. Even the previous government (DMK) made it clear that after implementing the *Annaithu Grama Anna Marumalarchi Thittam* (AGMT) every village ought to have adequate infrastructural facilities for the people to lead a decent human life. AGMT spent Rs. twenty five lakh in each village panchayat.[5] Even after implementing that scheme one could see the demands from the people for basic infrastructure facilities.[6] The reality is that in many villages, certain habitations have been neglected constantly while providing facilities.[7]

The AIADMK Government in the year 2012 introduced an innovative rural infrastructure development scheme which is popularly called 'THAI' (Tamil Nadu Village Habitations Improvement) to address the long felt but unattended demands of the neglected areas and segments. The basic objective of the scheme is to provide minimum infrastructure to the habitations which have remained excluded so far in providing basic infrastructure. The scheme activities have to be planned by the gram panchayats with the active involvement of the stakeholders. The above scheme is being implemented in Tamil Nadu for the past five years. Expenditure details estimated for the scheme over a period of five years are given in Table 15.1.

Table 15.1: Basic Details of the Habitations and the Funds Allocated

Sl. No.	*Habitation Range*	*No. of Village Panchayats*	*Total Population*	*Average Population per Panchayat*	*Allocation per Panchayat (Rs. in lakhs)*			*Total Requirement (Rs. in crore)*
					Minimum Basic Grant	*Additional Funds*	*Total Funds*	
1.	Below 5	6241	12534047	2008	20	0	20	1248.20
2.	5-15	5434	17392688	3201	20	10	30	1630.20
3.	16-25	637	3553429	5578	20	20	40	254.80
4.	Above 25	212	1864689	8796	20	30	50	106.00
	Total	**12524**	**35344853**	**2822**	-	-	-	**3239.20**
Fund for survey, IEC, preparatory activities and awards								160.80
Grand Total								**3400.00**

Source: Provide the source and then say 'computed by this author'.

Table 15.2: Year-wise Allocation of Funds and Activities of the Panchayats

Sl. No.	*Year*	*No. of Village Panchayats*	*No. of Habitations*	*Amount in Crores*
1.	2011-12	2,020	25,335	680.00
2.	2012-13	2,250	18,581	680.00
3.	2013-14	2,500	15,115	680.00
4.	2014-15	2,740	12,093	680.00
5.	2015-16	3,014	8,270	680.00
	Total	**12,524**	**79,394**	**3400.00**

Source: Computed.

After completion of five years since the time scheme was launched, it needs to be assessed whether it had made any difference to the quality of life of the people who got benefits under the 'THAI'. Hence, the State Planning Commission has decided to evaluate the impact of the scheme.

In this study, an attempt is made to critically analyse the objectives of the scheme; to study the planning and implementation process of the scheme and to evaluate the impact created in the life of the people who got benefits out of the scheme. With the above objectives this study has been conducted in Tamil Nadu.

Methodology

Impact Assessment Framework

For any impact analysis of rural development projects, people who received benefits out of the scheme in the rural areas are the key stakeholders to be involved right from initiating the planning process to the evaluation of the impact of the scheme.[8] Basically, the scheme details have to reach everyone. The stakeholders have to be properly sensitized because they have to participate in all the activities of the scheme from data collection, planning, prioritizing the activities, finalizing the works and carrying out the decided activities. All these steps are necessary steps but they are not sufficient.[9] Bringing them to the mainstream of development and governance activities is not a small task. Rural development schemes and programmes are not meant for the rich, but they are for the poor and the marginalised. These are the people who have always been in their livelihood struggles and they do not have time to participate in all those processes.[10] To make them to participate in the process of planning and implementation of development schemes, they are to be sensitized and facilitated.[11] In the beginning itself ownership has to be built among the stakeholders. Their daily wage has to be compensated or at least a sense has to be created that in equal measure of benefits they are also going to gain by attending the development initiatives and governance initiatives. They have to be involved in planning activities through a process of detailed discourse on development prioritization. Further, they should be involved in implementation and evaluation.

In this process any analysis of evaluation starts with triangulation, photo monitoring, transect walks and personal observation. The whole exercise revolves around the following questions: (a) whether the stakeholders recognize the changes since the inception of the project; (b) whether any learning took place as a result of the scheme among the stakeholders; and (c) what are the outcomes of the projects and the schemes in the life of the stakeholders.[12]

Stage–I : Informing the stakeholders
Stage–II : Sensitizing them for their participation
Stage–III : Enabling them for their participation in planning
Stage–IV : Their participation in decision making process
Stage–V : Their participation in the process of implementation
Stage–VI : Their participation in evaluation

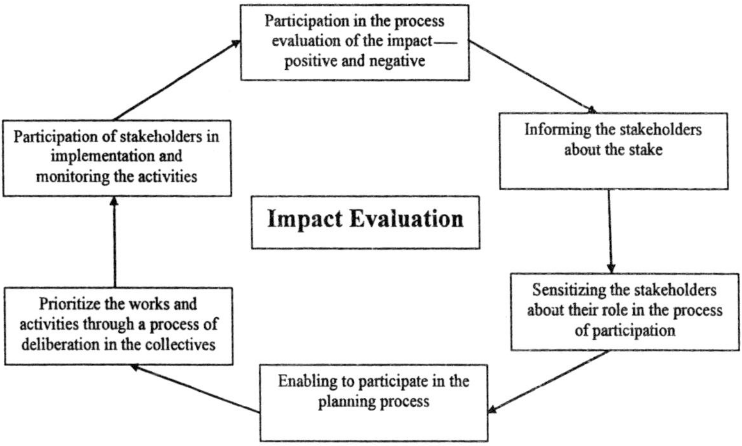

Fig. 15.1: Impact Evaluation.

A combination of methods has been adopted to collect data as it is an empirical study. Detailed one to one interaction has been conducted with officials and the elected representatives of the people in the local bodies. An exhaustive focus group discussion has been conducted with the beneficiaries of the scheme in every village panchayat. Apart from the above, a thorough verification of the records has been done. Physical verification of the infrastructure created through the scheme has been done. The whole exercise was carried in three districts, covering twelve panchayat unions and twelve gram panchayats. The gram panchayats are selected for data collection based on the following criteria: (i) range of habitations; (ii) headed by women, SC women, SC and general category of leaders; (iii) nature of the areas hills, coastal and plain. Details of the Gram Panchayats selected for data collection are given in Table 15.3.

Social backgrounds of the population of the selected village panchayats are given in Table 15.4.

From Table 15.4, one could easily understand that *dalits* are the prime beneficiaries in most of the villages.

We have drawn the beneficiaries of the scheme for Focus Group Discussions. The age, educational and occupational backgrounds of the participants are given in Table 15.5.

Prepared Activities in the Panchayats

Before starting the planning process, the officials and elected representatives involved in the plan preparation have been oriented

Table 15.3: Name of the Sample District, Panchayat Union and Village Panchayat and the Category of Reservation of Positions

Sl. No.	Sample District	Sample Union	Sample Gram Panchayat	Category of Reservation of Leadership Position in Gram Panchayats
1.	Dindigul	Athoor	Ambathurai	General
		Sanarpatti	Senthurai	Women (Gen.)
		Reddiyachatiram	Kasavanampatti	Women (Gen.)
		Kodaikkanal	Villpatti*	SC (Gen.)
2.	Pudukottai	Pudukottai	Vagavasal	General
		Thirumayam	Thulaiyanur	General
		Viralimalai	Viralur	Women (SC)
		Avudayarkovil	Mimisal**	Women (Gen.)
3.	Villupuram	Marakkanam	Singanur	Women (Gen.)
		Koliyanur	Thennamadevi	Women (SC)
		Kalrayan Hills	Vellimalai*	ST (Gen.)
		Vanur	Bommaiyarpalayam	Women (Gen.)

Note: * Hilly Village Panchayat.
** *Coastal Village Panchayat.*

Source: Computed.

Table 15.4: Population Details of Sample Gram Panchayats

Sl. No.	Name of the Gram Panchayat	Population			Scheduled Castes			Scheduled Tribes		
		Total	Male	Female	Total	Male	Female	Total	Male	Female
1.	Ambathurai	9,166	4,560	4,606	2,154	1,078	1,076	-	-	-
2.	Kasavanampatti	4,597	2,331	2,266	759	376	383	-	-	-
3.	Sendurai	15,055	7,635	7,420	1,871	924	947	-	-	-
4.	Vilpatti	15,820	7,924	7,896	4,028	2,046	1,982	221	114	107
5.	Vagavasal	3,852	1,956	1,896	790	400	390	4	2	2
6.	Thulaiyanur	5,685	2,845	2,840	1,165	575	590	2	-	2
7.	Viralur	4,090	1,987	2,103	951	471	480	1	-	1
8.	Mimisal	5,482	2,765	2,717	653	314	319	-	-	-
9.	Tennamadevi	2,842	1,446	1,396	1,104	537	567	19	11	8
10.	Singanur	3,255	1,572	1,683	2,496	1,199	1,297	-	-	-
11.	Bommayapalayam	8,266	4,095	4,171	614	295	319	4	2	2
12.	Vellimalai	6,603	3,278	3,325	14	6	8	6,363	3,167	3,196

Source: Computed from 2011 Census.

Table 15.5: Background Details of the Participants of FGD

Sl. No. Name of the Village Panchayats	No. of Participant			Age Group					Education						Occupation			
	Male	*Female*	*Total*	*Upto 25*	*26-35*	*36-45*	*46-55*	*56 above*	*Pri-mary*	*Sec.*	*Hr. Sec.*	*College*	*Technical*	*Illiterate*	*Agri.*	*Agri. Labour*	*Business*	*Others*
1. Villpatti	9	7	16	1	2	8	4	1	3	2	9	2	0	0	8	5	1	2
2. Sendurai	10	8	18	0	5	7	5	1	6	3	7	1	1	0	10	7	0	1
3. Kasavanampatti	11	3	14	2	4	2	3	3	4	2	3	2	1	1	2	3	1	8
4. Ambathurai	16	2	18	0	4	7	5	2	2	5	7	2	2	0	11	3	1	3
5. Viralur	10	5	15	2	3	7	3	0	5	1	8	0	1	0	7	4	4	0
6. Thulaiyanur	7	4	11	0	2	6	2	1	1	3	5	2	0	0	8	0	0	3
7. Mimisal	8	2	10	0	2	5	1	2	1	3	4	0	1	1	3	1	5	1
8. Vagavasal	6	2	8	0	2	2	3	1	2	2	3	1	0	0	7	0	0	1
9. Singanur	10	7	17	1	5	5	3	3	3	1	5	5	3	0	4	2	0	11
10. Bommaiyarpalayam	8	9	17	1	6	10	0	0	0	3	13	1	0	0	7	0	0	10
11. Thennamadevi	2	28	30	3	21	6	0	0	11	4	13	2	0	0	4	6	0	20
12. Vellimalai	17	13	30	0	10	15	5	0	11	3	12	0	0	4	28	0	0	2
Total	**114**	**90**	**204**	**10**	**66**	**80**	**34**	**14**	**49**	**32**	**89**	**18**	**9**	**6**	**99**	**31**	**12**	**62**

Source: Computed.

through a training programme. Since the planning and implementation of this scheme have to be done jointly by the elected representatives and the officials both have been trained. A well developed interview schedule has been used for data collection. The tool was prepared by the State Planning Commission. The tool developed by the State Planning Commission is exhaustive. Data collected through this instrument can be used by all and in future also. In such a way the tool has been designed. Preparatory exercises for data collection were done in the villages by mobilizing and sensitizing the people in the process of planning at the habitation level. People have been sensitized in such a way that it is going to help the groups so far neglected in accessing infrastructure facilities through this scheme. Here, it needs to be mentioned that in all the sensitization meetings, the officials unequivocally stressed that this scheme is meant for the habitations which have been neglected till now in providing basic minimum infrastructure facilities. It raised hope among the hopeless in the remote habitations. People in the main villages also started realizing the implications of exclusion. The officials have played an important role in convincing the people that this scheme is meant for the marginalised.

Planning Process

As per the guidelines of scheme, people from the selected hamlets participated in the planning process. The respective panchayats collected the basic data from the household and habitations for preparing the development plan. Data collection tools administered in the villages have brought volumes of data with minute details. Some of them are basic. The data collection methods and fields have been designed in such a way that the data can be used in future also. While preparing the plan details of each habitation have been analysed and works have been indentified based on the intensity of need. Technical experts too have helped the panchayats to make a thorough analysis of data to determine the works that can be carried out in the habitations. In this process works have been selected not because they are allowed in this scheme but based on the actual requirements of the people in the habitations. Works have been identified and they are prioritized when the above jobs have been done, care was taken to observe the long term implications. Decisions to identify the works were to be endorsed by a consensus evolved in the Gram Sabha. Another worth mentioning feature of the scheme lies in its flexibility to keep adequate provision for dovetailing the other schemes to be operationalised through a process of convergence, as convergence is a difficult task in rural development activities.[13] Panchayat being the responsible authority to maintain the assets created through the scheme, it has been mentioned in the scheme that all decisions have to be taken through the panchayat bodies. By doing so, it has been demonstrated that the areas populated by the marginalised, are the integral parts of the village administration and fulfilling the genuine demands of those people is also the prime responsibility of the village panchayats. They have hitherto been left out in the caste ridden hierarchical village communities. To an outside observer, the activities carried out in those habitations, will appear just like routine infrastructure facilities carried out in the villages. There is no innovation on the surface of things. But the process by which the activities have been carried out in the habitations is an eye opener for many since it will create curiosity as to how people of all segments have been involved in the decision making process. The details of the works carried out in the study villages are given in Table 15.6.

Table 15.6: Types of Work Carried Out—Water

Sl. No. Name of the Village Panchayat	Total No. of Habitation	No. of Habitation Work done	Water Supply					
			New Bore	Mini Power	Pipe Line	Hand Pump	OHT	Deepening of Well
1. Sendurai	24	6	3	4	0	0	0	0
2. Ambathurai	11	0	0	0	0	0	0	0
3. Vilpatti	26	1	0	0	1	0	0	0
4. Kasavanampati	11	9	0	4	7	0	0	0
5. Thulayanur	29	4	0	5	0	0	0	0
6. Mimisal	10	5	0	0	8	0	0	0
7. Vagavasal	16	6	0	5	1	1	1	0
8. Viralur	18	5	0	6	0	2	0	0
9. Bommaiyarpalayam	4	2	0	2	0	0	0	0
10. Singanur	3	1	0	2	0	0	1	0
11. Thannamadevi	4	1	0	2	0	0	0	0
12. Vellimalai	20	6	0	4	0	0	0	3
Total	**176**	**46**	**3**	**34**	**17**	**3**	**2**	**3**

Note 1: In all 62 water supply related works were carried out in the sample villages in 46 habitations.

Note 2: More attention was given to provide Mini power pump in 34 places and provision of Pipe Line Extension has been carried out in 17 places.

Source: Computed.

Table 15.7: Street Lights

Sl. No.	Name of the Village Panchayat	Total No. of Habitation	No. of Habitation where Work done	Street Light
1.	Sendurai	24	10	75
2.	Ambathurai	11	7	34
3.	Vilpatti	26	8	16
4.	Kasavanampati	11	6	9
5.	Thulayanur	29	8	18
6.	Mimisal	10	3	5
7.	Vagavasal	16	4	32
8.	Viralur	18	3	20
9.	Bommaiyarpalayam	4	2	13
10.	Singanur	3	2	10
11.	Thannamadevi	4	1	4
12.	Vellimalai	20	6	7
	Total	**176**	**60**	**243**

There are 243 new street lights provided in the sample villages at 60 habitations.
Source: Computed.

Table 15.8: Roads

Sl. No.	Name of the Village Panchayat	Total No. of Habitation	No. of Habitation where Works done	Road	
				CC	WBM & BT
1.	Sendurai	24	6	6 (6)	0(0)
2.	Ambathurai	11	6	10 (5)	3 (2)
3.	Vilpatti	26	9	10 (9)	19(1)
4.	Kasavanampati	11	3	0 (0)	3(3)
5.	Thulayanur	29	13	8 (8)	5 (5)
6.	Mimisal	10	5	2 (2)	3(3)
7.	Vagavasal	16	4	1 (1)	3 (3)
8.	Viralur	18	5	4 (4)	1(1)
9.	Bommaiyarpalayam	4	4	7 (4)	1(1)
10.	Singanur	3	3	3 (3)	0(0)
11.	Thannamadevi	4	1	0 (0)	1(1)
12.	Vellimalai	20	9	8 (8)	1(1)
	Total	**176**	**68**	**59 (50)**	**22 (21)**

* Number inside the parentheses shows total number of habitation.

There were 59 CC roads provided in 50 habitations.

There 22 WBM & BT roads and 2 layer WBM BT roads were provided under THAI in 21 habitations.

Source: Computed.

Table 15.9: Building Works

Sl. No.	Name of the Village Panchayat	Total No. of Habitation	No. of Habitation Work done	Buildings					
				Facilities in Cremation Ground	Bathing Ghat	Threshing Floor	Retaining Wall	Culvert	Drainage
1.	Sendurai	24	1	1(1)	0	0	0	0	0
2.	Ambathurai	11	1	1(1)	0	0	0	0	0
3.	Vilpatti	26	1	1(1)	0	0	0	0	0
4.	Kasavanampati	11	1	1(1)	0	0	0	0	0
5.	Thulayanur	29	11	1(1)	3	3	2	3	0
6.	Mimisal	10	2	1(1)	0	0	0	1	0
7.	Vagavasal	16	2	1(1)	0	0	1	0	0
8.	Viralur	18	6	6(6)	0	0	0	0	0
9.	Bommaiyarpalayam	4	1	0(0)	0	0	0	3	0
10.	Singanur	3	2	2(2)	0	0	0	0	0
11.	Thannamadevi	4	3	3(3)	0	0	0	0	0
12.	Vellimalai	20	1	1(1)	0	1	0	0	1
	Total	**176**	**32**	**19 (19)**	**3**	**4**	**3**	**7**	**1**

* Number inside the parentheses shows total no. of habitations.

There are 19 burial grounds in 19 habitations.

There are 3 bathing ghats, 4 threshing floors, 3 retaining walls at Oorani, 7 culverts and 1 drainage/culvert, provided under THAI.

Source: Computed.

RESULTS OF THE STUDY

For the first time in Tamil Nadu, after Independence, certain habitations have received regular drinking water supply to fulfil the needs of the households. Their houses have also been connected with electricity. Their streets have been improved through C.C. roads, streetlights have been provided in these areas. The people living in remote habitations had to wait for six decades to get such basic minimum facilities despite the pro-poor nature of the successive state governments. The importance of such a scheme could be realized only by those who have remained deprived of all those facilities so far.[14] For others, this scheme is only an infrastructural facilities creation. If anyone asks about utility, they are generally of multipurpose nature. But they are utilized fully. When their streets are provided with cement concrete roads, these are being used as meeting venue for women self-help groups, and many inhabitants find it comfortable to sleep on the roads. These inhabitants are mostly *Dalits* and for long they have observed the practice of sleeping in the open. When they were asked about the utility of the road, their immediate response is that they sleep comfortably on the C.C. roads. Moreover, it is a remote area. When their streets get lit, they are being used as playground for small kids. Once the streets used to be dark and dull and people's activities come to an end around six or six thirty in the evening. But now their day's activities continue up to 11 or 12 in the midnight. It has been narrated by an old man as a stakeholder that life has come to our living places, since the people of those habitations never entertained hope that they will get such facilities. Now it becomes a reality. To them it is unbelievable. Election after election, promises have been made, but nothing materialized. One senior inhabitant exclaimed, now we could not believe our own eyes as what we are seeing. We are now considered as citizens, added another villager. Their sentiments were expressed as, "someone in our government thought about us". An old man in one of the panchayat areas observed, "when many schemes were being implemented in our villages, our demands had not been considered and all along we were not considered. But now we have not demanded anything but a scheme come us by crossing many layers of power centre." It is because of the nature of the scheme 'THAI'. This scheme has given such a protection needed for them.[15] Because local elites always make design to capture programme.[16] It is an unbelievable surprise to many of the elders. Pathway to cremation ground and facilities in the cremation ground were the root cause for many caste conflicts in the villages between *dalits* and other communities. On many occasions, the *Dalits* faced hardship to burry or cremate the dead bodies of the SC communities. All these needs were attended to through this scheme. The plights of the *dalits* have been lessened and they have been relieved of such worries. Enthused by the activities in their habitations, *dalits* have started attending the meetings of Gram Sabha in large number as their hopes have been rekindled. When one notices the remote habitations with such infrastructure facilities where *dalits* are living, one gets the impression that the programme is designed to cater to the needs of the *Dalits*. One cannot measure the joy of the *dalit* women when they got pipeline for drinking water with borewell and mini pump station very near to their houses. They get enough water supply now. They fetch water whenever they need it. They save time and need not walk miles to fetch water. Unnecessary caste conflicts are also avoided. Because all along they had to walk during odd hours to fetch drinking water from the places where dominant communities were living. Time taken to fetch water has also come down from two hours to few minutes as everything is in their vicinity. When they found new roads, their happiness has increased manifold because previously these were full of wobbling and undulations and now these are smooth and clean. They got the tube lights on the roads which enabled the aged men and women to walk safely.

Till recent times, before the Government of Tamil Nadu evolved this scheme, village panchayats had received facilities but they did not reach these places because of programme capture culture.[17] Main village would get all such facilities. In the process of planning in the scheme, the involvement of the beneficiaries and others in the village panchayats resulted in huge mass mobilization while prioritizing the works for the marginalized and the neglected habitations. The panchayat representatives found it difficult to convince the people of other habitations mostly dominant communities. Addressing equity issue is not an easy task.[17] Very interestingly decisions for providing all basic infrastructure facilities to the *dalit* communities have been taken in the Gram Sabha meeting through a discourse. The lengthy deliberations brought a consensus decision. Majority in a multi-caste rural society have come to realize the plight of the marginalized and they have agreed to allow such facilities exclusively to them. It is an encouraging sign in the local governance that social justice and equity issues could be addressed through a deliberative process. Since government officials too participated in the deliberations of the Gram Sabha, they explained about the habitations in the remote areas of panchayats which have been neglected for a long. In order to provide them the basic facilities, this scheme has been introduced. This kind of official explanations in unequivocal term helped the panchayats to sensitize the people on social justice and equity issues. Even during prioritizing the works for the neglected areas, the amount is spent only for the feasible and impact making projects. The panchayats have not spent money as per their will. Since technical team has supported the village panchayats, the feasibility issue is addressed. Various stakeholders participated in the focus group discussion and endorsed that the money has been spent judiciously in this scheme. Unless it was utilized in addressing a problem, money has not been spent. The following paras convey the sentiments and views of the people in beneficiary habitations served under the scheme.

Box–I: Our voice is heard at last

Pachamuthu (name changed by the respondent himself) 83 informed that he had seen the British regimes and the governments in independent India. Many things have changed in India. But the living conditions of the *Dalits* have not changed as much as *dalits* expected. He further lamented that "road had come to our village panchayat but it failed to come to our habitation, electricity has come to our village, it did not come to our habitation, and water supply had come to our village habitations but it refused to come to our habitations. We led life by nursing the hope that someone will come and hear our plea. Now after sixty years of our Independence, this Amma has brought this 'THAI' scheme through which we have seen the electricity in our habitation, we have seen water supply to our habitation and we have seen C.C. road. It has come. We could not believe our own eyes. We feel that we are part of the society and part of our government". While making observation tears came from his eyes.

Box–II: We got benefits and we could use them now through THAI

Sowmya (name changed) has got bicycle from the Government of Tamil Nadu. She used the bicycle on the mud road up to main village to reach her school. She did not have electricity connection in her small house. Later she joined a college and thereby she got a laptop. She could not use the laptop in her house. She used the bicycle and studied up to plus two and now she is in a college. When she interacted with us she made the following observation: "I used to think why our colony is continuously denied of basic facilities such as roads, street lights, electricity connection, and piped water supply. When others are enjoying such facilities in the same village within half a kilometre. Amma enabled me to continue my studies, she further enabled me to learn computer and thereby my confidence level has gone up. I will easily get a job because of the computer knowlege. But now because of the THAI scheme our colony got all those facilities. Thanks to Amma." She did not even mention Chief Minister or J. Jayalalitha.

Box–III: Denial is accepted

Gurusamy (name changed) 74 years old, made a comment when we interacted with him on the utility of the scheme. He said that he never heard someone saying that "the *dalits* living in the remote area in the same panchayat are denied their due entitlements." This time the

(*Contd.*)

officials made it clear in the Gram Sabha that "this scheme is meant for those people who are denied access to many of the common facilities created for all to lead a decent human life." This statement I valued because over the years nobody came forward to make such a statement at the local level among the members of dominant caste groups. By hearing that statement I gained hope here is a government that works for me and realizes the feelings of the neglected and suppressed all through. Time and again our youth told us that our entitlements have to be claimed honourably. They used to lament on the provisions of the Constitution. We elders always felt that Constitution grants but community at the local level denies our share and entitlements. This scheme has brought a message to all that everyone has got his or her own entitlements. Really one has to be thankful to 'Amma' for her imaginative scheme to reach out to us."

Box–IV: Community is not communal

While interacting with an official who was involved with scheme, a significant observation was made based on his experience. He said that the community is not communal. "When the scheme was explained to the people of all caste groups, initially many made hue and cry. But when the officials patiently allowed them to express their opinion and argued with them the plight of the neglected segments in the same village in accessing the commons, many realized the plight of the *Dalits* living in the same village and working for them. What they need is information, deliberation, discourse, and patient hearing. In this scheme, panchayat is involved, Gram Sabha is involved, other line department officials are involved in planning and prioritizing the works to be executed in the village. People initially resist but later they understand through a process of deliberation. At the community level no effort is made to convert the Gram Sabha into deliberative and discourse body rather than keeping it as mutespectators' body."

Box–V: Lifelong misery comes to an end

Karupayee (name changed) a farm labourer aged 67, made an observation about this scheme and its implication. "As a *Dalit* I have to face volley of problems while living in a multicaste village panchayat. Being a woman, the problem is compounded and complicated. We are living in a remote area where there is no drinking water facility. When I got married 47 years ago I walked for about four miles to fetch water. Of course, at that point of time there was tank meant for it. We were allotted a share from the same tank, from which we had to draw our water. From that day onwards we had been walking at least

(*Contd.*)

three kilometres a day to fetch water, we could not get water as it is the last point and water was channelized towards our area after giving water to all other habitations. When we are unable to get adequate water, we have to walk down to main villages to fetch water for drinking purposes. While we go there we are treated badly by the elderly conservative women in the main village. Our dignity is always at stake. Now through this scheme we get water at our place as there is a mini pump fixed at our village. At one stroke our fate has been changed. Now within minutes I can get water to my need and quality and at my time. I am thankful to 'Amma' as she felt our miseries."

Box–VI: Now equality in Graveyard

Sukumar (name changed) 43, a *Dalit* working in a farm as farm labourer said that many a times he witnessed the ordeal that the *Dalit* families faced in this village while carrying the dead bodies to the cremation ground through a private land. Every time they cross the land of the owner, the *Dalit* families have to take permission. Granting permission is not regular. The *Dalits* have been at the mercy of the landlord. But now that problem has been solved by creating a road to reach the cremation ground. Yet another remarkable achievement made through this scheme is providing water facility and a shelter in the cremation ground meant for the *Dalits*. The above two facilities existed in the cremation ground meant for the dominant castes. But we did not have such facilities. This discrimination was ended by providing the above facilities in the cremation grounds meant for *Dalits*. Now we find equality at least at the last resting place. This kind of facilities provided to the *Dalits* made us think of the sensitivity of the government towards the plight of the *Dalits*. Now our worry is over.

Conclusion

"THAI" scheme is unique because of its objective to reach the unreached. Through the process of planning at the panchayat and keeping the focus on habitation as a planning unit, the apparent neglect of such areas are made visible and people of that village panchayat become sensitive to the issues of exclusion and marginalization. Without looking at the face of the beneficiaries, if one looks at the table it appears nothing more than spending money for laying roads to burial ground, providing streetlights, installing drinking water systems which are routine infrastructure facilities. But the noticeable fact is that all the above facilities have been created for the people who have been neglected for the past several years. In every Gram Panchayat money has been spent through a series of development schemes. But certain segments of the society have remained neglected. These neglected segments are the target groups for this scheme. Yet, it is not solely a target oriented scheme. It is both target and process oriented scheme in the sense, that it ensures felt needs of the people are attended to and in this process affected groups are involved at the planning stage. When the planning process was initiated from below, people from all sections and segments have been sensitized on the issues of exclusion. Tamil Nadu is pioneer in addressing the issues of the poor. Innovative pro-poor schemes have been implemented in Tamil Nadu earlier also. It is a model to other states. Likewise this "THAI" scheme is also a pioneering model to address the infrastructural issues of the marginalised.

The experience gained from planning and implementation of scheme will be very useful for introducing integrated development planning as well as for claiming the 14th Finance Commission awards for panchayats. The greater participation of the *Dalits* and other marginalised groups in the Gram Sabha meetings is yet another interesting feature one could observe in the process of planning and implementation of the scheme. Now they not only attend Gram Sabha meeting but also any other meeting organised by the panchayats. If one traces the reasons for such participation one could easily find out that this scheme has given hopes to the hopeless. They have found the benefit, scope and potentials of their participation. They get enormous information from the officials who attend the Gram Sabha meetings. Through their interaction with the officials they get to know the details about facilities and opportunities in other rural development schemes and programmes to improve the conditions of life of the *Dalits* and other marginalized groups.

This scheme goes a long way in restoring the dignity of people. Women who walked to fetch water for drinking purposes in the main village met with different kinds of unpleasant experiences, the main affront being verbal abuses by the caste Hindus. No doubt water is a common good meant for every household, but the source is in the main village dominated by the caste Hindus. But now they get water in their neighbourhood, which is also a succor to their self-respect and dignity. To cremate their dead, the *Dalits* had to walk to the cremation ground through the passage across the land of higher caste people. On every occasion they needed to seek permission from the landlord before carrying the dead bodies through their fields. This was a constant source of discomfiture and conflict. By laying separate road to the cremation grounds, their long pending demand has been met. In the same way, the

Dalits found difficulty in accessing facilities created in the cremation ground meant for the caste Hindus. Cremations during rainy season added to their miseries because, till the completion of the burial work, they had to stand in rains. The shelter created in the cremation ground meant for the caste Hindus cannot be used. They faced similar distress and difficulty in scorching heat during the hot summer days. Now water facilities have been created in the cremation ground meant for the *Dalits*. It has been a long pending demand but fulfilled through this scheme. The amount spent is not huge. But what the *Dalits* got through this scheme is the acknowledgement of their right to dignity. Now they feel the self-respect of the *Dalit* poor is intact.

The need of the hour will be to sustain the spirit and enthusiasm with which the scheme has been launched. The first five-year phase has meant a lot for the deprived people not only in terms of the basic facilities but more importantly for the sense of social inclusion which is writ large on the faces of beneficiaries spread across the state. The scheme has introduced innovations in planning and implementations. These innovations need to be sustained, fine-tuned and institutionalized. Funds are channelized to rural local bodies for development through a host of schemes and programmes, the experiences of THAI should be guiding spirit to utilize these resources equitably to fulfil the avowed objective of social justice.

Notes

1. In 1967 because of shortage of rice in public distribution system and in the open market, the opposition parties made it an election issue which had overthrown the Indian National Congress from power. It was a politics around rice. From 1967 onwards political regimes are sensitive on food especially rice.
2. At present the Central schemes are downsizing. But pro-poor schemes are increasing in Tamil Nadu. For details of the schemes refer to G. Palanithurai, *New Panchayati Raj System in Tamil Nadu: Act, Rules and Schemes* (in Tamil), Chennai: South Vision, 2012.
3. G. Palanithurai (2012). *Status of Dalits and Dalit Representatives in Rural Local Bodies*, New Delhi: Concept Publishing Company Pvt. Ltd.
4. Pranab Bardhan and Dilip Mookherjee (2000), "Capture and governance at local and national levels", *The American Economic Review*, 90(2): 134-139.
5. Government of Tamil Nadu, Rural Development Department, Website: www.tnrd.gov.in

6. Service Delivery Study.
7. S. Chandra, (2006). "Our Villages: Ground Realities and Future Prospects", In: Y.P. Singh (ed.), *Indian Village: 2020*, Vol. I, New Delhi: Concept Publishing Company Pvt. Ltd., pp. 104-110.
8. C. Roche (1999). *Impact Assessment for Development Agencies*, Bangalore: Oxfam.
9. Hoshiar Singh, (ed.) (1995). *Rural Development in India: Evaluative Studies in Policies and Programmes*, Jaipur: Printwell Publishers.
10. T. Scarlelt Epsteni, A.P. Suryanarayana and T. Thimmegowda (1998). *Village Voices. Forty Years of Rural Transformation in South India*, New Delhi: Sage Publications.
11. S. Paul (1987). "Community Participation in Development Projects" Discussion Paper No. 6, Washington DC: World Bank.
12. Katar Singh (2000). *Rural Development*, New Delhi: Sage Publications.
13. Kamal Taori (2006). "Convergence of Delivery System in Rural Areas", In: Y.P. Singh (ed.), *Indian Village: 2020*, Vol. I, New Delhi: Concept Publishing Company Pvt. Ltd., pp. 147-150.
14. Benjamin Powis (2007). *Systems of Capture: Reassessing the Threat of Local Elites*, (Social Development Paper no. 109). Washington DC: World Bank.
15. World Bank, (2011). *Social Protection for a Changing India*, Vol. II, New Delhi: World Bank.
16. J.P. Plattean (2008). *Information Distortion, Elite Capture and Task Complexity in Decentralised Development*, Belgium: University of Namur, Centre for Research on the Economics of Development.
17. G. Sreedhar and D. Rajasekhar (2014). *Rural Development in India: Strategies and Processes*, New Delhi: Concept Publishing Company Pvt. Ltd.

Section III

Environmental Justice and Entrepreneurial Development

16

Environmental Justice Discourses in India

Alternative Voices against Hierarchy, Patriarchy, and Inequality

Rajnish Saryal

The study of environment is a story of a relationship which mankind has with nature. Environment is constituted of all that nature bestows upon mankind. Nature does not distinguish and discriminate among its users and its resources are free for all to use. However, man has been consistently abusing nature by indiscriminately harnessing it and trying to secure full control over it. The indiscriminate development and industrialization has endangered the wholesomeness of the environment to a dreadful extent. Although everyone suffers the effects of pollution, global warming, and resource exploitation, it is well established that poor people are most vulnerable since they are less able to offset the effects of environmental degradation (Das, 2015; Ockwell and Mallett, 2012).

The recent water crisis in most parts of India and the long spell of heat wave above normal in the most parts of the north; north-west and central India during the summer of 2016 is a glaring example of global warming.[1] The worst affected are those who are poor and are not responsible for climate change.[2] The structure of modern development is such that poor are forced to pay the cost of development. The metabolism of modern industries is such that they require large quantity of natural resources to produce the symbols of development. These symbols do not fulfil the necessities of poor rather they pay in terms of shedding off their share to those natural resources which are pumped into the modern industries. For example, the potato chips that are produced with the inputs of huge raw material (potato, fuels etc.) do not cater to the survival needs of poor but the appetite of rich and capitalists. The production of such non-essential items leads to escalation of price of raw material and thus, eventually become out of reach of poor. Second, the poor also pay or bear the cost of industrial side effects. The poor who most often live on the margins or in the periphery of industrial hubs are ill-equipped to deal with industrial waste. Sometimes, the industrial waste is intentionally dumped near the site of habitation of poor people as they can hardly resist against this practice or they are meagrely paid for accepting industrial waste. This is a phenomenon that can be witnessed world-wide both at the national level and at the international level. In most of the cases, the poor people and the least developing countries accept dumping of industrial waste from the rich and developed countries simply to satisfy their immediate survival needs but they could hardly anticipate the long term effects of this hazardous waste. This is a plain case of environmental injustice. Over the period of time, a definitive vocabulary has developed to define and explain the cases of environmental injustice. In India, the Centre for Science and Environment, an ecological NGO has played a catalytic role in developing the concept like *Environmentalism of the Poor* and *Climate Justice* to highlight injustice done to the poor in cases of conflicts arising on account of ecological distribution (Martinez-Alier, *et al.*, 2016).

Throughout the world poor communities organized themselves to fight for environmental justice with the central idea for more equitable access to natural resources and environmental quality, including clean air and water, a 'right' based approach to environmental justice. The right based approach to environmental justice started in India with the active role of judiciary in environmental issues. A landmark judgement by the Supreme Court of India in *Subhash Kumar* vs. *State of Bihar* case is considered a cornerstone in the environmental justice movement in India. The Supreme Court observed that "right to live is a fundamental right under Article 21 of the Constitution, and it includes the right of enjoyment of pollution free water and air for full enjoyment of life." This judicial activism in environmental issues paved the way for series of protests and lawsuits by thousands of NGOs and advocacy groups on behalf of poor and vulnerable people. The issue of environmental justice, thus, appeared significantly in various environmental debates both at national and international level.

The proponents of environmental justice movement particularly focus on the existence of inequity in the distribution of likely benefits and burdens of any development project having its bearing on environment. Therefore, they demand the adoption of some criterion of distribution that takes into consideration the environmental cost and the social realities of poor people who are the major sufferer of environmental destruction. This chapter is an attempt to outline the discourse of environmental justice in India. Indian environmental justice discourse revolves around the concept of equity, fairness, survival needs and good governance. This is, however, different from that of the Western concept of environmental justice. The Indian concept of environmental justice focuses on the rights of poor peoples on natural resources in an equitable and just manner while the proponents of the Western concept of environmental justice raise their voices against the environmental pollution and its effects on the marginalised groups. Environmental justice movements in India are not for green or clean earth but for the very survival of the poor (Guha and Martinez-Alier, 1997; 2002).

Environmental Justice: Origin and Development

Environmentalism as a general term denotes various activities having their primary concern for the conservation, protection and improvement of natural environment. The publications of various reports and books on the subject like: *Silent Spring* (Carson, 1962), *Unsafe at Any Speed* (Nader, 1968) and *The Greening of America* (Reich, 1970) articulated the various environmental agenda in the Western World. All these publications focused on the apathy and silence of those who stood and watched the destruction occurring through the massive destruction of forests and wildlife, irresponsible spread of chemicals in nature and food chain and the gradual effacing of the community resource systems. With the gradual destruction and disappearance of the community resources, the first to be lost with them are those grassroots, aborigines and subaltern communities which had survived upon them through ages. Accordingly, a movement for environmental justice by these communities started all-over the World. The Environmental justice movement focused on the disproportionate sharing of environmental benefits and burden among different categories of person. Peter Wenz claims that environmental justice focuses "on the distribution of benefits and burdens among all of those affected by environmentally related decisions and actions" (Wenz, 1988:4). Similarly, Troy Hartley claims that environmental justice is "the fair distribution of environmental quality." (Hartley, 1995:287). Environmental justice is either stated or assumed to be about the fair or equitable distribution of environmental goods, services, and "resources". The first principle of environmental justice affirms the "sacredness of

Mother Earth, ecological unity, and the interdependence of all species" (Lee, 1992). Later, Julian Agyeman's (2003, 2005) work moved to bridge the differing ideas about environment and justice into a conception of 'just sustainability'. The studies that deals with the issue of environmental justice concern with the distribution of, and access to, resources, knowledge, power, representation and a clean, healthy living environment.

The concept of 'environmental justice', as it is presently understood, is by and large the consequence of the activities undertaken by the coloured and other marginalised groups in the USA. These groups have opposed the dumping of industrial waste from the factories and waste sites in residential areas inhabited primarily by the blacks and indigenous peoples. The U.S. Environmental Protection Agency (EPA) defines environmental justice as the "fair treatment for people of all races, cultures, and incomes, regarding the development of environmental laws, regulations, and policies" (Schlosberg, 2013:37-42). In 1994, the issue reached the White House when President Clinton issued Executive Order 12898: Federal Actions to Address Environmental Justice in Minority Populations and Low-Income Populations. This order reinforces the thirty year old Civil Rights Act of 1964 by requiring federal regulatory agencies to "make environmental justice a part of all they do" Activism and intellectual discourse on environmental justice in the US have led the way in developing the environmental justice approach in other parts of the world.

Environmental Justice in India

Environmental movements in India have grown particularly in the aftermath of Stockholm Conference in 1972 on 'Human Environment.' These movements were different in their character from that of their Western counterparts and had generally been designated as 'environmentalism of the poor' (Guha and Martinez-Alier, 1998). The Indian environmentalists focused more specifically on the questions of marginality, equity and patriarchal nature of the social order. The social order of a given society is based on the collective wisdom of inhabitants, although the collectivity is hard to achieve and is generally represented the majority. Every society try to justify its pattern of distribution of natural resources as well as the cost and benefits of developmental process as per its social order. The proponents of environmental justice, however, question the criterion of justification of distribution of natural resources conforming to the parameters of a given social order since the marginal groups or the ecological refugees hardly find place in that social order.

The idea of justice too is not a static phenomenon. It is a relative concept and keeps on changing with the change of time, space, culture, language etc. One thing, however, must bear in mind that the central component of justice is the criterion of 'right'. Each society with its own level of development of human faculty tries to define justice from the standpoint of its understanding of 'what is right?' Here, the usage of the term society does not explain the collective wisdom of the people because as I explained earlier collectivity is hard to obtain, it only represents wisdom of the majority. The scope for alternative worldview about the criterion of justice, therefore, always remains there not only between the societies but also within the society. The proponents of alternative worldview of justice emphasized on the need to dismantle the unjust social order by advocating their own scheme of distribution. The different environmental movements in India questioned the distribution pattern of natural resources and benefits and burdens of developmental process from their distinct perspective and advocate their own scheme of distribution.

In India, the diverse ideological strands represent the rich discourse of environmental justice in Indian. They represent the major intellectual underpinnings of Indian environmental justice movements. These movements drive their influence from Gandhian, Marxist and Eco-feminist ideas.

Rights of Native People in Resource Management

Environmental justice movements in India advocate the rights of native people in natural resource management. The central idea is that nature has bestowed its fruits on the mankind in common. Therefore, the share of natural resources should be based on equity and justice. The views of Mohandas Karamchand Gandhi—the Father of Indian Nation, on imperialism, Westernisation, resource use, rural reconstruction, ethics for simple living, village self-reliance etc. provide strong ideological underpinnings to this belief of ecological distribution. The environmental justice movements in India that advocate the distribution of fair ecological distribution of cost and benefits drive their ideological support from Gandhian views. The leaders of all these movements are highly influenced by the life and works of Gandhi. Gandhian ideology is held to be the site of inspiration for the supporters of almost all the social movements striving for the establishment of egalitarian society not only in India but also in the world at large.

Gandhian ideas on rural reconstruction and village self-reliance provide alternative worldview to the mainstream thinking on issues of distribution and justice. Ramachandra Guha called this strand of environmentalism *Crusading Gandhian* that, "rely heavily on a religious idiom in its rejection of the modern way of life. It upholds the pre-capitalist and pre-colonial village community as the exemplar of ecological and social harmony: Gandhi's invocation of Ram Rajya being taken literally, rather than metaphorically" (Guha, 1988:2578).

Gandhi had a great vision about India and her development. Gandhi, in fact, recognized the use of renewable sources of energy, evils of large-scale industrialization and dangers of environmental pollution eight decades ago, as he put more emphasis on non-violent development of village economy and the utilization of labour-intensive technique of production. In modern terminology, Gandhi's strategy is modified in terms of pattern of growth, with more emphasis on the use of renewable resources and a minimum utilization of non-renewable resources. Though concern for the environment was not the focus of such prescriptions, yet such strategy helped to minimize the degradation of environment. The Gandhian prescription of 'simple living' also attempts to put a check on unlimited consumption and unending exploitation of natural resources.

The Gandhian technique of *satyagraha* to resist the wrong and unjust actions has been most popular among the environmentalist as a mode of non-violent protest. The two world-renowned Indian environmental movements (Chipko and Narmada Bachao Andolan) have been widely acknowledged as being based on Gandhain principles. The Chipko movement although became popular in the 1970s, it has its genesis in the "long history of protest in Uttarakhand against government forest policy, stretching back to 1906" (Guha as cited in Hardiman, 2003:221). The local Sarvodaya workers actively participated in this movement. They established co-operative societies in the 1970s to obtain forest contracts so that the benefits would go to the local peoples and not to the outsiders. However, this endeavour did not earn much success as people who run these co-operative societies lacked both political as well as economic power. By that time, these *sarvodaya* workers developed an overall critical attitude towards forestry in general. The two best known leaders of the movement, i.e. Chandi Prasad Bhatt and Sunderlal Bahuguna exemplified the highest traditions of Gandhian constructive work to make this movement a success. Chandi Prasad Bhatt—one of the leaders, suggested of embracing the trees and thus 'Chipko' was born (Guha, 1989). This form of protest was instrumental in driving away the private company from felling the ash trees. This protest exemplified the alternative mode of distribution of natural resources that focused on empowering the native people. The Gandhian idioms were used to justify the central role of native people in deciding the distribution pattern of local natural resources.

In 1979, Sunderlal Bahuguna took a fast unto death force the authorities to consider their demands. On the 13th day of his fast, he was arrested by the police but he continued his fast in the jail. Ultimately, the authorities had to bow and agreed to discuss the issue on the 24th day of his fast. In 1980, Indira Gandhi banned all the commercial forestry in the Himalaya above altitude of one thousand metres for the next fifteen years (Hardiman, 2003:223) and thus recognized the rights of native peoples on their natural resource.

The Narmada Bachao Andolan also shows its high indebtness to the Gandhian ideals. The NBA leaders Baba Amte and Medha Patker have repeatedly underlined their own debt to Gandhi and they have relied heavily on Gandhian techniques of non-violent protest or *Satyagraha* in their struggle to save the Narmada. It has been carried out much in line with the Chipko movement, which is considered to be the precursor of environmental movement in India. The declared objective of the NBA is that of "creating an alternative political culture based on Gandhian principles" (Baviskar, 2003:225). The movement's leaders deeply rely on the Gandhian belief that the modern mega developmental projects do not cater the needs of villages and poor masses. Since these mega projects are supported by the state, which is an all-powerful institution, the only way to resist such an omnipotent institution is non-violent peaceful resistance. The protagonist of this movement asserted that state being the all-powerful central political institution rationalized such mega projects on the logic of large scale development. Benefitters of such mega projects, however, are not those who are poor. These mega developmental projects do not recognise the rights of native peoples who are displaced or suffer the loss of habitation and livelihood in process of execution of these projects. The compensation given to them in lieu of loss of habitation and livelihood does not bring their life back to the normal mode. These projects also fail on cost-benefit analysis if the ecological cost is to be counted (Khagram, 2004; Isaacman and Isaacman, 2013).

Beside these leaders there are number of environmental leaders who got influenced by the Gandhian views. J.C. Kumarappa, a lifetime associate and ardent supporter of Gandhi codified Gandhian views on rural economy from ecological perspective (Guha, 2001:82). He joined Gandhi in 1929 and at his behest "worked out a coherent ideological framework in justification of a 'village-centred economic order', of which resource conservation was an integral part" (Guha, 1992:58). "Another Gandhian with environmental ideas far in advance of her time was Mira Behn (Madeline Slade), the daughter of an English admiral who joined the Mahatma's Sabarmati Ashram in 1925" (Guha, 1992:73-74). Mira Behn set up an *ashram* at *Rishikesh* in 1947 and "drew attention of the public and of policy-makers to the intimate links between Himalayan deforestation, soil erosion and floods" (Guha, 1992:74). Mira Behn identified two lacunae in the forest management where the "necessary changes were too fundamental" for the Forest Department to make. The "first, the lack of involvement of villagers [in forest management]; and second, the replacement in many areas of oak with pine, a species with much less capacity to absorb and retain rainwater" (Guha, 1992:74). Thus, the vision of the Gandhian philosophy, i.e. village-centred economic growth with local people having control over their natural resources is the *mantra*, which provides blood to the vassals of most of the Indian environmental justice movements in India.

Alternative to the Mainstream Discourse of Environmental Justice

Indian environmental movements generally designated as "environmentalism of the poor" to distinguish them from the Western environmentalism calls for the division of environmental movements into two dialectically opposite groups at world level. This is much the same as the Marxist interpretation of political economy of the world, which divide the world into two opposite poles, i.e. north and south on economic grounds. The eco-socialist generally draws upon Marxist's analysis of capitalism and argued that capitalism is the main cause of all environmental problems. The main socialist ideas, which draw attention of the ecologists are: one, removal of private property and social ownership of resources. The ecologists argue, "if wealth is owned in common it will be used in the interests of all which means in the long term interests of humanity" (Guha, 1988:2578). Two, uncritical acceptance of Malthusian dogma—pointing out that unequal distribution of resources and the dynamics of capitalist expansion, rather than the 'tragedy of commons' (a euphemism for population growth) better explain the patterns and processes of environmental degradation (Guha, 1988). Therefore, any attempt to reverse this process would entail in it the radical social transformation or social revolution.

The ecological Marxists in India embraces a variety of groups, including some elements of the Naxalite movement and radical Christian groups, but they most closely identify themselves with the Kerala Shastra Sahitya Parishad—a People's Science Movement—whose initial concern was to take science to the people but later on also included environment in its ambit by widening its scope of action (Guha, 1988:2580). Amita Baviskar argues, "Among the various streams of environmentalism, ecological Marxism has been the most dominant. Its marring of two concerns—social justice and ecological sustainability—has made this ideology highly appealing to social activists working with tribal communities in western India" (Baviskar, 2004:289).

Although, the Indian Left is not anti-modern and generally reluctant to protest against the large developmental projects like damming of rivers, mining, commercialization of forests etc., it does not give unqualified support to these projects since it believes that the current development is exploitative in nature and serves the interests of only few rich peoples. Therefore, the Left Political Parties in India have emphasized that the main focus of such developmental projects should be on the designing and planning aspects so that the proper rehabilitation and resettlement of project affected peoples can be ensured beforehand. Archana Prasad pointed out that the Left mass movements in India does not support the 'temples of development' at the cost of large section of the peoples. This is well evidenced by the Kerala Shastra Sahitya Parishad (KSSP) led by Left movement "against the Silent Valley Project [which] started a debate on the nature of modern development within the left" (Baviskar, 2004:78).

Since 1990s, the CPI(M) has taken a consistent stand on the issue of damming Narmada. The party extended its full support to the project affected peoples and maintained its stand that the work on the Sardar Sarovar Dam should not start until the complete rehabilitation and resettlement of the project affected peoples took place. In August 2002, the CPI(M) placed certain demands regarding the rehabilitation and resettlement of project affected peoples (Baviskar, 2004:82-83). The party maintained the same position with respect to the other projects like Nathpa Jhakri wherein it argued that "Environmental Impact Assessment should be done by an independent panel of scientific experts so that a proper way of controlling the damage is found and alternative designs suggested on this basis" (Baviskar, 2004:84).

The Gender Perspective in Environmental Justice Movement in India

The gender perspective on environmental justice is a world movement.

Shiva and Maria Mies explain, we must acknowledge that we are part of the larger web of life that provides for our survival, and therefore, it is imperative that we protect that fragile web of life, not as dominators—men over women and humans over nature—but as partners with every other life form on the planet.

Although, Gender Perspective on environmental justice is a world movement, a line of distinction is made between the First World Ideas on environmental justice and feminist concerns and the Third World Ideas on the same.. The eco-feminism[3], as the perspective is generally known, addresses not only the environmental issues that concern women but also questions the dominant paradigm of justice. The supporters of this perspective "believe that the worldview that causes environmental degradation and inequality is the same that causes a culture of male domination, exploitation, and inequality for women" (Brikner and Shiva, 2009). There is a rich history of literature that establishes links between environmental justice and feminist ideas. Beth Berila argues, "Both environmental justice issues and feminist pedagogy address intersections of race, class, gender, sexuality, ability, and nation; both combine theory and practice; both involve radically rethinking deeply held assumptions; and both reveal the ideologies and power dynamics that inform language, policies, and practices" (Berila, 2006: 93).

Feminism in India is relatively a new intellectual practice and its history in this country can be traced back to the period of 1960s and 1970s. However, it has grown into its maturity during the early years of 1980s. Feminists in India in their attempts to locate historical example of women resistance, documented the historical movements of social transformation in which women played a leading role in the environmental protection. One such example is the Chipko movement, which was documented by many feminists' theorists as an ideal of feminism in India (Omvedt, 1993). The works of Vandana Shiva very well establish the link between the issues of injustice, women sufferings and environmental degradation. She explains, "We see the devastation of the earth and her beings by the corporate warriors, as feminist concerns. It is the same masculinist mentality which would deny us our right to our own bodies and our own sexuality, and which depends on multiple systems of dominance and state power to have its way" (Mies and Shiva, 1993: 14). Vandana Shiva distinguishes the Third World ecofeminism from that of the Western feminism and prefers to call it political or subsistence feminism for its central focus on equity and justice. She argues, "The new insight provided by rural women in the Third World is that women and nature are associated not in passivity but in creativity and in the maintenance of life" (Shiva, 1988: 47).

The Chipko movement in the central Himalayan region apart from being an environmental movement it was also a women's movement where women took up cudgels against the state to initiate effective forestry policies to protect the Himalayan environment. The ecofeminist see the feminist movement and ecological movement as interconnected and "believes that the worldview that causes environmental degradation and injustice is the same worldview that causes a culture of male domination, exploitation, and inequality for women" (Brinker, 2009). The Feminist in India prefer to designate their concerns for environment as 'Feminist environmentalism' instead of 'ecofeminism' (Aggarwal, 1992: 119-158).

The Feminist theorists argue that the effect of decay of natural resources have a location, class and gender specification. Bina Agarwal argues that in the context of India, the processes of environmental degradation, statization and privatization of natural resources, and the erosion of traditional system of knowledge and resource management have adverse effects on class as well as on gender. She argues that focusing only on class would provide a partial picture because there is a critical gender dimension of environmental degradation of which women and female children are most adversely affected. The 'class-gender effect' of environmental degradation, statization and privatization, according to her, relate to at least six critical aspects of women's life. These are—time, income, nutrition, health, social-survival-networks, and indigenous knowledge (Aggarwal, 1992: 130-36). She points out that although the Indian state has responded to the environmental degradation but this response has been 'piecemeal rather than comprehensive'. Most of the state initiatives like direct tree planting basically monoculture plantation for commercial use, wasteland development programme etc. are based on the top-down implementation method and does not recognize local knowledge of the forest dwellers or other group of peoples. These programmes are of little use to reverse the processes of environmental degradation and also far from being beneficiary to the poor peoples.

Feminist environmentalist argued that the woman who command and take part enthusiastically in the ecological movements in India speak not merely as the victims of environmental degradation but also represent the voices of emancipation. They demand from the government a recognition of their traditional rights and liberties over the forest. For example during Chipko movement when women gave the slogan 'Ecology is Permanent Economy', they were articulating their 'right to use'. The issue was more essentially related to a competition over the question of right to use between the state approved contractors and the community. The women hugged the trees because they needed them for firewood and fodders. The basis of fighting of these women against the state was the economic security for themselves and their family. "The Chipko struggle is a struggle to recover the hidden and invisible productivity of vital resources, and the invisible productivity of women, to recover their entitlements and rights to have and provide nourishment for sustained survival, and to create ecological insights and political spaces that do not destroy fundamental rights to survival"(Bahuguna,1990:112).

Feminist environmentalism provides a detailed critique to the developmental policy of Indian state. Vandana Shiva in her work *Staying Alive: Women, Ecology, and Survival in India* analyzes in details the contours of this critique. Shiva argues, "... modern science and development are projects of male, western origin, both historically and ideologically. They are the latest and most brutal expression of a practical ideology which is threatening to annihilate nature and the entire human species" (Shiva, 1988: xvi).

Shiva further exemplifies how the developmental ideology as implanted from above revolves around the market economy, which in turn primarily driven by transnational capital investment, undermines the natural economy. She argued that the social forestry scheme which was initiated in Kolar district of Karnataka by the State Government for plantation of eucalyptus trees was an attempt of indirect entry of global market domination. This policy of the government was severely opposed by women of the region who argued that the eucalyptus trees are harmful for soil, water and the food systems. This protest challenged "the domination of a forestry science that had reduced all species to one (the eucalyptus), all needs to one (that of the pulp industry), and all knowledge to one (that of the World Bank and forest officials)" (Gadgil and Guha, 1994).

Conclusion

To conclude we can argue that successful environmental justice movements in India have raised their voices primarily on the two ecological issues, i.e. forest destruction and major river valley developmental projects. The success of these movements is conditioned by the ability of movement's leaders to relate their agitation for ecological issues with that of the protection of social and economic rights of native people. The three perspectives that spearheaded the Indian environmental movements are concerned with those issues of environmental justice which are in one way or the other having their relevance with the livelihood of poor people. While the Gandhian philosophy proposed a village-centred economic growth with local people having control over their natural resources, the alternative voices to the mainstream thinking argued that the current development is exploitative in nature and serves the interests of only few rich peoples and therefore, any effort to secure environmental justice would require that developmental projects undertaken by government should focus on rehabilitation and resettlement of the project affected peoples, and finally, the Feminist environmentalist argued that there is a critical gender dimension of environmental degradation of which women and children are most adversely affected, and therefore, any attempt seek about environmental justice would require participation of woman in the policy-making decisions for the protection and conservation of the environment. These alternative voices that question the prevalent inequalities, hierarchies and patriarchies in the Indian state collectively "pose a serious challenge to the dominant ideology of the meaning and patterns of development" (Swain, 1977). Environmental justice movements in India are not necessarily for the 'green' or 'clean' earth but are for the very survival of the poor. They have been concerned with the issues of marginality, inequity, poverty, injustice and underdevelopment. For example, the primary objective of Chipko movement was to secure forest rights to the native peoples against the state sponsored commercial deforestation. In the same way, the NBA has been more concerned with the rights of the peoples who have been displaced due to the rise of water level and submergence of adjoining areas of the dam. The stand against deforestation as in the case of Chipko Movement and resistance to Sardar Sarovar Dam in the case of NBA were indirect repercussions of their struggle for rights and equity of the people concerned. Their struggle is not for protecting the environment for its intrinsic value. Indian environmentalists believe that issues of marginality, inequity, poverty, injustice and underdevelopment having a direct bearing on environmental sustainability, thus, pose a serious and immediate threat to development of native people.

Notes

1. In the summer of 2016, number of newspapers reported the water crisis in various parts of India. The news items like "Rain or Not India Faces Drinking Water Crisis", *Hindustan Times*, June 28, 2016, were eye opener. For detail reporting on the issue *see* Mishra, 2016; Bhasin, 2016.

2. Climate Change is caused by high concentration of Greenhouse Gases near the surface of the earth due to high emission of these gases from industrial activities, motor vehicle, thermal power plant etc. All this is required for the economic development of a given state but the benefits of this economic development are not distributed on the basis of some egalitarian principles of justice among the people.
3. "Ecofeminism" was a term first used by Francoise D'Eaubonne in 1980.

References

Agarwal, Bina (1992). "The gender and environment debate: Lessons from India", *Feminist Study*, Vol. 8 (1): 119-59.

Agyeman, J. (2002). "Constructing environmental (in) justice: Transatlantic tales", *Environmental Politics*, 11(3): 31-53.

Agyeman, J., Bullard, R.D., and Evans, B., (2003). "Joined-up thinking: Bringing together sustainability, environmental justice, and equity", In, J. Agyeman, R.D. Bullard, and B. Evans, (eds.) *Just Sustainabilities: Development in an Unequal World*, Cambridge, MA: MIT Press, pp. 1-18.

Bahuguna, Vimla (1990). "The Chipko Movement", In: Ilina Sen, (ed.) *A Space within the Struggle: Women's Participation in People's Struggle*, New Delhi: Kali for Nature, pp. 111-24.

Baviskar, Amita (2004). "Tribal politics and discourses of Indian environmentalism", In: Paul Greenough and Anna Lowenhaupt Tsing, eds., *Nature in the Global South: Environmental Projects in South and South-East Asia*, New Delhi: Orient Longman, pp. 289-318.

Berila, Beth (2006). "The links between environmental justice and feminist pedagogy: An introduction", *Feminist Teacher*, 16(2): 93-97.

Bhasin (2016). "Bombay HC: Can water from private dams be used for drinking purposes", *The Indian Express*, online edition, May 25.

Brinker, Rachel (2009). "Dr. Vandana Shiva and Feminist Theory", Conference on Earth Democracy: Women, Justice and Ecology posted online by *momentumfemininum* July 4, available at https://womenjusticeecology.wordpress.com/2009/07/04/dr-vandana-shiva-and-feminist-theory/accessed on July 10, 2016.

Carson, Rachel (1962). *Silent Spring*, Boston: Houghton, Mifflin.

Das, Saudamini (2015). "Effects of Climate Change and Heat Waves on Low Income Urban Workers: Evidences from India", In: Delgado-Ramos, Gian Carlo, ed., *Inequality and Climate Change: Perspective from the South*, Senegal: CODESRIA, pp. 171-192.

Gadgil, Madhav and Guha, Ramachandra (1994). "Ecological Conflicts and Environmental Movement in India", *Development and Change*, 25(1): 101-36.

Guha, Ramachandra (1988). "Ideological Trends in Indian Environmentalism", *Economic and Political Weekly*, 23(49): 2578-81.

Guha, Ramachandra (1989). *The Unquiet Woods: Ecological Change and Peasant Resistance in the Himalaya*, New Delhi: Oxford University Press.

Guha, Ramachandra (1992). "Prehistory of Indian Environmentalism Intellectual Traditions", *Economic and Political Weekly*, 27(1-2): 57-64.

Guha, Ramachandra (2001). *An Anthropologists Among the Marxists and Other Essays*, 2nd rpt. (2003). New Delhi: Permanent Black.

Guha Ramachandra, and Martinez-Alier J., (1997). Varieties of *environmentalism: Essays North and South*, Earthscan, London.

Guha, Ramachandra and Martinez-Alier, Joan (1998). *Varieties of Environmentalism: Essays North and South*, New Delhi: Oxford University Press.

Hardiman, David (2003). *Gandhi in his Time and Ours*, New Delhi: Permanent Black.

Hartley, Troy W. (1995). "Environmental Justice: An Environmental Civil Rights Value acceptable All World Views", *Environmental Ethics*, 17(3): 277-289.

Isaacman, Allen F. and Isaacman, Barbara S. (2013). *Dams, Displacement and The Delusion of Development: Cahora Bassa and its Legacies in Mozambique, 1965-2007*, Ohio: Ohio University Press.

Khagram, Sanjeev (2004). *Dams and Development: Transnational Struggles for Water and Power*, Ithaca: Cornell University Press.

Lee, C. (ed.) (1992). *Proceedings: The First National People of Colour Environmental Leadership Summit*, New York: United Church of Christ Commission for Racial Justice.

Martinez-Alier, Joan (2002). "The Environmentalism of the Poor", Paper presented in the conference on *The Political Economy of Sustainable Development: Environmental Conflicts, Participation and Movements*, Johannesburg: University of Witwatersrand.

Martinez-Alier, Joan, Temper, L. and Demaria, F. (2014). "Social Metabolism and Environmental Conflicts in India", *Indialogs*, Vol. 1, pp. 51–83.

Martinez-Alier, Joan, *et al.* (2016). "Is there a Global Environmental Justice Movement?", Colloquium Paper No. 16, International Institute of Social Studies, The Hague, Netherland, February 4-5, pp. 1-19

Mies, Maria and Shiva, Vandana (1993). *Ecofeminism*. Halifax: Fernwood Publications.

Mishra Garima (2016). "A Tale of Parched Maharashtra Village: Each Family in Shilantane Village Spends Rs. 100 a Day to Buy Water, *The Indian Express*, June 28.

Nader, Ralph (1965). *Unsafe at Any Speed*, New York: Pocket Books.

Ockwell, David G. and Mallett, Alexandra (2012). ed., *Low-Carbon Technology Transfer: From Rhetoric to Reality*, London: Routledge.

Omvedt, Gail (1993). *Reinventing Revolution: New Social Movements and the Socialist Tradition in India*, London: East Gate Book.

Patwardhan, Amrita, "Dam and Tribal People in India", 126 Contributing paper to the World Commission on Dam. See for details http://www.dams.org/

Pendharkar, Leena (2002). "Dam Being Built in India on Backs of Poor, Critics Say Huge Project is Uprooting Tribal People", San Francisco Chronicle, January 17, Avaliable at http://commondreams.org/cgi-bin/print.cgi?file=/headlines02/0117-01.htm accessed on May 15, 2016

Reich, Charles (1970). *The Greening of America*, New York: Random House.

Schlosberg, David (2013). "Theorising environmental justice: the expanding sphere of a discourse", *Environmental Politics*, Vol. 22(1): 37-55.

Sethi, Harsh (1993). "Survival and Democracy: Ecological Struggles in India", In: Wignaraja, Ponna, (ed.), *New Social Movements in the South: Empowering the People,* New Delhi: Vistaar Publications, pp. 122-48.

Shiva, Vandana (1988). *Staying Alive: Women, Ecology, and Survival in India,* New Delhi: Kali for Women.

Suchak, Kavita Y., "Development and Environment Issues with Special Reference to Gandhian Perspective", available at: http://www,mkgandhi-sarodaya.org/articles/kavita_suchak.htm accessed on May 15, 2016.

Swain, Ashok (1997). "Democratic consolidation? Environmental Movements in India", *Asian Survey*, 37(9): 818-32.

Wenz, Peter (1988). *Environmental Justice*, Albany: State University of New York Press.

17

Environmental Determinism in Entrepreneurial Development in Gujarat

An Indian Perspective

Ronald C. Zochin and *P.T. Aienla Lemtor*

Introduction

Abimbola *et al.* (2011) observes that entrepreneurship researches have established relationships between the business environment and entrepreneurial activities (Dobbin and Dowd, 1997; Borkowski and Kulzick, 2006; Carter and Wilton, 2006). The effective manifestation of the functions and roles of entrepreneurship in socio-economic development have often been attributed to the presence of certain factors in the external environment of the entrepreneur over which he has little or no control. Borkowski and Kulzick (2006) list the interplay between entrepreneurship and environment as follows:

(a) new venture strategies are formed in response to environmental forces;
(b) entrepreneurs are negative towards and will resist political interference; and
(c) unstable environments are negatively related to growth opportunities.

The entrepreneurial environment is inclusive of two types of environments, firstly, the physical infrastructure such as transportation, water and electricity as well as non-physical resources like regulatory policies, education, procedures and financial credit and secondly, the relational environment, which is normally made up of the natural, social and business networks and environment. This work attempts to examine the interface between the entrepreneurial environment and practice in India basing it on the latest evidence while anchoring it on an empirical work carried out by the researchers for four years—from 1999 to 2003.

To reveal the social background of the 168 entrepreneur respondents, some specific questions in this respect were made as to their caste, religion, nature or type of family (nuclear or joint), community occupation—whether business or non-business community; their region of origin, whether of urban or rural origin; from Gujarat or outside. All these are normally seen as part of the entrepreneur social background.

Entrepreneur's experience may come from early apprenticeship in the family business before joining it as an active participant or working in some business organization or another before starting one's business, setting up in partnership with persons of like interest or sometimes establishing a limited company if not joining it. There is an assumption that entrepreneurial success are determined by environmental factors like caste, religion, ethnic group, entrepreneur association, family type (i.e. nature of family) and such other social factors that contribute to the nurturing of the entrepreneur.

Besides, these factors determine the business field or the nature of business one sets up or joins and the organizational form the entrepreneur adopts in order to take advantage of these factors and the social network arising thereof. This natural support system sustains entrepreneurial initiatives and competitiveness. To test the validity of this theoretical determinism, the chi-square test has been applied.

Theoretical Perspectives

Goel Abishek *et al.* (2007) observed that interest in studying entrepreneurs and their activities had been recorded since early nineteenth century. Entrepreneurs and entrepreneurship are arguably the pillars on which societies were built. Entrepreneurial activity has been identified as one resource that needs to be tapped by developing countries to enable them to compete in a globalizing market economy (Kanungo, 1998; Khandwalla, 1998). The Commission of European Communities (2005) reported that entrepreneurship is very important for further social development through increased job opportunities and consequent economic prosperity. In developing economies like India and China promotion of entrepreneurs and entrepreneurship has become a priority for the governments, financial institutions, and academic institutions.

Partly because it is believed that such growth was made possible by efforts of the governments, institutions, and individuals who responded to calls for setting up business units.

In Indian Information Technology sector, for example, Small and Medium Enterprises (SMEs) in aggregate turned out to be largest employers ("SMEs largest employers: Skoch", 2002). An international consortium Global Entrepreneurship Monitor (GEM) carried out studies to measure entrepreneurial activities in several countries. It reported that India and China have consistently registered high entrepreneurial activities though the two countries had different patterns of support and investments in entrepreneurship (*GEM Hong Kong and Shenzhen Report, 2003;* Manimala, 2002). As the success stories of successful attempts at entrepreneurship became widespread, more and more people in China started their own businesses. In 2002, SMEs were responsible for about 60 per cent of China's industrial output and employed about 75 per cent of the workforce in cities and towns (China's small and medium enterprises: room to grow with WTO, http://www.usembassy-china.org.cn/econ/smes2002.html).

In an era of high economic growth the small and medium enterprises have continued to garner nearly 14 per cent share in the Indian GDP. These enterprises have continued to grow faster than the national economy and the employment had grown by over 4 per cent every year (GoI, 2006, pp. 151-152). The Government of India (GoI) has emphasized on the importance of giving boost to the attempted to make the proposition for entrepreneurship attractive support in three formats: (i) government policies favouring promotion of entrepreneurial activity; (ii) making financial support available; and (iii) setting up of academic or institutional support. In China multi-pronged strategies for promoting SMEs have been formulated by the Government.

Efforts in India to Promote Entrepreneurship

The Indian experience suggests that difficulties in starting up businesses and handling the pressures of entrepreneurship in the initial phases deter people from taking up entrepreneurship as means for livelihood. The grant of licences and policies and controls and taxations had been cited as one of the major hurdles in the setting up and running of new businesses (Awasthi & Sebastian, 1996; Gautam, 1979; Mokry, 1988; Sadhak, 1989; Singh, 1985). Thus, entrepreneurship had been encouraged in India by systematic attempts at removal of state imposed structural and regulatory roadblocks. More progressive governments have tried to make it easy for entrepreneurs to set up businesses. The growth of Bangalore, Hyderabad as hubs for organizations engaged in Information Technology business were direct outcomes of government's support in form of tax holidays to start-ups and sector-region specific concessions to start new ventures.

Second, there were attempts to make finances available to businesses. In the existing banking paradigm it was/is not so easy to get loans for starting new ventures or expanding current businesses. The Reserve Bank of India urged banks to consider easier lending to small and new businesses ("Banking not equipped to promote SMEs: RBI", 2002). The Government of India also increased efforts in this direction. Small Enterprise Development Bill of 2003 included guidelines for banks and other government agencies to ensure easy disbursement of loans to new ventures (Gopalakrishnan, 2004). Subsequently, lowering of borrowing rates from the banks also made it worthwhile of entrepreneurs to run profitable business. These steps were/are being taken in the direction of making easy finance available to entrepreneurs.

Another form of support and development of entrepreneurial talent by various institutions came in the form of setting up training institutions for entrepreneurs. Setting up of national institutions such as the Entrepreneurship Development Institute (EDI) at Ahmedabad is indicative of such thinking at the government level in India. Several institutions in the US, Singapore, the UK, and India set up special cells to support 'technopreneurs' and other innovators. These institutions provide basic management know-how and understanding of how to start and run a business, and also incubate new businesses till they are able to sustain themselves (*ibid.*).

Characteristics and Social Background of Entrepreneurs

Entrepreneurs belonging to the same geographical location and same social background are bound to display similar characteristics because of shared social values. Their temperament and the way they carry out business will reflect their social networks and affiliations.

Goitom Tesfom (2006) observes that studying the Characteristic of Entrepreneurs' social network may help shed light on new venture creation. Casson (1997) defines a network as a set of high trust relationship which either directly or indirectly link together in a social group. Social network analysis is based on an assumption of the importance of relationships among interacting units....Sociologists have for many years explored the resources embedded in social relations and social network structures (Kamman, 2000). Hence, entrepreneurial enterprises have been a productive area for application of the social network theory (BarNir and Smith, 2002).

The caste system of social hierarchy is indispensable in the Indian social structure. While there are many castes and sub-caste communities (*Jatis*) the main ones are about five. At the top of this hierarchy is the *Brahmin* (the priest group), the *Kshtriya* (the warriors), the *Vaishya* (the farmers) and the *Harijan* (or *Sudra*) at the bottom of the social status. But it must be noted that there are other castes, sub-castes and tribal networks in India.

There is presence of all these castes in the Gujarat state, just like in every part of India, except, in the Northern part of the Country (Nagaland, Mizorum, Assam, Sikkim, Meghalaya etc.). In Gujarat too, is the social group called the Patels and they form a strong social network. History has it that the Patels were some low caste but after the land reforms of the 1950s in India they obtained large chunks of land. This resulted in the Patels going into farming and as they grew in riches, they became a very powerful community both socially, economically and politically. The Patels, therefore, are land-owners and farmers. But they are also a very successful business community. Most of their sons have rose to the position of Chief Ministers and other political positions in the state. They are a dynamic entrepreneurial community who are not averse at taking risks. They are a tightly knit community and support each other.

The researcher while conducting the study inquired into this community's social characteristics. One very common significant characteristic is their unity. It is said that the Patels are a cohesive and with a strong sense of *"we feeling"*. It is said that when a Patel goes in search of opportunity within the country or overseas destinations, and discovers good opportunities or mere possibilities of success—in business or otherwise, he will make every effort to "import" members from his village—one by one to the new location.

They say a Patel may belong to a different political party, but when a Patel approaches another in a powerful position for help, the Patel receives attention first irrespective of his party affiliation. There is a Gujarati saying and expression, which runs, "*Patel Mate Patel*" (meaning, "*Patel for Patel*"). Though it may seem to have exaggerated overtones, it demonstrates a fellow intimacy and brotherhood. The Patels, like any closely knit group, therefore, are a united community that help one another;

and become a very effective network when in business or in politics for mutual self-help and co-operation.

There is yet another group called the *Bania*—they may be Hindu *Bania* or Jain *Bania*. Now these are said to be much superior in business, comparatively. It is said that they are calculative and good business strategists. Some respondents said that the *Banias* are very sly and cunning businessmen, something that, even if reference is made, does not annoy or hurt the *Bania* at all. Let me hasten to add here something interesting about the Indian *Gujaratis*. They are never annoyed when casually labelled by another as a "cheat", "Cunning", or any of such unkindly words. They take it in good spirit and lets it pass—something that would have annoyed other people. The researcher witnessed many such incidents of sportive abuse and sarcastic utterances, taken in jest and humour. They are, therefore, least irritated by negative overtures.

The *Bania* is a business community; and they are in virtually every other business especially in the textile and pharmaceutical line. As said earlier, they are calculative and smart in their approach. Many respondents who were interviewed said that the *Banias* can easily challenge and can out-smart the *Sindhi* businessman—that they can easily match them in a contest of supremacy and business acumen.

The *Sindhi* is another of the business community in Gujarat. They are considered the best in the art of business manipulation; and are said to have earlier come from Pakistan. This community would be literally called the business "warriors". It is said that they are shrewd, sly and manipulative in their deals and dealings. They can manipulate not only business deals but they can also manipulate the whole market (the economy of a whole city) to their advantage.

In the Gujarati business arena, we also have other communities which, in this study, we have categorized as "others". These include those who came from out of the state like the *Rajasthani* (the *Marwari*), Uttar Pradesh (UP) etc. This group, too, is not to be taken lightly. They are into all forms of businesses—small and big. The *Marwari* are well-known for being spread all-over India and have a large presence in Gujarat. In Gujarati characteristic chides, the Marwari is said to be mean and stingy. In the local Gujarati dialect they would say, "Kanchus Marwari" (the stingy Marwari)." The expression has been repeated so many times that it has become a form of truth. And a Gujarati behaving stingy would be called, "Marwari." But even then, it is taken in jest.

At one interesting occasion at Entrepreneurship Development Institute of India (EDII), where the researcher had received an in-house

4 month research fellowship, he had the opportunity to interact with the sons of businessmen who had come to undertake the one year rigorous postgraduate diploma in entrepreneurship and small business management—specializing in either new business creation (NBC) or family business management (FBM). On one such occasion as he was engaging a group of the students on the dominance of business groups in the state and in India, one *Marwari* young man said, "Actually, the economy of India is held and sustained by the *Marwari*", to which one humorous yet intelligent Gujarati young man from Surat city interjected, "No, that is not the case; the Marwaris, have actually, ruined the Indian economy", leading to thunderous laughter.

Through these stories and incidents, it becomes evident that the business communities are not only competing but are wary of one another; however, each group has their own survival tricks and strategies. The Patels have to unite, the *Banias* must lay strategies and executive them slyly. The Sindhi have to be shrewd and mercilessly manipulative. These characteristics and experiences make the Indian businessman uniquely competitive and therefore, can survive, wherever he settles—including in foreign lands. A typical Gujarati, irrespective of caste or community affiliation, is likely to adopt the Patel type of social networking, the *Bania* shrewd style and the Sindhi's "Entrepreneurial Judo" (Phrase borrowed from Drucker).

As mentioned in passing, there are other entrepreneurs who may come from non-business communities—who are included in the "other" category. This could be educated men who because of the business climate in Gujarat, where every young man talks business, and may have worked elsewhere and gained enough skills, experience and the confidence to set up business on his own. Some of whom, are likely to have some professional or technical background. Yet there are likely to be others who went into business by sheer force of circumstances. Such is the case with a petrol pump owner whose brother was in the Army and because of bad fate was killed during the Indian-Pakistan Kargil war of 1998.

The Government had set a policy for the compensation of the dependants or relations of such soldiers by providing them financial support through helping them set up petrol pump businesses. This is a good and benevolent policy and thrusts a non-business family into business by the attractiveness of the project and subsequent support by the government.

Research Method

The research was carried out in Ahmedabad, Gujarat state, India for the period between 1999 and 2003. The sample was drawn from small scale entrepreneurs in six business sectors across the city of Ahmedabad—Pharmaceuticals; Textile, enterprises selling and repairing of Motorbikes; Petrol filling stations; Cyber cafes; and electronic selling enterprises. A stratified sampling method was used and questionnaires were instituted to 168 entrepreneurs. Besides, a few of the respondents were interviewed through the use of unstructured questionnaires to seek clarifications. The questionnaires were analyzed to establish correlation between social factors and entrepreneurial success and development. The Chi-square was used for environmental determinism. The results are discussed here below.

Results

On the basis of the above background, we shall now provide the tabulated data and analysis accordingly, to make a sense of the factual realities of these research findings.

The Social Background of the Entrepreneur Respondents

Here we look at the entrepreneur(s) caste, nature of family, place of upbringing and the influence of community occupations. These variables provide a glimpse of the entrepreneur(s) social and business networks.

Table 17.1 gives the caste distribution of the entrepreneurs according to the six service sectors. The majority out of the 168 respondents came from "other castes" (32.10 per cent) other than the main ones: Jain *Bania*, Hindu *Bania*, Patels and the Sindhi. "Other Castes" were the majority at 32.10 per cent followed by Jain *Bania* (27.40 per cent). The third group was the Sindhi (14.90%) and the fourth was the Hindu *Bania* (14.30%) and finally, the Patels at 10.10 per cent.

But, if we combine the two *Banias* (Hindu and Jain) then they become the largest group at 41.7 per cent. We can, therefore, infer that the *Banias* are the leading business community in Ahmedabad and in Gujarat. Conversely, the "other" caste groups also demonstrate a remarkable presence at 32 per cent overall.

As mentioned earlier, this fifth group which has been categorized as "other castes" comprise caste groups from both business and non-business

Table 17.1: Caste Distribution of the Respondents

Sl. No.	*Business Field*	*No Response*	*Jain Bania*	*Hindu Bania*	*Patel*	*Sindhi*	*Other Castes*	*Total*
1.	Pharmaceuticals	-	11 (23.90)	7 (29.20)	3 (17.60)	3 (12.00)	4 (7.40)	28 (100)
2.	Textiles Cloth	2	9 (19.60)	6 (25.00)	2 (11.80)	-	9 (16.70)	28 (100)
3.	Motor Bikes	-	6 (13.00)	11 (45.80)	-	-	11 (20.40)	28 (100)
4.	Petrol Pumps	-	5 (10.90)	-	3 (17.60)	8 (32.00)	12 (22.20)	28 (100)
5.	Cyber Café	-	7 (15.20)	-	6 (35.30)	-	15 (27.80)	28 (100)
6.	Electronics	-	8 (17.40)	-	3 (17.60)	14 (56.00)	3 (5.60)	28 (100)
	Total	**2 (1.20)**	**46 (27.40)**	**24 (14.30)**	**17 (10.10)**	**25 (14.90)**	**54 (32.10)**	**168 (100)**

communities, some of whom are first generation entrepreneurs. In this group also, we have the traditional business community of the *Marwari* and a few others who migrated from states like Uttar Pradesh, among others. What is interesting to note is that this fifth group are spread in all the six sectors although very few are in Pharmaceutical business (7.40%) and in the electronic service sector (5.60%).

We can safely conclude that although there are some dominating business communities in Ahmedabad city and generally in the Gujarat state, it is also true that other communities, including the non-business communities are in business today. Some of the respondents had revealed that they had entered the business line(s) because of such reasons as availability of market, favourable commercial climate. Others cited the high profits margins—beside experience; and as we noted earlier, by being a beneficiary of a deceased relative and such reasons. This latter observation clearly shows that entrepreneurship can be engineered through a favourable business environment—which can be as a result of factors at the micro level (social networks) and at macro level by good economic policies. This evidence shows that developing countries can nurture environmental circumstances if they have to encourage many people, especially the young, to take up entrepreneurship.

Environmental Determinism—Belonging to Some Community

Social background and place of upbringing is also likely to have an influence on an entrepreneur; such origin would either be urban or rural.

Table 17.2: Urban and Rural Origin Distribution (Not adopt but conclude)

Sl. No.	*Place of birth and upbringing*	*No Response*	*Jain Bania*	*Hindu Bania*	*Patel*	*Sindhi*	*Other Castes*	*Total*
1.	No Response	2 (7.70)	7 (26.90)	2 (7.70)	-	3 (11.50)	12 (46.20)	26 (100)
2.	Urban	-	13 (23.60)	8 (14.50)	5 (9.10)	14 (25.50)	15 (27.30)	55 (100)
3.	Rural	-	26 (29.90)	14 (16.10)	12 (13.80)	8 (9.20)	27 (31.00)	87 (100)
	Total	**2** **(1.20)**	**46** **(27.40)**	**24** **(14.30)**	**17** **(10.10)**	**25** **(14.90)**	**54** **(32.10)**	**168** **(100)**

Table 17.2 gives the urban and rural origin and upbringing caste-wise distribution of the respondents. Of the total 168 respondents 55 (32.70%) are from urban origin and 87 (51.80%) are of rural origin. The majority, therefore, came from rural Gujarat or elsewhere. We can conclude that most of the respondents are of rural origin (57.80%) barring the 55 (32.70%) cases out of the 168 respondents. This probably is because of rural urban migration in search of employment, job opportunities or business opportunities.

However, it does not matter that an entrepreneur comes from urban or rural area in order to make it in business. But the social network (caste or otherwise) is helpful as far as networking is concerned. It is likely that some of the various caste fellows who had come to the city to set up shop later brought in others from their rural place thereby establishing a network of mutual help.

The data does not offer any support to the theory that the business field is determined by the caste affiliation as an explanation of success in entrepreneurship or in any business field. In the field of business, one's caste does not matter but what matter is that religious and caste affiliation which provides the necessary connections created by networking among community fellows who share the same religious beliefs and participate in communal social rites. Some of these forms of common rituals provide an opportunity to network. Being a member of business caste may make one enter not only business but also adopt same enterprise organizational form.

Table 17.3: Classification of Organizational form According to Caste of Respondents

Sl. No.	*Organization Form*	*No Response*	*Jain Bania*	*Hindu Bania*	*Patel*	*Sindhi*	*Other Castes*	*Total*
1.	No Response	-	1	-	-	1	1	3
2.	Self-Started Business	-	22	6	7	15	29	79
3.	Family Business	-	12	9	5	6	14	46
4.	Partnership	1	10	8	4	2	7	32
5.	Pvt. Ltd.	1	1	1	1	1	3	8
	Total	**2**	**46**	**24**	**17**	**25**	**54**	**168**

Chi-square = 24.083 (with df. = 20); significant at $\rho = 0.05$.

Table 17.3 above on the classification of organizational form of the business according to the caste factor of the respondents show significance at the chi-square value of $\rho = 0.05$. This confirms the environmental determinism of belonging to some community (or social network) in order to start or join some form of business or the other. To start your business and to remain in the field you need the support of the environmental network. This network enables the entrepreneur mobilize resources, identify and link with customers, suppliers and other important stakeholders and potential employees.

Joining, and subsequently running the family business puts one into an already existing business and social structure that determines one's success. So is the case to partnership and the setting up or joining the private limited undertaking. The partnership is a product of the social network which normally may be the commonality of the community (*Jati*) in which the partners come from. It would be difficult to find a native Gujarati running a partnership with a Marwari or a Sindhi or a Jain *Bania.*

Nature of Family—Nuclear or Joint

Marianne Bertrand (2006) writes that in the words of Giovanni Agnelli, the patriarch of Italian industrial dynast (as quoted in Betts, 2001): "The [family] company is an inheritance to be protected and handed on. It is the outcome of the next and each generation's commitment to the last." Dutta (1997) observes that business families in India can either be nuclear or extended. Nuclear families are quite common in the Indian business community as compared to the West. The element of close physical proximity in the Indian family has led to the development of traditions which require the conformity of all family members.

But times are changing and nuclear family businesses are slowly creeping in. Now, because of education, a girl gets married when mature and may find it difficult to submit to a mother-in-law who may be illiterate herself. This often leads to quarrels and conflict. This has led to increase in the erection of nuclear family units to physically disperse conflicting members (*ibid.*).

Table 17.4: The Nature and Type of Family

Sl. No.	*Nature of Family*	*No.*	*Percentage*
1.	Nuclear	29	17.30
2.	Joint	129	76.80
3.	No Response	10	6.00
	Total	**168**	**100.10**

Table 17.4 shows the nature of family the entrepreneurs belong to. The larger majority (76.80%) of the entrepreneur respondents belong to joint families. Only a mere 17.30 per cent are from the nuclear family type. It is evident here that in India and in Gujarat, the business family strive. These businesses, therefore, enjoy the cumulative family resources like skills, experiences and social capital and business network that sustain their growth.

Table 17.5: Classification of Organizational form of Business according to Nature of Family

Sl. No.	*Organization*	*No Response*	*Nuclear*	*Joint*	*Total*
1.	No Response	-	2	1	3
2.	Self-started Business	5	8	66	77
3.	Family Business	4	11	31	46
4.	Partnership	1	6	25	32
5.	Pvt. Ltd.	-	2	6	8
	Total	**10**	**29**	**129**	**166**

Chi-square = 11.502 (with df. =8); significant at $\rho = 0.05$.

Table 17.5, above, on classification of organizational form of business and according to the nature of family was found to be significant at 5 per cent and below. Therefore, it signifies that there is an association between the nature of family and organizational form it adopts—meaning there is a corelation between the two. The nature of family is one of the environmental factors that also determine what form of organizational form one adopts.

This is an assumption supported by the data and proves our hypothesis that there is need for supporting structures, social or otherwise for success in entrepreneurial development. An entrepreneur who belongs to a business family normally joints the family business or if he goes to start his own business is likely to adopt the same business organizational form. In India when a member of a joint family starts a business then as it becomes successful other members of the family joins him. An individual's business automatically becomes a family business.

Studies have shown that as many as 90 per cent entrepreneurs start business in the same market and industry as they are working in (Brackhaus, 1982); Bolton *et al.* (2000, pp. 18-21). Entrepreneurs coming from communities involved in some trade may later adopt the traditional occupation of the community.

Community Occupation and its Influence

It has been observed by many researchers that community occupation, especially those in the business field influence more entrepreneurial activities within the said community. Balton, W.K. and John Thompson (2000) as we earlier noted considered entrepreneurs' roots and their surroundings influences.

Community occupation is an important influence to becoming an entrepreneur, and a successful one for that matter. A question was posed to the entrepreneur respondents in the present study as to their caste occupation to find out whether they come from a business community or a non-business community.

Table 17.6: Community Occupation

Sl. No.	*Community Occupation*	*No.*	*Percentage*
1.	Business Community	130	77.40
2.	Non-Business Community	29	17.30
3.	No Response	9	5.40
	Total	**168**	**100.10**

Table 17.6 shows the background of the entrepreneurs—as to whether they are from business community or non-business community. Over three

quarters (77.40%) came from a business community and only 17.30 per cent are from a non-business background. The rest, 5.40 per cent did not respond. It is clear from these facts that to be a successful entrepreneur one must have a business background and a social support system. Such background provides the necessary skills, experiences and environment to learn and also motivates one to go into business. Besides, coming from a business background enables one to have access to business connections especially sources of resources like funds, markets, customers and supplier chain, and the goodwill established by one's family members, relatives and community network. The findings supports our *hypothesis* that to achieve entrepreneurial success, there is need for supporting institutions, guidelines, and supporting structures pertaining to entrepreneurial development—thus answering our research question: How important is the entrepreneur network, including the social environment, in the growth of SSEs?

Being a member of a business community, therefore, provides one with a ready network which functions as a supporting structure. Within this business network the entrepreneur accesses information on products, market trends and easily identifies threats and opportunities. This enables the entrepreneur adjust accordingly—for his survival and growth.

However, not belonging to a business community, does not bar one from becoming a successful entrepreneur if one lays his strategies of joining existing structures or associations. With proper skills, motivation and the support of available support structures, an entrepreneur can easily succeed. He will require some skills and may receive experience working in an earlier firm and getting exposed to ideas through various channels, which may include friends and acquaintances—being a member of a business association or knowing the right connections. Nevertheless, coming from a business background may become an advantage to becoming successful entrepreneur. The business values propagated by a business community may spark the much needed inspiration. This is demonstrated in Tables 17.7 and 17.8 respectively.

Tables 17.7 on the classification of respondents according to their community occupation was found, while applying the chi-square test, to be significant at $\rho = 0.05$ as shown under the two tables. The table confirms that belonging to a business community is an advantage to becoming a success in the field of entrepreneurship. Those who came from business background have the values and business culture engrained in their minds which determines their approach to social contact and relations, even in business.

Table 17.7: Classification of Respondents According to their Community Occupation

Sl. No.	*Business Field*	*No Response*	*Business Community*	*Non-Business Community*	*Total*
1.	Pharmaceuticals	1	26	1	28
2.	Textiles and Cloth	4	21	3	28
3.	Motor Bikes	1	21	6	28
4.	Petrol Pump	-	20	8	28
5.	Cyber Café	-	20	8	28
6.	Electronics	1	22	5	28
	Total	**7**	**130**	**31**	**168**

Chi-square = 13.882 (with df. = 8); significant at $\rho = 0.178$.

Gujarati conversation is often peppered with sayings and words of wisdom which are inclined towards business. A good example is: "Work is Worship", "Customer is God" (he decides whether you eat or starve), and many such others that make the entrepreneur call to memory any time when he is in mental distress. Businessmen are often under stress and tension. Therefore, a strong business philosophy, encouraging words of wisdom which can be expressed from time to time strengthens the resolve of the entrepreneur to pursue his business goals with focus, patience and determination; and with a sense of sure success.

Besides, the business community provides automatic support structures which we may call the social capital. The social capital is a network that avails opportunities to either the man in business or to one who intends to join business. The researcher observed several occasions where a businessman goes to a distant place to purchase products or supplies while accompanied by his five year old son. This is a very common phenomenon in Gujarat and seems to be a way of introducing the young boy to the business activities and most importantly to the business social network.

The young boy participates sometimes actively in the selection of products, and a close look at this two (the father and the son), will tell you that the boy is under instructions to keenly observe what is going on so as to learn the ropes of the trade. The Gujarati child undergoes through apprenticeship very early in life.

By the time the boy is 14 to 15 years his father can even seek his opinion on the quality of the product and his views are taken seriously. By the time he is 20 years of age, the Indian youngster is a semi-accomplished businessman of no mean capacity and capability.

On one such occasions, the researcher visited a shoe shop, where an old man was running the shop with the help of his grandson who seemed to be about 12 to 14 years old. The young boy played the errands of bringing the shoes from the shelves for the customers. The boy was very active in convincing the customer about the goodness and quality of the shoe and even its durability; he would say in local Gujarati language, "chabal, *Boodh Saras Che*" ("this shoe is very good"). The boy was well versed with the areas and words that could easily convince the customer. He mentioned things like: one year guarantee, concessional rate, repairable, and such finery in salesmanship.

These are the young men of the business community. Their joining the business or even starting their own becomes not so drastic a change, but a mere transition, and a very smooth and natural one. Bertrand (2006) writes that, knowledge about the business is easier between a founder and his children than between a founder and some outside manager. For example, family members may receive exposure to the business even before becoming formally involved in it. In an interview with L. Roberts, current CEO of Comcast and son of Ralph J. Roberts, the founder of Comcast, reports going to work with his father as a teen and "learning the nuts and bolts of the cable business." His father had "his teenage son sit in on some of significant deals in the making, positioning Brian at the back of the room and instructing him to quietly listen" (p. 77).

It is evident that community occupation, and for our purpose here, a business community, determine the success of an entrepreneur. There is a clear relationship between belonging to a business community and joining or starting an enterprise; but also, in succeeding in running and managing it. The support of the social network is critical and this is proven by the chi-square showing significance as we saw in Table 17.7.

Conclusion and Recommendations

Success in entrepreneurship requires an environment that is conducive for business activities. Besides, a cultural environment that recognizes and rewards enterprise is yet a very important factor for entrepreneurial development. The environment in the city of Ahmedabad and the Gujarat State is business oriented. Belonging to a business family attracts recognition and respect. More importantly is when one is involved in the family business or even having set up one's own.

The presence of traditional business families in large numbers in Gujarat, have made the social environment automatically supportive to enterprise. Entrepreneurs have a lot to learn from one another and even imitate and copy from each other. The caste factor also promotes entrepreneurship especially as relates to communities whose occupation is in the field of enterprise and trade. Most of the important castes in Gujarat—the *Banias*, the Patels and others are into business and for this reason business become part of the local culture.

Religious beliefs also play a significant role as far as enterprise and business activities are concerned. The Hindu culture and its religious values encourage the spirit of enterprise. It is believed in Hinduism that one cannot perform effectively his religious and social responsibilities and obligations without economic stability or economic wellbeing. For such beliefs, it becomes necessary to earn money through business activities. The Gujarati people, like all other Hindus, are a very religious community and performing of 'Pujas' (Religious rituals) is an integral part of their lives. Therefore, socio-cultural background that includes a philosophy that supports enterprise is important as far as entrepreneurship is concern.

References

Abimbola, Oluremi H. and Gbenga, Mayowa Agboola (2011). "Environmental Factors and Entrepreneurship Development in Nigeria", *Journal of Sustainable Development in Africa, Pennsylvania,* 13(4): 167.

BarNir, A. and K.A. Smit, (2002). "Interfirm alliances in the Small Business: The role of social networks", *Journal of Small Business Management*, Vol. 40, pp. 219-232.

Bertrand, Marianne, and Antoinette Scholar (2006). "The Role of Family in Firms", *Journal of Economic Perspectives*, Vol. 20, No. 2.

Bolton, W.K. and John Thompson (2000). *Entrepreneurs—Talent, Temperament and Technique*, Butterworth Heinemann, Oxford, pp. 18-21.

Casson, M.C. (1997). *Information and Organization: A New Perspective on the Theory of the Firm*, Oxford, Clarendon Press.

Chung, W. and A. Kalnins, (2004). "Social Capital, Geography and Survival: Gujarati Immigrant Entrepreneurs in the US Lodging Industries", American Sociological Association 2004 meeting proceedings.

Goitom Tesfom (2006). "The role of social networks in entrepreneurial drive of first generation of East African origin entrepreneurs in Seattle area", *Journal of Asia Entrepreneurship and Sustainability*, Vol. II, Issue 4.

Jenssen, J.I. and F.H. Koenig, (2002). "The effect of social network on resources access and business start up", *European Planning Studies*, 10(8): 1040-1046.

Kamann, D.J.F. (1998). "Modelling Networks: A long way to go", *Journal of Economy and Social Geography*, 89(3): 227-297.

Sharma, P.A. Dr. (2000). *Fundamental of Educational Research*, Merrut (India): International Publishing House, p. 350.

Borkowski, N. and Kulzick, R. (2006). *Perspectives from the Field: Will Recent Public Policies Reduce Entrepreneurship in the Healthcare Industry?*

18

Impact of Climate Induced Natural Disasters in Coastal Odisha focused on Socio-economic Vulnerability

Ashutosh Mohanty

Introduction

The state of Odisha which is known as the disaster capital of India situated on the eastern coast, periodically experiences loss of life and severe damage from tropical cyclones, floods and droughts (Dube *et al.*, 1994, 1997, 2000a, b; Das *et al.*, 1983). In the last 100 years, the state has been disaster affected for 90 years; floods have occurred for 49 years, droughts for 30 years and cyclones have hit the state for 11 years. Since 1965, calamities are not only becoming more frequent but striking areas that never had experienced such phenomena. In the last 10 years, calamities have claimed more that 30,000 lives mostly on the coastal belt (Infochange, 2001). A deadly cocktail of floods, cyclones and droughts have made Odisha the disaster capital of India. Agricultural land has turned into fallow land, and this in return has led to widespread malnutrition and even starvation in some parts of the state. Further, this is one of the poorest states in India where more than two-third of the population are below poverty line. Poverty has made the vulnerable segment of the population yet more vulnerable to the consequences of CINDs (Climate Induced Natural Disasters), especially for those living in high risk coastal areas and hilly western and southern parts of Odisha. CINDs have become a burden for the poor people of Odisha which leads to serious fiscal imbalances by heavy demands on revenue expenditure, expenditure on restoring assets. There is a significant reduction of revenue in terms of taxes and duties, due to the crop loss and property loss.

CINDs turning into severe disasters are mediated by the social vulnerability entwined into a complex interrelationship of social, economic, political, technological and institutional factors that render an exposure unit vulnerable or resilient in the face of extreme events. Understanding as to how different societies will respond to and adapt to these changes is thus a key element of research and policy relating to global environmental change (Vincent, 2004). All individuals or social groups exposed to hazard are not equally vulnerable rather affected human being show a pattern of differential loss (Wu *et al.*, 2002). Vulnerability are social conditions of measuring the coping ability and also as combination of social resistance (the ability to absorb the damaging impacts of the hazard and continue functions) and resilience (the ability to recover from the loss quickly). (Dow, 1992; Cutter 1996; Clark, *et al.*, 1998 and Wu *et al.*, 2002). The purpose of the chapter is to build a theoretical framework and developing a methodology in establishing Composite Index of Social Vulnerability to CIND. The framework of methodology relies upon the structural functionalist paradigm targeting social systems and regional systems as units of analysis. In the context of this chapter, the units of analysis are districts of Odisha. The challenges for development are considerable, not least because the impacts are complex and highly uncertain.

Factors Influencing Social Vulnerability

The climate change impact and vulnerability give insight that several demographic attribute, social aspects and economic wellbeing factors are important indicators of climate induced vulnerability. Demographic attributes cited most often throughout the literature include age (Cutter *et al.*, 2000; O'Brien and Mileti, 1992; Hewitt, 1997; and Ngo, 2001), gender (Blaikie *et al.*, 1994; Enarson and Morrow, 1998; Enarson and Scanlon, 1999; Morrow and Phillips, 1999; Fothergill, 1996; Peacock *et al.*, 1997, 2000, Hewitt 1997, and Cutter, 1996), race, ethnicity and caste (Pulido, 2000; Peacock *et al.*, 1997, 2000; Bolin and Stanford, 1998; and Bolin, 1993). These demographic variables play important role in quick assessment of households to recover (Bolin and Bolton, 1986; Morrow, 1999; Enarson and Scanlon, 1999). The social vulnerability is driven by structure of family, social cohesiveness among the community, social capital and social networking (Blaikie *et al.*, 1994; Morrow, 1999; Heinz Center for Science, Economics, and the Environment, 2000; and Puente, 1999). There are several additional vulnerability factors associated with personal limitations and special needs population. Those vulnerability indicators include restrictions in mobility, the ability to care for oneself, and the ability to work, and the persons usually affected by these variables are those with disabilities, transients, homeless or the institutionalized (Morrow, 1999). Lastly, there are a number of economic factors that can also increase vulnerability, such as poverty (Dhanani and Islam, 2002; Clark *et al.*, 1998 and Blaikie *et al.*, 1999), level of education (Cutter, 1996), occupation and employment type (Cutter, 1996; Hewitt, 1997; Mileti, 1999), natural resource dependant population (Adger, 2000a).

Selection of Variable for Composite Index of Social Vulnerability

Eight indicators like dependant population (DP), per cent of rural population (PRP), social dependant population (SDP), special need population (SNP), per cent of illiterate population (PILP), per cent of population dependent on natural resources (PPSDEN), per cent of marginal workers (PMW) and human health (HH) have been considered for constructing composite index of social vulnerability.

1. Dependent Population

The two demographic groups are tend to be more susceptible to climate induced natural disasters— children and the elders. In general population with a low dependency ratio (high proportion of working age adults) and in good health are likely to have the widest coping ranges and thus be least vulnerable in the face of climate change exposure. The underdevelopment status of Odisha, which by definition has high birth rates and declining death rates. The result is expanding population and high dependency ratio formed largely out of under 15 age groups rather than over 65 age groups.

2. Natural Resource Dependant Population

The extreme events induced by CIND may create significant disturbances and immediate threats to natural resources of state in twenty first century. Odisha has more climatic sensitive economy than any other state in the country because more than two-third of population depend upon natural resource for their livelihoods. The immediate impact of CIND inform of change in water availability may increase baseline vulnerability because of high percentage of population of state belong to natural resource dependant livelihood category such as primary industries (agriculture, fishing and forestry) and the productivity of which is a function of water availability. This is a potent indicator to measure social vulnerability to ongoing environmental changes in the state.

3. Poverty

This is most apparent indicator to show vulnerability in the space. It shows the economic condition of the people in terms of size of operational landholding, type of houses they possess, availability of clcths, food security, sanitation, ownership of consumer durables, literacy status, status of household labour force, means of livelihood, status of children (going to school), type of indebtedness, reason for migration from household and preference for assistance. CIND will compound existing acute and persistent poverty (47.15% of population BPL, Planning Commission, Government of India) of the state by further reducing there accesses to drinking water, negatively affects their health and poses a threat to food security where livelihood choices are limited. Hence, it is important indicator to measure the ability to cope with CIND.

4. Marginal Workers

The marginal workers are defined as the percentage of landless labourers in the agricultural workforce, provides an indication of inequality in landholdings. Landless labourers are generally poor and have little security of income; in times of agricultural distress, labourers are the first to lose their income due to CIND. The state of Odisha has largest share of landless labourers in the agricultural workforce in the country and are thus more vulnerable to shocks generated by CIND because of social and economic disruption as a result of droughts, floods, cyclone or other climatic stresses.

5. Illiteracy

Education is the principal attribute for assessing quality of population and plays an important role in linking social and economic development. Increased literacy levels reduce vulnerability by increasing people's capabilities and access to information, thus their ability to cope with adversities. More the percentage of illiterate people the more vulnerable to CIND because lack of awareness about the global changes affecting the climate of the state.

6. *Socially Dependant Population (SC+ST)*

About 23 per cent of the population comprise the indigenous tribal population, mostly concentrated in the north-western and south-western districts of the state with traditional means of livelihood. They solely depend on the forests for livelihood. The population belonging to Scheduled Caste constitutes little more than 16 per cent of the state's population. The processes of modernization and CINDs have largely marginalized them in economic terms, threatening their livelihood security. Hence, it is a suitable indicator for understanding the dynamics of social vulnerability.

7. *Rural Population*

Rural households of Odisha tend to rely heavily on climate-sensitive resources such as local water supplies and agricultural land; climate-sensitive activities such as arable farming and livestock husbandry; and natural resources such as fuelwood and wild herbs. CIND will reduce the availability of local resources, limiting the option of rural household and compelling them to migrate to urban area as alternative strategies. This can be an indicator for assessing the lack of resilience and also have narrow coping ranges for villagers to cope CIND in Odisha.

8. *Human Health*

Health is an important determinant of wellbeing in the broadest sense of the term. Improved health is desirable not only in itself, but also because it leads to enhanced capability to work and improve adaptive capacity in climate change scenario. Improved health and nutritional status contribute to increased life expectancy. The state of Odisha is one of the malaria prone belts of India. A little more than one-fifth deaths in Odisha is caused by infectious and parasitic diseases. Hence, number of people affected by different diseases are taken as indicator to measure status of heath in the state to cope with CINDs.

Data Source

Sl. No.	*Name of Indictors*	*Source of Data*
1.	Dependent Populations	Census of India (2001)
2.	Natural Resource Dependant Populations	Directorate of Economics & Statistics, Bhubaneshwar, Odisha (2002)
3.	Household below Poverty Line (BPL)	Department of Panchayati Raj, Government of Odisha (1999)
4.	% of population affected by diseases	Director of Health Services, Bhubaneswar, Odisha (2002)
5.	Marginal Workers	Census of India (2001)
6.	Socially Dependent Population (SC+ST)	Directorate of Economics & Statistics, Bhubaneshwar, Odisha (2002)
7.	Illiteracy	Census of India (2001)
8.	Rural Populations	Directorate of Economics & Statistics, Bhubaneshwar, Odisha (2002)

Methodology

A wide variety of multivariate statistical techniques are available to derive a composite index from set of indicators. The choice of most appropriate method depends upon the type of problem, the nature of data and objective of the analysis. In vulnerability science, indicators are in general correlated and researchers are not in a position to study the dynamic of social vulnerability with set of independent variables. It has been criticised by researchers in constructing composite index using method like ranking and indexing because of arbitrariness and allocation of equal weights (Kundu and Raza, 1982; Dandekar Committee, 1984; and Sarkar, 1985). Hence, one has to look into alternative dimension reduction technique which would enable to summarize the whole set of information into a manageable form without much loss of information content of the original data. The theme of multivariate analysis is simplification and to summarize a large set of data by means relatively few indicators (Chatfield & Collins, 1980).

Kendell (1939) had earlier developed a composite index formula by using interdependent indicators to agricultural productivity which is called as 'first principal component' by Hotelling (1933). In principal component analysis (PCA), a set of original variable is transformed to set uncorrelated variables called principal components. The new variables are linear function of original variables and derived in decreasing order of importance. The objective is to find the principal components which account the most variation in the original data set. According to Chatfield and Collin (1980), there is generally a little point in carrying PCA unless the variables have similar variance. The conventional way of getting the unit variance is to standardize the variable, i.e. making the variable scale free. In the present study, the indicators are made scale free by dividing each by their respective mean. This method unlike the other approaches of scale transformation (ranking, standardization, normalization and division by standard deviation) does not lead to shift in origin of the indicators in a given space. The Eigen vector corresponding to largest Eigen value of the projection matrix gives the required weight for the indicators. The weights of the indicators are given in Table 18.1.

Table 18.1: Weight assigned to indicators by Principal Component Analysis

Indicators	*PCA - 1*	*PCA - 2*
DP(CH+OLD)	0.708	0.543
PRP	0.558	0.768
SDP(SC+ST)	0.772	–0.488
SNP(BPL)	0.805	–0.037
PILP	0.889	–0.157
PPSDEN	0.844	0.472
PMW	0.858	–0.079
HH	0.65	–0.585
% of Variation	**64%**	**25%**

Results and Discussion

The weights are multiplied to the standardize indicators and then placed in an additive model to produce the composite index of social vulnerability score for each district and ranked according to hierarchy of their variables as shown in Table 18.2. More than half (60%) of districts of Odisha exhibit moderate to least vulnerable levels of social vulnerability and 40 per cent having high to extreme vulnerability. The CISV ranges from 0.443 (low social vulnerability) to 1.107 (high social vulnerability) with mean vulnerability score of .760 (SD –0.184) for all districts of Odisha. The coping ability of 16 districts are less than state average (0.741) to resist or handle any kind of climate induced natural hazard in Odisha.

Table 18.2: Districts having least coping ability to CIND

District	*CISV-Score*	*Rank*
Nabrangapur	0.993	5
Rayagada	1.009	4
Kandhamal	1.079	3
Nuapara	1.099	2
Malkangiri	1.107	1

Analysis reveals that the district having least coping ability is Malakangiri (1.107) followed by Nuapara (1.099), Kandhamal (1.079), Rayagada (1.009) and Nabrangpur (0.993) to the occurrence of any kind of climate induced natural disasters in Odisha. These districts have less potential to cope with any kind of extreme events. These districts are most vulnerable to climatic variability due to high percentage of dependent population, high reliance on natural resources, limited ability to adapt financially and institutionally, low per capita GDP and high poverty, and a lack of safety nets. The district of Malkangiri covered with steep Ghats, plateaus and valleys sparsely inhabited by primitive tribes like Bondas, Koyas, Porjas and Didiyas, have least potential to cope with CIND in Odisha. The coping ability in this district is least due to presence of high percentage of SC&ST (78.32%) population, level of illiteracy is high (68.74%), prevalence of high level of poverty and also majority (91.3%) of the population depend upon primary activities for their livelihood. It is also one of the malaria prone belts of Odisha. Malkangiri is one of the most backward districts of Odisha and deserves a special attention and proper planning to enhance the capability to cope with upcoming climatic shocks. The tribal hilly district of Nuapada has 2nd least potential cope with natural disasters in Odisha. The coping ability is low because of 85 per cent of families live below the Government of India poverty line of Rs.15,000 (US $ 300) per annum, high percentage of dependant population (24.69%), majority of the population depend upon natural resource for their livelihood and 46.12 per cent belong to marginal workers having no agricultural land. This is one of the poorest districts of Odisha where 50 per cent of families are 'very poor' with an income of only Rs. 6,000 (US $ 120) per annum (Ministry of Rural Development, BPL survey, 2002). Kandhamal district, in the heart of Odisha, is God's own country — an area of great natural beauty, dotted with springs, waterfalls, lush forests and green hills back in headline as symbol of religious strife ranked 3rd in coping ability to counter CIND. Almost 66 per cent of the land area of the district is covered with dense forest and towering mountains which provide shelter to more than half (52%) of population of aboriginal people like Khandas classified under the ancient Gondid race of proto Austroloid group have high dependency ratio (24.13%), whereas more than two-third population depend upon solely on forest product and is also one of the malaria prone belt of Odisha. Almost 78.48 per cent of populations live below poverty lines which further reduce the ability to cope with any kind of natural hazards. The social and religious divide artificially created will further reduce their ability to cope because thousands have been rendered homeless and without hope or sustenance. The district of Rayagada has been the homeland of various tribal communities with their sub-tribes rank 4th position having less coping ability to counter CIND in Odisha. Majority of population (70.32%) belong to marginalized section of society having very low literacy level (35.61%), health status is very poor and also depend upon pre-agricultural economy based on foraging, hunting and gathering but they now primarily depend on a subsistence agriculture, i.e. shifting cultivation or slash and burn cultivation or *Podu* are the factors playing role in creating inability of the district to cope with climatic stresses in Odisha. District of Nabarangpur has mostly tribal, nomadic and aboriginal ranked 5th position having least potential to cope natural hazard in Odisha. This district has high dependant population, high degree of poverty, high level of illiteracy and also depend upon agriculture and forest product for their livelihood are the criteria for least ability to counter natural hazards in Odisha.

Table 18.2: Composite Index of Social Vulnerability and Human Development Index for districts of Odisha

Districts	*CISV*	*Rank*	*District*	*HDI*	*Rank*
Khurda	0.443	30	Khurdha	0.736	1
Puri	0.520	29	Jharsuguda	0.722	2
Jagatsinghpur	0.525	28	Cuttack	0.695	3
Kendrapara	0.557	27	Sundargarh	0.683	4
Bhadrak	0.564	26	Debagarh	0.669	5
Cuttack	0.581	25	Angul	0.663	6
Jeypore	0.500	24	Puri	0.657	7
Nayagarh	0.600	23	Bhadrak	0.646	8
Balasore	0.614	22	Mayurbhanj	0.639	9
Ganjam	0.645	21	Kendrapara	0.626	10
Angul	0.652	20	Kalahandi	0.606	11
Jharsiguda	0.656	19	Dhenkanal	0.591	12
Baragarh	0.678	18	Sambalpur	0.589	13
Dhenkanal	0.684	17	Nuapada	0.581	14
Odisha	0.741		Odisha	0.579	
Sonepur	0.743	16	Nayagarh	0.571	15

(Contd.)

Districts	*CISV*	*Rank*	*District*	*HDI*	*Rank*
Boudh	0.770	15	Sonepur	0.566	16
Bolangir	0.772	14	Bargarh	0.565	17
Sambalpur	0.778	13	Baleshwar	0.559	18
Keonjhar	0.820	12	Jagatsinghpur	0.557	19
Kalahandi	0.852	11	Ganjam	0.551	20
Mayurbhanj	0.859	10	Bolangir	0.546	21
Deogarh	0.891	9	Jeypore	0.54	22
Sundergarh	0.899	8	Baudh	0.536	23
Gajapati	0.914	7	Keonjhar	0.53	24
Koraput	0.943	6	Rayagada	0.443	25
Nabaragapur	0.993	5	Nabaragapur	0.436	26
Rayagada	1.009	4	Koraput	0.431	27
Kandhamal	1.079	3	Gajapati	0.431	28
Nuapara	1.099	2	Kandhamal	0.389	29
Malkangiri	1.107	1	Malkangiri	0.37	30

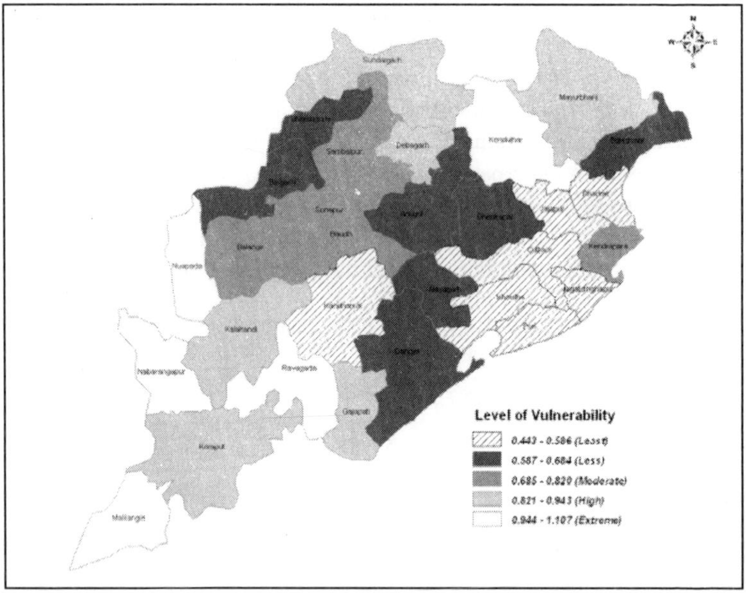

Fig. 18.1: Composite Index of Social Vulnerability.

Districts having high coping ability to CIND

The top five districts having more potential to cope with CIND in Odisha are Khurda, Puri, Jagatsingpur, Kendrapara and Bhadrak. These districts of Odisha have high capability to cope any kind of climate induced

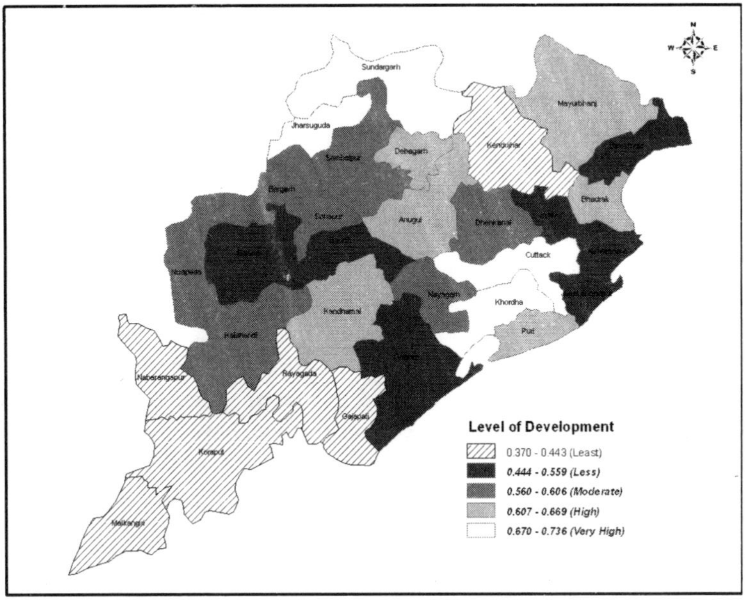

Fig. 18.2: Human Development Index.

Source: Human Development Report-2004.

District	*CISV-Score*	*Rank*
Khurda	0.443	30
Puri	0.520	29
Jagatsingpur	0.525	28
Kendrapara	0.557	27
Bhadrak	0.564	26

extreme events because of less reliance on natural resources, less percentage of population belong to marginalized section of the society, less prevalence of poverty and have wide range of capacity to adapt financially and institutionally. The district of Khurda topped the list because of less degree of poverty (59.17%), high percentage of urbanization (42.93%), having access to alternative source of income, low dependency ratio (19.86), well communicated and informed and less percentage population from marginalized section. The coastal district of Puri is famous for its historic antiquities, religious sanctuaries, architectural grandeur, sea-scape beauty and moderate climate secured 2nd position in the row having potential to cope CIND. The district of

Puri has less prevalence of poverty, less percentage of ST population, high level of literacy rate, larger percentage of population is working class are engaged mainly in the secondary sector and the income generated from tourism sector plays indirect role making the district economically sound than other districts to cope with natural disaster in the state. The district of Jagatsingpur rank 3rd in coping ability is because of low percentage of SC & ST (22.23%), low level of poverty, high literacy rate and health condition in this district also very good. The district of Kendrapara and Bhadarak rank 4th and 5th position, respectively in hierarchy in coping ability to CIND in Odisha. The coping ability of both the districts are quite high in ranking are because of high level of urbanization, low percentage of ST population, low amount of poverty, diversified economic activity and access to good education and information technology. These coastal districts have high potential to absorb the climatic shocks and stresses in the whole state.

Comparison between CISV and HDI

The relation between CISV and HDI are inverse, i.e. the district having high human development index should have low social vulnerability, i.e. coping ability should be high and *vice versa*. There is a moderate, negative association (-.635) between CISV and HDI as shown in Table 18.3.

Table 18.3: Correlation

Correlations

		CISV	HDI
CISV	Pearson Correlation	1	–.635**
	Sig. (2-tailed)		.000
	N	31	31
HDI	Pearson Correlation	–.635**	1
	Sig. (2-tailed)	.000	
	N	31	31

**Correlation is significant at the 0.01 level.

The HDI only measures the wellbeing taking only few socio-economic indicators but not a different kind of non-conventional social indicators. The reason for using CISV instead of the HDI for measuring coping ability for climate induced natural disaster as follows: First, one of the stated goals of the HDI is to achieve a stable indicator; therefore, the HDI may mask much of the variability in Social Vulnerability that can be identified by the CISV. Second, the CISV has a much stronger theoretical base in measuring both potential of society to cope with disaster and also developmental aspects than the HDI. The CISV tries to give different weight using multivariate technique (PCA) to indicators for the construction of better index. This is not to suggest that the CISV does not need much refinement, but only that it is a better and more interesting indicator than the HDI, particularly while developing composite index at micro-level study (district, block and villages).

Conclusion

The academia do not have consensus within their community about social vulnerability or its correlates. These correlates are largely derivative from local case studies of climate induced natural disasters and community responses. There have been few attempts to develop larger theoretical or conceptual understandings the dynamics indicators of social vulnerability, instead the clear need to develop such a robust and replicable set. The work on the Composite Index of Social Vulnerability demonstrates that there is a considerable potential for such an index when used in the context of measuring sustainability, development, climate change impacts, disaster managements and any other kind of spatially change. The CISV can assist local decision-makers in pinpointing those factors that threaten the sustainability and stability of the districts (or community). Using this index in conjunction with biophysical risk index, help in mitigating efforts or empower the manager of disaster management who can target the most vulnerable groups or districts. Whilst the index, therefore, has important academic and policy applications, its development has also raised a number of potential directions for further research. It has to be used with appropriate regard to the limitations and it marks the first robust and systematic assessment of relative levels of social vulnerability in Odisha. This is the first index constructed on micro scale and complimentary index to Human Development Index constructed by UNDP. There is a need to try and validate the index by applying the model (with appropriate data) to past historical hazards to explain why they did or did not translate into impacts (disasters). The researchers should try in developing robust indicators and indexes which can really capture the ground reality. As international agreements such as the UN Framework Convention on Climate Change incorporate the goals of sustainable development and human threats as key provisions, there will be a need for additional research on indicators for measurement and prediction. The CISV presents a major effort towards meeting this need.

References

Adger, W.N. (2000a). "Social and ecological resilience: are they related?" *Progress in Human Geography,* 24: 347-364.

Blaikie, P., T. Cannon, I. Davis, and B. Wisner. (1994). *At Risk: Natural Hazards, People's Vulnerability, and Disasters*. New York: Routledge.

Bohle, H.G. (1994). "Climate change and social vulnerability. Toward a social and geography of food insecurity", *Global Environmental Change* 4: 37-48.

Bolin, R. (1993). *Household and community recovery after earthquakes*. Boulder, Colorado: Institute of Behavioural Science, University of Colorado.

Bolin, R., with L. Stanford. (1998). *The Northridge Earthquake: Vulnerability and Disaster*, London: Routledge.

Bolin, R.C. and P. Bolton. (1986). *Race, religion, and ethnicity in disaster recovery*. Boulder, Colorado: University of Colorado.

Chatfield, C., and Collins, A.J., (1980). *Introduction to Multivariate Analysis*, London; Chapman and Hall.

Clark, G.E., Moser, S.C., Ratick, S.J., Dow, K., Meyer, W.B., Emani, S., Jin, W., Kasperson, J.X., Cutter, S.L. (1996). "Vulnerability to environmental hazards", *Progress in Human Geography* 20(4): 529-539.

Cutter, S.L., J.T. Mitchell, and M.S. Scott (2000). "Revealing the vulnerability of people and places: A case study of Georgetown County, South Carolina," *Annals of the AAG* 90 (4): 713-737.

Dandekar Committee (1981). Report of the facts Finding Committee on Regional Imbalance in Maharastra, Government of Maharashtra, Planning Department, Bombay.

Dhanani, S. and Islam, I. (2002). "Poverty, vulnerability and social protection in a period of crisis: The case of Indonesia", *World Development*, 30(7): 1211-1231.

E. Enarson and B.H. Morrow (1998). "Women will rebuild Miami: A case study of feminist response to disaster," pp. 185-200 in *The Gendered Terrain of Disaster*.

Enarson, E. and J. Scanlon (1999). "Gender patterns in flood evacuations: A case study in Canada's Red River valley", *Applied Behavioural Science Review* 7(2): 103-124.

Fothergill, A. (1996). "Gender, risk, and disaster", *International Journal of Mass*, 14(1):33–56.

Hewitt, K. (1997). "Regions of Risk: A Geographical Introduction to Disasters". Essex: Longman.

Hotelling, H. (1993). "Analysis of a complex of statistical variable into principal component", *Journal of Educational Psychology*, 24:417-27.

Intergovernmental Panel on Climate Change (2001). *Summary for policy makers. Intergovernmental Panel on Climate Change,* Third Assessment Report.

IPCC (2001). *Impacts, Adaptation and Vulnerability*, Summary for Policymakers, WMO.

Kasperson, R.E., and Schwarz, H.E. (1998). Assessing the vulnerability of coastal communities to extreme storms: The case of Revere, MA. *Mitigation and Adaptation Strategies for Global,* Change 3:59 82

Kendell, M.G. (1939). "The geographical distribution of crop productivity in England", *Journal of the Royal Statistical Society,* 102: 21-48.

Kundu, A. and Raja, M., (1982). *Indian Economy: The Regional Dimension*, New Delhi: Spectrum Publishers and Distributors.

Mileti, D.S. (1999). *Disasters by Design*, Joseph Henry Press, Washington DC.

Morrow, B.H. (1999). "Identifying and mapping community vulnerability", *Disasters,* 23(1):11–18.

Morrow, B.H., and B. Phillips. (1999). "What's gender 'got to do with It'?" *International Journal of Mass Emergencies and Disasters,* 17(1):5–1.

Ngo, E.B. (2001). "When Disasters and Age Collide: Reviewing Vulnerability of the Elderly", *Natural Hazards Review* 2(2):80–89.

OSDMA, *Orissa Disaster Management Authority Report, 2011.*

O'Brien, P. and D. Mileti (1992). "Citizen participation in emergency response following the Loma Prieta earthquake". *International Journal of Mass Emergencies and Disasters,* 10: 71-89.

Peacock, W., B.H. Morrow, and H. Gladwin, eds. (1997). "Hurricane Andrew and the Reshaping of Miami: Ethnicity, Gender, and the Socio-Political Ecology of Disasters", Gainesville, Fla.: University Press of Florida.

Pulido, L. (2000). "Rethinking Environmental Racism: White Privilege and Urban Development in Southern California." *Annals of the Association of American Geographers*, 90:12–40.

Sarker, P.C. (1998). *Regional Disparities in India: Issue and Measurement*, Bombay: Himalaya Publishing House.

Thomas, D.S.G. and Twyman, C. (2005). "Equity and justice in climate change adaptation amongst natural-resource-dependant societies", *Global Environmental Change A,* 15(2), 115-124.

Vincent, K., (2004). Creating an Index of Social Vulnerability to Climate change of Africa, *Working paper.*

19

E-Governance Model to Deliver Citizen Centric Services

Madhu Thawani

Introduction

Paul H. Appleby has defined public administration as "public leadership of public affairs directly responsible for executive action". Today in the era of modern age different approach of Governance is required. Traditional approach of Public Administration was 'Weberian' 'Bureaucratic' is no more relevant today. Public agencies following bureaucratic set up led to centralization of activities wherein customer have no say and it functioned like machine and were rigid and impersonal in their approach.

In real life, the bureaucratic mode of organization is not the most efficient or effective model of Governance. Today we talk about new public administration and management, it is a digital era, value loaded, market oriented wherein utmost importance is given to citizens. They are to be provided quality service without any delay, at their door step and are to be involved in decision-making process. Thus, the major concepts of traditional public administration are now challenged on the fronts of efficiency, effectiveness, accountability, transparency and responsiveness. With the rapid changes in technology and societal demands different paradigm of administration is required, i.e. smart governance. One of the ways of smart Governance is E-governance.[1] This chapter focuses on how SMC through E-Governance has moved from Bureaucratic Governance to Smart Governance.

E-Governance is an activity of economic, political and administrative authority to manage a country's affairs at all levels. "E-governance is not just about government website and e-mail nor is it just about digital access to government information or electronic payments. Rather, it brings forth new concepts of citizenship, both in terms of needs and responsibilities. It can be defined as the application of information technology to the processes of government functioning in order to bring about SMART (Simple, Moral, Accountable, Responsive and Transparent) governance. E-governance also involves transformation from being passive information and service provider to active citizen involvement.... It provides a common framework and direction in the implementation of government policies for G2G (government to government), G2B (government to business) and G2C (government to citizen) communication.[2] At the service level, e-governance features include being open for business 24 hours a day, greater accessibility, lower costs and not having to visit government offices; it also aims to provide government information.[3]

Traditional Service Delivery Process

Prior to development of e-governance model adopted by government departments, citizens used to visit each department to avail a service provided by that department. As the number of staff available in each department was much less than required and each citizen was to be provided face to face services, long queues of citizens outside each department were seen. Apart from this they had to travel long distance as the departments are established in different corners of the city or town. For example, if a person wants to pay electricity bill and water bill, which are regular activities for every citizen, first he has to go to the electricity department, stand in the queue, pay the bill and then travel a long distance to arrive at the water resource department, again stand in a queue and then pay the water bill. Due to this disintegrated service offering, the citizen used to spends nearly half of the day for paying these utility bills. To overcome these problems slowly and gradually most of the states adopted E-Governance model to deliver citizen centric services.[4]

Surat Municipal Corporation

Surat is Gujarat's second-largest city with a population of 4.6 million (2011 Census). It has an average literacy rate of 89 per cent, higher than the national average of 79.5 per cent: male literacy is 93 per cent, and female literacy is 84 per cent. Males constitute 53 per cent of the population and females 47 per cent.[5] There are three main governing bodies within Surat, namely, Surat Municipal Corporation (SMC), Surat Urban Development Authority (SUDA) and Hazira Development Authority (HADA) governing the industrial hub of Hazira. Approximately 326 square kilometres of the city comes under the jurisdiction of SMC. The Surat Municipal Corporation is responsible for maintaining city's civic infrastructure as well as carrying out associated administrative duties. The rapid growth of the city has put lot of pressure on the SMC to provide basic civic services to match with the increasing demand of the citizens. For this the whole Surat city has been divided into 7 zones.[6]

Census Data S.M.C. Zone-wise

Sl. No.	Zone	Area Sq.Km.	Population		Density per Sq.Km.	Decade Growth 2001-2011 (% age)
			2001 Census	*2011 Census		
1.	Central	8.18	413641	408760	49971	–1.18
2.	South West	111.912	242466	347447	3105	43.30
3.	South	61.764	407980	695028	11253	70.36
4.	South East	19.492	397257	748304	38390	88.37
5.	East	37.525	711516	1137138	30303	59.82
6.	North	36.363	416370	705163	19392	69.36
7.	West	51.279	287144	424986	8288	48.00
	Total	**326.515**	**2876374**	**4466826**	**13680**	**55.29**

* Detail Population of Enumeration Block of Census-2011 is not available, so Zone-wise Population is approximate.

Source: https://suratmunicipal.gov.in/TheCity/city/stmt3.shtml

Surat Municipal Corporation Journey to Smart Governance

Area under Surat has increased threefold from 112 sq. km. to 326 sq. km. in 2006. Apart from this it can be seen from the above table that Surat population decadal growth rate is 55.29 per cent (Census 2011). This in future would have put lot of burden on SMC to deliver civic services if it would have continued with same bureaucratic set up wherein each customer is to be entertained face to face. So SMC planned to do away with traditional system of governance and adopted e-governance model of governance.

1979 Start of computerization

1982-85 Development and implementation of Computerised payroll, property tax, vehicle tax

1990-92	Property Tax Computerized Receipt System Computerised accrual based double accounting system
2000	Birth & Death System implemented
2001	IT Plan for computerization at SMC
2003	Started City Civic Center (CSCs/CFCs)
2007-08	e-Tendering adopted/Information Kiosks
2009	m-Governance started with Vaccination Alert System
2010	Single No. Helpline
2011-12	Revision of IT Plan/Virtual Civic Center
2013	Mobile App
2014	Whats app

IT Environment at Surat Municipal Corporation

IT Environment components are stakeholder, computerized system and application and delivery channels.

Stake Holders

Citizens, Business & Service Sector, SMC Employees.

Computerised Systems and Applications

G2C Services

- Property Tax & User Charges
- Birth & Death Registration
- Marriage Registration
- Water Billing & Accounting System
- Complaint Redressal System
- Building Plan Approval System
- Software for RTI Act, 2005

G2B Services

- Shops and Establishment System
- Profession Tax System
- e-Procurement System
- Food Licence

G2E Services

- Personnel Information System
- Employee and Officer Portal

G2G Services

- Finance & Accounts System
- Material Management System
- Asset Management System
- Audit System

Service Delivery Channels

- Civic Centres
- Kiosks
- Virtual Civic Centres
- M-governance
- Mobile apps
- Single helpline number
- Mobile Van
- E-tendering
- Whats app
- E-Magazine

Surat Municipal Corporation E-governance Model of Governance to Deliver Citizen Centric Civic Services

SMC have started its journey to smart governance by adopting e-governance model to delivery Citizen Centric Civic Services through the following delivery channels.

1. Civic Centres

Civic Centres were opened to provide access to citizens at their door step. It facilitated single visit solutions, speeded the processing of transaction, standardized delivery of services and eliminated *babu* system and promoted transparency and accountability. First Civic Centre was opened in May 2003. Eight more Civic Centres opened in the same year.

At present there are 16 functional civic centres. Each zone has two or more civic centres.

Features of Civic Centres

- Single Window Clearance.
- Clean Modern Offices with air-conditioned environment.
- All the processes are computerized.
- String of sufficient computers are installed on the network to handle the task.
- Acceptance of payment through Credit/Debit Card.

Civic Centre Usage

Particulars	2007-08	2008-09	2009-10	2010-11	2011-12	2012-13	2013-14
Transaction count	12,32,706	13,81,916	14,45,631	15,24,096	16,88,041	18,94,116	19,54,424
Transaction amount in Rs. in cr.	235.47	244.91	276.43	311.49	442.56	532.07	703.37

KIOSKs at City Civic Centre

SMC has placed the Information KIOSK for the self-help of the citizens. This helps the citizen in accessing the useful information on their own without the help of SMC's employees. Over 2.5 lakh hits have been registered through this Kiosk. It provides the following information:

- Details related to individual's Property Tax.
- Birth & Death registration details.
- Details about Shops & Establishment Licence, its renewal etc.
- Details about Profession Tax.
- Functions of Zone office; contact details of zone and office bearers.
- Functions of ward office and contact details of ward office.
- Information related to various facilities like libraries, reading rooms, swimming pools, health centres, vaccination centres, gardens, fire stations etc.
- Details of all Employees and Pensioner of SMC including salary information.
- Complete details of the elected wing.

- "How do I?" information.

Features

- Touch screen functionality.
- User friendly and intuitive interface.
- No specialized computer skills required for usage.
- Bilingual support (English & Gujarati).

Virtual Civic Centres

Number of barriers were faced by the people even when civic centres were established in different zones like: necessity to visit city civic centres, geographical barrier in terms of reach, time barrier, services accessible during working days and working hours overlaps with working hours of business and offices, limitation in terms of citizens that can be served at a time (one to one relation), heavy rush during rebate and peak billing period (despite of extra counters). To overcome these problems of citizen SMC started Virtual Civic Centre in April 2012.

Surat Municipal Corporation has always aspired to achieve total customer satisfaction and has endeavoured the same through various methodologies. With this objective in mind, S.M.C. started an e-governance project through virtual city civic centres. This is further integrated with an in-house Management Information Systems (M.I.S.) that gives an instant and as—is report on all activities of City Civic Centre on Municipal Commissioner desktop.

Features of Virtual Civic Centres

- Services are offered through SMC's portal www.suratmunicipal.gov.in
- Accessible 24 × 7
- Facilitates citizens to pay their dues from their convenient place and at their convenient time.
- The facility is offered free of cost.
- Wider Coverage (100+ payment option)
  - 48 banks are covered for Net Banking Facility.
  - 64 Debit Cards accepted.
  - Master & Visa Credit Cards.

- Ability to cater many request at a time, one to one barrier is overcome.
- It provides a single point payment facility.

Virtual Civic Centre Usage

Particulars	*2012-13 (yearly)*	*2013-14 (Yearly)*	*2014-15 (1st Quarter)*	*Total*
Transaction Count	16,959	30,469	10,336	57,764
Transaction amount (Rs. in Cr.)	3.68	10.09	4.44	18.21 c

M-GOVERNANCE VACCINATION ALERT SYSTEM

SMC was the first ULB to start m-Governance with Vaccination Alert System in January 2009. Citizen can now know their Property Tax, Professional Tax, Complaint Status by sending SMS to '9274222222'. For vaccination alert at the time of Birth Registration parents are asked to provide the mobile number if they wish to get the SMS alerts. Parents are sent SMS alert for periodic immunization/ vaccination. SMS intimates and informs:

- The Birth Registration No. of child and from where the first Birth Certificate can be obtained.
- BCG & Polio Vaccination required after birth.
- DPT & Polio Vaccination required after — 1.5 months of birth, 2.5 months of birth, 3.5 months of birth.
- Measles vaccine & Vitamin-A dose required after 9 months of birth.

SMS Service Count

Vaccination Alerts	13,19,263
Birth Registration	1,82,607
Complaint Management	1,61,102
Interactive Service	12,602
Monsoon Alerts	38,618
Tax Reminder	52,380
Audit, MIS, Recruitment Exam Intimation and other	31,847
Total	**17,98,41**

SMC MOBILE APP

SMC App is a mobile application developed by Surat Municipal Corporation. It enables the service delivery and information sharing using the latest mobile technology. This mobile app does not collect Personal Information. One can generally visit the mobile app without revealing personal information, unless one wants to use app for Complaint Registration, Feedback, etc. It can be downloaded free of cost from Google Play Store and Apple App Store. It is first ULB in India to launch Mobile App in August 2013. It has received the Award for Citizen's Connect – SMC Mobile App Skoch Order of Merit 2014, by Skoch Group.

Current Downloads

- 44,124 from Google Play Store.
- 6,210 from Apple App Store.
- 4.6 out of 5 rating based on 1296 reviews.
- Downloaded from more than 15 countries.
- Over 14 lakh requests so far.
- Over 3 lakh requests during the flood like situation in the month of September 2013 for three days.
- 25% of total complaints received through mobile app.

Single No. Help Line (Call Centre)

Single help line number system was started by SMC from September 2010. It helps the citizen to register complaints irrespective of the department and zone. Once the citizen register complain he is sent an SMS stating the Complaint ID, its brief description and the name and contact details of the concerned nodal officer. The concerned nodal officer also receives the SMS stating the Complaint ID, name and contact details of complainant and the brief of complaint and its location. Complainant is notified for any updates on his/her complaint by SMS.

Other Initiatives

E-Tendering

It was started from September 2007. Till date 4356 tenders of over 11,860 crore have been processed. It helped in containing the malpractice which used to take place in awarding and getting tenders.

Mobile Tax Collection Van

Area under Surat has increased threefold from 112 sq. km. to 326 sq. km. in 2006. To cater to the citizens of newly merged area where civic centres are not available Mobile Tax Collection Van services was started in 2009. It is useful to people who do not use mobiles, internet and for the people who do not have convenience to reach civic centres.[7]

WhatsApp

SMC is now available on whatsApp also. Through whatsApp SMC is receiving everyday about 2000 complains along with photographs. Here the citizen gets the immediate solution to his problem as complain directly reaches specifically to the concerned department. SMC is also planning Twitter and Facebook debut in future.

E-Magazine

E Magazine was started by SMC in 2005. This gives the information of various activities carried out by SMC. The citizen can subscribe to receive weekly issues of e-Magazine by e-mail.

Health Centres Computerized

All the health centres are computerized from 2002. Web based disease surveillance system (DocNet) was launched in May 2004.

Summary

Surat Municipal Corporation has received various awards like for Use of e-Governance for Improved Service Delivery, Skoch Gold Award & Skoch Order-of-Merit, by Skoch Group 2013 and For Best Website under the category "Transparency & Accountability" by Janaagraha Centre for Citizenship and Democracy. This shows that SMC has started its journey of smart Governance and has reached to a common man and is trying to align its services with the changing needs of different stakeholders.

References

http://www.mu.ac.in/myweb_test/SYBA%20Study%20Material/pol_sc-III.pdf

Narayana Raju Swamy, Effective e-Governance and Development:Case Studies from Kerala. http://www.csi-india.org/c/document_library/get_file?uuid=bcc74b5f-ce7d-4798-ba58-112713d25225&groupId=10157.

Gilmore & D'Souza, 2006 Service excellence in egovernanceissues: An Indian case study, *JOAAG*, Vol. 1. No. 1. http://joaag.com/uploads/1-_Gilmore_D_Souza.pdf

Chakravarti, B. & Venugopal M. Citizen Centric Service Delivery through e-Governance Portal—Present Scenario in India—A White Paper, National Institute for Smart Government Hyderabad, India, 2008. http://nisg.org/files/documents/D01010001.pdf

http://en.wikipedia.org/wiki/Surat

www.sgcci.in/download_file.php?download=19.

http://www.amdaindia.org/PDF/arc/ppt/7/e-Governance%20at%20SMC%20-%20AMDA%20Workshop%207-8%20Aug.%202014.pdf.

Index